MW00574540

A SHAU VALOR

A SHAU VALOR

AMERICAN COMBAT OPERATIONS
IN THE VALLEY OF DEATH

1963–1971

THOMAS R. YARBOROUGH

CASEMATE

Philadelphia & Oxford

Published in the United States of America and Great Britain in 2016 by
CASEMATE PUBLISHERS
1950 Lawrence Road, Havertown, PA 19083
and
10 Hythe Bridge Street, Oxford OX1 2EW

ISBN 978-1-61200-354-2
Digital Edition: ISBN 978-1-61200-355-9

Cataloging-in-publication data is available from the Library of Congress and
the British Library.

10 9 8 7 6 5 4 3 2 1

Printed and bound in the United States of America.

For a complete list of Casemate titles please contact:

CASEMATE PUBLISHERS (US)
Telephone (610) 853-9131, Fax (610) 853-9146
E-mail: casemate@casematepublishing.com

CASEMATE PUBLISHERS (UK)
Telephone (01865) 241249, Fax (01865) 794449
E-mail: casemate-uk@casematepublishing.co.uk

CONTENTS

This book is dedicated to the memory and incomparable fighting spirit of the American soldiers, sailors, Marines, airmen, and Coast Guardsmen who willingly marched to the sound of battle in the Valley of Death. All gave some, some gave all.

Vietnam—The A Shau Valley,
The Valley of Death

Welcome to the jungle,
You've arrived, watch out for its wrath,
It lives on our dead, broken bodies,
Reeks of blood and death.
This valley is quite beautiful,
It hides under cloudless skies,
Takes its toll of fighting men,
Doesn't choose who lives . . . who dies!

No villages on its landscape,
Fighting, while explosions sound.
Rifle shots, mortar rounds,
Soldiers dying,
Soldiers killing,
Some bodies never found.

The stench of death is the valleys' perfume,
Our blood feeds the growing palms,
This is where we fought and died,
A place of courage,
Where we fought with pride.

There is where,
We left a little sign,
A place to fear . . . nowhere to hide,
Deep, dark thoughts,
Attack our mind.
Written it holds the valleys' psalm,
Welcome to the A-Shau Valley,
Republic of Viet-Nam.

—Philip Lore

GLOSSARY

A-1 SKYRAIDER: A Korean War-vintage prop attack aircraft capable of carrying large ordnance loads and used extensively for search-and-rescue missions as well as in support of SOG long-range reconnaissance teams.

A-4 SKYHAWK: A single seat light attack jet aircraft used by Navy and Marines.

AIRMOBILE: Helicopter-borne infantry.

AH-1 COBRA: Army helicopter gunship used extensively throughout Vietnam.

AK-47: The standard automatic assault weapon used by North Vietnamese and Viet Cong soldiers.

AO: Area of operations, usually a specific sector assigned an air or ground unit.

ARC LIGHT: Code name for B-52 operations in Southeast Asia, usually flown in three-plane cells.

ARVN: Army of the Republic of Vietnam, South Vietnamese Army.

BDA: Bomb damage assessment, the reported results of air strikes.

BILK: Call sign of Air Force FACs assigned to support the 101st Airborne Division.

BINH TRAM: North Vietnamese supply complexes along the Ho Chi Minh Trail, the largest located adjacent to the A Shau Valley.

BRIGHT LIGHT: Code name for a 12-man Special Forces team dedicated to recovering POWs, downed pilots, or reconnaissance teams in Laos, Cambodia, or North Vietnam.

CAR-15: Submachine gun version of the M-16 rifle, with folding stock and shortened barrel.

CBU: Cluster bomb unit. An area-coverage, anti-personnel ordnance dropped by fighter aircraft, used extensively in Southeast Asia.

CCN: Command and Control North, the Da Nang-based regional headquarters for all cross-border operations, a subunit of Military Assistance Command's Studies and Observations Group, SOG.

CHARLIE: A slang term for enemy soldiers, probably stemming from "Victor Charlie," the phonetic alphabet words used for the letters VC, or Viet Cong.

CHINOOK: Nickname for the U.S. Army's CH-47 medium lift helicopter, a venerable workhorse in Vietnam.

CIA: Central Intelligence Agency

CIDG: Civilian Irregular Defense Group, South Vietnamese paramilitary force composed primarily of Montagnard tribesmen.

CINCPAC: Commander in Chief, Pacific, headquarters in Hawaii.

CLAYMORE MINE: A directional anti-personnel M18 mine packed with C-4 explosive that shoots a pattern of steel balls into a kill zone like a shotgun blast.

COBRA: Nickname for the AH-1G helicopter gunship.

COMBAT ASSAULT: The movement of ground forces via helicopter to seize and hold key terrain and to attack enemy forces. In Vietnam CAs were normally carried out by airmobile units such as the 1st Cavalry Division and the 101st Airborne Division.

COSVN: Central Office of South Vietnam, the nominal communist military and political headquarters in South Vietnam.

COVEY: Call sign of the USAF special-mission FACs flying sorties into Laos from Da Nang and Pleiku in direct support of SOG cross-border missions.

COVEY RIDER: Highly experienced Special Forces member who flew with Prairie Fire FACs to help direct air strikes and team inserts and extractions.

CP: Command post.

CS: Tear gas. A riot control agent, it was discovered by two Americans, Ben Corson and Roger Stoughton in 1928; the chemical's name is derived from the first letters of the scientists' surnames.

DANGER CLOSE: Term used by ground commanders authorizing ordnance (bombs, artillery) well inside the recognized minimum safe distances.

DMZ: Demilitarized Zone, the no-man's-land between North and South Vietnam at the 17th Parallel.

DUST-OFF: Call sign of Army UH-1 medical evacuation helicopters.

F-4 PHANTOM: State-of-the-art fighter bomber flown by Air Force, Navy, and Marines in Vietnam.

FAC: Forward air controller (pronounced "Fack," as in pack). In South Vietnam and Laos, virtually all tactical air strikes were directed by FACs.

559TH TRANSPORTATION GROUP: Secret North Vietnamese command that operated the Ho Chi Minh Trail, with its forward headquarters located in Target Oscar Eight adjacent to the western edge of the A Shau Valley.

FLAK: Air bursts from antiaircraft fire.

FOB: Forward Operating Base.

FSB: Fire support base, a temporary military encampment widely used during the Vietnam War to provide artillery support to infantry units operating in areas beyond the normal range of fire support from their own base camps.

GRUNT: Affectionate nickname for the infantryman in Vietnam.

HE: High-explosive, normally referring to rockets fired by fighters, FACs, or helicopter gunships.

HO CHI MINH TRAIL: An extensive network of Laotian trails and roads used by the NVA to move men and supplies to South Vietnam and Cambodia. Between 1966 and 1971, intelligence analysts estimated that North Vietnam moved 630,000 NVA troops, 100,000 tons of food, 400,000 weapons, and 50,000 tons of ammunition down the Trail.

HUEY: Nickname for the versatile UH-1 helicopter.

I CORPS: The five northern most provinces in South Vietnam, later renamed Military Region 1.

JOLLY GREEN: Call sign of Air Force HH-3 or HH-53 rescue helicopters, known as "Jolly Green Giants."

KBA: Killed by air. Refers to casualties inflicted by aircraft bombing or strafing.

KIA: Killed in action.

LAM SON 719: The ARVN invasion of Laos in February 1971.

LLDB: Luc Luong Duc Biet (Vietnamese Special Forces).

LRRP: Long-range reconnaissance patrol.

LZ: Landing zone, usually an open area large enough to accommodate a helicopter. A "hot LZ" indicated a landing zone under enemy fire.

MACV: Military Assistance Command, Vietnam, headquarters in Saigon.

M-16: Standard U.S. 5.56mm automatic rifle.

MIA: Missing in action.

MK-82: A general-purpose 500-pound bomb widely used on missions throughout Southeast Asia.

MONTAGNARD: French name for ethnic minority tribes in Vietnam located primarily along the Lao-Vietnamese border. They developed a special rapport with U.S. Special Forces.

NLF: National Liberation Front, a Vietnamese political organization to orchestrate the overthrow of South Vietnam's government in order to reunify the North and South.

NUNG: Ethnic Chinese minority in Vietnam noted for their prowess as fighters. As anti-communists, they sided with the Americans.

NVA: North Vietnamese Army.

ONE-ZERO: Designation for the leader of a SOG reconnaissance team.

OV-10 BRONCO: A twin-engine light-attack aircraft used by forward air controllers; also flown by specialized Marine and Navy units.

PAVN: People's Army of Vietnam (NVA).

POINT MAN: The first and most exposed position of a combat patrol through hostile territory, usually the first soldier to take enemy fire during a firefight or ambush.

POW: Prisoner of war.

PROJECT DELTA: This special reconnaissance organization consisted of South Vietnamese commando troops and U.S. Army Special Forces advisors. Under the auspices of the 5th Special Forces Group, Delta teams worked targets throughout South Vietnam.

RPG: Shoulder fired, rocket-propelled grenade used extensively by NVA forces.

PRAIRIE FIRE: Code name for top secret cross-border ground reconnaissance missions into Laos. When used tactically by team leaders, the term indicated a dire condition requiring immediate helicopter extraction.

RIF: Reconnaissance-in-force, a patrol technique used by U.S. Army units in Vietnam.

ROE: Rules of engagement. A lengthy, complicated list of limitations and conditions applied to a ground target before ordnance could be dropped or enemy forces engaged.

ROLLING THUNDER: The American bombing campaign against North Vietnam from 1965–1968.

RT: Reconnaissance team. Each SOG team had a distinctive name, usually after a snake or a state.

SANDY: Call sign for Air Force A-1 Skyraiders dedicated to search-and-rescue missions.

SAR: Search and rescue.

SEARCH AND DESTROY: The U.S. strategy in Vietnam of seeking out the enemy to inflict casualties in a "war of attrition." Whatever the name, for the first time in modern warfare the goal was not territory—it was body count.

SF: Special Forces.

SLICK: Affectionate nickname for the UH-1 Huey.

SOG: Studies and Observations Group, the Vietnam War's covert special warfare unit used primarily in top secret cross-border operations.

III MAF: III Marine Amphibious Force, located at Da Nang and headquarters for all Marines in Vietnam.

TIC: Troops in contact, a situation where friendly troops engage enemy forces in a close-quarters firefight.

VC: Viet Cong, enemy soldiers belonging to indigenous South Vietnamese communist forces.

VIET MINH: Communist military forces in the French-Indochina War, 1946–1954.

VIETNAMIZATION: Nixon policy to curtail the U.S. combat role and turn the fighting over to South Vietnamese forces.

VNAF: (South) Vietnamese Air Force.

VR: Visual reconnaissance, performed either on the ground or in the air.

WIA: Wounded in action.

WILLIE PETE: Slang for white phosphorous, an explosive round from artillery, mortars, rockets, or grenades. When the rounds exploded, a huge puff of white smoke would appear from the burning phosphorus. Willie Pete burns at 5,000 degrees Fahrenheit.

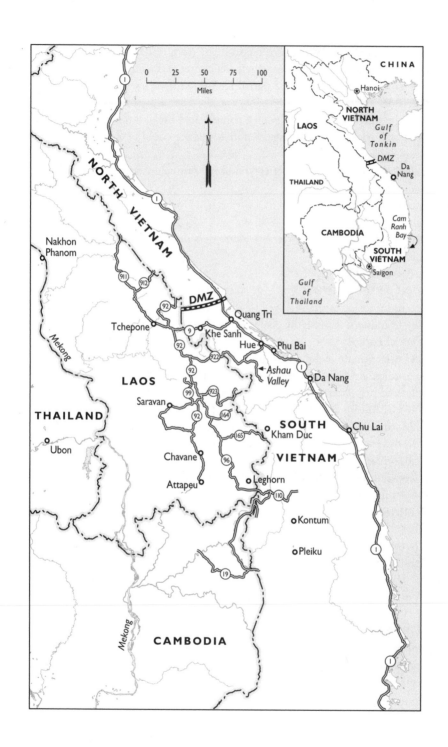

PREFACE

*Many of us will have to pass through the
valley of the shadow of death again and again
before we reach the mountaintop of our desires.*
—NELSON MANDELA

The Vietnam War was contested in ten thousand places, from the U
Minh Forest in the Mekong Delta to the Ia Drang Valley in the Central Highlands, from Tay Ninh Province near the Cambodian border
to the rugged mountains framing Khe Sanh on the Laotian frontier, from
the Ho Chi Minh Trail in Laos to the deadly skies over Hanoi. And for
the millions of combatants—whatever their allegiance—every battle played
out differently, each experience proved to be unique. Except for the ubiquitous fighting and dying, the 1964 guerrilla clashes in the rice paddies of
the Delta bore little resemblance to the 1968 head-to-head urban slugfest
in Hue during the Tet Offensive. Contrasting as their experiences were,
however, one constant emerged: every soldier, every marine, every guerrilla,
every airman, every general was aware of and personally affected by an ill-omened piece of real estate and battleground in Thua Thien Province
known to one and all as the Valley of Death—the A Shau Valley.

Approximately 25 miles long, running roughly northwest to southeast,
the A Shau lay hidden between rugged ridgelines over 5,000 feet tall, covered with dense double canopy jungle and impenetrable stands of thick
bamboo, deep ravines, saddles, draws, and treacherous, forbidding cliffs.
The narrow A Shau Valley, 27 miles southwest of the old imperial capital
of Hue, 25 miles southeast of Khe Sanh, and only a scant few kilometers
from the Laotian border, had been formed over millennia by the erosion

of the Rao Lao River. Thick, razor-sharp elephant grass over eight feet high covered most of the valley floor except around leech-infested pools and streams where tangled brush, bamboo, ferns, low trees, and "wait-a-minute" vines made travel next to impossible. Numerous constricted animal trails meandered through the A Shau and one primitive, man-made road extended the length of the valley with lesser trails connecting to it and radiating out in all directions. Some of those trails were and still are traveled by the reclusive but deadly Indochinese tiger, also referred to as "Corbett's tiger," named after hunter turned conservationist, British Army Colonel Edward James Corbett.[1] In addition to 400-pound tigers, the A Shau and surrounding environs are home to over 100 different types of venomous snakes, and American soldiers who campaigned in the area were warned that "Over 97 percent of the snakes in the A Shau are deadly poisonous; the other three percent will eat you."[2]

In a strange meteorological quirk, the prehistoric Valley of Death exists in the transition zone between two dominant weather phenomena: the northeast and southwest monsoons. For that reason the entire valley does not experience the typically alternating dry and rainy seasons associated with a monsoon climate, but instead tends to be shrouded in fog and low clouds most months of the year; annual rainfall on the A Shau's west wall approaches 120 inches. Consequently, the valley has long been both revered for its primordial beauty and feared because of its dangerous weather and the daunting physical geography of the environment, a setting so remote that it has sometimes been referred to as "a place from the beginning of time."[3]

From its very creation the region around what evolved into the A Shau Valley held center stage for scenes of Nature's violence and cataclysmic geological events. The formation of the Truong Son Mountain Range along the current Vietnam-Laos border, also called the Annamite Chain, occurred some two hundred million years ago in connection with powerful tectonic activity. The huge tectonic plates pushing against each other created intense pressure; therefore, the only direction for the folded mountains of the forming Annamite Chain to move was up. Worn down by myriad seismic events, massive lava flows, and violent weather, these now ancient eroded mountains remain rich in deposits of granite and limestone and abound with early plant and dinosaur fossils. The subsequent erosion along the

Truong Son Range produced a wild, spectacular landscape, ultimately defining the inhospitable terrain that witnessed some of the most brutal battles of the Vietnam War.[4]

As the topography of the locale evolved from the Mesozoic period across scores of millions of years, the introduction of the human element over 7,000 years ago ushered in a new and often contentious component to the reputation of the A Shau. There is little information about the factual history of the first permanent residents in the land that time forgot: the Katu tribe. Evidently they originally lived in Bronze Age southern China before being driven out approximately 700 BC. They settled in the coastal area of Vietnam and were forced into the upland region of their present territory along the Laotian border by the expansion of the ethnic Vietnamese sometime around 900 AD. Living much as they had for 1,000 years, the Katu became accomplished slash-and-burn farmers (dry rice being the staple with cassava and maize as the main supplementary crops) as well as proficient hunters and fishermen.[5]

Ethnically, the Katu were close relatives of the Montagnard tribesmen, members of Vietnam's largest minority of "mountain dwellers." Organized along tribal lines similar to American Indians, the Katu, Jarai, Rhade, Sedang, and Bru each had its own culture and dialect. All the Montagnard tribes were natural jungle fighters, and coincidentally, there was no love lost between most of the tribes and the Vietnamese—North or South. Contempt for Montagnards, manifested in the Vietnamese term *moi,* meaning savages, had fueled a long tradition of distrust and suspicion between the tribes and their Annam rulers.[6]

The exception proved to be the Katu. In the 1940s–50s during the first Indochina War, various Katu villages, especially those in and around the A Shau, formed a loose alliance with Ho Chi Minh's forces. That informal collaboration with the communist North continued throughout the American phase of the conflict. It is not entirely clear how or why the Katu were drawn into the war, but it is evident that the People's Army of Vietnam (PAVN) and communist cadres were more successful in penetrating the area and rallying the Katu to their cause than the Army of the Republic of Vietnam (ARVN) and its American allies. One explanation as to why the Katu were more susceptible to the propaganda of the North rather than that of the South was probably the distinctly negative influence that the colonial French had left in Katu minds. The Americans were apparently regarded as akin to the French and, in fact, old Katu chieftains often did not clearly differentiate between the two nationalities of white men.[7]

Some Katu elders, however, when asked to explain why they had decided to side with the communist forces, stated that it was not so much because of any particular animosity against the French or Americans as it was due to the xenophobic policies of South Vietnam's regime, first propped up by France, then by the United States. One village elder noted that, "The soldiers from the South would come here and ask the Katu to carry their luggage. But after the Katu had finished helping them, instead of paying them, the soldiers would shoot them."[8]

The North Vietnamese cadres also gained the sympathy of the Katu by supplying them with a new type of fast-ripening rice seed (the "three-moon rice"), significantly easing the labor burden of Katu men and women during the harvest period.[9] And while the communist agenda clearly was not entirely altruistic—the North Vietnamese Army (NVA) and Viet Cong (VC) soldiers were no strangers to using violence to coerce villages to loyalty—it served to gain an ally, or at least a sympathetic party, in the escalating war along the western edges of Thua Thien Province. By all accounts the average Katu guide, tracker, and soldier, armed only with a crossbow, was a very efficient jungle fighter, indeed, and a force multiplier for the NVA. Their inherent value comes as no surprise given that the knowledge possessed by the indigenous Katu fighters of the imposing jungle and mountain terrain in their homelands was absolutely vital for the NVA's and VC's ability to control the mountainous inland and repeatedly repel the combined efforts of American and ARVN forces.[10] By contrast, American units were never able to rally Katu villages to side with the South, but they were quite successful in recruiting other Montagnard tribes, especially the Bru. The best part of that alliance was the genuine rapport, respect, and even love that developed between the United States Special Forces and the Montagnards. They formed a unique brotherhood of warriors, willing to sacrifice and even die for each other.[11]

Even though the A Shau Valley had probably been part of the human landscape for at least 5,000 years, its tactical and strategic importance did not really take root until 1959 when North Vietnam's ruling Lao Dong Party adopted Resolution 15, calling for support of the National Liberation

Front (NLF) movement in South Vietnam. With that watershed decision, PAVN Colonel Vo Bam inherited the monumental task of "organizing a special communication line to send supplies to the revolution in the South." From that moment on the crux of the entire Vietnam War hinged on Hanoi's efforts to sustain the vital logistics supply line down the Ho Chi Minh Trail, and American attempts to interdict and cut it.[12] So, by a quirk of fate and the vagaries of geographic location, the A Shau was transformed into a massive logistical complex for infiltrating NVA supplies and soldiers into the I Corps Tactical Zone, referred to by most as "Eye" Corps. The stage was set. Between 1963 and late 1971, the Valley of Death became a bloody battleground and final resting place for thousands of American and Vietnamese soldiers locked in mortal combat in and around a remote valley—a place from the beginning of time.

Just as the A Shau has evolved without much alteration over countless millennia, so too has the unique character of the military profession evolved, slowly, ponderously. At Saratoga, Antietam, the Argonne, Bataan, Bastogne, and Inchon, young American soldiers and Marines were prepared to face death out of love for friends, family, and country. In that same tradition many trudged into I Corps' Valley of Death armed with a weapon, physical stamina, and personal valor, and far too many perished in the effort—a strange, fragmented effort that replicated itself each year for nine long years.

While a few may have admired the tropical beauty of the A Shau, most American combat troops loathed the place. Over the years it became a frightening location to operate in, and its very name sent chills down the spines of even the most hardened warriors. To them, the A Shau probably represented the most NVA-infested area south of Hanoi, and it was not a place for the faint of heart. They saw it as a haunted jungle of impenetrable secrecy and spookiness, a forbidding, mythical place where death lurked and the mist never lifted. One Special Forces non-commissioned officer (NCO) captured the general attitude about the A Shau when he noted, "I've known about this place since Bragg in 1968. The bogeyman for us. The place they send you when you say 'whatcha gonna do, send me to Nam?' I'd rather go to Hell. At least once you're there, you're already dead. Somethin' like 25 to 30 percent of all the teams that ever went in there didn't come back."[13] Tagged with that sort of reputation and in the best traditions of wartime gallows humor, GIs early on began referring to it as "Ah Shit Valley."

And the NVA were not the only dangers lurking in Ah Shit Valley. One of the most bizarre war stories substantiating that point involved a young Marine whose rifle company had just begun operations along the northwest corner of the valley right on the Laotian border. That first night, a cold and rainy one, he was asleep wrapped in his poncho on the edge of the perimeter when he awoke to something grabbing his foot. "I start screamin' and hollerin' and this tiger is all over me. I mean it's big as I am." The other squad members heard the commotion but could not shoot "cause me 'n the tiger's wrestlin' around the tent tryin' to kill each other, see?" At some point in the melee the big cat bolted away into the darkness, and the young Marine ended up with 63 stitches. His take on the A Shau? "I ain't ever going out there again. Ever."[14]

No matter the threat, whether man or beast, the A Shau wasn't the first valley of death in the Vietnam War. The original, a remote land-locked basin in the northwest corner of Vietnam encircling a place called Dien Bien Phu, gained world-wide attention in May 1954 when the French forces under Colonel Christian de Castries fell to a Viet Minh army commanded by General Vo Nguyen Giap. During the 56-day siege the French lost over 1,700 men killed, 5,000 wounded, 1,700 missing, and 11,700 prisoners. Viet Minh casualties included almost 8,000 killed and 15,000 wounded.[15] The bloody battle in the deadly valley at Dien Bien Phu, while extremely costly to General Giap's forces, nevertheless ended France's colonial reign in Indochina, foretold American involvement in the region, and offered pointed lessons that were ultimately ignored. Prophetically, the war in 1954 Indochina in general and the battle at Dien Bien Phi in particular had become very unpopular with French citizenry; the indecisiveness of the Fourth Republic signaled that France was both politically and militarily unable to extract itself from the conflict.[16] Yet the French experience in their war was significant to the United States if for no other reason than it somberly demonstrated the ominous reality that a Western colonial power could indeed be defeated by a third-world, indigenous revolutionary force, or that God forbid, a super power could be cowed by a peasant army.

Eleven years later and some 650 miles to the south of Dien Bien Phu, the U.S. Army engaged in its own struggle in another valley of death; this time the scene was the Ia Drang Valley in II Corps' Central Highlands, only a few miles east of the Cambodian border and 14 miles west of the Special Forces camp at Plei Me. From November 14–18, 1965, in the first major battle between U.S. and NVA forces, three battalions from the 1st Cavalry Division combat assaulted into the valley and engaged 2,500 soldiers of the NVA 320th, 33rd and 66th regiments. The 1st Cav troops pioneered a brand new idea and rode into battle not on the horses suggested by the division's name, but rather in UH-1 "Huey" helicopters; the concept was called Vertical Envelopment. In the savage fighting around the Ia Drang Valley, the Americans lost 234 killed and 242 wounded at landing zones (LZ) X-Ray and Albany. The NVA, in their first direct showdown with Americans, suffered an estimated 1,800 killed and many more wounded. At the end of the battle both sides claimed victory, and both sides ostensibly drew lessons from the encounter in their valley of death. In its wildest dreams, however, the United States never imagined that the war would drag on another ten long years.[17]

But North Vietnam did. The Democratic Republic of Vietnam was in it for the long haul, and General Vo Nguyen Giap's 'peasant army,' made up of dedicated followers bent on fighting a protracted war, was willing to absorb enormous casualties to achieve its goals. As early as 1950, Giap served notice that the strategy for victory involved decades, not years. In Giap's own words:

> The enemy will pass slowly from the offensive to the defensive. The *blitzkrieg* will transform itself into a war of long duration. Thus, the enemy will be caught in a dilemma: he has to drag out the war to win it and does not possess, on the other hand, the psychological and political means to fight a long drawn-out war.[18]

Even though not mentioned specifically by name, the French were obviously the focus of his remarks, yet he paradoxically chose the word "enemy" rather than the name of a specific foe. Ironically, his prediction might just as easily have applied to American military policy 15 years later.

Although the battles at Dien Bien Phu lasted about two months and Ia Drang only five days, the slugfests in the A Shau Valley intermittently spanned nine years and more nearly characterized Giap's prediction of "a long drawn-out war." This book does not pretend to provide a day-by-day, comprehensive account of those nine years, but rather it is episodic, singling out for special attention a series of American combat operations encompassing the entire length of the valley and a 15-mile radius around it. Beginning in 1963, Special Forces A-teams established camps along the valley floor, followed by a number of top-secret Project Delta missions through 1967. Then, U.S. Army and Marine Corps maneuver battalions engaged in a series of temporary and sometimes controversial thrusts into the A Shau designed to disrupt NVA infiltration into I Corps and to kill enemy soldiers, part of what came to be known as Westmoreland's 'war of attrition' strategy. The various campaigns included Operations Prairie Fire and Pirous in 1967, 1968's Operations Grand Canyon, Delaware, and Somerset Plain, 1969's Operations Dewey Canyon, Massachusetts Striker, and Apache Snow with the infamous battle of Hamburger Hill, culminating with Operation Texas Star and the vicious fight for and the humiliating evacuation of Fire Support Base Ripcord in the summer of 1970. By 1971 the fighting had once again shifted to the realm of small Special Forces reconnaissance teams assigned to the ultra-secret Studies and Observations Group—SOG. This book, then, chronicles a frustrating military involvement, the battles, and most of all, the associated courage, sacrifice, and valor in and around the remote and lethal A Shau Valley.

In presenting this story, I struggled with a perennial dilemma faced by virtually every author who tries his/her hand at writing military history: how to fashion a comprehensive account of the facts without getting bogged down in minutiae and repetitious details. In the end I settled on a relatively innocuous literary device—I combed numerous military archives for individual cases of conspicuous gallantry in action, to include Medal of Honor, Distinguished Service Cross, Navy Cross, and Air Force Cross citations. A total of 15 Medals of Honor were awarded for deeds in and around the A Shau—more than any other single location in the Vietnam War. In effect those heroic actions, those incredible acts of bravery, provided the framework for the story I wanted to tell. That methodology ultimately suggested the title for the book: A Shau Valor.

I have also attempted to convey the distinctively tropical character of a conflict in a location that if not unique was certainly extraordinary. The A Shau spawned its own peculiar war without fronts where terrain, weather, and people triumphed over technology. For me, the challenge was to communicate not only the essential elements of the battles but also to supply a sense of the sights, sounds, and even the smells of the battlefield so that the reader feels engaged and, at least figuratively, experiences the mosquitoes, the mud, the oppressive heat, the leeches, the agony, the frustration, the fear.

In addition, I feel compelled to point out that the nine-year struggle around the A Shau Valley did not occur in a vacuum and cannot be understood or viewed as a series of stand-alone battles devoid of historical and societal context. Other political and military events—large and small—impacted the battles and strategies associated with the Valley of Death. For that reason it was necessary to at least touch on other consequential episodes and decisions. Therefore, I have attempted to expand the story by including relevant background information, newly declassified facts, and bits of pertinent historical perspective from key players such as Presidents Johnson and Nixon, Robert McNamara, and General William Westmoreland. I hope that discerning readers will find these historical detours presented responsibly, with care, and as essential digressions.

Any book that includes factual accounts of a war is by necessity a collective endeavor. Numerous books and articles have been written by key participants and scholars on various aspects of the Vietnam War, many of which I have been able to consult in the course of my research. They are listed in the bibliography at the end of *A Shau Valor.* But as a compulsory underpinning for understanding the individual unit operational summaries and after action reports, each filled with hour-by-hour accounts of missions and firefights, perhaps the most indispensable documentary sources are the inspiring valor citations themselves, riveting accounts of the heroes who defined the battles. The best documents, however, cannot replace direct accounts of men in battle. Consequently, in order to flesh out the story I felt obliged to include recollections and interviews with some of the warriors, for as author Herman Wouk so eloquently observed, "The beginning of the end of War lies in Remembrance."

Additionally, I have had the unique opportunity to study the battle for the A Shau through several disparate lenses: from a detached status as a college faculty member; from an inquiring position as a graduate student; from the viewpoint of a young Air Force forward air controller supporting

SOG teams in the A Shau. I gained a unique perspective by flying daily over the Valley of Death—we FACs had a god's-eye view of the action. And working with the men who were engaged in life or death battles on the ground, I came to know and admire them: warriors, human beings on two feet, soldiers, crawling on their bellies up the steep slopes of the primordial A Shau, with racing minds and fearful thoughts and short futures. They were the finest men I have ever met, and I am proud to count these warrior-friends as my knights in shining armor—forever the quintessential heroes of my memory.

The guiding principle in my research, no matter how painful the process might be to national pride or to widely held prejudices, has been to present the facts and data as they are and not as one wishes them to be. Any conclusions stated are based on meticulous examination of the historical evidence, not on widely circulated popular myths or preconceptions. Moreover, the persons and events depicted in this book are in all cases true and authentic to the best of my knowledge. And while I had access to a mind-boggling number of official primary sources and records at the National Archives, the U.S. Army Center of Military History, the United States Marine Corps History Division, the Air Force Historical Research Agency, the U.S. Army Military History Institute, and the Texas Tech University Vietnam Center and Archive, any mistakes or misinterpretations that remain are my responsibility alone.

chapter 1

INTO THE VALLEY OF DEATH

Act in the valley so that you need not
fear those who stand on the hill.
—DANISH PROVERB

Beginning in 1963, ARVN units and American military advisors essentially ignored Machiavelli's celebrated admonition to always control the high ground. Instead, they focused more or less exclusively on several small settlements along a remote valley floor. A nearly deserted Katu village, namesake for the entire area, was positioned at the southeastern end of a valley measuring roughly 40 kilometers in length and only several kilometers across at its widest point. On each side of the valley, steep, jungle-covered mountains rose thousands of feet and offered a spectacular view of the basin below. From the heights VC and NVA lookouts kept a watchful surveillance over all activities. A small river, the Rao Lao, ran past the village, and a single lane dirt road paralleled the stream, providing the only travel route through the tall elephant grass. The Katu inhabitants called the place A Sap. To the Vietnamese and Americans, it was known as A Shau.

All participants in the war—NVA, Viet Cong, ARVN, and American military advisors—recognized that the valley was indeed strategically positioned. The Laotian border, running along the peaks of the A Shau's west wall, was only several kilometers away, the narrow ravine representing the only passage through the largely impassable mountain region. The valley also served as the junction of three routes: Route 548 running the length of the A Shau; Route 547 running east toward Hue; and Route 922, snaking its way west from the Ho Chi Minh Trail to the north end of the valley. Whoever controlled the valley, so the thinking went, controlled the

23

region and the entry from Laos into Thua Thien Province and Hue; whoever owned the A Shau Valley could set the terms of battle. A major clash was inevitable.

Due to 1,000 years of Chinese rule, Vietnamese traditions had been strongly influenced by Chinese culture in terms of politics, government, and Confucian social and moral beliefs. As an example of that cultural sway, according to the Chinese calendar—revered in both North and South Vietnam—the year 1963 did not herald a particularly propitious time: it was the Year of the Rabbit, celebrated by some Vietnamese as the Year of the Cat. In Chinese lore the Rabbit did poorly in conflict, as it was often overly sensitive in times of confrontation. Likewise, those born under the Rabbit sign had a tendency to dwell on negative events in the past, at times to an obsessive extent. Given over to cultural bias, an assortment of fortune-tellers, Buddhist priests, and shamans employed the Chinese zodiac calendar to interpret events and personalities in 1963. In Saigon they made much of the fact that South Vietnam's president, Ngo Dinh Diem, was born in the Year of the Rat, and that President John F. Kennedy had been born in the Year of the Snake. More auspiciously, soothsayers in Hanoi crowed that Ho Chi Minh was born under the sign of the Dragon.[1]

While the year 1963 witnessed the first American ventures into the A Shau, initially by U.S. Army advisors to ARVN units, followed by Special Forces A-teams from Okinawa, the timing of those movements proved to be particularly inauspicious for several reasons. Besides being the Year of the Rabbit, political squabbles in both Washington and Saigon cast a cloud over policy direction and commitment to the war. For one thing, the assessments of the commander of the Military Assistance Command Vietnam (MACV), General Paul D. Harkins, proved to be overly optimistic to the point of fault, which became the basis for his ongoing problems with reporters who found his assessments sharply different from the accounts provided by American advisors in the field. As a result, MACV unofficially assigned all media the roll of opposition, a label that stuck throughout the war. In spite of that bone of contention, General Harkins and his faction staunchly maintained that ARVN pushback against the Viet Cong was going so well that MACV could plan for phasing out U.S. forces beginning with the withdrawal of 1,000 advisers by year's end.[2] Other official reporting channels saw it differently. They, along with the press, did not concur that the war was progressing well and did not see the South Vietnamese showing evidence of being reliable. For example, CIA Director John Mc-Cone felt certain the U.S. had received very inaccurate information from the South Vietnamese who tended to report what they believed Americans wanted to hear. He wrote, "The Province and district chiefs felt obliged to 'create statistics' which would meet the approbation of the Central Government."[3]

At about the same time, American attention was brutally yanked away from various military concerns to a political and religious crisis that bubbled to the surface across South Vietnam. Buddhist monks upset at the Diem regime's crackdown on religious freedom staged protests in Hue that led to deadly retaliation by the local military commander. When thousands marched in protest against a government order banning parades and the display of Buddhist flags, army troops fired into the unruly crowds; nine protesters were killed and scores wounded. A month later Buddhist monks in Saigon shocked the world when one of their number, Thich Quang Duc, doused himself in gasoline while sitting in the lotus position on a main thoroughfare and struck a match. The reek of funeral pyre smoke and burning flesh hung over the location like a dark shroud. Then, over the summer of 1963, six more monks and one Buddhist nun also immolated themselves in protest. The events shocked and appalled leaders in Washington and made Diem's regime, top heavy with Catholics and French-trained bureaucrats, more suspect than ever. After seeing reporter Malcolm Browne's photograph of the first monk's fiery death, President John F. Kennedy remarked, "No news picture in history has generated so much emotion around the world as that one."[4]

In spite of the political and religious turmoil that diverted attention away from the insurgency, the American military nevertheless initiated limited moves into the A Shau Valley. One of the first U.S. advisors with "boots on the ground" was a young Army captain assigned to the 2nd Battalion, 3rd Infantry Regiment, 1st ARVN Division posted along the Laotian border near the village of Ta Bat, situated in the middle portion of the A Shau. Arriving on January 17, 1963, the young officer, a native of the Bronx and an ROTC graduate from the City College of New York, settled into the sensitive job of advising his "counterpart," Captain Vo Cong Hieu, without intruding on the prerogatives of the Vietnamese commander.

When the American advisor inquired about their mission, he was told it was to protect the newly constructed airfield—little more than a primitive dirt runway carved out of the valley floor. In response to the question, "what's the airfield for?" Hieu replied that the airfield was there to resupply the outpost. On that January day in 1963, the experience proved to be the advisor's first—but not his last—exposure to Vietnamese circular thinking.

The American advisor's life settled into an endless series of patrols and movements down the valley. On a regular basis, small, unseen pockets of VC initiated ambushes against the ARVN column or harassed it with sniper fire and booby traps. Aggravation and casualties mounted. Aside from those adrenalin-pumping episodes, the daily grind also ate away at morale. Living conditions in the jungle were miserable; an odious smell hovered around each soldier, an overpowering stench of mud, sweat, body odor, and decaying vegetation. The patrols also trudged through blinding clouds of gnats, flies, or mosquitoes, and every encounter with a puddle or stream meant leeches. The advisor reported, "Worse were the leeches. I never understood how they managed to get through our clothing . . . biting the flesh and bloating themselves on our blood. We stopped as often as ten times a day to get rid of them."[5]

The 2nd Battalion of the 3rd Regiment was ambushed almost daily, usually in the morning soon after the point squad moved out. The American advisor's own words capture best the strain and frustration of those early engagements in the A Shau:

> I found it maddening to be ambushed, to lose men day after day to this phantom enemy who hit and ran and hit again, with seeming impunity, never taking a stand, never giving us anything to shoot at. I often wondered if we were achieving anything. How did we fight foes who blended in with local peasants who were sympathetic or too frightened to betray them? How did we measure progress? There was no front, no ground gained or lost, just endless, bloody slogging along a trail leading nowhere.[6]

The American advisor who wrote those prophetic words was Colin L. Powell, future Chairman of the Joint Chiefs of Staff and Secretary of State. In late March Captain Powell moved with his battalion to the southeast corner of the A Shau to establish a new camp at Be Luong. The ARVN troops normally used axes or dynamite to clear trees for landing zones (LZ), a time-consuming and exhausting effort in the debilitating heat and humidity of the jungle. The resourceful Powell, however, found a better way. He had several power tools airlifted in, which dazzled the Vietnamese who had never seen a chain saw before.

After six months of "humping through the A Shau boonies," Captain Powell and his battalion received orders to leave Be Luong and move to a Special Forces camp at Nam Dong, 15 miles to the east. On July 23 the point squad, with Powell near the front, was slogging along a creek bed when the big American soldier stepped in a concealed Viet Cong punji trap. The dung-tipped spike pierced the sole of his boot and penetrated clear through his foot to the top of the instep. In a matter of minutes his foot was hugely swollen and turned purple as the poison from the buffalo dung spread. Powell managed to limp into Nam Dong where the Special Forces medic took one look at the wound and called for an evacuation helicopter—Colin Powell's tour in the Valley of Death was over. Ironically, Powell probably spent more actual time on the ground in the A Shau than any other American soldier.

In the spring of 1963, with most of MACV's focus on widespread Viet Cong attacks in IV Corps, known to all as "the Delta," U.S. Army Special Forces detachments began building several new camps in the A Shau Valley. The effort became part of a border surveillance program administered by the Central Intelligence Agency and operated by Special Forces detachments from the 1st Special Forces Group Airborne (SFGA) in Okinawa. The program's primary objectives were to "recruit and train border surveillance personnel, establish intelligence nets, gain the border zone population's loyalty to the South Vietnamese government, and conduct guerrilla warfare—long range patrol activities in the border zone to deny the areas to the Viet Cong."[7]

To set the program in motion, in March, Special Forces Detachment A-433 constructed the first camp at Ta Bat. In addition to border surveillance, the new camp became part of the country-wide Civilian Irregular Defense Group (CIDG) program. Focusing on local defense and civic action, the Special Forces teams conducted the training for CIDG activities whereby villagers were instructed and armed for self-defense, while localized strike force companies served as a quick reaction unit to respond to larger Viet Cong attacks. The vast majority of the CIDG camps were initially manned by inhabitants of ethnic minorities, especially Montagnards, who disliked both the North and South Vietnamese. Once in place, the 12 Green Berets of A-433 conducted a number of patrols to determine CIDG training potential in the Ta Bat area. Between operations, the newly trained strike force began receiving advanced training with automatic weapons, mortars and immediate action drills, and during the month of August another strike force company was requested for operations to the west where air reconnaissance had spotted many villages. According to the 1st SFGA monthly operational summaries, throughout this early start-up period there were no reported engagements with the VC.

On November 3, 1963, another detachment, A-434, took over at Ta Bat and established a new forward operating base (FOB) at A Shau. Enemy response was immediate. VC initiated actions included 6 attacks, 1 probe, and 17 ambushes, and unfortunately, with only partially trained troops pitted against tough and experienced Viet Cong fighters, the "good guys" came out on the short end with 1 SF team member wounded, 3 CIDG killed in action (KIA), and 10 others wounded in action (WIA).[8] From that point on the tempo and frequency of engagements increased, resulting in a predictable rash of desertions among the CIDG personnel. The sporadic firefights in the A Shau also portended the deadly combat that was to occur there during the next nine years.

While the skirmishes at the remote A Shau FOB did not warrant more than a single line in the daily MACV situation reports, the escalating political turmoil in Saigon made the entire world gasp and hold its collective breath. The drama played out before the critical eyes of the international press corps and worried officials at the American Embassy. On November 1, 1963, the top South Vietnamese generals, with the apparent implicit approval of the CIA, staged a *coup d'état* against President Ngo Dinh Diem. The CIA station in Saigon reported that Diem and his brother Ngu were shoved into an armored personnel carrier with their hands tied behind their backs. When the personnel carrier arrived at the Joint General Staff headquarters, Diem and Ngu were dead. Both had been shot and Ngu had been stabbed several times. Inconceivably, the South Vietnamese reported that the brothers had committed suicide. Back in Washington President

Kennedy was deeply shaken by Diem's death, but his national security advisor, McGeorge Bundy, commented dryly that "it seemed uncommon for individuals to shoot and knife themselves with their hands tied behind their backs."[9] Three weeks later the unthinkable happened. John F. Kennedy, 35th president of the United States, was assassinated in Dallas.

JFK's principal foreign affairs advisors on Vietnam urged Lyndon Banes Johnson to reaffirm the continuity of policy and direction as the new president. Therefore, LBJ's first important decision on Vietnam as president, only five days after taking the oath of office aboard Air Force One, was to approve National Security Action Memorandum 273 which stated:

> It remains the central objective of the United States in South Vietnam to assist the people and government of that country to win their contest against the externally directed and supported communist conspiracy. The test of all U.S. decisions and actions in this area should be the effectiveness of their contribution to this purpose.[10]

Following the assassination of Diem, the government of South Vietnam spiraled into a series of coups and power struggles among various military and religious factions. It came as no surprise to anyone that the NLF jumped at the opportunity to exploit the unstable political environment to achieve both political and military gains. The depth of the problem was not completely apparent in late 1963, but in Washington, Saigon, and the A Shau, everyone was relieved to see the end of the Year of the Rabbit.

With the beginning of the Year of the Dragon, several exasperating holdover elements from the Diem regime complicated life for American advisors around the A Shau, especially for the Special Forces A-teams. Diem had established a kind of "palace guard" named the *Luc Luong Dac Biet,* or LLDB, a term which translates into Airborne Special Forces. Instead of being the elite unit its name implied, the LLDB initially consisted of members who had obtained their positions through family influence or the payment of bribes. In a highly questionable move, LLDB units took command of many of the border surveillance camps, including those in the A Shau, creating very strained relations for the American advisors. First and foremost, the early LLDB commanders were inexperienced, irresponsible, and reluctant to perform their jobs, although once free from President Diem's influence, many became excellent warriors. Additionally, the upper echelons of Vietnamese society frowned on service with savage Montagnards in remote areas, and the I Corps outposts, in close proximity to North Vietnam and the dreaded A Shau Valley, were the most feared assignments. Consequently, Special Forces advisors were initially hard pressed to get LLDB units to even associate with CIDG strike forces. Furthermore, VC activity usually occurred at night; the LLDB generally refused to patrol at all during darkness. At any rate, aggressive patrolling often did not work because the A Shau was full of pro-Viet Cong sympathizers who tipped off NVA or VC units about LLDB patrols or ambushes.[11]

Another problem plaguing the border surveillance camps involved an insufficient local recruiting base for their CIDG units. Camps manned by Montagnards imported from other regions of the country suffered from low morale and desertions, and partially for that reason the camp at Ta Bat shut down in March 1964, with all CIDG and LLDB forces consolidated at Camp A Shau. Inadvertently, however, one of Diem's schemes became an asset. In an effort to rid Saigon of some of its less desirable elements, Diem had emptied the city jails containing thugs, violent criminals, juvenile delinquents, and army deserters, turning them all over to the Special Forces for service at border camps. Oddly enough, the A-teams won the grudging respect of the transplanted hoodlums and turned many of them into valuable fighters.

By mid-1964, Camp A Shau and others like it had assumed a unique Special Forces flavor, a tropical version of a French Foreign Legion outpost straight out of *Beau Geste*, complete with a cast that included superstitious Montagnards, self-absorbed LLDB companies, and a motley collection of former prison inmates. In a particularly apt observation, one detachment commander described a typical camp as "a hodge-podge of males; laborers, mechanics, contractors, soldiers, mercenaries, interpreters, officers, Montagnards, Nungs, pimps, card sharks. Some were patriots, some criminals. All were selfish. All were tough."[12]

While the almost daily CIDG skirmishes with the VC never made headlines, one incident that did indeed capture the attention of MACV and the press occurred at Camp A Shau in May, 1964. Shortly after his arrival in Vietnam, General William C. Westmoreland, referred to unofficially as 'Westy,' visited Camp A Shau along with several American Embassy officials. At the conclusion of the stopover, his CV-2 MACV Caribou taxied to the end of the crude runway for takeoff. At that moment the VC opened fire, the first rounds ripping into the Caribou's nose, shattering the instrument panel and wounding both pilots. Somehow they managed to gun the engines and take off. At liftoff, bullets were still penetrating the aircraft cabin, wounding the crew chief, several ARVN soldiers, and missing General Westmoreland by inches. The Special Forces Detachment B-420 commander, Major George A. Maloney, was also wounded while returning fire from inside the aircraft. Miraculously, the VIP-toting Caribou, flown by two wounded pilots, made a safe landing at a more secure airfield. The incident proved to be Westmoreland's closest call during his four and a half years in Vietnam, and prophetically, it happened in the remote, deadly A Shau Valley.[13]

Six weeks after Westy's close call, VC units upped the ante by staging a large-scale attack against the Special Forces camp at Nam Dong, 15 miles from the foothills forming part of the A Shau's eastern wall. Originally a French outpost during the Indochina War, the site had become a strategic hamlet in 1962, designed to protect some 5,000 tribesmen and 9 villages—mostly hostile—on a key VC infiltration route from Laos to Hue and Da Nang. By 1964, Special Forces surveys indicated that the Nam Dong location was not only dangerous but indefensible. Low ridges covered by dense jungle surrounded the camp, the Katu villagers were uncooperative, the Vietnamese company included a number of suspected VC sympathizers, and there was bad blood between the Vietnamese soldiers and the Nung mercenaries. Trying to keep a lid on the volatile situation, Captain Roger H.C. Donlon, commander of Detachment A-726, made plans to close out the camp and turn it over to the ARVN. The circumstances were made even worse because a large cache of weapons was stored at Nam Dong awaiting transfer to other locations.[14]

In addition to his American team members, Donlon's camp included 60 Nung mercenaries, 381 predominately Vietnamese CIDG, 7 LLDB, 1 Australian advisor, and 1 American anthropologist under contract to the Rand Corporation to study hill tribes. That study included the Nungs, who were a minority group of ethnic Chinese descent from southern China and had been fighting the communists since World War II. After being chased out of China, they fought for the French, and during the Vietnam War the Chinese Nung soldiers were best-known for their devoted loyalty to U.S. Special Forces with a well deserved reputation as the most-feared fighters of all the minority groups trained by the Americans. On July 5 the bad feelings between the Nungs and the Vietnamese strike force members of Company 122 erupted into a brawl over a camp prostitute, an argument that culminated in threats, rock throwing, fights, and firing of weapons before Capt Donlon could re-establish order.

Acting with the intuition of an experienced warrior, Donlon sensed that the earlier quarrels possibly masked a more sinister threat to the camp, so that night he remained awake, personally patrolling the perimeter mortar pits and machine gun positions located along the camp's two concentric defensive ovals, each fortified by trenches and barbed wire. In support, the Nung guard force remained at their assigned battle posts on full alert. The Vietnamese strikers and LLDB, on the other hand, seemed apathetic or lax with most turning in for the night.

Donlon's intuition had been spot on. The Viet Cong attack began at 2:26 a.m. on July 6, 1964, when the first mortar rounds crashed into the A-team's mess hall and team quarters, setting them both on fire. At the same instant, two VC battalions, approximately 900-strong, assaulted the camp from all four sides, with the largest attack pressing in from the southeast. There was no advance warning because the six-man CIDG outpost just beyond the outer perimeter had their throats cut in their sleep. During the initial onslaught, 45-year-old Master Sergeant Gabriel R. Alamo from Lyndhurst, NJ, sprang into action and promptly directed the team radio operator to transmit an emergency message requesting support, then rushed into the burning command post to assist in the removal of weapons and ammunition. Ignoring the burns he received while in the blazing structure, Alamo, known to everyone as "Pop," then ran through a hail of enemy gunfire to a 60mm mortar pit partially buried below ground with sides protected by sandbag parapets, and readied the weapon for firing. When he saw the enemy attempting to breach the main gate, he again dashed through a heavy volume of automatic weapons fire to meet the threat head on. Although Pop sustained a serious wound in this courageous action, he reached the gate and took out the enemy troops with his AR-15. Bleeding badly from a shoulder wound and a fresh hole in his right cheek just below the eye, Pop returned to the 60mm mortar pit, refused evacuation for medical treatment, and directed the fire of the 60mm mortar while simultaneously manning a 57mm recoilless rifle. As the waves of VC broke through the outer perimeter trenches and barbed wire with suicidal fanaticism, Alamo cranked his mortar to maximum elevation, bringing the rounds practically down on to his own position. Undaunted by the vicious VC assault, Pop Alamo remained in the mortar pit defending the camp until mortally wounded by the enemy.[15]

At the height of the battle the enemy resorted to psychological warfare. From the edge of the outer perimeter a loudspeaker blared out in English and Vietnamese, "Lay down your weapons. We are going to annihilate the Americans in your camp. Surrender or you will all be killed." Exchanging anxious looks with several other A-726 teammates, Sergeant Thomas Gregg, one of the team medics, summed up the feelings of everyone when he said, "We'll lay down our weapons when we're too dead to pick them up." At that point Sergeant Thurman Brown, a Korean War veteran, calmly adjusted his mortar while Sergeant Vernon Beeson indicated where the loudspeaker voice was coming from. Brown fired ten high explosive and white phosphorus rounds against the target. The voice abruptly stopped.[16]

When the first VC mortar rounds hit the camp, 22 year-old Sergeant John L. Houston from Winter Park, FL, immediately began removing the radio equipment from the burning hut in order to save it. Although blown to the ground and wounded by a large explosion, Houston climbed out of the debris to continue the fight. As he was moving through the darkness, he noticed that one of his team members, Sergeant Terrance Terrin, had been knocked down by an exploding mortar round. With complete disregard for his own safety, Houston rushed through a hail of small arms fire and grenade blasts, succeeded in reaching the unconscious soldier, placed him in a covered position, and stayed with Terrin until fully conscious before proceeding to his battle station. After he had moved only a few yards and was injured for the second time by shrapnel from an exploding mortar round, Sgt Houston climbed to the top of a large seven foot mound of dirt which afforded him excellent observation and fields of fire. From this exposed position he single-handedly broke up the vicious human wave assaults in his sector and killed many of the enemy troops who had completely overrun Strike Force Company 122 and were at the inner perimeter barbed wire. While the outgoing mortar and automatic weapons fire kept the VC pinned down, they were still within grenade throwing distance, tossing the Chinese-made old-fashioned "potato mashers." As the hostile forces continued to assault Houston's position, he again blunted the enemy action with his deadly fire. Although his ammunition was running out, he refused to take cover, called out to a fellow soldier to throw additional rounds to him, and reloaded the magazine while exposed to extraordinarily heavy VC gunfire. Undaunted by the overwhelming onslaught, John Houston remained in this dangerous position for over two hours until cut down by the marauding enemy.[17]

Throughout the five-hour battle at Nam Dong, Roger Donlon was the glue and inspiration that held the camp together. The 30-year-old captain from Saugerties, NY, directed the defense operations in the midst of a coordinated enemy barrage of mortar shells, hand grenades, and extremely heavy automatic weapons and small arms fire. During the initial onslaught, he swiftly marshaled his forces and ordered the removal of the needed ammunition from a blazing building. Donlon then dashed through a hail of bullets and exploding hand grenades to repulse an attack near the camp's main gate. En route to this position he detected an enemy sapper team and quickly annihilated them. Although exposed to an intense grenade attack, he then succeeded in reaching a 60mm mortar position despite sustaining a severe stomach wound when he was within five yards of the gun pit. Donlon stuffed a handkerchief in the wound, cinched up his belt, and kept fighting. When he discovered that most of the men in this mortar pit were also wounded, he completely disregarded his own injury, directed their withdrawal to a location 30 meters away, and again risked his life by remaining behind and covering their movement. Noticing that his wounded team sergeant, Pop Alamo, was unable to leave the pit under his own power, the detachment commander crawled toward him; Donlon got one of Alamo's arms around his neck and started to straighten up. At that instant an enemy mortar shell exploded, killing Alamo and inflicting a debilitating wound to Capt Donlon's left shoulder. Although bleeding profusely from multiple wounds and realizing that Alamo was beyond help, he then carried the abandoned 60mm mortar tube to a new location 30 meters away where he found three wounded Nung defenders. After administering first aid and encouragement to these men, he left the weapon with them, headed toward another position and retrieved a 57mm recoilless rifle. Then, with great courage and absolute coolness under fire, he returned to the abandoned gun pit and while recovering and dragging the urgently needed ammunition, he was wounded a third time in the leg from an enemy hand grenade. Disregarding his injuries, he crawled 175 meters under fire to an 81mm mortar position and directed firing operations which protected the seriously threatened east sector of the camp.

Donlon then moved to another location and upon determining that the vicious enemy assault had weakened, crawled back to the gun pit with the 60mm mortar, set it up for defensive operations, and turned it over to two defenders with minor wounds. Without hesitation he left this sheltered mortar pit and moved from position to position around the beleaguered perimeter while hurling hand grenades at the enemy and inspiring his men to superhuman effort. As he continued to move around the perimeter, another mortar shell exploded, wounding him in the face and body. Undeterred, he kept fighting, leading, and inspiring his men. At daylight the enemy forces began a retreat back to the jungle, leaving behind 54 of their dead, many weapons, and grenades. Donlon immediately reorganized his defenses, administered first aid to the wounded, and waited for the relief force to arrive. His dynamic leadership, fortitude, and valiant efforts inspired not only the American personnel but the friendly Vietnamese defenders as well and resulted in the successful defense of Nam Dong against overwhelming odds.[18]

At 9:45 a.m. Marine H-34 helicopters arrived with 100 Special Forces and CIDG reinforcements. When the choppers landed, many of the camp's CIDG began to storm the helicopter pad, forcing members of the relief team to brandish their weapons to keep the panicky mob at bay so the wounded could be loaded.

What the relieving force found was incredible. Virtually all the American survivors had been wounded, their faces and bodies covered with blood and blackened from explosions and thick smoke. They were barely able to move. Two A-726 members were dead along with the Australian advisor, Warrant Officer Kevin G. Conway. The strike force companies lost 55 dead and 65 wounded, and during the battle approximately 100 of the CIDG had stripped off their uniforms and rallied to the VC. In addition to the 54 dead attackers left behind, as many as three times that number of VC were believed killed and many more wounded. Almost every building in the camp had burned to the ground, so all members of A-726 were evacuated to Da Nang. A few days later anthropologist Gerald Hickey, fluent in Vietnamese, debriefed with General Westmoreland in Saigon. When Hickey described the attackers as having North Vietnamese accents, there was no comment.[19]

For their heroic actions, both Master Sergeant Gabriel Alamo and Sergeant John Houston were awarded the Distinguished Service Cross posthumously. Captain Roger Donlon became the first American in the Vietnam War to receive the Medal of Honor.

Unfortunately, the battle for Nam Dong ended on a bureaucratic sour note. Warrant Officer Kevin Conway, veteran of the Malaya and Borneo emergencies and the first Australian killed in Vietnam, was recommended by his Australian commander for the Victoria Cross, the equivalent of the Medal of Honor. Conway, a member of the Australian Army Training Team Vietnam, was alone in his pit at Nam Dong firing his mortar into the assaulting enemy in ever decreasing range until he was forced to bring his mortar fire upon himself to save the perimeter of the camp. Warrant Officer Conway never received the valor ward. According to several sources, his commander suggested that because of the award to Donlon, Special Forces politics denied Conway his Victoria Cross. No proof was ever found to substantiate that claim. The U.S. Army awarded Kevin Conway the Silver Star for gallantry in action.[20]

Immediately after his post-battle visit to Nam Dong and his meeting with American anthropologist Gerald Hickey, General Westmoreland and the MACV staff began contemplating several disturbing revelations. First, while ARVN and CIDG forces were winning a few victories like Nam Dong, it was becoming clear that they were being out-gunned. Throughout 1964, VC units attacked with a new weapon, the AK-47, a superior assault rifle provided by the Soviet Union. And as Capt Donlon and A-726 discovered, the enemy had also been issued modern rocket launchers, mortars, and recoilless rifles. Against these new weapons, the ARVN still used World War II models, including the Garand M-1 rifle, whose powerful kick when firing often knocked the small Vietnamese soldiers off balance. For regional and CIDG forces, the light semiautomatic M-1 carbine proved to be little more than a "pea shooter" against the AK-47.

The firepower imbalance was disturbing enough, but intelligence sources confirmed a second, more unsettling fact. As Gerald Hickey had suspected, infiltrators included separate North Vietnamese units. At its core, that information revealed a decision by Hanoi that went beyond mere support for the NLF; it indicated direct intervention by units of the NVA—and the point of infiltration for those units was the A Shau.[21]

Just one month after the battle at Nam Dong, American focus once again shifted away from fighting in the A Shau to an event that ultimately committed the United States to war in Southeast Asia. On August 2, North Vietnamese patrol boats attacked the U.S. Navy destroyer *Maddox* operating in international waters. Two days later the Pentagon received a message that patrol boats had attacked again, this time engaging the *Maddox* and the destroyer *C. Turner Joy*. Although there was and still is controversy concerning the veracity of a second attack, President Johnson nevertheless ordered a retaliatory airstrike against the North Vietnamese patrol boat base and on a major oil storage tank facility. On August 5, aircraft from Seventh Fleet carriers *Ticonderoga* and *Constellation* destroyed the oil storage facility at Vinh and damaged or sank 24 enemy naval vessels along the North Vietnam coast. In the attack the North Vietnamese downed two American strike aircraft; Lieutenant J.G. Everett Alvarez, Jr. was captured and endured eight years and seven months of brutal captivity. Then on August 7, Congress passed the Gulf of Tonkin Resolution that gave the President authorization "to take all necessary measures to repel any armed attack against the forces of the United States and to prevent further aggression." The resolution further empowered the President "to take all steps necessary, including the use of armed force, to assist any member or protocol state of the Southeast Asia Collective Defense Treaty requesting assistance in defense of its freedom." The vote in the Senate was 88 to 2, while in the House the vote was 416 to 0.[22]

Throughout the remainder of 1964, the 1st and 5th Special Forces Groups' monthly operational summaries documented activity in the A Shau, consisting primarily of recruiting and training new strike force members, construction, and defoliation. The danger, however, was ever-present. Typical of the action was a combat patrol on August 21 conducted by Detachment A-421 when a VC sniper killed Sergeant First Class William R. Patience, Jr. Then, on September 14–15, Typhoon Violet slammed into the coast of Vietnam and damaged or destroyed most of the buildings at Camp A Shau, forcing a curtailment of all operations.

Following the typhoon, and indeed for the remainder of 1964, operations in the A Shau remained below the official radar screen, and that suited Washington fine. With 1964 being an election year, Washington had obviously decided, according to General Westmoreland, "to play the war in a low key." While there was genuine concern about the shaky political stability of the coup-prone South Vietnam regime, LBJ nevertheless pursued a policy of extreme caution regarding any hint of escalating the war, fearful that his Republican opponent, Senator Barry M. Goldwater, might capitalize on the situation. In the process, the Johnson administration even withheld the fact that North Vietnamese regular troops were infiltrating into the South through the A Shau. As the MACV commander confided, he viewed Washington's cautious approach as a means to insure "minimum rocking of the political boat."[23] Yet the political climate in Washington suggested much deeper issues, prompting President Johnson to begin questioning the long-term prospects of the struggle in Vietnam. In a private 1964 conversation, LBJ confided to his national security advisor, Mac Bundy, "It looks like to me we're getting into another Korea. I don't see what we can ever hope to get out of there . . . once we're committed. I don't think it's worth fighting for and I don't think we can get out."[24]

Perhaps because of the charged political atmosphere, there was practically no mention made about a sharp action against a VC platoon in the A Shau where on December 23 Sergeant Emmett H. Horn of Detachment A-113 lost his life, or when on December 31 Sergeant First Class Edward R. Dodge of the 5th SFGA and his pilot went missing during an O-1 Bird Dog reconnaissance flight over the Valley of Death. The aircraft failed to return to Da Nang, never to be found.[25] And like the missing O-1 crew, the A Shau remained out of sight—and out of mind.

chapter 2

THE RISE AND FALL
OF CAMP A SHAU

*The bravest are surely those who have the
clearest vision of what is before them, glory and danger
alike, and yet notwithstanding go out to meet it.*

—THUCYDIDES

F or the Special Forces teams stationed in and around the A Shau,
1965 proved to be yet another year in the shadows where the coun-
terinsurgency and unconventional warfare environment remained
not only low key, but also low priority. Nevertheless, in May, Special
Forces Detachment A-102 opened a new forward operating base at A Luoi
at the northern end of the A Shau and a new camp at Ta Bat near the center. From the new locations, Civilian Irregular Defense Group units deployed over a wide area of the surrounding valley, running patrols in search
of North Vietnamese, yet being hunted themselves. And although heavy
NVA infiltration into I Corps through the A Shau continued unabated,
both Washington and MACV remained preoccupied with the politically
weightier issues of reprisal airstrikes against North Vietnam and the introduction of U.S. combat troops into South Vietnam. The escalation began
on February 7 when members of the VC 409th Sapper Battalion initiated
a deadly mortar attack in the Central Highlands on an American helicopter unit at Camp Holloway near Pleiku. The strike killed 8 American soldiers, wounded 126, and destroyed 10 aircraft, although Hanoi claimed
100 "U.S. imperialists" killed and 20 aircraft destroyed. Three days later
the VC struck an American compound at Qui Nhon, killing another 23
U.S. military personnel.[1] In response, the U.S. launched "tit-for-tat" retaliatory airstrikes against North Vietnam, but bowing to pressure from the

A SHAU VALLEY

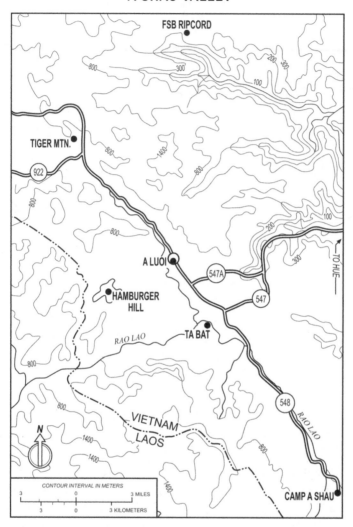

Joint Chiefs of Staff (JCS), President Johnson finally approved a sustained bombing program against the North, code named "Rolling Thunder." The first mission launched on March 2, 1965; the bombing campaign continued until November 1968, dropping a total of 643,000 tons of bombs on North Vietnam. During the 44 months of Rolling Thunder, the U.S. Air Force lost 506 aircraft in the deadly skies over the North, the U.S. Navy 397, and the Marine Corps lost 19.[2]

Out of concern for the steady buildup of enemy troops in I Corps, General Westmoreland requested and ultimately received permission to deploy U.S. Marine units as close-in security for the big air base at Da Nang. On March 8 the entire complexion of the war changed when Marines from the 3rd Battalion, 9th Regiment executed an amphibious landing at Da Nang Bay just a few miles northwest of the city. Instead of facing a fanatical enemy as they had on Tarawa, Saipan, or Iwo Jima, the Marines on Red Beach 2 were greeted by pretty Vietnamese school girls who presented them with flower leis made of gladioli and dahlias. The mayor of Da Nang recorded the event with his new Polaroid camera, snapping pictures of the unsmiling and obviously embarrassed Brigadier General Frederick J. Karch, commander of the expeditionary landing force. Later that same afternoon, members of the 1st Battalion, 3rd Marines arrived at Da Nang Air Base from Okinawa aboard Air Force C-130 transports. Although snipers fired at the aircraft on their approach, none was damaged.[3]

Apparently General Westmoreland was appalled by the spectacle on Red Beach 2; he had expected the Marines would maintain a low profile. He later learned that the public landings were LBJ's personal idea. Ambassador Maxwell Taylor in Saigon was also upset by the introduction of U.S. Marines. Taylor had warned that a landing by the Marines would be perceived as a public escalation of the war and would further give the impression that the Americans had inherited the old French role of colonizer and conqueror. The ambassador also doubted whether 'white-faced Americans' could do any better in the jungles of Southeast Asia than French troops had.[4]

In one of the strange quirks of history, this was not the first time U.S. Marines had landed at Da Nang. One hundred twenty years earlier, in May 1845, a detachment of Marines from the USS *Constitution* stormed ashore near Monkey Mountain to rescue a French priest being held prisoner and condemned to death by the Vietnamese. Following 16 days of scuffles, several broadsides from "Old Ironsides," and a series of unsuccessful negotiations, Captain John Percival of the *Constitution*, known throughout the Navy as "Mad Jack," sailed away leaving the situation much as he had found it. Of the incident, one of the *Constitution's* officers, Lieutenant John B. Dale, wrote in his journal: ". . . it seems, I must say, to have shown a sad want of 'sound discretion,' in commencing an affair of this kind, without carrying it through to a successful conclusion."[5] Whether that entry portended coincidence or providence, Lieutenant Dale could not have known then how eerily prophetic his words would resonate over a century later.

Throughout the remainder of 1965, the principal American focal point remained the introduction and deployment of U.S. combat ground forces in Vietnam, especially in the Central Highlands of II Corps. There General Westmoreland deployed the 1st Cavalry Division (Airmobile) in the first "big unit battle" against NVA regulars: the battle of Ia Drang Valley. Only two months after that historic November fight, the spotlight shifted north. The battle of Camp A Shau was about to begin.

Nineteen sixty-six ushered in the Year of the Horse, a period Chinese astrologers had predicted would be characterized by volatility and impulsiveness. What the astrologers could not predict was that the volatility would take the form of a fight to the death in the A Shau. In early January, in a foreshadowing of what was to come, a 50-man CIDG patrol ventured about 3 kilometers northeast of Camp A Shau before setting up a night defensive position in the foothills along the eastern wall of the valley. In spite of posted sentries and a protective line of claymore mines, security was apparently lax, because at 5:30 a.m. a company of NVA regulars, supported by Viet Cong guerrillas, ripped into the CIDG patrol, killing 6 of the irregulars, capturing 8, and wounding 12 more. Both of the Special Forces advisors were also wounded. The exchange killed 4 of the enemy.[6]

That attack proved to be typical of the NVA/VC probes in and around Camp A Shau during the winter of 1965–1966. With the ever-increasing enemy activity, Captain John D. Blair IV, commander of Detachment A-102, and his LLDB counterpart, Captain Chung Uy Dung, decided to close the untenable FOBs at A Luoi and Ta Bat in order to consolidate forces for defense against large enemy units. The A Shau fort, triangular in shape, consisted of walls approximately 200 meters long with barbed wire perimeter defenses. A series of strong points defended by machine gun positions anchored each corner and the center section on each wall. Each was connected by fighting trenches and protected by numerous electrically detonated claymore mines. The center of the camp housed the operations hut, communications bunker, medical bunker, team house, and ammunition bunker. The inner perimeter also contained an assortment of

81mm and 60mm mortar pits protected by sandbag parapets. A 2,300-foot airstrip of pierced steel planking ran just outside the eastern perimeter.

Well outside the range of friendly artillery support, the camp required resupply by air and relied on close air support and interdiction to keep the enemy at bay. Blair suspected that the NVA 325B Division had infiltrated through Laos and into Thua Thien Province where it was to spearhead the elimination of Camp A Shau, strategically located on top of a major line of communication and infiltration route into the region. To the North Vietnamese the camp had to go, and to accomplish its destruction, the 325B Division moved several infantry regiments into the area and reinforced them with reconnaissance and engineer battalions. The division also deployed a full artillery regiment consisting of one mixed battalion of 120mm and 82mm mortars, with one battalion of 12.7mm anti-aircraft machineguns, and one battalion of 75mm recoilless rifles.[7]

When weather permitted during January and February, the forward air controllers (FAC) and helicopter pilots flying around the valley always spotted enemy forces on the move. For example, on February 17 a FAC observed an entire company of khaki-clad NVA soldiers wearing their ubiquitous pith helmets just a few kilometers southwest of the camp. Upon being observed, they disappeared into the tall elephant grass.

For the airmen supporting the camp, the sky proved to be a dangerous place. Virtually every aircraft landing or taking off at Camp A Shau drew numerous rounds of sniper fire; more than a few were hit. Additionally, the Air Force C-123K "Ranch Hand" defoliant aircraft repeatedly came under fire as they sprayed the valley and surrounding ridges with herbicides, more commonly known as Agent Orange. The antiaircraft fire became so bad that heavily armed A-1 Skyraiders began escorting the Ranch Hand flights on their runs over the valley. Yet in spite of the added protection, the C-123s seldom returned from a mission without bullet holes, largely because the defoliant spray had to be applied from a height of 150 feet at a speed of 130 knots. At that altitude they were sitting ducks, fair game for any bad guy with a gun or a slingshot. Perhaps the most famous Ranch Hand C-123, Patches, got its nickname the hard way. During the course of its service, Patches received almost 600 hits from enemy gunners in Vietnam.[8]

Operating under the call-sign "Hades," the Ranch Hand unit's motto would have shocked ecologists: "Only you can prevent a forest." Unfortunately, the herbicides were ineffective against the elephant grass, and the defoliation efforts on the ridgelines east and west of the camp were only partially successful—only the leaves on the higher canopy of trees were removed by the Agent Orange sprayings. And because of the climate and rainfall in the valley, the trees and plants grew back rapidly, necessitating frequent follow-up sprayings.[9]

By February, VC ambushes had become so frequent that Camp A Shau was forced to resort to new tactics. As part of its patrol scheme, Detachment A-102 introduced the use of ARVN scout dogs and handlers. Interestingly, the scout dogs proved useful in the prevention of VC ambushes along the valley floor, but on the rugged, jungle-covered ridges it was a different story. The dogs were ineffective because they were not physically capable of navigating the steep terrain. On two patrols the handlers had to break out poncho liners to carry the exhausted scout dogs back to camp.[10]

The evidence pointing to a major attack kept mounting. On February 18 a combat patrol operating about five kilometers north of the camp stumbled into a pair of ambushes sprung by a squad of VC trail watchers. Neither side sustained any casualties, but shortly after noon the CIDG patrol surprised a solitary NVA soldier, trousers around his ankles, in the act of defecating. The startled soldier ditched his khaki uniform trousers and scampered away amid a hail of bullets from the equally surprised CIDG irregulars. In the hastily abandoned trousers they found a detailed written reconnaissance report of what he had observed while scouting Camp A Shau. Later that night, a CIDG squad on a local security patrol ambushed a squad of NVA soldiers about 200 meters east of the airstrip. One CIDG irregular was killed. The enemy withdrew with undetermined casualties, although an inspection of the site the following morning revealed two blood trails and two blood-spattered magazines for an AK-47 assault rifle.

Then on the 25th, a patrol surprised approximately a dozen NVA soldiers in the valley about two kilometers northwest of camp. In the brief skirmish that followed, two NVA soldiers were killed and one CIDG irregular was wounded. The real significance of the action surfaced when a Green Beret advisor with the patrol found a diary on one of the bodies. Translated, the diary revealed that Camp A Shau was being meticulously reconnoitered in preparation for some sort of attack. According to Capt Blair, this spate of close-in enemy probes made the A-102 team members feel alarmed and worried, although the CIDG irregulars appeared somewhat complacent. They responded to the nightly sniping and probes around the camp perimeter by opening fire with all their automatic weapons and by firing dozens of mortar illumination flares in the air. By doing so the CIDG companies disclosed the exact locations and fields of fire of their automatic weapons and mortar positions, and once they started firing, it was difficult to get them to stop. They wasted an enormous amount of ammunition, a precious commodity which could only be replaced via airlift.[11]

All signs lent themselves to one inescapable conclusion. The reconnaissance report captured on February 18, the diary recovered on February 25, the numerous sniping incidents at aircraft, and the firefights between local security patrols and enemy probes convinced Capt Blair that his position was not only going to be attacked, but that the NVA were determined to overrun and wipe out the little CIDG-Special Forces camp brazenly sitting on the valley floor.

A bizarre event occurred at mid-afternoon on March 5 when two khaki-clad NVA soldiers stepped out of the tall elephant grass and walked with raised arms onto the A Shau airstrip in front of a jeep being driven by a Vietnamese mechanic. The startled mechanic, who was unarmed, took the defectors into custody and escorted them into the camp. They claimed to be members of the 6th Battalion, 95B Regiment, 325B Division, and that their unit was alerted to participate in an attack on March 11. They had decided to give up after hearing about the *chieu hoi* open arms amnesty program, a 1963 initiative by the South Vietnamese to encourage defection by the Viet Cong and their supporters to the side of the Government. The two defectors, both "city boys," indicated that among their motives for switching sides were fear of being killed in the forthcoming battle and their demoralization resulting from hunger, illness, and hardship while living in the jungle. The defectors said many members of their battalion felt the same way. They even taped an appeal urging other NVA soldiers to participate in the *chieu hoi* program. On March 7, in an attempt to capitalize on the situation, an Air Force psychological warfare U-10 Helio Courier dropped thousands of leaflets on suspected enemy positions in the area and broadcast the taped defection appeal via loudspeaker. The results of that effort were nil; no more NVA or VC soldiers switched sides.[12]

Armed with the intelligence from the NVA defectors, the Detachment A-102 commander sent an urgent message to Lieutenant Colonel Kenneth B. Facey, Detachment C-1 commander in Da Nang requesting immediate reinforcement of the camp. Specifically, the message asked for two infantry companies and a battery of 105mm howitzers, along with immediate delivery of an emergency resupply of ammunition and medical supplies. For unknown reasons the ARVN commander of I Corps, Lieutenant General Nguyen Chanh Thi, rejected Facey's request for reinforcements. General Thi, a flamboyant, ambitious man and born agitator, was popular with his men but believed to be politically aligned with the strong Buddhist movement around Hue. According to *Time* magazine, Thi ran I Corps 'like a warlord of yore, obeying those edicts of the central government that suited him and blithely disregarding the rest." Not surprisingly, the support from the Buddhists, his troops, and regional alliances gave Thi a dictator's strong power base and made it difficult for Saigon and the Americans to oppose him. On a particularly tense occasion in February 1966 when Premier Nguyen Cao Ky, himself a flamboyant general, arrived in I Corps to reproach the maverick commander, Thi openly insulted the premier by turning to address his staff and mockingly asked, "Should we pay attention to this funny little man from Saigon or should we ignore him?"[13]

The outspoken Thi also had a reputation as the general most likely to question and speak out against U.S. policy, so he most definitely was not a favorite at MACV. Whether the I Corps commander's denial of reinforcements to Camp A Shau represented an intentional slap at Americans in his tactical zone will probably never be known, but on the last day of the A Shau battle, the ruling junta in Saigon—led by Ky—fired Thi. This provoked major unrest in I Corps, where some units joined with Buddhist activists supportive of Thi and hostile to Ky in defying his junta's rule. Three months of large-scale demonstrations and riots paralyzed parts of the country, and after much maneuvering and some military skirmishes, Ky's forces finally put down the uprising and Thi was exiled from the country.

With General Thi's refusal of more troops, a frustrated 5th Special Forces Group at Nha Trang decided to reinforce with a company from its own Mike Force, a country-wide quick reaction unit. Late on the afternoon of March 7, one Mike Force company from Nha Trang consisting of 143

Nungs, 6 interpreters, and 7 Americans from Detachment A-503, arrived at Camp A Shau to shore up the threatened outpost. The company was under the overall command of Captain Tennis H. Carter, known to most by his nickname, "Sam." That same afternoon Caribous and C-123 Providers delivered the emergency resupply of ammunition. It wasn't enough, but it was better than nothing.

During the night and early morning hours of March 8–9, Camp A Shau remained on full alert, its defenders, including CIDG companies 131, 141, and 154, totaled 180 men. Augmenting this force were the 143 Mike Force Nungs, 30 Combat Reconnaissance Platoon Vietnamese, 6 LLDB, 8 interpreters, 51 civilians, and 17 Americans. The Green Berets armed themselves with M-16s; those CIDG and Mike Force personnel not armed with BARs or light machine guns used .30 caliber M-1 carbines. Backing up these individual weapons, the camp deployed 14 mortars, 29 Browning .30 caliber machine guns, and one 57mm recoilless rifle. As a further precaution, at dusk Capt Chung Uy Dung sent three security patrols of approximately 10 men each to outpost positions about 200 meters from the camp, with the mission of warning of the approach of enemy forces. After the defenders settled in, they heard digging noises at 11 p.m. near the camp's south wall and at 1:30 a.m. the sounds of concertina wire being cut along the southern perimeter.[14]

The attack began at 3:50 a.m. on March 9 when devastating mortar fire crashed into the camp—the heavy barrage continued without letup until 6:30 a.m. The exploding mortar and recoilless rifle rounds blasted the compound with deadly shrapnel: huge chunks of red dirt, barbed wire, and debris from shattered buildings ripped through the night sky. The explosions appeared to zero in on the American part of the compound and destroyed many of the camp's structures and temporarily disabled all radios. When the attack started, the senior medic, Staff Sergeant Billie A. Hall, grabbed his weapon and aid kit and ran from his quarters. Seeing many wounded, he ran through heavy enemy fire to assist in dragging the injured to safety and treating them. Spotting two Americans lying on a road in the center of the camp, SSgt Hall dashed to their aid. With enemy mortar rounds bursting all around him, he reached Sergeant First Class Raymond Allen and Sergeant John W. Bradford, dragged them into a ditch, and gave them medical aid. Raymond Allen was among the first in the camp to die when the Rossville, GA native took a direct hit from a mortar round. The same explosion also blew both of Hall's legs off. Several American team members carried him to the dispensary, and although in extreme pain and weak from blood loss, SSgt Hall, through an interpreter, directed indigenous medics in caring for the wounded. Billie Hall continued to give instructions for treating the other wounded until he lapsed into a coma and died. For his extraordinary heroism, he was posthumously awarded the Distinguished Service Cross.[15]

As the heavy shelling continued, at approximately 4:30 a.m. two companies of the NVA 95B Regiment began probing the south wall. What appeared to be an all-out assault was actually an onslaught by sapper squads using Bangalore torpedoes to blow gaps in the concertina wire. They accomplished their mission. Unfortunately, the bad breaks for Camp A Shau kept right on coming. A few minutes later, at dawn, the three CIDG security patrols came slinking back into the besieged camp. Not only had each patrol spotted the enemy forces before the mortar shelling began, but they had not fired on the NVA troops or otherwise given an alarm for fear they would be discovered and attacked.

Early on during the barrage, a series of explosions knocked out all camp radios, preventing any communication or emergency requests for help. At dawn when the shelling ended, Detachment A-102 radio operators inspected the damage to the communications bunker and assumed that the radios had been jarred out of commission by exploding mortar rounds. Instead, what they discovered infuriated them. The underground antenna wire had been cut with a knife. This was the first overt indication of subversion among the Vietnamese irregulars, although it had been suspected that the CIDG units at the camp, particularly Company 141, might have been infiltrated by Viet Cong agents. By 9 a.m. the communications supervisor repaired the sabotaged antenna and re-established contact with Detachment C-1 at Da Nang, although communication was initially only possible via Morse code since the generators powering the single side band radio had been destroyed in the mortar attack.[16]

At around 11 a.m., as the camp survivors dug out and regrouped during a morning lull after the attack, two Army Bird Dogs dropped below a 400-foot ceiling and made a hazardous approach and landing on the airstrip. Capt Sam Carter and Sergeant First Class Bennie G. Adkins, both wounded from the mortar shelling, braved sporadic sniper fire to carry critically wounded Master Sergeant Robert L. Gibson to the runway. As they unceremoniously stuffed Gibson into the O-1 for evacuation, they received a heavy volume of small arms fire from the southeast corner of the camp. Thinking that the enemy had infiltrated between the airstrip and the east wall, Carter and Adkins moved a 2-1/2 ton truck in front of the O-1 for protection, but at that point Sergeant First Class Victor C. Underwood watched in disbelief from inside the camp as some of the CIDG Company 141 troops emptied their weapons at the Bird Dogs and the personnel on the airstrip. He and several other A-503 team members instantly interceded. According to Underwood's matter-of-fact explanation, "the firing stopped when several of the Vietnamese were killed." He then stationed a Nung platoon behind Company 141 to prevent a recurrence. Once the firing died down, both O-1s gunned their engines and took off.[17]

At 11:20 a.m. Captain Willard M. Collins piloted his AC-47 gunship, call sign Spooky 70, into the valley in a desperate attempt to aid the camp's weary and bloodied defenders. Throughout Vietnam, everyone knew about and respected these venerable old World War II cargo planes turned gunship, affectionately called "Puff the Magic Dragon" for the stream of red tracers that spewed from its threesome of side-mounted 7.62mm mini-guns. Collins, assisted by his co-pilot, 1st Lieutenant Delbert R. Peterson, made two unsuccessful attempts to get under the low clouds that socked in the entire A Shau—and masked the treacherous mountain peaks lining either side of the valley. Finally on the third attempt they found a small hole and guided the AC-47 into the area at an altitude of 400 feet above the ground. Hugging the terrain on a southerly heading, Spooky 70 executed a firing pass down the west side of the perimeter; everyone inside the camp stood and cheered. Then, for the men in the camp, one of the most demoralizing incidents of the battle occurred right before their eyes. As Collins turned to the north for a second run, enemy antiaircraft positions on the east and west ridgelines opened up with a vengeance. The gauntlet of fire from .51 caliber machine guns tore the right engine from its mount. Seconds later another burst knocked out the left engine. With superb airmanship and unbelievable composure, Collins and Peterson brought the bullet-riddled gunship in for a crash landing on a mountain slope roughly three kilometers north of the camp. All members of the crew survived with minor injuries except Staff Sergeant Robert E. Foster, whose legs were broken by the impact.

From the heavy movement and signal shots in the area, Capt Collins instinctively realized that an enemy attack was inevitable. When he found out that SSgt Foster could not be moved, Collins, rather than leaving the injured crewmember and moving to more favorable terrain, set up a defensive perimeter around the crash site and dug in to wait for a rescue helicopter. Fifteen minutes after the crash the crew repulsed the first probe by NVA soldiers. Minutes later Collins valiantly led his crew in fending off a second attack by a much larger force, but during the fierce firefight he and Foster were both gunned down and killed.[18]

Just as an Air Force HH-43 helicopter arrived overhead, a third attack began. Muzzle flashes from a .51 cal machine gun that had been moved to within yards of the small perimeter were clearly visible to Lt Peterson, now in command of the crew. If the gun were not silenced, he reasoned, the chopper would likely be downed before it could rescue the four airmen. Firing his M-16 on full automatic, Del Peterson charged the gun, which went silent as the HH-43 dropped down to pick up the surviving crewmembers. The young co-pilot from Maple Plain, Minnesota was not among them. For extraordinary heroism and superb airmanship, both Captain Willard Collins and Lieutenant Delbert Peterson were posthumously awarded the Air Force Cross.[19]

Following the unsettling loss of Spooky 70, the defenders at Camp A Shau concentrated on regrouping and repairing their battered perimeter and fortified fighting positions for the all-out attack they knew was imminent. Low on ammunition and desperate to get his many wounded medically evacuated, Capt John Blair repeatedly requested supplies and reinforcements from Da Nang. As Detachment C-1 processed the urgent appeals, the action shifted back into the air.

When he received word that an AC-47 had been shot down in the A Shau, Major Bernard F. Fisher, from the 1st Air Commando Squadron at Pleiku, diverted his flight of two A-1E Skyraiders to the area. Locating a small hole in the overcast approximately five miles north of the camp, Fisher led his flight at just 500 feet above the valley floor, all the while dodging an intense barrage of antiaircraft fire. At that point he got instructions to destroy the Spooky 70 wreckage to prevent enemy retrieval of the aircraft's three lethal mini-guns. Assigning his wingman to handle that mission, Fisher pressed on to the camp and immediately enlisted the services of a second set of Skyraiders. After directing their ordnance around the perimeter, Major Fisher climbed back above the overcast and escorted two C-123s down through the weather and into the valley where they parachuted much needed medical supplies and ammunition to the defenders. As the two C-123s made their low-level drops, Bernie Fisher and his wingman suppressed the enemy ground fire with 20mm strafe. And he wasn't finished yet.

Earlier that afternoon a Marine H-34 attempted a landing to evacuate the wounded, but as the chopper began to settle into the camp, it was hit repeatedly by machine gun and small arms fire, bringing it down. At that point Major Fisher escorted an Air Force HH-3 to the camp and once again suppressed enemy fire while it landed. Under Fisher's covering guns, the Air Force helicopter, piloted by an unflappable crew, successfully evacuated the 26 wounded defenders and the Marine helicopter crew. One of the wounded, Sgt John Bradford, refused to sit down inside the crowded chopper. Although the crew demanded he take a seat, Bradford insisted on remaining standing; he had been severely wounded in both buttocks.

A pair of B-57 Canberra bombers then joined the battle, being led through a hole in the overcast by Bernie Fisher, who by that time was dangerously low on fuel and ended up making an emergency landing at Da Nang with almost dry tanks. Just before dark, the B-57s dropped a series of cluster bombs (CBU) on enemy positions around the camp. Throughout that long day on March 9, a scant 29 sorties launched in support of Camp A Shau, mainly because of bad weather: 17 by the USAF, 10 by the USMC, and two by the South Vietnamese Air Force (VNAF).[20]

In yet another act of betrayal, two members of CIDG Company 141 were observed firing at the C-123s and Caribous as they airdropped supplies. At gunpoint one of the Americans took the men to Capt Blair, who turned them over to Capt Chung Uy Dung with the recommendation that they be executed for their treachery. The LLDB camp commander refused, expressing the opinion that Company 141 was loyal. Under the circumstances, the only realistic action Blair could take was to instruct the Nungs to keep a close watch on the company and to fire on it if any further signs of subversion occurred.[21]

At 2:30 a.m. on March 10, NVA Regiment 95B opened fire on Camp
A Shau with everything they had: heavy mortars, rocket propelled grenades
(RPG), recoilless rifles, and automatic weapons. The ferocity of the enemy
barrage stunned and horrified the camp's survivors, the heavy bombard-
ment continuing without letup until about 7 a.m., pulverizing what was
left of the camp and inflicting heavy casualties among the defenders. All
of the bunkers on the walls took several direct hits from recoilless weapons
or RPGs, which destroyed about half of the machine gun emplacements.
The heavy shelling also killed most mortars crews and put their weapons
out of action. In the 81mm mortar pit, three direct hits by in-coming
enemy shells killed 7 Vietnamese and wounded 6 men, including Bennie
Adkins. Although bleeding profusely, he repeatedly relaid the mortar tube
each time it was knocked down by hits or near misses and continued to
service it alone. In short order, SFC Adkins was the only man left in the
camp firing a mortar.[22]

Around 5 a.m. under cover of darkness, three massed battalions of
NVA infantry attacked the south and east walls. The defenders held fast
and mowed the enemy infantry down—except in one area. When the
enemy hit CIDG Company 141's sector, that unit folded. Many members
stopped fighting altogether and even assisted the attackers in getting over
the wall. As the NVA troops poured into the gap created by Company
141's defection, they began placing enfilade fire on the defenders along the
south and east walls. Sergeant Owen F. McCann died at his post trying to
stop the onslaught. To plug the gap, the Nung platoon and the civilians in
the reserve force positioned in the center of the camp, attempted a counterattack but could not repel the masses of enemy soldiers assaulting through
the smoke and rubble. Coming to the assistance of the Nungs, Specialist
5th Phillip T. Stahl manned a machine gun, killing numerous attackers as
they threw wave after wave against his position. His devastating fire helped
the Nungs stall the main enemy assault. Although seriously hurt in the
previous day's attack with a painful wound that partially paralyzed his left
arm and another wound to his right leg, Stahl refused medical treatment
and held his ground as once more the enemy mounted another full scale
assault. He resisted the onslaught by killing scores of attackers and continued firing his machine gun until the barrel glowed red hot. As the human
waves inched ever closer, Specialist 5th Phillip T. Stahl was mortally

wounded by an NVA grenade blast. For his extraordinary heroism, he was posthumously awarded the Distinguished Service Cross.[23]

As the deadly pre-dawn slugfest continued, Bennie Adkins, although painfully wounded, continued to blunt the fanatical waves of infantry attempting to storm his mortar pit. Finally withdrawing to a communications bunker where several Americans were attempting to fight off an entire company of NVA, SFC Adkins plunged into the firefight, killing numerous enemy soldiers with his suppressive fire. Running extremely low on ammunition, he returned to the mortar pit, gathered the vital ammunition, and ran through intense fire back to his colleagues at the communications bunker. Wounded yet again, he kept right on fighting.[24]

The gut-wrenching battle also spilled over into a third dimension. In the pre-dawn darkness above the east wall, a warrior from outside the camp rushed to help. Attempting to work under a parachute flare dropped by an Air Force C-123, Marine Lieutenant Augusto "Gus" Xavier piloted his A-4 Skyhawk below the foul weather and low overcast to drop his bombs "danger close" on nearby NVA troop concentrations. On his second low-level pass, he died in a fiery explosion when his jet plowed into the side of a mountain.[25]

As the close combat continued to rage inside the camp, Capt Blair ran from position to position to check on his meager forces and to assess the deteriorating situation. Reorganizing the men, the A-102 commander led them in three counterattacks across the open terrain of the camp but was forced to order his small force to withdraw each time because of the murderous fire. By 8 a.m. only the north wall and the American communications bunker were still in friendly hands. Shortly after that, the one remaining 81mm and 60mm mortars were either destroyed or ran out of ammunition. Blair had no choice but to regroup along the north wall and to call in airstrikes against the enemy troops occupying the rest of the camp.

While waiting for the close air support, Capt Sam Carter, SFC Vic Underwood, and SFC Vernon A. Carnahan, using an M-79 and M-16s, took on a wave of infiltrators and killed a tremendous number of NVA in front of their position. Sam Carter said of the fight, "Three of us knew we killed 50 of 'em in a tiny area. I laid in one hole in the wall and killed twelve. Just in that one hole."[26] In Underwood's debriefing, he noted that the enemy soldiers "didn't seem to know what to do when they got inside the camp. They would stand up to look around, making good targets." Underwood and Carnahan then rallied some of the badly shaken Vietnamese and launched another counterattack, charging through the rubble and debris around the communications bunker, only to be wounded by a grenade-throwing enemy soldier. Vic Underwood recounted, "I jumped around Carnahan and saw the VC who threw the grenade running back toward the south wall. I hit him in the back with our last grenade [M-79] and blew him all to pieces. We then pulled back to the north wall and Carnahan took care of our wounds which were all in our legs—he had a broken leg."[27]

Huddled along the north wall clogged with their dead and wounded, the survivors sat bleeding, dog tired, covered from head to foot with red dirt and soot, their eyes burning and tearing from the thick smoke, their ears ringing from the constant mortar explosions, their nostrils filled with the pungent smell of cordite, their mouths bone dry with that peculiar taste of metal brought on by adrenalin and fear. The defenders' hearts sank when, through the acrid smoke, they observed another NVA battalion massing on the airstrip for a final push against Camp A Shau. Before the hostile force could launch the charge, however, two B-57s roared over them at 800 feet dropping CBU. The slaughter and mayhem inflicted by hundreds of CBU explosions literally stopped the momentum of the NVA assault in its tracks.

Capt Blair's urgent calls for napalm airstrikes against the camp resulted in the dispatch of six A-1 Skyraiders to the scene. Fresh off his mission from the day before, Major Bernie Fisher led the three flights of two aircraft each into the Valley of Death. Using the call sign Hobo 51, Fisher led his wingman, Captain Paco Vazquez, Hobo 52, to the besieged camp at an altitude of 800 feet. Right behind Hobo Flight, Major Dafford W. "Jump" Myers and his wingman, Captain Hubert King, followed in trail formation. On the second pass, Jumps Myers' aircraft took a pounding from the concentrated ground fire; his engine froze and his cockpit filled with smoke. At only 400 feet Myers was too low to bail out, so he decided to land his burning A-1 on the airstrip. Miraculously the big Skyraider bellied in and skidded to a stop as Myers climbed out and took cover in a weed-covered ditch along the east side of the runway. Myer's wingman, Hubie King, watched his leader go down and made a low level run at 30 feet above the runway, but he never saw the gun that shattered his front canopy windscreen and peppered him with shards of glass. King's A-1 received multiple hits and broke off the mission to make an emergency landing at Da Nang. Inside the camp some of the defenders saw Myers get out of his burning aircraft and run to the edge of the runway. Vic Underwood and four Nungs raced toward the airstrip to rescue the downed pilot, but the enemy fire was so heavy the American was pinned down and all four Nungs killed.

Fisher called in the third set of A-1s and led the low-level attacks against NVA troops converging in the direction of the downed pilot. The antiaircraft fire was intense and disarmingly accurate. In describing the scene, one of the A-1 pilots observed, "It was like flying inside Yankee Stadium with the people in the bleachers firing at you with machine guns."[28]

When Bernie Fisher learned that a rescue helicopter was at least 20 minutes away, he instinctively understood that his old friend Jump Myers would be captured or killed prior to the chopper's arrival. He decided to land and make the pickup himself, realizing full well that such an attempt in the face of the murderous enemy ground fire would be suicidal. With the other A-1s covering him, Hobo 51 dropped his landing gear and touched down on the hazardous runway, dodging shell craters, fuel drums, debris, while being the target of heavy small arms and automatic weapons fire. In spite of the fusillade, Fisher taxied 1,800 feet back down the airstrip to Myer's general location and brought the A-1E to a halt. Myers bolted from his hiding place, climbed on the right wing, and dived headfirst into the cockpit. His first words to Fischer were, "You dumb son of a bitch, now neither of us will get out of here."[29]

Turning his aircraft around, Bernie Fisher gunned the engine. Once again dodging debris, he coaxed the Skyraider off the ground at the very end of the runway as bullets slammed into the fuselage. The camp defenders cheered as Hobo 51 roared down the airstrip and into the air. When the plane landed at Pleiku, the maintenance crews counted 19 bullet holes in the bird. For his conspicuous gallantry at the risk of his life above and beyond the call of duty, Major Bernard F. Fisher became the first Air Force member in Vietnam to receive the Medal of Honor.[30]

For Capt John Blair, by late afternoon on March 10 there seemed little more that could be done except to hold on and hope reinforcements would arrive in time to prevent the complete loss of the camp. Heavy explosions from enemy 82mm mortars constantly blasted the survivors while NVA riflemen and machine gunners continued to fire within the camp itself. Practically all of the remaining defenders were "walking wounded," all hungry and thirsty, for there had been no food or water available for 36 hours. Complicating the situation, ammunition was dangerously low, and the remaining CIDG personnel were frightened and demoralized. At Camp A Shau no further offensive capability existed. At about 5 p.m. Blair was ordered to abandon the camp.

Marine Medium Helicopter Squadron 163 (HMM-163) based at Phu Bai got the call to evacuate the survivors of Camp A Shau. Under the command of Lieutenant Colonel Charles A. "Chuck" House, the squadron launched all its H-34 Choctaw helicopters with the daunting task of flying under the nasty weather in the valley and making the pickup, probably against heavy antiaircraft opposition. Without any hesitation, Chuck House led his section of eight H-34s escorted by several "Huey" gunships under the 200-foot ceiling and into the valley well north of the camp. Unfortunately, the other eight Choctaws ran into a solid wall of weather and returned to Phu Bai.

In preparation for the evacuation, Captains Carter and Blair, under heavy fire, crawled out to open a wire barricade on a path from the north wall. With a few other able-bodied men they set up a position to cover the withdrawal. SFCs Underwood and Carnahan were sent about 400 meters north of the camp to secure a landing zone in the elephant grass for the approaching choppers. Their other job was to see that the badly wounded got out first. Almost immediately the plan fell apart. In Vic Underwood's own words, "When the Vietnamese saw us and the Nungs head for the landing zone they lost complete control and swarmed out of the camp in a mob, led by the Vietnamese camp commander. They ran past us, separating Carnahan from me and the Nungs. I was wounded in the legs and couldn't move very fast. I tried to shoot the Vietnamese camp commander but someone always kept getting in the way."[31]

As the HHM-163 helicopters landed on the LZ, the frantic mob of CIDG irregulars rushed the choppers and fought among themselves to get on board. The H-34s were immediately overloaded to the point where they were too heavy to lift off. "We tried to drag 'em off, beat 'em off, kick 'em off," House said, "but they just came back. It was mass panic. Finally, we had to shoot 'em off." When Chuck House finally lifted off, he only managed to get about ten feet in the air before enemy fire—or perhaps panicky CIDG troops—shot his tail rotor off; out of control, his bird crashed. As the crew crawled out of the wreckage, shaken and bruised but otherwise unharmed, House realized that in the rapidly approaching darkness and the low cloud ceilings a rescue was no longer feasible. He started planning to evade on foot.[32]

As the remaining Americans in the rear guard broke out and raced through a hail of bullets for the north wall gate, Specialist George E. Pointon, who had both arms shattered and had suffered a large open chest wound during the early morning firefight, ran by himself all the way to the landing zone—almost 400 meters—only to find all the H-34 helicopters gone. Seeing Pointon's predicament, Vic Underwood flagged down a Huey gunship that dropped its empty rocket pods and landed. As told by Underwood, "I helped Pointon on board and he pulled a pistol and pointed it at me; I side-stepped and he shot a Vietnamese off my back." Underwood then loaded 14 other wounded men aboard, and the Huey evacuated them to safety. All told, the valiant helicopter crews lifted out a total of 69 personnel, including 4 gravely wounded Americans.[33]

As the last of the walking wounded moved toward the LZ, the NVA infantrymen renewed their assaults. The rear guard action became extremely violent, but the Americans and Nungs succeeded in holding the north wall until everyone who was still alive got out of the camp. Among the last out were Lieutenant Louis A. Mari and SFC Bennie Adkins. Fighting their way through heavy fire, they carried Sergeant James L. Taylor who had been critically wounded earlier in the day. As they worked their way through the north wall trench line, Adkins killed an enemy soldier who blocked their way. Under fire the entire way, the two men carried Sgt Taylor on a stretcher to the LZ only to find all helicopters had gone. Jimmy Taylor died several hours later during the evasion, his body hidden in the heavy brush by his fellow Green Berets.

By the time the last of the rear guard reached the landing zone, all helicopters except for two that had been shot down were gone. All that remained on the LZ were 8 Marine helicopter crewmen, about 50 wounded CIDG irregulars, 40 Nungs, 7 Americans, and 2 women. Enemy fire continued to sweep the landing zone, and NVA soldiers could be heard shouting to one another in preparation for a final assault. Under the circumstances it became obvious that further chopper rescue was not possible. The only course of action was to begin evading.

As the senior combat arms officer present, Lt Col Chuck House, armed with a map and a compass, took command and began leading the A Shau garrison survivors in a northerly direction. His plan was to evade across Laos to Thailand. About two hours after dark the evaders stopped to rest; extreme fatigue, hunger, thirst, and wounds had made the column's movement slow and painful. The evaders rested until 2 a.m. on a mountainside about two kilometers northwest of the camp. While in that location, the Special Forces officers advised Lt Col House that the run-down physical condition of most of the evaders would prevent their being able to make it to Thailand over 100 miles away and that a move to Hue, only 25 miles northeast, was the better choice. Taking their recommendation under advisement, House set out heading north. During this portion of the trek, the party became separated in the dark—whether by accident or on purpose—with Capt Carter, SFC Adkins, and approximately 8 Nungs continuing to evade northeast on their own.

Around noon on March 11, House's column spotted several Marine H-34 helicopters circling around Ta Bat. Lt Mari approached Lt Col House about a route he knew to a suitable LZ for helicopters. House refused, stating that it would be too dangerous for the helicopters to land. Apparently at that point a heated disagreement developed between Lt Mari and Lt Col House. The lieutenant told House he didn't care what House did, but that the A Shau people were going to signal the helicopters, move to a suitable landing zone, and go for a pickup. The young lieutenant, wounded and exhausted, then struck out toward Ta Bat, leaving Lt Col House standing there fuming and threatening to have Mari court-martialed. Seven of the Marines and all of the other men followed Mari; Chuck House then reluctantly rejoined the column. Needless to say, it had not exactly been a red-letter day in the annals of inter-service cooperation.[34]

The HHM-163 helicopters made up for the discord on the ground. With the help of an O-1 Bird Dog, the choppers spotted the main column and began lifting the men out individually using a "horse collar" sling, the previous day's mob scene still fresh in their minds. By 3:15 p.m. they had picked up Lt Col House and all the Marines, SFC Underwood, who was barely able to walk, four seriously wounded CIDG, and the two women. The remaining SF soldiers and about 50 Vietnamese and Nungs could not be picked up and had to continue evading.

Late in the afternoon, Capt Carter's small group also contacted a Bird Dog and put the wheels in motion to be rescued. Second Lieutenant Donald J. Berger piloted his H-34 under the heavy weather and through an intense barrage of enemy fire to reach Sam Carter. Since jungle growth prevented landing, Berger, totally exposed and vulnerable, went into a hover and was attempting to hoist the defenders aboard when hostile automatic weapons fire damaged the tail pylon of his aircraft, causing complete loss of tail rotor control. Exhibiting outstanding flying skill and great presence of mind, Lt Berger executed a text-book perfect forced landing and promptly ordered the co-pilot and one of the crewmembers to board another rescue helicopter. Due to darkness and inclement weather precluding further rescue attempts, he remained on the ground and guided the outpost defenders through difficult terrain where they encountered and successfully fought off an enemy patrol. In the brief skirmish one Nung was KIA. After helping set up a night defensive position, Berger stayed on watch throughout the night, giving the exhausted soldiers a chance to rest. However, during the long night a tiger continuously circled around the perimeter and frightened the Vietnamese. Undoubtedly the stench of the wounds attracted the tiger and whetted its appetite. Much to the relief of the evaders, the big cat eventually gave up the hunt and went to find easier prey. At first light on March 12, Berger guided the group to another location, then signaled for help and succeeded in getting a rescue chopper to hoist the exhausted men aboard. For his extraordinary heroism in the air and on the ground, Lieutenant Donald J. Berger was awarded the Navy Cross.[35]

At approximately 10:30 a.m. on March 12, Marine H-34 helicopters from HHM-163 returned to the perimeter held by the main column and began hoisting men aboard by sling. In a repeat performance of the mob scene at the camp two days earlier, the CIDG, fearful of being abandoned, began killing one another in their stampede to get to the sling and be hauled aboard the hovering helicopters. The first to start shooting were some of the men on the perimeter, but soon everyone was shooting at everyone else, and the Americans could not stop the indiscriminate firing.

Someone even threw a hand grenade into the mob crowding around the sling, the explosion killing and wounding several of the Vietnamese. In desperation, the three Americans grabbed the collars of the helicopter slings and were snatched to safety, being hauled aboard the choppers as they rapidly climbed for altitude.[36]

That same day word came in that another A-1E had been shot down over the A Shau Valley. Major Monroe E. "Buzz" Blaylock was strafing an antiaircraft position near the fallen camp when the heavy fire damaged his Skyraider, forcing him to bail out. Luckily for Blaylock, a flight of H-34s from HHM-163 plucked him out of harm's way and flew him to Phu Bai.[37]

In one of the most bizarre episodes in the immediate aftermath of the battle, Lt Col Chuck House gave an incredibly candid interview to reporter John Laurence in which he described the rescue and giving orders to shoot the panic-stricken Vietnamese mobbing the helicopters trying to evacuate the camp survivors. When the reporter asked if House would be willing to repeat the story on camera, he responded, "Yeah, what the hell, I've been passed over for promotion twice. So I'm on my way out anyway." His words proved prescient. For his role during the rescue at Camp A Shau, Lieutenant Colonel Charles A. House, USMC, received the Navy Cross for extraordinary heroism. For emotionally charged statements to the press, he received a letter of reprimand and was relieved of command of HHM-163.[38]

On March 18, 1966, Special Forces Detachment C-1 at Da Nang conducted Operation Blue Star, a body recovery mission to the abandoned Camp A Shau. The bodies of the Americans, along with those of 200 NVA, lay scattered about the compound undisturbed. Evidently the Katu tribesmen had not entered the camp for fear of ghosts. The remains of Raymond Allen, Billie Hall, Owen McCann, and Phillip Stahl were retrieved. The body of Jimmy Taylor, who had died during the evasion, was never found.

By any standard of measurement, the 1966 battle in the Valley of Death resulted in a traumatic ordeal for both sides. Estimated enemy losses were 1,000 killed, with many more wounded. But they now owned the valley, and that undisputed fact suggested much larger ramifications. Indeed, the fall of Camp A Shau had a major bearing on the future course of the entire war. After its fall, mainstream American Army units would not return to the Valley of Death for two years. But the valor of the men who fought there was forever immortalized in their citations for bravery. In addition to the posthumous awards to Staff Sergeant Billie Hall and Specialist 5th Phillip Stahl, the Distinguished Service Cross was also awarded to Captains John Blair and Sam Carter, First Lieutenant Louis Mari, and Sergeants First Class Victor Underwood and Bennie Adkins. Some 48 years later, the circumstances surrounding Bennie Adkins' Distinguished Service Cross were reevaluated—and with good reason. In reexamining the 38-hour battle, it was determined that Adkins fought ferociously with mortars, machine guns, recoilless rifles, small arms, and hand grenades, killing an estimated 135–175 of the enemy and sustaining 18 different wounds. His DSC was upgraded to the Medal of Honor and presented to him at the White House on September 15, 2014.

Although the camp had been lost, the horrendous struggle by the small outpost against the human wave attacks by 1,000 NVA and VC determined soldiers ironically received a modicum of public attention thanks to Hollywood. For John Wayne's 1968 film *The Green Berets,* the screenwriter contacted Ken Facey, the former Detachment C-1 commander, who briefed him on the events at Camp A Shau. The screenwriter then based the film's battle scenes on that briefing—except for the "heroism" of the LLDB commander.[39]

Of all the recaps on the fall of Camp A Shau, perhaps the most insightful belonged to reporter John Laurence when he wrote:

> The A Shau Special Forces camp is closed. But the story of what happened there—the overwhelming attack, the evacuation and dramatic rescue, the panic and confusion, and especially the shooting of South Vietnamese soldiers—will be debated for months to come. It has been said that this is a strange and ugly war. It has never been worse than at A Shau.[40]

To be sure, in some respects it was a strange and ugly war—all wars are. But what Laurence neglected to mention was that American valor and sacrifice shown through above all else like a shining beacon. It has never been more inspirational than at A Shau.

chapter 3

PROJECT DELTA
INVADES THE A SHAU

*Deeds of great courage were done in the
darkness and never seen or recorded.*
—PIERRE CORNEILLE

Nineteen sixty-seven ushered in what Americans would call the "year
of the big battles." To the Vietnamese it was also the Year of the
Goat, in particular, the Fire Goat. For Vietnamese and Chinese
astrologers, the year suggested a cautionary time when one might be drawn
into complex predicaments. Under that zodiac sign the powerful usually
shied away from confrontation, pulled back when faced with heavy deci-
sion-making, and blatantly refused to take an unpopular stand in a conflict.
Those predictions may well have colored Saigon's thinking in the Year of
the Goat, but they had little if any bearing on Washington—and none at
all on Hanoi.

After the battle and loss at Camp A Shau, the U.S. military focus in
South Vietnam shifted away from unconventional warfare and the border
surveillance missions involving Special Forces detachments and CIDG
companies. Instead, to facilitate the large-scale destruction of the VC and
NVA units flooding into the country, MACV launched a new tactical doctrine, backed up by a powerful American ground force consisting of seven
U.S. Army and Marine divisions, two airborne and two light infantry
brigades, and one armored cavalry regiment, in addition to the 5th Special
Forces Group. The strategy sought to exploit American firepower and mobility by forcing major engagements with NVA/VC main force units,
thereby thwarting the enemy's capability to threaten and destabilize Saigon.
While American units attempted to destroy the main force units, ARVN

units were to focus their efforts on the pacification effort in the populated areas. General Westmoreland made it clear that it was never his intention to keep U.S. troops in a defensive posture. Specifically, he planned to employ them to wipe out insurgency in War Zone C and the Iron Triangle, drive the VC out of populated areas, and to attack enemy strongholds along Vietnam's borders, especially in the II and III Corps tactical zones.[1] Surprisingly, the plan did not address combat operations in I Corps or the A Shau.

Westmoreland's strategy was new, bold, and from the beginning controversial. Some referred to it as a strategy of "search and destroy," while others called it a "war of attrition." In any case the strategy had its roots in both the present and the past: first, General Westmoreland latched on to the lopsided kill ratio of ten North Vietnamese to one American. But since he was also a product of the meat-grinder campaigns of World War II and Korea, he also came to the conclusion that he could bleed the enemy to death over the long haul, especially in large-unit battles. Whatever the name, for the first time in modern warfare the goal was not territory—it was body count.

Operation Cedar Falls kicked off the first of the year's big battles, running from January 8–26 and had the distinction of being the first corps-sized American action of the war. The objective was a 60-square-mile chunk of real estate known as the Iron Triangle, an NLF stronghold just 20 miles north of the capital, often characterized by the Vietnamese as "a dagger pointed at Saigon's heart." The target area included dense jungle and wet rice paddies, all occupied by the VC since the mid-1950s.

Operation Cedar Falls called for a "hammer and anvil" tactic. The 25th Infantry Division with the 196th Infantry Brigade attached to it was to assume blocking positions west of the Iron Triangle while one brigade of the 1st Infantry Division was assigned the same task east of the area of operations. The remaining units were then tasked to hammer the VC 9th Division's 272nd and 165th Regiments against the anvil by rapidly moving through the Iron Triangle, combing it for enemy troops and installations, and clearing it of civilians. Unfortunately, the treatment of civilians created a public relations uproar.

An air assault on Ben Suc, a key fortified VC village, took place on D-day. The civilian inhabitants of Ben Suc and surrounding villages, some

6,000 individuals, were physically uprooted along with their belongings and livestock and moved to relocation camps. After the deportation of the civilian population, American engineers systematically razed Ben Suc, first burning the village's buildings to the ground and then leveling the area and crops with bulldozers. Although the villagers were moved as humanely as possible, the episode generated criticism, especially among the press. Even some senior officers within the military reacted to the forced movement. Brigadier General Bernard Rogers, assistant division commander of the 1st Infantry Division during Operation Cedar Falls, conceded that "It was to be expected that uprooting the natives of these villages would evoke resentment, and it did." The sight of the refugees from Ben Suc with their carts, chickens, hogs, and rice was "pathetic and pitiful."[2]

As the first of the big unit battles, Operation Cedar Falls was viewed by most as an unqualified victory, even though the fighting had been sporadic and comparatively sparse. American and ARVN units ultimately drove the VC—at least temporarily—out of the Iron Triangle and accounted for nearly 750 confirmed enemy dead and 280 prisoners. By comparison, U.S. casualties were relatively light totaling 72 killed, 337 wounded. The 1st Infantry Division's commander, Major General William DePuy, called Cedar Falls a "decisive turning point in the III Corps area; a tremendous boost of morale of the Vietnamese Government and Army; and a blow from which the VC in this area may never recover."[3] Some military historians, however, disagreed with that assessment. For example, Shelby Stanton has argued that the battle in the Iron Triangle had disturbing long-range strategic consequences. He noted, "Instead of pushing the NVA/VC into the more 'vulnerable posture' as MACV had envisioned, the 9th VC Division had simply been pushed into Cambodia, where it was immune to any attack whatsoever."[4] Because of LBJ's "hands-off" policy on Cambodian sanctuaries, MACV was relegated to fighting a war of attrition within the geographical boundaries of South Vietnam. Not surprisingly, enemy units returned at will from across the border, and the same region was thus fought over repeatedly. Nowhere was that scenario more pronounced than in the A Shau.

Just 27 days after Cedar Falls, MACV launched its second big battle of 1967, Operation Junction City, a search and destroy mission into the VC stronghold in Tay Ninh Province known as War Zone C. For the most part thick jungle defined the area, but the 3,200-foot-high Nui Ba Den Mountain dominated the landscape. With the Big Red One—1st Infantry Division—and the men of the "Tropic Lightning" 25th Infantry Division leading the charge, the operation also included separate brigades equal to a third division, to include the 173rd Airborne Brigade which executed the only major combat parachute jump of the Vietnam War. Operation Junction City had three main objectives: to search out and destroy the 9th VC Division and the 101st NVA Regiment; to destroy the Central Office for South Vietnam (COSVN), the supreme headquarters in the South which tied together the various elements of insurgency and provided direction to both the military and civilian communist organizations; and to establish a Special Forces-CIDG camp at Prek Klok. At the end of the 82-day operation, the scorecard showed mixed results. Unlike Cedar Falls, extremely heavy fighting characterized the much longer campaign, and while the enemy forces had not been wiped out, they most certainly received a bloody nose: 2,728 killed. By comparison, the U.S. suffered 218 KIA and 1,576 WIA. North Vietnamese sources, in a heavily propagandized account of the battle, claimed 14,000 U.S. killed or wounded, 801 tanks or APCs destroyed or damaged, and 167 aircraft shot down or damaged.[5] Hanoi's practice of publishing preposterously inflated numbers is evident in these figures; that habit continued throughout the war.

In spite of fierce ground assaults by VC and NVA units, MACV did establish the Special Forces camp at Prek Klok but never located the much sought after COSVN headquarters. One of the most disheartening results of Operation Junction City was that shortly after American units redeployed to other areas, the VC crossed back into South Vietnam and quickly returned to War Zone C. The essence of the North's "hit and run" tactic was perhaps best summed up by Ho Chi Minh himself when he observed:

> It will be a war between an elephant and a tiger. If the tiger ever stands still, the elephant will crush him with his mighty tusks. But the tiger does not stand still. He lurks in the jungle by day and emerges only at night. He will leap upon the back of the elephant, tearing huge chunks from his hide, and then he will leap back into the dark jungle. And slowly the elephant will bleed to death.[6]

While debate about the relative success of Operation Junction City continues into the present, there can be no argument over the valor and dedication of the American soldiers and airmen who carried the fight to the enemy in War Zone C. The story of Sergeant First Class Matthew Leonard from the Big Red One drives the point home. Near the village of Suoi Da on February 28, his platoon was suddenly attacked by a large enemy force. When the platoon leader and several other key leaders were among the first wounded, SFC Leonard, from Birmingham, Alabama, quickly rallied his men to throw back the initial enemy assaults. Spotting a wounded platoon member outside the perimeter, he dragged the man to safety but was struck by a sniper's bullet which shattered his left hand. Refusing medical attention and continuously exposing himself to the withering fire as the enemy again assaulted the perimeter, SFC Leonard moved from position to position to direct the fire of his men against the onslaught. To make matters worse, during the attack the enemy moved a machine gun into a location where it could sweep the entire perimeter. This threat was magnified when the platoon machine gun malfunctioned. SFC Leonard quickly crawled to the gun position and was helping to clear the stoppage when the gun crew was wounded by fire from the enemy machine gun. At that point SFC Leonard rose to his feet, charged the enemy gun and destroyed its crew despite being hit several times by enemy fire. He then moved to a tree, propped himself against it, and continued to engage the enemy until he died from his many wounds. For his conspicuous gallantry and intrepidity at the risk of his life above and beyond the call of duty, Sergeant First Class Matthew Leonard was posthumously awarded the Medal of Honor.[7]

As the big unit battles wound down in III Corps, in April 1967 a detachment of the 5th Special Forces Group saddled up and headed back into the A Shau Valley, scene of their humiliating defeat 13 months earlier. The detachment was officially known as B-52, but throughout Vietnam, combat units knew it as Project Delta. Never numbering more than 100 officers and enlisted men at any one time, Delta would become the most highly decorated unit of its size in the Vietnam War, and the second most highly decorated unit in the conflict.

From 1965 through 1970, Delta teams ranged throughout South Vietnam conducting long-range deep penetration reconnaissance missions into

VC sanctuaries, collecting strategic or tactical intelligence, directing air-strikes against camouflaged enemy strongholds, performing bomb damage assessments (BDA), initiating reconnaissance-in-force missions against special NVA/VC targets, capturing NVA prisoners, running wire taps on enemy communications lines, and even rescuing downed aircrew members. The heart of the operation consisted of approximately 16 reconnaissance teams each manned by three hand-picked Special Forces personnel and three Vietnamese LLDB members. Project Delta also ran a unique platoon made up of eight teams of four specially trained CIDG soldiers, who performed their missions wearing NVA or VC uniforms with the intention of actually infiltrating enemy patrols or units. Since the teams deliberately traveled along trails deep in NVA sanctuaries, they were called "Roadrunners." Backing up the reconnaissance teams and Roadrunners, the Vietnamese 81st Airborne Ranger Battalion served as a quick reaction force for emergencies or for exploiting special targets. Rounding out the organization was an American-led Security Company of 124 Nungs and a BDA Platoon consisting of four U.S. and 24 CIDG.[8]

Although assigned to the 5th SFGA, Project Delta came under the operational control of the commanding general, MACV. If any Corps Tactical Zone commander ran up against a tough reconnaissance target, especially those in enemy controlled areas, he would put in a request through MACV for Delta to run the mission. The various elements of Delta consequently evolved into a "first responder" role for obtaining critical covert intelligence deep within enemy territory throughout South Vietnam.

The concept of long-range reconnaissance missions was not a new one; the predecessor to Project Delta had attempted the same mission in Laos. Code-named Leaping Lena and originally organized and funded by the CIA, the program initially consisted of several all-Vietnamese reconnaissance teams who were trained by U.S. Special Forces personnel on temporary duty from the 1st SFGA from Okinawa. In the summer of 1964, five of those small teams parachuted into Laos just north of the A Shau along Route 9, west of Khe Sanh. Immediately the operation ran into trouble. Despite being warned about going into villages, most teams ignored the orders—with catastrophic results. Of the 40 Vietnamese team members initially dropped into Laos, most were either killed or captured soon after their insertion. Only five survivors straggled back weeks later. From that disastrous effort it became embarrassingly clear that without American leadership and expertise on the ground, the Leaping Lena missions were doomed to fail. Still intrigued by the potential, however, planners realized that for deep penetration missions of this type to succeed, highly trained Special Forces would have to lead indigenous soldiers on the ground. Therefore, in late 1964 the decision was made to train combined reconnaissance teams by employing both Green Berets and LLDB personnel. With the American presence on teams, Laos was no longer a viable target, but there were plenty of "bad guy" areas in South Vietnam. The revamped organization and mission became Detachment B-52, Project Delta.[9]

Project Delta teams entered the A Shau Valley on April 18, 1967, to conduct reconnaissance and surveillance as part of Operation 5-67, also known as Operation Pirous. The operations order tasked Project Delta to infiltrate recon teams, Road Runner teams, and Ranger recon platoons into the area of operations (AO) to detect, identify, and interdict enemy targets by tactical airstrikes and to commit airborne Ranger reaction forces in support of recon teams or against targets of opportunity. On paper Operation Pirous appeared to be straightforward, but in reality the operation included a political as well as a jurisdictional component. The I Corps Tactical Zone was hardcore "Marine country," under the command of Lieutenant General Lewis W. Walt, the III Marine Amphibious Force (III MAF) boss. While deployed to I Corps, Delta teams fell under the operational control of III MAF—and that arrangement set the stage for indirect high-level friction. Ostensibly, the III MAF commander reported to the MACV commander, but he also reported through Marine channels to include the Commandant. In the ensuing jurisdictional squabble, senior Marine commanders proved to be less than shy about expressing strong disagreement with the conduct of the war by the leadership of MACV. While the Marines pushed for a small-scale unit pacification program along the populated coastal areas, the Army leadership in Saigon advocated large unit search and destroy operations against North Vietnamese units; it was hoped Delta would locate and identify those big units. As a MACV assigned detachment, Delta was, inopportunely, caught in the middle.[10]

Fortunately, Delta functioned first and foremost as a self-contained ground unit, operating with dedicated Air Force forward air controllers and committed helicopter assets from the 281st Assault Helicopter Company (AHC). The Delta FOB at Phu Bai also enjoyed an excellent working relationship with the Air Force Tactical Air Control Party and elements of the 1st Marine Air Wing (MAW), both essential to the insertion and extraction of Delta teams in and around the A Shau AO. Although there was no hard and fast rule, most Delta recon and roadrunner teams were inserted at twilight using four UH-1 Hueys from the 281st AHC, escorted by two Huey gunships. In the vernacular of the Vietnam War, Army Hueys were dubbed "Hogs" when sporting rocket pods, while troop-carrying Hueys became "Slicks." On each mission the command helicopter led the formation to the LZ, followed by the insertion bird carrying the team and by two recovery Slicks. If the insertion bird could not actually land, the team climbed down shaky chain ladders, repelled into the target, or jumped from heights approaching 15 feet. The recovery Hueys were along to extract the team in case of enemy detection—as often happened—or to rescue the crew of a downed chopper, also a frequent occurrence around the heavily fortified Valley of Death. In most scenarios a dedicated Delta FAC also orbited the scene, ready to call in airstrikes at a moment's notice. In bigger operations involving a Delta Ranger company, the larger CH-46 Sea Knights from the 1st MAW joined the missions.

Operation Pirous was slated to kick off on April 17, but bad weather over the A Shau caused a 24 hour delay. On the 18th, the Delta FAC performed a visual reconnaissance (VR) over the southern end of the valley; what he observed was not encouraging. The FAC spotted two trucks stopped along Route 548 with 27 enemy troops in khaki standing around the trucks—one truck covered with a camouflaged tarpaulin and the other loaded with large boxes, roughly 5x8 feet in size. Nearby, the sharp-eyed pilot picked out two additional trucks parked under trees near the road. The Delta FAC quickly expended several flights of fighters on the target, severely damaging three trucks and setting off one large secondary explosion with heavy black smoke. The bombs also silenced a .51 cal machine gun position which had opened up on and hit two of the F-100 Super Sabre strike aircraft. Despite heavy enemy activity throughout the AO, Recon Team 7 and Roadrunner Team 102 repelled into the A Shau without incident at last light.[11] The essential elements of information the teams were tasked to find out were as follows:

(1) What is the location, strength, identity, and disposition of the enemy in this area?

(2) How effective is the enemy security and early warning system? What measures are used?

(3) What activities are being carried out by enemy units in the area?

(4) What use is made of trails, roads, and waterways in the area? Type traffic, volume, frequency, origin and destination, and routes used?[12]

Several days later Roadrunner Team 102 reported sighting an enemy company in black and khaki uniforms with carbines and Thompson submachine guns. They also reported being tracked by an NVA squad, but through a series of maneuvers and cutbacks the team managed to lose their pursuers. Recon Team 10 was not so fortunate when, on April 22, the six men infiltrated into the valley at last light. Staff Sergeant Herbert Siugzda, the senior team advisor, was seriously injured during a 15-foot jump from the hovering Huey. He landed on a large punji stake that penetrated through his groin and into his stomach. At that point the team came under intense small arms fire from a large enemy force around the LZ. SSgt Siugzda estimated 60 to 70 enemy troops within an area 20 to 100 meters on all sides of their besieged team. He observed that the enemy wore NVA khaki uniforms, but the type of weapons could not be positively identified because of darkness, although they were assumed to be AK-47s. As a hail of bullets ripped through the leaves and branches around him, SSgt Siugzda, immobilized from his injury and in great pain, nevertheless directed the perimeter defense and then orchestrated the successful helicopter recovery of his team through a wall of hostile fire. Herbert Siugzda spent three months on a hospital ship recovering from his wounds, but when released he insisted on returning to Project Delta.[13]

At almost the same moment, in the northern end of the valley Roadrunner Team 103 reported that it had become split and was surrounded. Since it could not be extracted due to poor weather conditions, the tiny team evaded and hid during the night as numerous NVA patrols searched the terrain and fired shots into bamboo thickets in an attempt to flush the team into the open. Somehow the roadrunners reunited at daylight and were rescued.

Delta intelligence estimates suspected that the NVA's 324B and 341 Divisions had infiltrated south of the DMZ, but because of the year-long American absence from the A Shau, one of Delta's primary missions was to determine the "who and where" of enemy unit dispositions, a very dangerous assignment under the best of circumstances. According to veteran Delta team leader Donald J. Taylor, Project Delta's long-range reconnaissance patrols:

> were intended to be uneventful operations, and most of them were. A recon team was expected to infiltrate undetected by the enemy, remain undetected while it collected the intelligence it had been sent in to gather, and finally to exfiltrate, still undetected by the enemy. These were the successful patrols and there were many, but they are seldom remembered, mentioned, or written about. Recon patrols we still remember in vivid detail are the few patrols where things went wrong, our recon team was detected, and we wound up fighting for our lives.[14]

After the insertion of over half a dozen Delta teams on the ground between April 18 and April 23, the wily enemy quickly caught on to the pattern and deployed an equal number of counter-recon units around the A Shau. With so many NVA trackers and LZ watchers on alert, Delta teams found it almost impossible to remain undetected—and that usually resulted in ferocious, close-quarter firefights against at least 10 to 1 odds. It was in just such a scenario that the members of Recon Team 9 wound up fighting for their lives.

On April 23, Sergeant First Class Orville "Robbie" Robinette led Team 9 onto the A Shau's east wall at the north end of the valley and began the deadly cat and mouse game with the enemy. On that first night the only incident occurred around 9 p.m. when the team heard six single rifle shots fired in the distance. At an agonizingly slow pace, involving frequent stops to listen and to cover its back trail, Team 9 had only traveled about 1,500 meters by April 26, but more importantly, the team remained undetected. Yet in addition to the constant fear of being found out, each team member had to endure the debilitating tropical heat and humidity. Leech-infested streams and malaria-contaminated rain forests caused the best of men to come down with burning fevers and incapacitating chills, all aggravated by carrying heavy rucksacks on their backs while slogging through ankle-deep mud. Drenched in their own jungle sweat and covered with filth and vermin, the teams became the target of every flying insect known to man, and ever-present sores festered as creepy-crawly parasites found homes in skin ripped open by "wait-a-minute vines" and razor-sharp elephant grass. And there was no relief through the normal time-honored GI process of vocal bitching or griping. While moving as silently as possible through the A Shau's unforgiving terrain, they only communicated with hand signals or with occasional whispers. The psychological toll proved to be every bit as perilous as the physical environment because teams were completely cut off and isolated from everything, particularly during the hours of darkness.

That evening Robbie Robinette suspected they had located some sort of enemy way station when the team heard the distinct sounds of domestic animals, women and children, along with chopping and digging sounds throughout the night. He was right. Early the next morning while crossing a well-used trail, the team spotted a lone lookout jump from a tree and bolt at a dead run to the northwest. Since they had been spotted, Team 9 opened fire on the fleeing soldier, but he disappeared into the jungle. With his team now compromised, Robinette knew it was time to get out. That instinct was confirmed a few minutes later when Robbie detected approximately 25 NVA moving swiftly in his direction, so he radioed for an extraction.

As the enemy took Team 9 under attack and attempted to surround them, SFC Robinette dodged the heavy fire and moved into a small clearing to place a marker for the incoming helicopters. The first 281st Huey only hoisted out two LLDB members before an intense antiaircraft barrage damaged the chopper so badly that it was forced to leave the scene. A second Huey fared even worse, crashing into the clearing after being battered by heavy small arms and automatic weapons fire. With complete disregard for his own safety, Robbie ran through the gauntlet of molten lead and pulled the crewmembers from the burning Huey. After organizing his men into a defensive perimeter, SFC Robinette then radioed for reinforcements and began calling in tactical airstrikes as close as 25 meters from his position.

The "cavalry" arrived in the form of Delta's Ranger Company 5 aboard three Marine CH-46 Sea Knights. The first two platoons made it in safely, but the third CH-46 crash-landed nearby with only minor injuries to the platoon and crew. As the ranger company moved toward Team 9, Robinette set up an ambush against an enemy squad of a dozen men attempting to flank the friendly position. With death only a few yards away he charged the squad and at a distance of 15 feet took out all 12 soldiers. Once the ranger platoons linked up with Team 9 and the downed aircrew members, Robbie continued to call in devastating airstrikes around his perimeter. His courageous leadership and fighting skills disorganized the enemy force and facilitated an extraction under fire by five CH-46s. For his gallantry in action, Sergeant First Class Orville G. Robinette was awarded the Silver Star.[15]

Recon teams often remained out of sight without engaging enemy forces, and by simply observing they turned up attention-grabbing pieces of intelligence, some operationally important and some bizarre. On one occasion a roadrunner team smiled in disbelief when they spotted 30 NVA soldiers walking along a trail. Yet the most intriguing observation stretched right behind the procession. The enemy column had in tow a wheeled 37mm antiaircraft gun—pulled by two large water buffalos. On another occasion, recon Team 6 observed a column of about a dozen enemy soldiers moving on a road with weapons but no packs or web gear. What was in the column with them grabbed everyone's attention and piqued curiosities. Marching with the group in the center of the column was a Caucasian female! She wore a white shirt and dark pants that appeared to be clean and neat. She was a strawberry blonde with roughly shoulder-length hair. The team estimated her to be about five feet six inches tall, and from all indications she was under no duress. She seemed well fed and in good health. The team report did include the perceptive observation that she had a large bust.[16]

Whether teams in the A Shau were compromised or remained undetected, they all enjoyed the privilege of serving under one of Detachment B-52's legendary commanders, Major Charles A. Allen. A huge SF trooper weighing in at 250 pounds with the build of an NFL linebacker, Chuck Allen loved his men, but the mission always came first. He instilled that same attitude in the members of Project Delta, and because of his physical stature, most Delta men simply referred to their boss by his radio call sign: Bruiser. There was one exception; General Westmoreland always called him "Big Un." Before joining the Army, Bruiser had played a little semipro football and worked as a bouncer in a few bars. His career in the military hit a snag in no less a place than the office of the 82nd Airborne Division commander at Fort Bragg. According to various accounts, the higher ups attempted to put pressure on Allen to play Service League football. When he refused and turned to leave the commander's office, a colonel blocked his exit and placed his hand on Allen's chest to stop him. Chuck Allen's maverick legend started right there when he cold cocked the colonel. Some claim that the episode was the reason the big man remained a captain for 12 years.

As head of Delta, Bruiser was a no-nonsense sort of guy, but one with a slightly irreverent demeanor who commanded the undivided loyalty of his clannish, unconventional warriors. They came to love his lopsided grin, his chipped front tooth, the perpetual gleam in his eyes, and the sight of the "Big Un" wearing his tiger-striped fatigues. But most of all the men of Project Delta came to genuinely admire the man who led them from out front, personally taking charge of every insertion/extraction by flying over 1,500 missions in his command and control helicopter. All his men smiled broadly when they recounted stories about their leader, especially the occasion when a young, newly assigned officer radioed Bruiser circling overhead and requested an extraction because he had inadvertently left his weapon on the chopper during the insertion. The answer the young officer received was classic Chuck Allen: "Cut a fucking spear and continue the mission."[17]

By May 4, Delta had inserted 12 teams into the A Shau. That same afternoon Roadrunner Team 8 detected two persistent enemy tracking squads about 75 meters to its rear. When a blocking squad moved to the team's front, the leader requested and received the help of gunships from the 281st "Intruders." All through the ensuing extraction the nimble gunships suppressed heavy enemy fire with the lethal placement of 2.75-inch high explosive (HE) rockets and machine gun fire within mere meters of the friendlies. During the operation a Marine F-8 from Da Nang ran afoul of the formidable network of triple A positions along the valley's west wall and was shot down. The pilot, Major Edward F. Townley, ejected and was rescued by a 281st AHC Huey and a Delta FAC.[18]

For SFC Robbie Robinette, multiple missions into the Valley of Death went with the territory and the job, but his adventures with a brand new recon team leader tested his mettle. In a demonstration of excellent judgment, the young lieutenant from the tiny town of Speed, NC, decided to run his first mission with Robbie Robinette as his assistant. Primarily he chose Robbie because he was a veteran of many Delta missions, but the second reason was much more personal. At six feet five inches tall, the big lieutenant wanted a strapping, powerful man like Robinette who was strong enough to carry him in case he was wounded.

The team inserted at last light on the east wall of the A Shau opposite the abandoned Special Forces camp at A Luoi. As they jumped free of the helicopter, the flat crack of small arms fire greeted them from a tree line about 200 meters down the slope to their left. As the lieutenant led his team in a dead run into the tall elephant grass, one of the LLDB troopers began to cough loudly, while just below them the NVA pursuers shouted back and forth and began shining flashlights into the approaching darkness. In an effort to throw off the enemy, the team changed directions several times and even reversed course and moved back down the steep slope. Finally, masked by the total darkness, the team once again climbed up the slope and away from the agitated enemy voices. After running for what seemed like hours, the team finally fell exhausted into a thick clump of bushes. As they lay there gasping for breath, the LLDB trooper continued his noisy cough. The lieutenant grabbed the Vietnamese lieutenant's arm and said, "If you don't keep him quiet, he'll get us all killed."

The Delta recon team evaded throughout the next day with the NVA in hot pursuit; the soldier almost never stopped coughing. By sunset of the second night they were already completely out of water and beginning to feel the effects. Their tongues became sticky and swollen, yet the ARVN soldier kept right on hacking. After a sleepless night, as they saddled up to move out at dawn, the lieutenant and Robinette realized that the coughing had stopped. On inspection, the reason quickly became obvious. Sometime during the night the Vietnamese lieutenant had either strangled or smothered the man, an act that was grisly but necessary.

After evading all through the second day without water, the team's physical condition deteriorated rapidly as severe dehydration set in. Their skin began to shrivel while each man experienced intermittent dizziness and confusion. As they doggedly continued to move, the team stumbled across an NVA base camp with rows of neatly placed pith helmets on the ground next to small cooking fires. It appeared to be a bivouac area for at least a battalion, and the owners of those helmets had to be close by.

As the team cautiously moved away from the camp, the lieutenant suddenly heard a rustling noise in the brush directly ahead. There in front of him was a huge tiger not ten feet away. The big cat dropped to a crouch, its ears back and its striped tail swishing nervously. After a few agonizingly long seconds of ocular sparing, the tiger snorted and moved off in another direction. Still unnerved from the encounter with the tiger, the team had not moved more than 50 meters when there was a loud crashing sound overhead. Instinctively putting his CAR-15 selector switch to auto, the tall lieutenant anxiously looked up to see a large, furry animal swing through the tree branches. "What the hell was that?" he whispered to Robinette.

"Beats the shit outta me, sir. Orangutan maybe," he said with a weak grin.

On a high ridge near a clearing the exhausted and desperately thirsty team flopped to the ground. They had finally reached the breaking point. At that exact moment thunder rumbled and rain began to pelt down through the jungle canopy. They rolled their ponchos into makeshift funnels and caught enough rain to fill their canteens.

That third night the team rigged an antenna wire and tapped out a brief message in Morse code pinpointing the location of the NVA base camp and arranging for a helicopter extraction. It took most of the next morning to reach the LZ, a small clear area not large enough for a Huey to land. When he at last heard the wop-wop-wop of the approaching Huey, the team leader talked the bird into his location. At that point the daring pilot extended his winch cable to its full 165-foot length, went into an incredibly vulnerable hover, and began hoisting the Delta team aboard using a jungle penetrator, a metal, bullet-shaped steel contraption with three spring loaded fold-down seats, each big enough for one person to straddle. Just as the team leader, the last on the ground, grabbed the jungle penetrator for his ride to salvation, blasts from multiple AK-47s ripped through the foliage around him. As green tracers zipped by, the lieutenant just managed to grab the chopper's right landing skid and hang on for dear life. Half way back to the FOB the crew chief finally hauled the lanky team leader inside.[19]

The lieutenant who had just survived his first mission in the Valley of Death as a Project Delta team leader was none other than Henry "Hugh"

Shelton, a future four-star general and Chairman of the Joint Chiefs of Staff. Just like young Colin Powell four years earlier, Hugh Shelton's baptism of fire took place in the A Shau Valley.

During Operation Pirous, Delta's harrowing intrusion into the A Shau confirmed at least two undeniable trends. First, the place was crawling with bad guys. It became painfully obvious that team firefights were not just against a few NVA trackers or LZ watchers. Rather, the frequent and deadly encounters often involved entire companies of well-armed and disciplined enemy soldiers bent on wiping out Delta teams. The second trend was equally disturbing. NVA antiaircraft units had deployed automatic weapons around all likely LZs, and therefore took a terrible toll on the helicopters of the 281st Assault Helicopter Company. Between April 27 to May 14, enemy gunners shot down four helicopters supporting Delta and damaged twice that many. In spite of the high risk to the choppers, to a man the Delta teams knew that during an emergency extraction the 281st AHC aircrews would either rescue them or die trying. This was indeed a brotherhood of warriors.

Although many Delta missions in other areas of South Vietnam went undetected, that scenario did not hold true for Operation Pirous. The battle on May 14 in the southeast corner of the A Shau characterized the unique dangers faced by both recon teams and the helicopters that supported them while operating in a North Vietnamese-controlled sanctuary. Sergeant First Class Joseph M. Markham's adventures on that date proved to be typical.

Late on the afternoon of the 14th, Recon Team 1 attempted infiltration near the village of Be Luong. As the Huey approached the LZ flying at 75 feet above the ground, it encountered a heavy volume of automatic weapons fire from several .51 cal machine guns. The 281st AHC bird received a number of hits causing it to lose oil pressure completely, but the pilot managed to keep the aircraft flying long enough to make a controlled crash-landing. SFC Markham's recovery helicopter quickly descended into the intense fusillade and picked up the crew and a portion of the team. When he realized that the aircraft was overloaded, Markham voluntarily jumped 15 feet to the ground to lighten the load. He found three members of Recon Team 1, organized a hasty defense, and began returning fire. During the fight, as Markham guided another recovery helicopter into his position,

enemy gunners blasted the bird, causing it to crash near the first downed
Huey. In spite of the intense and highly accurate small arms fire, SFC
Markham led his men across open ground to the crash site and pulled the
crew from the wreckage. He then contacted the Delta FAC and coordinated suppressing fire from several Intruder gunships, two F-4s, and an
orbiting Spooky gunship. When a third recovery helicopter arrived, Markham remained on the ground alone holding off the advancing enemy soldiers while the crew and remaining team members scrambled up the rope
ladder dangling beneath the hovering Huey. Only when they were safely
aboard did Joe Markham grab the rope ladder and signal the pilot to depart
while he was still climbing the swaying ladder, all the while taking fire from
every NVA soldier in the immediate area. For his gallant actions, Sergeant
First Class Joseph M. Markham was awarded the Silver Star.[20]

Around the hot LZs in the A Shau, extractions under fire were the rule
rather than the exception, and the Delta teams literally owed their very
lives to the unwavering valor of the crews from the 281st Assault Helicopter
Company. Arguably the best tribute to the Intruders was written by long-
time Delta recon team leader Don Taylor about a spectacular rescue in the
A Shau. Here is the story in his own words about two old friends he had
first met at Fort Bragg in 1963:

> Probably the greatest bit of flying expertise of the Vietnam War
> was when CWO-2 Donald Torrini, a 281st pilot, pulled Jerry L.
> Nelson out of the A Shau Valley. It is highly doubtful that if any
> helicopter unit other than the 281st had supported the Project
> during that deployment, a pilot would have gone to such an ex-
> treme effort to extract a recon team from what had appeared to be
> a hopeless situation.
>
> Jerry had been inserted with his six man recon team to "snatch"
> a POW, and on the second day in, he saw an opportunity to do
> so. He had observed two and three man groups of NVA moving
> down a trail in one or two hour intervals and had decided to go
> for it. He selected a good ambush site beside the trail and moved
> his team into position to ambush the next group that came along.
>
> However, the next group to come down the trail was a 15-man
> point element of a much larger NVA unit, and after a brief interval

of the customary claymore popping, shooting, stabbing, kicking, and grenade chunking, Jerry had destroyed the point element and had his POW. Jerry's POW snatch technique was simply to try his level best to kill everyone in the kill zone and then look for a survivor; somehow, there always was at least one.

But now, Jerry had a company plus of pissed off NVA after him, as he dragged his badly wounded POW toward his extraction LZ. As luck would have it, Jerry found his route blocked by a flanking NVA element, while the main NVA element pushed him towards the river and away from his LZ.

When Jerry arrived at the river, he found himself facing a 75-meter wide river too deep to ford, too swift to swim with gear and surrounded by triple canopy too thick and too high for either ladder or McGuire rig extraction. Near the river, the canopy thinned just enough for Jerry to obtain a "shiny" [signal mirror] fix from Sheriff [FAC call-sign], and an extraction helicopter flown by Torrini, already on station, immediately descended into the trees to recover Jerry and his team. Torrini attempted to chop the treetops out with his rotor blades in order to get down low enough, but he failed.

By this time, Jerry was in a fierce firefight to his front, most of his team was wounded, his back was to the river, extraction appeared to be impossible, and the enemy was too close to effectively use TAC air support. All seemed to be hopeless for Jerry and his team, but Torrini had not given up.

While Torrini had hovered high over Jerry's position trying to get down low enough to extract him, he had noticed that the trees, though thick along the river bank, only hung over the river and there was space enough under the tree branches and along the surface of the river for his helicopter to narrowly fit. Torrini flew up and down the river looking for a hole in the tree canopy over the river large enough for his helicopter to drop into until he finally found one about 500 meters down river from Jerry, and he dropped into it. Torrini put his skids in the water and flew his ship up river and under the overhanging tree branches, with his rotor blades, at times, only clearing the branches above by a few feet.

Jerry could not believe his eyes when the helicopter suddenly appeared behind him in the river, with its skids completely submerged, its troop deck awash in the swiftly moving water, and the M-60 delivering over-head fire into enemy positions to his front. Torrini moved his helicopter as close to Jerry's team as possible, and with the rotor blade tips chewing into the bark of the tree trunks along the river bank, and the door gunner's M-60 firing closely over their heads, Jerry swam his team, with POW, the short distance out to and into the waiting helicopter.

But now there was another problem to deal with; there was not enough room to turn the helicopter around, and Torrini would have to back the helicopter out in reverse hover to return to the hole in the canopy that he had previously entered. As the gunships made repeated runs down each side, Torrini slowly backed his helicopter down the river.

All along the way, the NVA continued to appear on the riverbank and were met by fire from the door gunners and from Jerry's team. By the time the helicopter finally reached the hole in the canopy and Torrini lifted them up and out of the river, both door gunners and Jerry's team had expended all of their ammo.

The helicopter was so badly shot up and the rotor blades, transmission, and engine were so badly damaged from tree strikes and enemy fire that Torrini determined that it probably would not make it back to Phu Bai. So he sat his faithful helicopter down in a clearing, transferred his crew and Jerry's team to other helicopters, and the brave little bird was destroyed in place; it was the only U.S. casualty of the day.[21]

For his conspicuous gallantry in the remarkable rescue of the recon team, Chief Warrant Officer-2 Donald G. Torrini was recommended for the Medal of Honor. The award was subsequently downgraded, and he received the Silver Star.

Of all the teams put on the ground during Operation Pirous, perhaps the most costly engagement for both Delta and their supporting helicopters occurred between May 21 and May 23. During the attempted extraction of Roadrunner Team 107, enemy gunners zeroed in on a 281st recovery

Huey flown by a veteran Intruder pilot. As he slowed to a hover, the pilot suffered a head wound and the recovery NCO was hit in the arm by shrapnel from the shattered instrument panel. The damaged bird managed to limp out of the area and return to Phu Bai. On the second recovery attempt, a 281st AHC gunship was shot down by heavy small arms and automatic weapons fire. The aircraft crashed on a very high ridge along the west wall of the A Shau; on impact it rolled into a ravine and burst into flames. Observers doubted that anyone had survived.

While an Air Force HH-3 Jolly Green helicopter extracted Roadrunner Team 107, a Marine CH-46 from the 1st MAW located a crash survivor, Crew Chief Craig Szwed, and lifted him to safety. He was convinced the other crewmembers died in the violent crash. However, several hours later, orbiting aircraft spotted signals from possible survivors. When a 281st recovery chopper approached the area and began to hover ten feet off the ground, it was hit by a heavy volume of enemy fire, killing the left door gunner.

At first light on May 22, the command and control chopper spotted signals from two possible crash survivors, and Ranger Company 1 was inserted under fire to search for the two crewmembers. One of the CH-46s exchanged bursts with a .51 cal position with one enemy killed, but a stream of green tracers hit the Sea Knight's rear engine, causing it to crash on the LZ. Fortunately, a second CH-46 immediately rescued the crew. On the ground the ranger company located a very lucky door gunner, Specialist 4th Gary D. Hall, and had him extracted. The rangers then moved on, searching for the two remaining crewmembers.

On May 23, the rangers finally linked up with gunship pilot Chief Warrant Officer Donald L. Corkran. An attempt to extract him was unsuccessful due to intense ground fire, so the rangers, with "Corky" Corkran in tow, moved to another LZ. En route they were caught in an ambush by an NVA platoon and during the 15-minute firefight, suffered 3 rangers KIA, 2 WIA, and a translator WIA. After heavy saturation bombing by Air Force and Marine fighters, CH-46s finally extracted Ranger Company 1 and the incredibly lucky downed pilot. The co-pilot of the gunship, CWO Walter F. Wrobleski, was never found.[22]

As in the earlier 1967 big unit battles like Operation Junction City, Operation Pirous terminated with mixed results. During the two-month long campaign, Project Delta inserted a total of 48 teams along the length and breadth of the A Shau Valley. Those teams confirmed that Route 922 entering South Vietnam from Laos at the northern end of the A Shau, and Route 548 running southeast through the valley, were indeed connected and had been improved to accommodate heavy truck traffic along their entire length to the southernmost portion of the A Shau. Evidence of truck traffic and road repair work had been reported daily, as well as six instances of actual truck sightings along those routes. Project Delta teams additionally discovered numerous previously undetected trails, all in good shape and recently used. The teams also observed that the enemy only used the roads and trails at night or during inclement weather when detection by strike aircraft was limited. The teams furthermore confirmed that the concentration of enemy forces proved to be much larger than earlier intelligence studies had estimated. Those NVA units moved at will throughout the AO, their counter-recon companies displaying a remarkable ability to track and anticipate the moves of Delta recon teams. The 90 incidents involving exchanges of fire between Delta and hostile units emphatically verified the effectiveness of enemy tactics.[23]

In addition to the important intelligence gained between April 17 and June 13, Operation Pirous chalked up a notable score against the opposition. Delta assets accounted for 17 enemy soldiers confirmed killed and 29 killed by air (KBA). During that period, teams called in 44 pre-planned and 117 immediate air strikes which resulted in 14 structures destroyed, 2 vehicles destroyed and 6 damaged, 88 automatic weapon positions destroyed or silenced, and 68 secondary explosions and fires. Unfortunately, those statistics came at a steep price. In the fierce fighting, Delta lost 1 American KIA, 7 WIA, and 1 MIA. The Vietnamese Rangers suffered 4 KIA, 9 WIA, and 1 MIA. NVA gunners shot down four Hueys, two CH-46s, and one F-8, along with numerous aircraft and helicopters damaged by the intense ground fire.[24]

Throughout the operation, the valor displayed by all Project Delta components was undeniable; they took the fight to the enemy no matter the risk, and in the A Shau that risk registered as high if not higher than in any other arena in South Vietnam. But the burning question remained: was the price too high?

chapter 4

SOG: WEST OF THE A SHAU

There are roads which must not be followed, armies which must not be attacked, towns which must not be besieged, positions which must not be contested.

—SUN TZU

D
elta recon teams were not the only intrepid souls who ventured into the sinister and always dangerous Valley of Death. While Delta ran missions in the A Shau on the Vietnam side of the border, a top-secret joint service organization performed an almost identical mission across the border in Laos. That unit was known as MACSOG: Military Assistance Command, Studies and Observations Group. Usually referred to as SOG, the unit was formed to carry out covert action against North Vietnam, Laos, and Cambodia, but in reality the name 'Studies and Observations Group' conveyed about as thin a cover as had ever been devised. Instead of the academics and scientists the name suggested, the personnel were actually Green Berets borrowed from the 5th Special Forces Group, while the various SOG commanders read like an Army who's who of legends in the special operations world: Clyde Russell, Donald "Headhunter" Blackburn, Jack Singlaub, Arthur "Bull" Simons, Steve Cavanaugh, and John "Skip" Sadler. The organization also included several Air Force Air Commando units as well as members of the U.S. Navy's elite SEAL Team One. Virtually all of these highly trained unconventional warfare troops participated in one of SOG's four core operational missions: Agent Networks and Deception, Covert Maritime Operations, "Black" Psychological Warfare, and Covert Operations against the Ho Chi Minh Trail.

By far the largest effort within SOG, and one of the most dangerous, was OP 35, tasked with the insertion of American-led covert reconnaissance teams against the Ho Chi Minh Trail, first in Laos and later in Cambodia. The teams, routinely commanded by Special Forces personnel, performed a variety of missions deep within enemy territory, to include identifying NVA base camps and supply caches, bomb damage assessment of B-52 strikes, wire tapping, sabotaging logistics supply lines, directing air strikes against lucrative targets of opportunity, counting trucks moving down the Trail, and on occasion, snatching NVA prisoners. SOG was even tasked with rescuing U.S. crewmembers evading capture, or rescuing American or allied personnel being held as prisoners. The political sensitivity surrounding these hairy missions stemmed from the 1962 Geneva Accords which declared Laos to be "neutral." As a result, all foreign forces were required to leave. They all did—except the North Vietnamese. In total disregard of the international agreement, NVA strength along the Trail rose to 60,000 support troops, 40,000 security troops, and over 10,000 antiaircraft gunners. Clearly the major network for infiltration, the Trail would eventually transport 20,000 NVA soldiers a month from the North into South Vietnam.[1]

A steadfast concern among senior American policy makers included the distinct possibility that a Green Beret on one of SOG's covert recon teams would be captured and put on public display, thus exposing American duplicity, not to mention our overt, albeit comparatively modest, violations of the Geneva Accords. Faced with a delicate balancing act of measuring the legal, political, and ethical ramifications attached to honoring the Geneva Accords, against the critical requirement to find out what Hanoi was up to in Laos, President Johnson reluctantly approved SOG covert missions across international borders. Originally code named "Shining Brass," SOG's cross border missions became "Operation Prairie Fire" in early 1967. That same year covert operations were extended into Cambodia; they were code named "Daniel Boone," later changed to "Salem House." Through it all the United States government staunchly denied that any American military combat personnel were on the ground in neutral Laos or Cambodia.

The covert nature of the Prairie Fire mission, coupled with heavy losses among SOG reconnaissance teams, created sticky political problems requiring elaborate secrecy. Consequently, SOG missions were among the most

NVA BASE AREAS

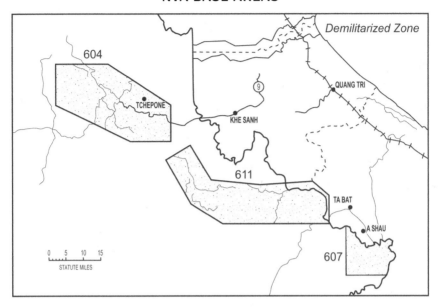

highly classified of the war and therefore came under intense high-level scrutiny. The approval process also evolved into a bureaucratic nightmare. At a minimum of 30 days in advance, SOG submitted a planned mission up the chain of command. First stop was MACV, followed by Pacific Command Headquarters in Hawaii. Next came the Joint Chiefs of Staff and the Office of the Secretary of Defense for review and approval. From there, SOG's planned mission went to the National Security Council's 303 Committee for coordination with State Department, the CIA, and finally to the White House for authorization. Much to the disgruntlement of SOG, at any point in the process a mission could be altered or rejected.[2]

To fend off and partially mollify concerns and criticisms from State Department officials who definitely balked at the notion of permitting the American military to set up camp in neutral Laos, SOG teams went to extraordinary lengths to conceal their identities on missions. When crossing the border into Laos or Cambodia, team members completely sanitized themselves: no dog tags, no military ID cards, no personal items of any sort that might identify them as American. Their weapons, often foreign, had untraceable serial numbers; their uniforms, devoid of any patches or insignia, were non-regulation and locally produced; if they smoked, even their American cigarettes were replaced by Asian brands. All this deception served one purpose: plausible deniability. If team members were killed or captured in Laos, the U.S. government would deny any association. The cover story included a flimsy explanation that the individuals had inadvertently strayed across the ill-defined border. In the event of a fatality, families back home were simply told that their loved ones had been killed "in Southeast Asia." The subterfuge even went so far as to hide missions from Ambassador William H. Sullivan in Laos. When Sullivan initially imposed a ban on helicopter insertions of teams deeper than five kilometers into Laos, SOG legend Colonel Arthur "Bull" Simons solved the problem by simply drawing in a new border 20 kilometers farther west and issuing the new maps to his recon teams. As far as can be determined, the State Department never found out about the switch.[3]

In I Corps, SOG ran its cross-border operations from Command and Control North, or CCN, its regional headquarters located at Da Nang. CCN reconnaissance teams, called RTs, worked all cross-border operations from Chu Lai north to the DMZ. Within CCN several FOBs operated, including those at Phu Bai, Khe Sanh, Quang Tri, and one at Nakhon Phanom, Thailand. At the tactical level, CCN assigned Operation Prairie Fire targets to a specific recon team, then shipped the team off to the FOB for the actual mission. Depending on the assignment, an RT could range in size from four to twelve men, usually with two or three Green Berets. The teams also included mostly Nung and Montagnard tribesmen, members of Vietnam's largest ethnic minority. And like Project Delta, SOG "borrowed" Slicks and gunships from U.S. divisions in I Corps, along with helicopter assets from the Vietnamese Air Force (VNAF). RTs also operated under the protective cover of their own dedicated FACs, call sign Covey.

Because of the secrecy involved, Prairie Fire missions into Laos were totally non-attribution affairs—nobody admitted the U.S. had teams operating there. The primary objective was to scout the Ho Chi Minh Trail, a sprawling, twisting network of paths, trails, and secondary dirt roads snaking through Laos and Cambodia. Running approximately 600 miles north to south and stretching 20 to 30 miles east to west, the Trail belonged exclusively to the North Vietnamese following the 1962 Geneva Accords. For that reason the U.S. had to find out what was going on along the Trail network, called by the North Vietnamese the Truong Son Strategic Supply Route.

Laos, best described by Bernard Fall as a "political convenience," had become a quagmire of intrigue as various factions within Premier Souvanna Phouma's Royal Lao neutralist government vied for power. In that vacuum the North Vietnamese and the Laotian Communist Pathet Lao virtually owned the Trail from North Vietnam's Mu Gia Pass south through Laos and into Cambodia. Their logistics infrastructure included a staggering 100,000 troops. Consequently, American military activities in Laos constituted a top-secret war in one of the most remote areas of the world—and it was brimming with enemy soldiers and weapons. The ground fire in South Vietnam, where pilots flew through a hail of small arms and automatic weapons fire, was highly dangerous as loss rates among Delta helicopter units showed, but in Laos and Cambodia, low-flying, slow-moving FACs and helicopters also flew against the same big guns that defended Hanoi, murderously accurate 23mm, 37mm, and 57mm antiaircraft artillery—AAA or "triple A" for short. Things got even worse with the 1968 termination of America's sustained bombing campaign against North Vietnam, called Operation Rolling Thunder, when there were virtually no U.S. air strikes north of the DMZ. Safe from that threat, Hanoi upped the ante by increasing its antiaircraft inventory along the Trail by 600 percent; they simply moved 2,000 of their triple A weapons from the North to locations in Laos, making the Ho Chi Minh Trail the most dangerous and heavily defended stretch of road in the world. A single round from any one of those guns could blow an aircraft to bits; from what SOG and its aircrews experienced, the gunners on the Trail also had plenty of ammunition. There were even rumors that North Vietnamese gunners were chained to their weapons: kill or be killed![4]

To counter the success of the American ground reconnaissance efforts, Hanoi had fielded a huge security force of dedicated troops to neutralize and destroy SOG teams, many stationed along trail segments near the A Shau's west wall. As a result, most sites contiguous to the Trail and capable of receiving helicopters were under permanent observation by LZ watchers. When a SOG helicopter approached on a Prairie Fire mission, the LZ watcher signaled the alarm and set the deadly stalking game in motion. A local NVA reaction force of 100 men or more immediately moved toward the team's insertion point, while professionally trained tracking teams, often with dogs, began the hunt. Not only did the counter-recon companies spread out and search carefully selected areas for the RTs, they also staked out nearby LZs to thwart the extraction of the team. Often, that meant concealed .51 caliber antiaircraft machine guns designed to ambush the rescuing helicopters and FACs. Although SOG teams used their radios sparingly, enemy troops also employed sophisticated radio detection-finding devices to track team positions to within yards of their actual location.

The small SOG teams, statistically outnumbered several hundred to one, still jumped at the chance to embark on their decidedly dangerous missions. Their success was primarily a direct result of two important attributes: quality over quantity and unmitigated audacity. Anxiety and uncertainty are among war's most contagious diseases, and the men of SOG suffered from neither affliction. SOG RTs epitomized stealth in the jungle, and they prided themselves on being able to move unseen and unheard right under the enemy's nose. They called it "being good in the woods." If a firefight did erupt, however, the team instantly transformed itself into one of the most highly trained, lethal light infantry units in the world. Rather than cower, the team leader, known as the One-Zero, almost always struck the critical first blow, then led his team toward a pre-determined defensive position or LZ. If the RT had to stay and fight it out, hopefully the supporting Covey FAC orbiting overhead could bring in air strikes to help even the incredibly long odds.[5]

The Air Force FAC for each mission always teamed up with one of a small number of experienced Special Forces NCOs known as "Covey riders." Together they flew every sortie, the Covey pilot controlling the airborne assets while the Covey rider coordinated the map reading and radios; they talked to the team on the ground, and interpreted the tactical situation for his pilot and for the FOB listening on the same radio frequency. These SOG veterans had survived numerous recon missions, so they had firsthand knowledge of exactly what a team was experiencing on the ground. When a team got in trouble, the Covey rider's soothing voice on the radio not only provided a distinct psychological lift, tactically it also said, "We're here for you, and we're gonna get you out."[6]

Against such odds the teams also had some tricks of their own, all of which came in handy in the remote A Shau. To discourage and throw off the trackers, teams often left small M-14 "toe popper" mines along the egress route. And to confuse the tracker dogs, SOG teams effectively employed CS tear gas powder shaken on the ground as they moved. To further confuse the enemy, some RTs wore NVA uniforms. Thus disguised, a Vietnamese-speaking member of the team might actually pass for an NVA soldier. Even if the disguise caused an enemy sentry to hesitate for only a few moments, those critical seconds were probably his last on earth.

In early 1967, MACV initiated a new concept for SOG operations in Laos known as SLAM: Seeking, Locating, Annihilating, and Monitoring enemy infiltration to and through the Laos Panhandle. Prairie Fire reconnaissance teams were tasked to locate enemy units and installations, direct tactical air attacks against them, and assess damage if possible. When appropriate, SOG exploitation resources—Hatchet forces—were then deployed via helicopter to execute attack, destruction, and mine-laying missions in key target areas. Specifically, SOG focused on two major infiltration areas immediately west of the A Shau Valley. The first, designated Base Area 611, stretched west from the northern end of the A Shau along Route 922. The second, Base Area 607, butted up against the southwest corner of the A Shau. Both areas were hotbeds of NVA logistic and counter-recon activity, and the danger for SOG teams working those targets was vividly illustrated on two costly missions.[7]

As Project Delta's Operation Pirous wrapped up, on June 2, 1967, CCN launched a Hatchet Force company into an ominous place called Target Oscar Eight, roughly 15 kilometers inside Laos due west of the A Shau. Alleged to be the largest depot outside of Hanoi, the complex located within Oscar Eight served as the forward headquarters for the 559th Transportation Group, responsible for maintenance and security of the entire Ho Chi Minh Trail. In addition to the headquarters, this was also a *binh tram*, or logistical support base and trans-shipment point for arms, food, ammunition, medical supplies, and reinforcements destined for NVA units throughout South Vietnam. National Security Agency (NSA) listening posts had suspected for some time that a major headquarters operated in that area because they intercepted an incredibly high volume of radio transmissions from Oscar Eight—over 1,500 each day.[8]

The mission against Oscar Eight began at dawn on June 2 when an Arc Light formation of nine B-52s dumped over 200 tons of bombs on the target. Before the smoke had even cleared, nine VNAF H-34s, call sign Kingbee, and five Marine CH-46 Sea Knights inserted a SOG Hatchet Force company of 100 men with the mission to conduct BDA of the strike, capture any wounded NVA, and to destroy enemy equipment in the area.

By early the following morning the NVA forces had fully recovered from the Arc Light pounding. Hundreds of them swarmed around the vastly outnumbered, predominately Nung Hatchet Force which had taken cover in several bomb craters. The SOG leaders on the ground immediately began calling in gunships and airstrikes—danger close. To complicate matters further, Oscar Eight amounted to an NVA defensive marvel with the only LZs located in a shallow basin with jungle-covered hills all around them, and those hills were thick with triple-A of every caliber from 12.7mm, to 37mm, and 57mm radar controlled guns; they constituted one of the most sophisticated complexes of interlocking antiaircraft defenses in Southeast Asia. The bitter truth registered for the Hatchet Force when the first two Marine UH-1 gunships were immediately shot down. Next, two A-1E Skyraiders from Pleiku pressed in on the deck to attack the surging NVA forces. As Lieutenant Colonel Lewis M. Robinson came around on his second napalm run against the horseshoe shaped ridge, multiple .51 cal machine guns blasted his Skyraider with a stream of green tracers. On the ground, Sergeant First Class Charles F. Wilklow in the Hatchet Force watched in horror as the stricken A-1 pitched up violently, crashing into his wingman whose big propeller sliced the tail off Robinson's plane. The A-1 entered an inverted spin, exploding when it hit the ground approximately five miles east of the battle area. There was no parachute.[9]

On the ground the Hatchet Force, reasonably well protected in their bomb craters, managed to keep the enemy at bay, although they were pinned down by steady volleys of small arms fire. The Nungs possessed too much internal firepower for the NVA to mount a frontal assault, but neither did the Hatchet Force have the ability to counter attack against the large enemy contingent. The situation spelled stalemate. The only hope for the stranded troops was close air support and helicopter extraction. In the middle of the melee, two F-4 Phantoms attempted to come to the rescue by dropping their loads of "snake and nape"—slang for snake-eye retarded fin high-drag bombs and napalm—along the horseshoe shaped ridge. As the Phantoms executed their low-level passes, a barrage of flak greeted both birds, and according to several witnesses one of the jets received a hit in the right wing, nosed over, and crashed in a huge orange fire ball.[10]

By that time a rescue fleet consisting of Marine CH-46s from HMM-165 Squadron and H-34 Kingbees from VNAF Squadron 219 had launched from the Khe Sanh FOB. A Kingbee was the first to approach the hot LZ but burst into flames when raked by the heavy ground fire before crashing on Route 922. Another H-34 rescued that crew. Next, a Sea Knight ran the gauntlet of fire and although hit multiple times, it managed to land near the bomb craters and lift out almost an entire platoon. The second CH-46 was not so lucky. Shark 03, piloted by Captain Steven P. Hanson, landed on the LZ under fire, ultimately lifting out 24 Nungs and 3 SOG sergeants: Billy R. Laney, Ronald J. Dexter, and Charles F. Wilklow. While lifting off, the pilot was wounded, lost control, and hit the trees in a violent crash about 350 meters from the LZ. Many aboard were killed or severely injured.[11]

As SFC Charlie Wilklow attempted to climb out of the wreckage, he saw SFC Billy Laney on the floor with a massive chest wound, a broken ankle, and probably dead. SFC Ron Dexter appeared uninjured and was helping wounded Nungs out of the twisted wreckage. The wounded pilot, Capt Hanson, crawled outside the helicopter but climbed back in to get his carbine. He was never seen again. Throughout the ordeal the enemy continued to fire on the crash survivors and even tossed grenades toward the downed chopper, apparently with no intention of capturing the personnel inside. As Wilklow dodged the small arms fire ripping into the fuselage, he saw the Marine door gunner, Lance Corporal Frank E. Cius, receive a wound to the head and slump over his gun. Seconds later Charlie Wilklow took a slug in the right leg as he rolled out of the helicopter.[12]

Unable to walk, SFC Wilklow began crawling away from the wreck, unaware that SFC Dexter, wounded Lance Corporal Frank Cius, and 12 Nungs had set up a defensive perimeter 200 meters away and were fending off assaults by the enemy. Weak from loss of blood, Wilklow finally passed out. When he came to, he looked up to see an NVA soldier sitting on a wooden platform beside a .51 cal machine gun, watching him from 60 feet above. Similar platforms were in the trees all around him. At that point he realized that he had crawled into the middle of an enemy base camp. Wilklow expected to be captured or more likely shot, but NVA soldiers simply walked over, saw his condition, and left him there. At some point he passed out again. When he woke up, enemy soldiers had moved him into a clearing and placed an orange signal panel beside him in an obvious attempt to use him as bait to lure other helicopters into a flak trap. They left him there all day.[13]

Wilklow came to on the second day weak and terribly thirsty. When he tried to lap water from a muddy puddle, enemy soldiers strolled over and urinated in the puddle. Lying in the scorching sun during the day and shivering from the cold rain at night, Charlie Wilklow knew he was dying. The following night, with no one bothering to watch him anymore, the valiant SF trooper mustered what little remaining strength he had and slowly, painfully, began to crawl. He slid face-first down a muddy hillside, passing out occasionally, but he somehow found the willpower to keep going. By sunrise he had dragged himself about two miles. He crawled into a small clearing on the western edge of the A Shau and placed the signal panel beside himself before passing out yet again. When he next came to, he was looking into the face of SOG Staff Sergeant Lester Pace. SSgt Pace dragged the nearly dead Wilklow to a nearby clearing where a Kingbee lifted them both to safety. General Westmoreland personally flew to the hospital at Da Nang to present the Purple Heart to SFC Wilklow.[14]

For SOG, the raid on Oscar Eight had been unimaginably costly, with 23 Americans killed or missing, about 50 Nung raiders lost, and 7 aircraft shot down. After the fierce battle, Lance Corporal Frank Cius was listed as MIA, but in actuality he had been captured. When he was released in 1973, Cius told debriefers that SOG SFC Ronald Dexter had also been captured but died in captivity on July 29, 1967. The pilot, co-pilot, and crew chief of Shark 03 were initially listed as MIA, but that status was later changed to presumed dead.[15]

At home, the American public knew nothing of these costly raids into Oscar Eight, a blessing for the military since the tempo of anti-war protests had already escalated considerably; had protesters known about SOG battles in Laos, a national mob scene might well have been set in motion. As it was, on October 21, 1967, a huge throng of 50,000 protesters marched from the Lincoln Memorial to the front steps of the Pentagon where the predominately young, college-educated marchers achieved worldwide press coverage of their planned civil disobedience activities. Among the 650 protesters arrested during the march on the Pentagon were such social activist notables as Normal Mailer, Allen Ginsberg, Abbie Hoffman, and Jerry Rubin. The march on the Pentagon was only the beginning. Two years later the Vietnam Moratorium Committee staged what is believed to be the largest anti-war protest in United States history when as many as half a million people attended a mostly peaceful demonstration in Washington. The *New York Times* described the crowd as "predominantly youthful" and a "mass gathering of the moderate and radical Left . . . old-style liberals; Communists and pacifists and a sprinkling of the violent New Left." The *Times* went on to characterize the demonstration by saying, "The predominant event of the day was that of a great and peaceful army of dissent moving through the city."[16] After the Washington demonstrations, everyone, whether hawk or dove, young or old, could better relate to Bob Dylan's 1964 classic song, "The Times They Are A-Changin."

Against the backdrop of anti-war protests and despite the costly Hatchet Force debacle in June, SOG could not resist the lure of another mission into Oscar Eight—in spite of Chinese military strategist Sun Tzu's 2,500-year-old dire warning about "armies which must not be attacked." On the afternoon of November 8, 1967, a VNAF Kingbee flew across the A Shau and inserted RT Utah on a grass-covered hilltop in the sinister target area. The team consisted of Master Sergeant Bruce R. Baxter, Staff Sergeant Homer Wilson, Specialist 4 Joseph G. Kusick, and five Montagnards.

Approximately two hours after inserting, while moving through dense jungle shortly before nightfall, RT Utah was cornered by hundreds of enemy troops. MSgt Baxter quickly directed the fire of his men on the hostile forces, disrupting the large but ragged attack. He was seriously wounded by a blitz of enemy grenades during the firefight that followed, but he refused aid and led his men to a landing zone for extraction. The team was about to be overrun when Huey gunships and Kingbees arrived for the extraction, and under murderous fire the first H-34 made it into the LZ. MSgt Baxter refused to be evacuated, directing instead that SSgt Wilson and half of the team board the aircraft while he remained on the ground. A second Kingbee was downed after being riddled by the devastating ground fire, but Bruce Baxter completely disregarded his own safety by rushing through the hail of bullets to rescue the crew. Next he requested a hoist extraction for the rest of his team, and as soon as the Air Force HH-

3 came in, Baxter placed three of his men aboard before the ship abruptly took off under heavy small arms fire. When a second HH-3 helicopter elected to land in near-darkness despite the heavy salvos, MSgt Baxter attempted to climb in only after he was sure that the rest of his team was aboard. Peppered by a barrage of AK-47 fire, both Baxter and Joe Kusick were mortally wounded just as the helicopter was lifting off; it was shot down in an attempt to fly out of the area. For his extraordinary heroism, Master Sergeant Bruce R. Baxter was posthumously awarded the Distinguished Service Cross.[17]

As night fell, the surviving crewmembers huddled together not far from the crash site while a lone Huey gunship flown by Warrant Officers Kent Woolridge and William Zanow made one final pass to help, but in a hail of antiaircraft fire it too was shot down. In the darkness the forlorn survivors waited, but the enemy did not move in for the kill. "Instead of finishing off the survivors," an Air Force debrief noted, "the communists used them for bait to bag more rescue choppers."[18]

In 1967, night vision goggles had not been perfected, so SOG team extractions during darkness rarely occurred. But just after midnight on November 9, 1967, two "Jolly Green Giant" Search and Rescue (SAR) helicopters from the Da Nang-based 37th Aerospace Rescue and Recovery Squadron (ARRS) agreed to give it a shot. Supported by an orbiting Covey FAC, two Army gunships, and a Blind Bat (a C-130 flare ship), Jolly Green 29 moved into position for the pickup. Fully aware that three other helicopters had already been shot down, Captain John B. McTasney nevertheless flew his big HH-3 chopper through a curtain of small arms fire, and with complete disregard for his personal safety, set his left landing gear against the steep mountain slope. Illuminated by the flares from the C-130, he maintained this position and picked up three survivors before hostile fire severely damaged his helicopter. As Jolly Green 29 staggered out of the area, enemy ground fire knocked out both generators and the intercom system, cut two fuel lines, and caused the cargo compartment to flood with fuel. Warning lights flashed in the cockpit, sparks lit the bird's interior, and the engine instruments fluctuated wildly. Capt McTasney, demonstrating a remarkable degree of coolness and professional skill, flew the crippled HH-3 to Khe Sanh and landed safely in the dark despite the loss of one engine during descent and 30 bullet holes in his aircraft. For his extraordinary heroism Capt John McTasney received the Air Force Cross.[19]

A few minutes behind Jolly Green 29 and en route to Oscar Eight, Captain Gerald O. Young unhesitatingly piloted Jolly Green 26 into the fray. Even though McTasney advised him not to try it, Young decided to attempt the rescue of the remaining team members when he replied simply, "Hell, we're airborne and hot to trot."[20] Under the eerie, wavering yellow illumination from the parachute flares, and bracketed by streams of green tracers, Capt Young eased his big bird into the steep mountain slope and went into a hover with his right landing gear resting on the ground and his rotor blades barely clearing the bank above him. Enemy troops brazenly moved into the open and sprayed Jolly Green 26 with automatic weapons fire as several Montagnards, all wounded, attempted to climb aboard with the bodies of Baxter and Kusick. Only seconds after Young lifted off, an RPG streaked out of the tree line and exploded against the left engine, setting it on fire. CWO Kent Woolridge, whose Huey gunship had been shot down earlier, witnessed the terrifying crash of Jolly Green 26. According to Woolridge, "He came off the ground, dropped the nose and rose about 60 feet into his departure path. Suddenly the nose pitched up and J.G. 26 slipped aft. It descended tail first until the aircraft contacted the ground and exploded in flames."[21]

What Kent Woolridge observed from the ground was the force of the RPG explosion flipping the HH-3 inverted, causing it to fall on its back, slam into the steep slope, and careen down the hillside. At that point the engine fire engulfed the entire aircraft. Hanging upside down in his harness, his flight suit on fire, Capt Young finally escaped through the broken windshield and rolled down hill about a 100 yards to extinguish the flames. He received second and third-degree burns on his legs, back, arms, and neck. Spotting a Montagnard lying nearby who had been tossed clear of the crash, Young crawled over and with his bare hands extinguished the flames on the young soldier's clothing. Young, fearing that others might be trapped in the burning wreckage, crawled back up the slope only to be driven away by intense enemy fire and unbearable heat from the blazing wreckage.

At first light, a flight of A-1 aircraft, call sign Sandy, arrived over Oscar Eight to soften up enemy defenses so Jolly Green rescue choppers could hopefully lift the survivors to safety. The badly burned Young realized that the NVA intended to use him as bait for a flak trap, so he hid the unconscious soldier, and in a display of amazing courage, yelled and shouted at enemy troops he could see setting up machine gun positions. Fully aware that his actions meant almost certain capture or death, Capt Gerald Young took off into the jungle leading his pursuers away from the crash site. With all enemy troops in pursuit of Young, an HH-3 slipped in to rescue the Army and VNAF survivors, also permitting the insertion of a small SOG Hatchet Force. While Young led the NVA farther and farther away, the Hatchet Force quickly searched the crash site and found the charred remains of Bruce Baxter and Joe Kusick. Capt Young, in the meantime, stumbled and crawled a distance of six miles. Only when he was sure he had eluded his pursuers did he use his survival radio to call in a rescue helicopter for himself—17 hours after the crash.[22] Unfortunately, before they could retrieve the bodies from Jolly Green 26 for evacuation, the Hatchet Force engaged in a running gun battle with a large NVA unit; the SOG force was not extracted until November 11 and none of the dead from the crash was ever recovered.

The gutsy pilot of Jolly Green 26 spent six months in the hospital recovering from his burns. In May 1968, for conspicuous gallantry and intrepidity at the risk of his life above and beyond the call of duty in Oscar Eight, Captain Gerald O. Young attended a White House ceremony to receive the Medal of Honor from President Lyndon Johnson.[23]

In retrospect, on its 1967 ventures into Oscar Eight, SOG failed to achieve any of its goals, and although there has been considerable post mortem debate as to the root cause of the failure, it most certainly was not because of a lack of effort, determination, or valor on the part of the brave warriors who fought and died west of the A Shau. At the time, however, SOG viewed its missions into Oscar Eight—disastrous though they were— as beneficial. The SOG command history for 1967 even justified the raids by noting that "Of particular interest, the A Shau salient continually evidences intense enemy activity and is known to harbor enemy base areas."[24]

The real issue, however, was in effect left hanging. SOG teams could well have served as both scouts and the vanguard for major attacks on Oscar Eight by larger conventional forces, forces that could have wiped out a major NVA supply area; however, because of rigid political restrictions imposed by Ambassador William H. Sullivan in Vientiane, no such large-scale cross border attacks were ever going to happen. Instead, the A Shau remained a major enemy stronghold and transshipment point, virtually ignored by MACV except for pinprick attacks by SOG's daring teams.

chapter 5

ANNUS HORRIBILIS: 1968

Even in the valley of the shadow of death, two and two do not make six. —LEO TOLSTOY

In early 1968, deep in the shadows of the A Shau, as was indeed true throughout Vietnam and the United States, a discordant, ill-omened wind blew. Even the American troops in Vietnam sensed it, although evidently MACV did not. Recuperating in a hospital near Saigon from a nasty punji stick wound, a young infantry officer, Lieutenant Mike Sprayberry, had time to reflect on the war, arriving at a conclusion that many other soldiers shared. In a letter home he prophetically wrote, "This war will not be won on the battlefield within the next five years unless something happens politically. It's going to be worse before it's better." Mike Sprayberry's intuition was correct; it did get worse—much worse. Three months later he found himself fighting for his life in the A Shau.

Coincidentally, in Saigon the soothsayers for the Chinese astrological calendar predicted a less than auspicious phase. In the Year of the Monkey, the powers that be were forecast to be lethargic, concentrating on marginal matters while ignoring more important issues. They would close their eyes to complications, finding them beneath their consideration.

One day after the beginning of the Lunar New Year, the price of ignoring important issues or concentrating on small matters reverberated through the country with catastrophic results. On January 31, VC and NVA forces launched one of the largest military campaigns of the Vietnam War, a coordinated series of surprise attacks against military and civilian command and control centers throughout South Vietnam. Approximately 80,000 communist troops simultaneously struck more than 100 towns and cities, including 36 of 44 provincial capitals, 72 of 245 district towns, and the crown jewel itself, Saigon. Perhaps Hanoi's greatest military success occurred at Hue when an entire NVA/VC division infiltrated through the nearby A Shau Valley to capture the old imperial capital and hold it for over three weeks, committing unspeakable atrocities against the civilian population in the process. Enemy forces there and throughout the country, however, paid an extremely high price for this bold adventure. An estimated 45,000 had died by the end of February, substantiating MACV's contention that by any standard what came to known as the Tet Offensive represented a massive military defeat for the Viet Cong and the North Vietnamese.[1]

By far the heaviest street fighting followed the Marines of Task Force X-Ray, a brigade-size component of the 1st Marine Division. For almost a month, X-Ray battled block by block from south of the Perfume River right up to the walls of the Imperial Palace in the Hue Citadel. Typical of the vicious fighting was the combat endured by Company A, 1st Battalion, 1st Marines, 1st Marine Division. Less typical but just as representative were the exploits of a member of the 3rd Platoon, Sergeant Alfredo Gonzalez. On January 31, 1968, shortly after crossing the Dai Giang River ten miles southeast of Hue, Sgt Gonzalez's "Bald Eagle" reaction force was hit by intense enemy fire. One of the Marines on top of a tank fell to the ground wounded. With complete disregard for his own safety, Sgt Gonzalez ran through the murderous crossfire to the assistance of his injured comrade. He lifted him up and although receiving serious fragmentation wounds during the rescue, he carried the injured Marine to safety. When a fortified machine gun bunker pinned down the entire company, Sgt Gonzalez, fully aware of the danger involved, charged across the fire-swept "Street without Joy" and destroyed the hostile position at point-blank range with grenades. Although seriously wounded again on February 3, he steadfastly refused medical treatment and continued to supervise his men and lead the attack. On February 4, the enemy had again pinned the company down, inflicting heavy casualties with automatic weapons and rocket fire. Sgt Gonzalez, utilizing a number of light antitank assault weapons, saved his entire platoon when he fearlessly moved from position to position firing numerous rounds at point blank range into the heavily fortified enemy emplacements. He singlehandedly knocked out the rocket positions and suppressed much of the enemy fire before falling mortally wounded. For conspicuous gallantry and intrepidity at the risk of his life above and beyond the call of duty, Sergeant Alfredo Gonzalez was posthumously awarded the Medal of Honor.[2]

Staff Sergeant Joe R. Hooper was yet another shining example of American valor at Hue. A member of Delta Company, 2nd Battalion, 501st Airborne Infantry, 101st Airborne Division, he received the Medal of Honor for personally knocking out seven enemy bunkers and killing 22 enemy soldiers on February 21, 1968.[3] While SSgt Hooper and Sgt Gonzalez were singled out to receive the Medal of Honor, many more fighting in the ferocious battle at Hue deserved it.

A little known fact about the battle for Hue was that Hanoi attempted a rare instance to employ its own airpower to support its soldiers, another indication of how serious the communists were about the campaign. On February 7, the North Vietnamese sent four IL-14 twin-engine cargo aircraft south to the battle area carrying explosives and field telephone cables. Faced with terrible weather, they airdropped their cargo into a lagoon roughly ten kilometers north of Hue. Three of the aircraft returned safely, but the fourth crashed into a mountain killing all aboard. Five days later two more modified IL-14s attempted a second mission to bomb Hue, but bad weather prevented them from finding the target. Both aircraft radioed that they were heading out to sea to jettison their bombs; they were never heard from again.[4]

The 25-day battle for Hue cost all sides dearly. USMC units sustained 142 KIA and close to 1,100 wounded. For their part in the battle, the 1st Cavalry Division (Airmobile) listed casualties of 68 killed and 453 wounded while the 1st Brigade, 101st Airborne Division reported 6 KIA and 56 WIA. All told, including ARVN losses, allied military casualties totaled more than 600 dead and nearly 3,800 wounded and missing. The enemy, likewise, did not escape unscathed. MACV estimated that 5,000 communist troops met their deaths in the bitter house-to-house fighting in Vietnam's traditional cultural capital.[5] Additionally, over 5,000 Hue civilians died in the fighting, most of them brutally executed by the NVA/VC. After the battle, the allies discovered mass graves containing approximately 3,000 civilians. Some had their feet and hands tied, and many showed signs of having been shot at close range execution style. At least 600 had been buried alive. The communists also abducted several thousand civilians to serve as porters during the battle; most vanished, never to be heard from again.[6]

Tactically, Hue signified an allied victory because the NVA and VC forces were driven from the city, paying a heavy price for their offensive, but was it a strategic victory? MACV claimed as much, yet on the home front such a notion did not take hold. Sizable segments of the public were confused, rattled, and skeptical of General Westmoreland's rationalization regarding the overall surprise of Tet. He contended that while intelligence reports had foreseen a major enemy offensive, "nobody anticipated the extent to which attacks on towns and cities actually developed throughout the country." Apparently General Westmoreland never did fathom why the surprise of Tet so upset the American public. Furthermore, the MACV commander wrote after the fact, somewhat bitterly, it would seem, that neither he nor his staff foresaw that "press and television would transform what was undeniably a catastrophic military defeat for the enemy into a presumed debacle for Americans and South Vietnamese."[7] Nor did Westmoreland or his staff ever foresee, as indicated by the enemy's losses during Tet, the horrendous casualties that Hanoi was willing to absorb to achieve its goals, a miscalculation which may well have called into question MACV's entire strategy of attrition, a stratagem that measured success not by positions taken and held but by the all-important body count.

In spite of various interpretations regarding the efficacy of that strategy, it is reasonable to assume that following Tet, with televised coverage of the dramatic fight at the U.S. Embassy and the battle of Hue fresh on their minds, Americans were understandably caught off guard and rocked back on their heels by the turn of events in Vietnam. Without question, the Tet Offensive cast doubt on the accuracy, if not the candor, of General Westmoreland's optimistic forecasts about the war. For example, just three months earlier during a November 21, 1967 speech at the National Press Club in Washington, DC, General Westmoreland got a lot of coverage for saying, "With 1968 a new phase is starting . . . we have reached an important point where the end begins to come into view."[8] The general went on to tell his audience that the enemy was "certainly losing" and that their hopes "were bankrupt." At a follow-up news conference he even used the phrase "light at the end of the tunnel" to describe the outlook for the war, repeating almost word-for-word French General Henri Navarre's optimistic though doomed May 1953 prediction about France's long campaign in Indochina. For all practical purposes, the contrast between Westmoreland's optimistic assertions and what appeared to be happening on Vietnam battlefields served as a major catalyst for precipitating a dramatic downturn in the American public's willingness to support the war.

In some measure, the bombshell of the Tet Offensive in general and the battle for Hue in particular did, indeed, herald a pronounced paradigm shift in American public opinion; in many ways Hue symbolized that erosion of support. For example, a Marine captain who commanded a 100-man rifle company during the battle for Hue unintentionally articulated the feelings of many Americans when he asked: "Did we have to destroy the town in order to save it?"[9] From that time forward, American support for the war in Vietnam declined.

Rarely, however, can the reason behind a complicated event—or opinion—be attributed to a 'single causation' explanation. Nevertheless, after Tet and during the years since, countless Americans, including the MACV commander and many a Vietnam veteran, have cited the "liberal press" for continually misreporting the war to the American people; apparently the only true stories came from authorized MACV sources in Vietnam. A prevalent attitude argued that slanted news reports prompted the change in public opinion regarding support for the war.

Yet blaming the press for that shift by painting all journalists with the same tar brush smacked more of singling out scapegoats than facing head on the mistakes of omission or commission, or the realities of a frustrating and challenging military campaign, complicated by international and domestic politics. For many Americans, perhaps nothing captured the revulsion of the Tet Offensive and the war itself more than the disturbing televised images of South Vietnam's national police chief, Nguyen Ngoc Loan, pistol in outstretched hand, executing a suspected Vietcong guerrilla with a bullet through the head on a busy Saigon street. Moreover, the disconcerting sight of Viet Cong insurgents storming the grounds of the American Embassy in Saigon was in no way the fault of the Fourth Estate; pointing the 'blame finger' at reporters for whipping up anti-war sentiment was in most cases analogous to 'shooting the messenger.'

In any event, prior to Tet the majority of Americans thought we were winning in Vietnam; however, the massive, coordinated communist attack throughout the country shook that belief right down to its core. But in truth it was not shaken by any single cause brought on by liberal bias on the part of the press. Obviously, news reporting about Vietnam influenced public opinion, yet it was never the stand-alone basis for the shift in attitude, even though Gallup polls taken between February and March 1968 reported a drop in "hawks," or supporters of the war, from 60 percent to 41 percent, and a corresponding leap in "doves" from 24 percent to 42 percent.[10] Clearly, attitudes were changing. For the first time, a sizable percentage of Americans had begun to conclude that the war was unwinnable.

These national doubts manifested themselves in a series of disconcerting questions. If we were winning, how could that massive attack have happened? If we were winning, why had General Westmoreland requested 206,000 more troops? If we were winning, why did a disgruntled Robert McNamara resign under fire as Secretary of Defense? If we were winning, why did Walter Cronkite, arguably the most trusted man in America, broadcast on February 27, 1968 that:

> To say that we are closer to victory today is to believe, in the face of the evidence, the optimists who have been wrong in the past. To suggest we are on the edge of defeat is to yield to unreasonable pessimism. To say that we are mired in stalemate seems the only realistic, yet unsatisfactory, conclusion. . . . But it is increasingly clear to this reporter that the only rational way out then will be to negotiate, not as victors, but as an honorable people who lived up to their pledge to defend democracy, and did the best they could.[11]

While network television news anchors, various political pundits, and high-level administration officials in Washington debated the "deeper meanings of the deeper meanings" concerning how Tet had happened and why, American combat forces in Vietnam pressed on with the grim job at hand in the single most deadly year for Americans in the entire war. Nowhere was the fighting more intense than in the two northern-most provinces at the big battles of Hue and Khe Sanh.

Intertwined throughout the Tet Offensive was the specter of Khe Sanh, an obscure, isolated plateau base just below the DMZ and only a few miles west of the Laotian border. The 77-day siege, where 6,000 Marines were surrounded by more than 20,000 NVA from the 325C and 304 Divisions, lasted from January 20 to April 8 and constituted one of the longest and largest battles of the entire war. Known as Operation Scotland, the defense of Khe Sanh Combat Base and the hilltops surrounding it fell to Colonel

David E. Lownds and his 26th Marine Regiment. With the only road into Khe Sanh, Route 9, cut and held by elements of the enemy's 320th and 324th Divisions, Lownds and his men were forced by circumstance to rely totally on resupply by air. Coupled with the distinct possibility that the four NVA divisions in the area were massing for a large set-piece battle, comparisons to 1954's stunning Viet Minh victory 14 years earlier at Dien Bin Phu were bound to occur.

Ironically, much of the argument about defending Khe Sanh came from the Marines themselves. By tradition and doctrine they had a natural distaste for static defense, insisting that the real danger in I Corps came from a direct enemy threat to Quang Tri City, not from massed NVA forces around the isolated Khe Sanh outpost. As was to be seen throughout the Vietnam War, multiple layers of disagreement often surfaced, not only between different participating services, but also within each unit. Nowhere was that dispute more pronounced than between the Marines and MACV. For example, in spite of Westmoreland's orders to reinforce and hold Khe Sanh, Brigadier General Lowell E. English, assistant commander of the 3rd Marine Division, complained that defense of the remote outpost was ridiculous. He viewed Khe Sanh as "a trap to expend absolutely unreasonable amounts of men and material to defend a piece of terrain that wasn't worth a damn."[12]

Operation Niagara, a massive tactical air campaign for the defense of Khe Sanh, set off the next confrontation between General Westmoreland and the Marines. The MACV commander insisted on centralizing Niagara under a single manager for air, Air Force General William W. Momyer; the Marine Corps balked. They possessed their own aviation squadrons that operated under their own close air support doctrine and were extremely reluctant to relinquish authority over their aircraft to an Air Force general. According to Westmoreland, that was "the one issue during my service in Vietnam to prompt me to consider resigning."[13] He got his way. By the end of Operation Niagara, more than 24,000 tactical air strikes and 2,700 B-52 sorties dropped 110,000 tons of bombs on NVA forces in and around Khe Sanh, squashing entire NVA units and killing an estimated 10,000 enemy soldiers.[14]

On the ground, some of the bloodiest small unit fights of the Vietnam War occurred on several of the key hills approximately seven kilometers west of Khe Sanh Combat Base. Hills 861, 881 North and 881 South, named for their height in meters, formed the prominent terrain around the Khe Sanh plateau. Climbing the steep slopes of Hill 881 South, 2nd Lieutenant Michael H. Thomas engaged in one of those fights on January 20, 1968. Lt Thomas led his 2nd Platoon from Company I, 3rd Battalion, 26th Marines, against a battalion-sized force of enemy soldiers occupying a series of reinforced bunkers dug into one of the hill's ridges. From those locations the platoon was immediately taken under intense automatic weapons fire, wounding several of the Marines. When a medical evacuation helicopter approached to extract the wounded, it was hit by highly accurate machine gun fire and crashed. Lt Thomas quickly organized a rescue team and led his men through murderous small arms fire to the crash site and dragged the crew to cover.

Learning that the adjacent platoon was pinned down and that its leader was wounded, the Pawnee, Oklahoma native maneuvered his unit through the concentrated enemy fire across 500 meters of open terrain to reinforce the beleaguered platoon. Lt Thomas then repeatedly exposed himself to a withering hail of bullets as he moved from one position to another, encouraging and directing his men's return fire. Discovering that an eight-man patrol was cut off, he organized and personally led a search party into the killing zone, successfully locating the patrol, all its members wounded. One at a time, he hoisted each man on his back and moved them to positions of relative safety. Although wounded in the face while carrying a sixth Marine to cover, he refused medical assistance and elected to continue his rescue efforts. Despite his painful wound, loss of blood, and sheer exhaustion, the intrepid platoon leader, with complete disregard for his own safety, again crawled through the savage barrage in an attempt to rescue the two remaining casualties who were lying in the open. At that point he received multiple wounds and was killed. For his extraordinary heroism, Lieutenant Michael H. Thomas was posthumously awarded the Navy Cross.[15]

Once the Marines had secured Hill 881 South, they taunted the enemy each morning by raising an American flag on a makeshift flagpole, complete with a bugle call, "To the Colors." One of the Marine officers observed that they did it so the NVA "would observe the colors being raised and know that the ragged, dirty, and tired marines were still full of fight and were there to stay." And every morning the enemy responded to the ceremony with a concentrated barrage of artillery and mortar fire.[16]

Even as the large, newsworthy battles raged around Hue and Khe Sanh, most of the firefights in I Corps were short, furious clashes between platoon or squad-sized units, and the majority only lasted a few minutes. In the A Shau Valley, the small, clandestine, unpublicized clashes were even more ferocious and bloody, frequently involving Special Forces reconnaissance teams consisting of only six to ten men—against hundreds.

Since the beginning of 1968, CCN's forward operating base at Phu Bai had been tasked with a dicey intelligence collection effort in the A Shau Valley, code-named Grand Canyon. NVA supply depots in and around the valley fed and armed most of the enemy troops in central and southern I Corps; consequently the supplies that sustained the 1968 Tet Offensive against Hue had arrived through the valley. Ordered by General West-moreland, Grand Canyon inserted numerous SOG teams into the valley to determine the extent of the infiltration—only to have the teams chewed up by NVA counter-recon companies. Losses became so heavy that some SOG team leaders balked at going back into the Valley of Death. In an attempt to shore up the reconnaissance effort and sagging morale, a new commander took over as FOB boss on March 3. The veteran SF officer arrived at Phu Bai apparently infuriated by the number of failed or aborted A Shau missions and incensed by the attitudes of team leaders, so to motivate his men and lead by example, the new commander accompanied a team into the A Shau on March 4. Two days later he was killed on the valley's east wall during a helicopter insert when the CH-46 he was aboard was shot down.[17]

Three weeks later, SOG sent another team into the Valley of Death—with almost identical results. On March 27, Staff Sergeant Johnny C. Calhoun was leading his team just south of Ta Bat when it was attacked by a large NVA force. SSgt Calhoun stood alone providing covering fire for the rest of the patrol as they withdrew. During the bitter fighting at point blank range, the Newman, Georgia native was hit several times in the chest and stomach, and when last seen by interpreter Ho-Thong as he slumped to the ground, Calhoun pulled the pin from a grenade and clutched it to explode among the enemy soldiers swarming around him. Even though the rest of the team was eventually extracted, Johnny Calhoun rests forever in the A Shau. For his extraordinary heroism, he was posthumously awarded the Distinguished Service Cross.[18]

On March 4, Project Delta reconnaissance teams once more entered the A Shau for a month-long mission designated Operation Samurai IV. While the primary focus in I CTZ (I Corps Tactical Zone) remained on Khe Sanh, the III Marine Amphibious Force headquarters sought details regarding enemy infiltration from Laos across the A Shau, and since virtually all maneuver battalions were already committed, Delta inherited the job. Delta recon teams were tasked "to conduct reconnaissance, surveillance, and interdiction missions primarily along highway 547 in Western Thua Thien Province and to determine if alternate routes exist linking A Shau Valley and Hue."[19]

At III MAF headquarters there was some speculation that NVA strength in the A Shau might have been depleted by the heavy fighting in I Corps at Khe Sanh. Reality proved that assumption to be wide of the mark. The entire AO was still crawling with company-sized enemy units, and if anything, the antiaircraft fire proved to be more concentrated than ever. Furthermore, little had changed for Project Delta since Operation Pirous a year earlier. NVA counter-recon companies still hunted down Delta's six-man recon and four-man road runner teams mercilessly, frequently triggering David vs. Goliath confrontations—only during Operation Samurai IV, Goliath would often win. In retrospect, Delta's most pronounced successes occurred when an entire ranger company inserted into the AO, because in most cases the larger unit was capable of taking care of itself—or at least holding its own.

One such mission occurred during the late afternoon of March 7 when Delta's 5th Airborne Ranger Company air assaulted into a suspected hot area in the eastern A Shau near the intersection of Routes 547 and 547A. The mission was to ascertain the condition of the road and to estimate the type and frequency of traffic. Elements of the company observed a stream, approximately 15 meters wide, flowing north to south. At that point a road, four meters wide and well traveled, crossed the stream via an underwater bridge. The bridge was roughly three meters wide and 15 meters long, constructed of log revetments and rock fill, with its surface less than a foot beneath the surface of the water. The road approaches to the bridge had apparently been cut out by a bulldozer, and vehicles had recently crossed the bridge heading east as evidenced by V-shaped tractor tire tread marks. Most interesting of all, overhanging foliage on both banks of the stream had been tied together, partially concealing the bridge from aerial detection.

As the 5th Ranger Company inspected Route 547 along the valley floor, a ranger sighted one NVA soldier without a weapon approaching along the road. The company point man fired at the enemy, but his weapon malfunctioned. The single North Vietnamese soldier fled north, apparently frightened but unhurt. Within 15 minutes, however, the ranger company began receiving small arms and automatic weapons fire from the northeast at a distance of only 30 meters. The company returned fire and the enemy force disengaged, but not before wounding two SF advisors, Specialist 5 Little J. Jackson and Staff Sergeant Philip S. Salzwedel. A short time later, Jackson died of his wounds. One enemy was killed in the skirmish.

Normally when a Delta unit's position was compromised, they extracted before an enemy force attempted to surround them, but the 5th Airborne Ranger Company pressed on with the mission. In this case, as deep shadows just before sunset swallowed up the area, a peculiar event surprised the Delta raiders. Out of nowhere a lone NVA soldier came up to the company perimeter and asked in a loud voice, "What company is this?" Playing along, the company executive officer (XO) answered, "This is 5th Company." The enemy soldier departed and returned several minutes later, illuminated his face with a flashlight and asked, "5th Company from where?" At that point the XO promptly shot at the dark figure from a distance of ten meters but apparently missed. A short time later the company stumbled across four enemy soldiers sitting around a cooking fire on the edge of the road. The lead element of the company opened fire, hitting two of the NVA. The next morning they found blood trails at both locations; however, none of the enemy could be confirmed as killed.

Just before midnight the rangers heard several trucks on the road evidently heavily loaded and moving uphill in low gear. Almost immediately they observed two enemy soldiers with flashlights, one behind the other at an interval of five meters, moving along the road past the company's concealed position. The rangers let them pass, but it was obvious to all that the NVA owned Route 547 and operated with impunity.

Early the next morning the rangers heard an unknown number of NVA soldiers shouting to each other about an enemy battalion. Two hours later the 5th Airborne Ranger Company was ambushed by heavy automatic weapons fire at a distance of 35 meters to their east. The rangers returned fire, the probe ceasing after two minutes with no casualties. A few minutes later an estimated enemy squad opened fire from the same location. In short order the Delta force heard a whistle and the enemy yelling, "Attack, Attack," this time firing a fresh volley from the south. During the brief firefight the rangers suffered five WIA. Through the remainder of the morning the ranger company continued to receive sporadic sniper fire, and in one exchange killed an enemy soldier armed with a Soviet SKS semi-automatic carbine and dressed in yellow khaki uniform with pith helmet, pistol belt with ammo pouches, and rubber sandals. At the same location the company observed an enormous puddle of blood, indicating that at least one more NVA soldier had been severely wounded and probably killed. Rather than press its luck against a force of unknown strength, the 5th Ranger Company called for a helicopter extraction and departed the area without incident.[20] When they returned to Phu Bai following their short stay in the A Shau, the exhausted rangers sported uniforms that were filthy, ripped to shreds, covered with mildew, and literally rotting off.

The experiences of Recon Team 7 proved to be more typical of Delta reconnaissance missions in the A Shau. Just after noon on March 13, the six-man team inserted into the same treacherous area the 5th Airborne Ranger Company had worked a week earlier. Right away the mission got off to a shaky start. Approaching the LZ, the 281st Assault Helicopter Company Hueys carrying the team ran into a heavy volume of .51 cal machine gunfire. Under the circumstances the Delta FAC should have called off the insert, but instead he had A-1s lay down a smoke screen 300 meters north of the LZ to mask the insert. The covering white phosphorus smoke—known as Willie Pete—helped the UH-1 make it into the LZ, but within minutes after leaving the chopper two of the SF personnel, Staff Sergeant James H. Zumbrun and Sergeant First Class William H. Bruno, had been wounded by persistent small arms fire.

After evading for three hours, Recon Team 7 observed an enemy platoon 50 meters south of their position advancing toward them in a skirmish line. The enemy wore khaki uniforms, web gear, soft hats, jungle boots, and carried AK-47s. Interestingly, two enemy soldiers appeared to be unusually light-skinned, suggesting that these individuals might be Chinese or even Russian. Initially the team did not think the enemy had observed them in the heavy foliage, but at point blank range the enemy force opened fire with small arms, automatic weapons, and rifle grenades. The team returned fire, the three minute firefight ending with SSgt Zumbrun and SFC Richard A. Conaway wounded and one LLDB missing, while the NVA suffered six killed. Once contact was broken, Recon Team 7 evaded 300 meters south to an LZ for extraction.

Just before dark 281st AHC helicopters arrived overhead and dropped ladders to extract the surrounded team. In the twilight, tracers filled the air as the choppers received intense ground fire from 4 different positions and approximately 30 weapons, all within 150 meters of the extraction LZ. SFC Bruno and two Vietnamese team members scampered up the ladder just as the Huey began taking heavy fire. One Vietnamese team member was shot and killed after climbing in the aircraft, while the enemy salvo knocked the other Vietnamese team member off the ladder as the Huey jinked away from the murderous crossfire. The remaining team members on the ground set up security on the LZ and waited until the next Huey arrived, about 15 minutes later. This aircraft also received intense ground fire and was forced to move away. A third UH-1 was hit by an enemy barrage and crash-landed east of the LZ; the crew was rescued. With darkness now upon them, the half-strength recon team realized they would spend another night next to Route 547, so they carefully started to hunt for their missing team member. The team moved south and began searching in a figure-8 pattern, each time increasing the size of the 8 while moving farther south. Throughout the night, from the time the team moved off the LZ, they could hear sounds of the enemy pursuing and searching for them.

By 11:30 a.m. the next morning, Recon Team 7 watched as F-4 Phantoms delivered airstrikes immediately to their west as part of the effort to extract them. Under the umbrella of the covering airstrikes, a Huey arrived and dropped a hoist to extract the three remaining team members. As the team was being lifted up, the aircraft began receiving automatic weapons fire from a distance of 50 meters to the southwest. With all the ground fire and helicopter maneuvering, SSgt Zumbrun, already wounded twice, fell off the hoist to the ground, some 30 feet below, injuring his back. Fortunately, he was lifted out again, and at 12:45 p.m. the extraction was finally completed.[21] At that point, however, the battle shifted from saving Recon Team 7 to rescuing the rescuers.

On March 14 in a dramatic battle above the A Shau, large caliber flak brought down Gunfighter 41, an F-4D from the 366th Tactical Fighter Wing at Da Nang. The two-man crew had been hit by 37mm fire while executing their fourth napalm run along the east wall in support of Project Delta Recon Team 7. Both pilots ejected successfully, although the back-seater suffered a broken leg on landing. During the first rescue attempt, one Jolly Green initiated a hover about 50 feet above one of the downed pilots, but ground fire forced the HH-3 to limp away when bullets pummeled the rotor blades and smoke belched out of the engine. Next, an Army Huey went in for the pickup but was driven off and crash-landed about a mile away. Then an Army OH-6 Loach, riddled with bullet holes, also went down; an HH-3 managed to rescue both helicopter crews. While A-1 Sandys and an F-100 Misty FAC peppered enemy positions with 20mm strafe and CBU, a Jolly Green maneuvered into a hover and lowered a pararescue jumper (PJ) to the ground to assist the injured F-4 pilot. A Misty pilot watching the PJ brave a veritable shower of enemy lead while descending on the hoist commented, "That guy has the biggest balls I've ever seen." Within minutes the PJ had the injured pilot safely inside the Jolly Green.[22]

On the ground in the middle of the A Shau Valley with enemy troops rapidly closing in, the second F-4 pilot faced a situation characterized by equal parts panic and cool desperation. As A-1s and the Misty continued to attack targets only a few meters away from the downed pilot, he kept asking them to put their ordnance closer. Finally, he shouted over his survival radio, "Put it on me. They're all around me." Seconds later the pilot announced, "I'm breaking my radio. See you after the war." Then the shooting stopped. First Lieutenant James E. Hamm was never seen again.[23]

The saga of Recon Team 7 calls into question the true effectiveness of small reconnaissance patrols attempting to operate in an NVA stronghold like the A Shau. Without question, Project Delta teams gave their all to collect invaluable intelligence throughout South Vietnam, but they rarely succeeded in the Valley of Death. In the specific case of Recon Team 7, its valiant members acquired little if any hard intelligence other than to confirm that enemy forces saturated the entire area, a fact already made painfully obvious by earlier missions. Was the cost too high? With two thirds of Recon Team 7 members as casualties, including one KIA, one MIA, and nothing concrete to show for it, the argument against small team missions into the A Shau becomes compelling. Factor in the additional loss of three helicopters, one F-4, and one MIA pilot, and the evidence seems undeniable. By comparison, reconnaissance-in-force missions by ranger companies, mobile strike force companies, or even Nung platoons fared significantly better against the NVA counter-recon and security units infesting the A Shau. That should have been a clue. Still, Project Delta took its orders directly from MACV and executed its mission no matter what the odds.

While the individual Delta ranger company apparently epitomized the optimum unit size for reconnaissance operations during Samurai IV, on one occasion a significantly larger unit fared poorly. On the morning of March 29, two companies of the 91st Airborne Ranger Battalion boarded an armada of Marine CH-46 helicopters and inserted near the intersection of Route 547 and 547A, the identical area where the 5th Airborne Ranger Company and Recon Team 7 had patrolled two weeks earlier. Totaling more than 200 rangers and advisors, the insertion required three separate lifts into the LZ, each opposed by heavy antiaircraft fire. Since there was no possibility of achieving surprise in light of multiple helicopter inserts on the same LZ, enemy security forces responded quickly and with a vengeance, seemingly assaulting the two companies at will. During the 36-hour mission, NVA elements initiated attacks against the rangers on 18 separate occasions, wounding 7 SF advisors, 32 rangers, and 2 chopper crewmembers. Three helicopter crewmen were KIA, two MIA, along with five rangers KIA. The NVA lost six confirmed killed. All through the insertion and extraction, concentrated enemy ground fire brought down four Hueys and two CH-46s. The subsequent attempted rescue of those crews triggered phase two of the battle.[24]

From the 6 choppers shot down, 14 American crewmembers lay huddled in two bomb craters, some wounded, others injured from the crashes, and all miserable and frightened. The incessant rain and low clouds left them wet, despondent, and suffering from hypothermia brought on by cold night temperatures in the high mountains along the A Shau's east wall. They had no food or water and only a few weapons with limited ammunition for protection. Each survivor realized that it was only a matter of time before the NVA got around to launching a full-scale attack, an assault they could not defend against—or survive. Their only hope was rescue by their fellow helicopter pilots, and the foremost question resonating in their minds was,

'What chance did a rescue force have against the deadly enemy antiaircraft fire spewing from this remote valley perpetually shrouded in mist?'

With most of the CH-46s from Marine Squadron HMM-165 dedicated to the extraction of the 91st Airborne Ranger Battalion, the III MAF called on the services of the rescue experts, the Air Force HH-3 Jolly Greens from the 37th ARRS at Da Nang. At about noon on the 30th, Major Joe B. Green led four HH-3s through terrible weather into the Valley of Death. Initially the overcast was so low and the visibility so poor that tactical fighters could not work. As two Huey gunships attempted to suppress the murderous antiaircraft fire, enemy gunners blasted one of the Jolly Greens, forcing it to stagger out of the area. At that point Major Green made an attempt to pick up the survivors who were hiding in bomb craters on a steep slope, but the ground fire was so intense that the Marine crewmembers on the ground waved him off. Undaunted, Joe Green attempted a second approach from the southwest, dropping over a hill on a fast approach into a risky hover. He continued to receive heavy ground fire despite the best efforts from two Army gunships.

As Green courageously remained in a stationary hover, a large, juicy target for every armed NVA soldier in the immediate area, the enemy fired a B-40 rocket at his bird. In describing the incident he recalled, "I was sitting in the right seat when a rocket came over my right shoulder from about our 1 o'clock. It was probably fired from about 200 yards out and I guess it passed right through the rotor blades." By the time the four most seriously wounded were on board, the Jolly Green had been hit multiple times and warning lights flashed all over the cockpit instrument panel. With his aircraft almost out of fuel, Major Green nursed his shot-up HH-3 out of the valley toward Hue as his PJ treated the wounded Marines.[25]

As Joe Green and his riddled chopper lurched out of the valley, Major Jerry M. Griggs piloted his Jolly Green into the deadly antiaircraft barrage, receiving substantial battle damage from intense opposing ground fire before he even located the downed crewmembers. Fortunately, the clouds lifted enough for a flight of A-1 Sandys to pound the enemy surrounding the remaining survivors. Covered by their suppressing fire, Major Griggs, with indomitable courage and professional skill, held his already shot-up bird in a dangerous hover until he rescued four more survivors, even though the HH-3 sustained further hits and damage from the intense hostile ground fire. With all guns trained on Major Griggs, a third Jolly Green quickly snatched the remaining Marine crewmembers from the jaws of death. For their extraordinary heroism on March 30, 1968, Majors Joe Green and Jerry Griggs were both awarded the Air Force Cross.[26]

Half a world away the following night at 9:01 p.m., March 31, President Johnson in a nationally televised address talked to the American people about Vietnam. He shocked the country and indeed the world with two announcements designed to deescalate the war. First, he said, "Tonight, I have ordered our aircraft and our naval vessels to make no attacks on North Vietnam, except in the area north of the demilitarized zone, where the continuing enemy build-up directly threatens allied forward positions and where the movements of their troops and supplies are clearly related to that threat." Then LBJ dropped the political bombshell. "I do not believe," he said, "that I should devote an hour or a day of my time to any personal partisan causes or to any duties other than the awesome duties of this office—the Presidency of your country. Accordingly, I shall not seek, and I will not accept, the nomination of my party for another term as your President."[27]

Reactions to the presidential pronouncements were mixed. Some viewed LBJ's address as a genuine move toward peace and the unselfish gesture of a brave man, while others saw it as an abdication speech by a lame-duck commander-in-chief. Many more were confused and baffled. Yet the war continued.

That war most certainly escalated on April 1 in I Corps Tactical Zone when two Marine battalions and all three brigades of Major General John J. Tolson's 1st Cavalry Division jumped off to lift the siege of Khe Sanh, just 25 miles north of the A Shau. Under Operation Pegasus, the Second Battalion, 1st Marine Regiment and 2nd Battalion, 3rd Marine Regiment, initiated a ground assault from Ca Lu, 16 kilometers east of Khe Sanh, westward along both sides of Route 9, while three brigades of the 1st Cavalry Division air-assaulted into key terrain features along Route 9 to establish fire support bases to cover the advance into Khe Sanh. The 11th Marine Engineers followed right on their heels, repairing the road and refurbishing the bridges to open the land route.

As with earlier MACV plans involving the Marines, Operation Pegasus also generated some friction, if not open inter-service bickering. Incongruously, General Westmoreland's planned relief effort ruffled the feathers of

Marines who had not wanted to hold Khe Sanh in the first place. The Marines had persistently hitched their argument to a technicality, claiming Khe Sanh had never been under siege since it had never truly been isolated from resupply or reinforcement. General Robert E. Cushman, Jr., III MAF's new commander, was appalled by the "implication of a rescue or breaking of the siege by outside forces."[28]

General Cushman's indignation may well have stemmed from an earlier difference of opinion over MACV policy. It was no secret that General Westmoreland had long considered I Corps to be the most critical and dangerous area of Vietnam, so in late January 1968 he transferred the 1st Cavalry Division and the 101st Airborne Division into I CTZ—"the heart of Marine land." On March 10 he even established a full-blown subordinate headquarters, Provisional Corps, Vietnam (PCV), under the command of Army Lieutenant General William B. Rosson at Phu Bai—much to the annoyance of the Marines.

In a strange interpretation of the prevailing III MAF view, General Westmoreland denied any friction and instead blamed the misunderstanding on press reports to the effect that the Marine Corps resented Army presence. He was particularly irked by what he labeled a "blatantly speculative account" in the *Los Angeles Times* written by noted Vietnam correspondent Bill Tuohy and went on to say, "That and the other accusations were patently false, a marked disservice to everybody involved."[29] While Westy may have chosen to spin it that way, his take was not shared by the Marines, many of whom believed that Tuohy had been correct in his assessment. For example, one Marine staff officer recalled, "Those of us at III MAF regarded it [establishment of PCV] as a transparent effort to diminish the importance of III MAF. We . . . saw it as a power grab."[30] Ironically, Bill Tuohy's articles on the Vietnam War received the 1968 Pulitzer Prize for International Reporting.

In spite of the acrimony bubbling just beneath the surface, the combined forces worked well together at the operational level, pushing on to Khe Sanh ahead of schedule. While there were countless small, sharp firefights, enemy resistance proved to be lighter than expected, in part because NVA units had been decimated by the air campaign Operation Niagara and because the air mobility of the 1st Cav kept them off-balance—both victories for Westmoreland in his war of words with the Marine Corps.

On April 4, the 26th Marines at Khe Sanh added to the pressure by launching their own offensive attack to the southeast against a well-defended enemy stronghold, Hill 471, where members of the 1st Battalion, 9th Marines secured the position by late afternoon. Early the following morning, in one of the highlights of Operation Pegasus, elements of the NVA's 66th Regiment launched a rare counterattack against Hill 471; the fight proved to be utterly one-sided. Assisted by artillery and close air support, the Marines on Hill 471 cut down large numbers of the attackers while suffering few casualties themselves. Then, on the morning of April 8, the 1st Cav's 2nd Battalion, 7th Cavalry, marched into Khe Sanh Combat Base and linked up with the 26th Marines.[31]

Because of events unfolding in the United States there was scant attention paid to the relief of Khe Sanh. Domestically, the nation reeled over the assassination on April 4 of its preeminent civil rights leader, Nobel Peace Prize Laureate Martin Luther King, Jr., in Memphis. In 110 cities across the country a wave of racially fueled riots broke out, sparking violent confrontations with police. Labeled by some the "Holy Week Uprisings," the rioting climaxed in Washington, DC, where out-of-control protesters torched 1,200 buildings, including over 900 stores. Elsewhere, Doctor King's assassination not only led to unruly disturbances and civil disobedience, but also triggered blatant unrest in communities that were already discontented over race, inequality, and the war in Vietnam. One of the largest and most public demonstrations up until that time occurred on April 23, when Columbia University students seized the campus for a week while protesting university collaboration with the U.S. military through the Institute for Defense Analyses, a think tank involved with weapons research that contributed to the war in Vietnam. In the wake of the Columbia student protests, campuses across the country exploded.

Against the emotional backdrop of Doctor King's tragic assassination, on April 14 Operation Pegasus terminated and the siege of Khe Sanh was over. In many respects the operation amounted to a Dien Bien Phu in reverse—this time the besieged garrison held out and won. After flying into Khe Sanh by helicopter, General Westmoreland told the assembled press, "We took 220 killed at Khe Sanh and about 800 wounded and evacuated. The enemy by my count suffered at least 15,000 dead in the area."[32] Buoyed by those statistics, Westmoreland practically gushed with self-con-

gratulation since he clearly viewed the stand at Khe Sanh as a major vin-
dication of his signature strategy regarding big unit battles engaged in a
war of attrition. The Marines had a different opinion—as did others. An
up-and-coming staff officer in Vietnam and a future Chief of Staff of the
Army, Colonel Edward C. Meyer, observed, "We just didn't think we could
do the job the way we were doing it." A fellow colonel who had pleaded
with Westmoreland to end the big unit war advised, "We're just not going
to win it doing this." Even a key White House staffer reporting from Vietnam insisted that "chasing after victory through attrition is a will-o'-the-
wisp that costs us too much in dollars, draft calls and casualties, makes it
too hard to stay the course."[33]

Shortly after that press conference Westy returned to the States to become Army Chief of Staff, replaced by his deputy, General Creighton W.
Abrams. And with that command change the war was supposed to change.
Apparently General Abrams intended to bring a markedly different outlook
to the conflict and how it ought to be conducted. Under Westmoreland,
the emphasis had been almost exclusively on large-scale, big unit combat
operations intended to inflict crippling casualties on the NVA, based on
the premise that heavy losses would eventually cause Hanoi to cease aggression against the south—bleed the enemy to death over the long haul. In
contrast, according to military historian Lewis Sorley, Creighton Abrams—
known to most as 'Abe'—viewed Vietnam as 'One War' in which combat
operations, improvement of South Vietnamese forces, and pacification
were all of equal importance.[34] Realistically, however, there was more continuity than change in Vietnam after Abe succeeded Westy. In all future A
Shau operations, only American combat campaigns took center stage, and
the Westmoreland strategy of attrition and body count remained alive and
well whether General Abrams intended it that way or not. Furthermore,
the Abrams strategy of "clear and hold" somehow went astray in the A
Shau Valley. While American units attempted repeated clearing operations
in the Valley of Death, they captured the ground for short periods—then
abruptly left.

Unfortunately, the lifting of the siege at Khe Sanh did not signal a happy
ending to an otherwise dramatic story. During the two and a half months
following Operation Pegasus, 413 more Marines died in fighting around
the rescued combat base, and at that point the story took on a decidedly

controversial twist. In June, shortly after the siege had been lifted, the new MACV commander, General Abrams, sided with the Marines and decided to dismantle the remote base rather than risk a similar siege. Therefore, on July 5, the last of the Marines left Khe Sanh and it was officially closed. By contrast, the NVA's 304th Division official history noted that "on 9 July 1968, the liberation flag was waving from the flag pole at Khe Sanh airfield."[35] Predictably, the new ending did not sit well with the American public, whether hawk or dove.

As Operation Pegasus wound down, General Tolson and the 1st Cavalry Division received surprise new orders on April 10. Two of the division's three brigades were to pull out of their east-west thrust toward Khe Sanh to conduct one of the most audacious air mobile operations in the history of the Vietnam War: an air assault into the infamous A Shau Valley, the most intimidating NVA sanctuary in South Vietnam. Code name for the attack was Operation Delaware.

The timing for Operation Delaware hinged on several key yet seemingly unrelated circumstances, all intersecting by chance or fate. First, by March 1968, over 50 percent of all American maneuver battalions in Vietnam were crowded into I Corps' provinces: the 1st and 3rd Marine Divisions, the 1st Cavalry Division, the Americal Division, and elements of the 101st Airborne Division. Convinced that enemy infiltration through the A Shau into Thua Thien Province still presented a deadly menace and the possibility of a North Vietnamese capture of the northern half of I Corps, General Westmoreland finally had the manpower at hand to do something about it, by striking deep and eliminating the huge NVA staging area. He also took advantage of the unique air mobility capabilities of the redoubtable 1st Cav. Because of terrain and remoteness, the A Shau could only realistically be invaded by employing vertical envelopment, and with 450 helicopters assigned internally, the horse soldiers of the 1st Cav constituted the ideal force. Led by Major General John Tolson, a rugged paratrooper who had made numerous combat jumps during World War II, the 1st Cavalry Division was a first-rate outfit noted for its panache and fighting ability against crack NVA units.

Ultimately, the urgency in attacking the A Shau was due to calculations about the weather. According to old French records, there existed a brief interval between monsoons when the unpredictable weather in the A Shau might be workable. Therefore, MACV planners settled on mid-April to mid-May as the logical window for Operation Delaware.[36]

For the raid into the A Shau, General Rosson, commander of Provisional Corps, Vietnam, dispatched the 1st and 3rd Brigades of the 1st Cav, along with the 1st Brigade of the 101st Airborne Division and an airborne task force from the ARVN 1st Division. Operation Delaware was to be a coordinated airmobile and ground attack on two axes using elements of the designated three divisions: the 101st Airborne and the ARVN task force were to attack along and astride Routes 547 and 547A from the east wall, while the main attack was the helicopter assault by the 1st Cav on the valley floor into the northern A Shau and into A Luoi.[37]

The kickoff of Operation Delaware began on April 16 with extensive aerial reconnaissance by light observation helicopters from the 1st Squadron, 9th Cavalry. Facing marginal weather and low cloud ceilings, the crews nevertheless swept along the length of both valley walls at low level, attempting to pinpoint dug-in enemy artillery batteries and antiaircraft positions. Indeed, the reconnaissance helicopters found what they were searching for: dozens of powerful crew-served 37mm antiaircraft guns, some of them radar controlled. They also encountered the rapid-firing ZU 23-2, a twin-barreled 23mm antiaircraft weapon capable of firing in excess of 200 rounds per minute, along with scores of .51 caliber machine guns. In that deadly environment the squadron choppers performed magnificently, but they paid a hefty prince: a total of 50 aircraft hit by ground fire, 5 shot down, and 18 others damaged beyond repair. Using the information gathered by the intrepid 1st Squadron crews, 209 preliminary tactical airstrikes and 21 B-52 Ark Light strikes attempted to soften up the enemy positions.[38]

General Tolson's original plan called for the 1st Brigade to air assault into the central part of the valley around the old airfield at A Loui, but the antiaircraft fire coming up from that area proved to be so heavy that it was decided to work it over with more suppressive airstrikes. Instead, on April 19 a swarm of 1st Cav helicopters lifted the 3rd Brigade through the marginal weather and intimidating flak into the northern section of the valley where Route 548 crossed into Laos. As the helicopter formations descended into LZ Tiger, also known as Tiger Mountain, a veritable torrent of red and green antiaircraft tracers tore through the vulnerable choppers, damaging 23 and sending 10 crashing into the ground. A company commander from the 5th Battalion, 7th Cavalry, captured the mood on that first air assault into the A Shau Valley when he observed:

> The feeling the majority of the men had upon first coming into the valley was a sort of fear, distinctly different from that felt at Hue or Khe Sanh. We had heard so many stories about A Shau, like the possibilities of running into large concentrations [of flak]. We had a fear of the unknown. We thought that just around any corner we would run into a battalion of North Vietnamese.[39]

The helicopter crews transporting the 1st Cav soldiers into the Valley of Death experienced much the same feelings of foreboding. In the past, the crews had often dealt with streams of menacing tracers from small arms and automatic weapons fire, but for most of them it was their first time to face the "big stuff"; the chopper crews were naturally somewhat unnerved dodging the frightening white and gray flak airbursts from 23 and 37mm guns. In addition to the deadly antiaircraft fire, the most intense the aviators from the 1st Cav had ever encountered, the weather during Operation Delaware was unbelievably poor. Thick cloud layers, fog, thunderstorms, and low ceilings hampered the operation from the beginning. Not only were the conditions bad over the valley, but even the weather around Camp Evans forced the helicopters to climb up through an overcast on instruments to heights of 10,000 feet, reassemble the formation on top of the clouds, fly to the target area, and then search for some sort of hole in the clouds to make a hazardous descent. What normally amounted to a 20-minute flight often took over an hour—according to some of the pilots, "60 minutes of sheer terror." The nerve-wracking twin challenges of weather and flak prompted one helicopter crewmember to confess during an interview:

> From the moment the assault on the A Shau Valley began, the radio was full of talk about aircraft taking hits and getting shot down. All that day, we went into LZ after LZ knowing in our minds that it was probably our last sortie before we got killed. I had never been so afraid in all my life, but we all kept going.[40]

The morning assault on the 19th, through a barrage of antiaircraft fire, lifted the 1st and 5th Battalions of the 7th Cavalry into LZs Vicki and Tiger respectively, and while neither battalion was initially opposed once on the ground, they found themselves socked in by the rapidly deteriorating weather. The 5th did manage to receive its direct support artillery battery before the weather closed in, but not without opposition. A CH-47 helicopter was downed by small arms fire as it attempted to land on LZ Tiger. Then a second CH-47 sustained hits from 37mm and .51 cal machine guns. With the bird burning and out of control, the flight engineer and the crew chief jumped from an altitude of 50–100 feet above the jungle canopy. Their bodies were never found, but the other crewmembers survived the crash. Minutes later ground fire downed a CH-54 Sky Crane attempting to lift a bulldozer into LZ Tiger. All told, five crewmen survived and nine were listed as MIA.[41]

On LZ Vicki, the 1st of the 7th immediately ran into trouble. Fog and zero visibility shut down all flights, leaving the battalion marooned with no support and no way to be evacuated. Fortunately, no enemy probes or attacks materialized. The only appreciable action took place that first night when the 5th of the 7th spotted a convoy of nearly 100 enemy trucks and opened fire with their small artillery battery. Results were negligible.

Farther to the east, the 1st Brigade of the 101st Airborne Division initiated operations out of Fire Support Base Bastogne, roughly halfway between Hue and the A Shau, with the 2nd Battalion of the 327th Infantry attacking overland to the southwest. Later in the morning of the 19th, the 1st Battalion of the 327th air assaulted into LZ Veghel near the strategic road junction of Routes 547 and 547-A. Each battalion encountered light to moderate contact with the enemy throughout the day.[42]

Radio communication in the valley would be a vital element during Operation Delaware, so General Tolson's staff planned ahead for the contingency. Since both walls of the A Shau featured 5,000-foot peaks, effectively blocking line-of-sight radio transmissions between deployed units on the valley floor and Camp Evans near the coast, the planners selected a 4,878-foot peak on the eastern wall known as Dong Re Lao Mountain. They dubbed the radio relay site "Signal Hill."

The job of securing Signal Hill fell to the long-range reconnaissance platoon (LRRP) of Company E, 52nd Infantry. Since the mission required specially trained and equipped soldiers who could rappel from helicopters into an unsecure area, clear an LZ with explosives and hold the ground until a security force arrived, Lieutenant Joseph Dilger's LRRP platoon was the obvious choice. On April 19 the platoon headed into the A Shau loaded aboard Hueys from the 227th Assault Helicopter Battalion. Approaching the target area, the choppers went into a hover approximately 100 feet above the top of Dong Re Lao Mountain as the LRRP members jumped off the skids to begin the long repel, via rope, into the dense jungle below. But in the thin air above the mountaintop, one of the Hueys experienced a loss of engine power brought on by the high-pressure altitude, and plummeted out of control with two platoon members still dangling 50 feet above the ground. One team member was seriously injured when the Huey crashed and pinned him under the skid. All of the Huey crew were badly shaken up.[43]

Deep in enemy territory, the LRRP platoon dived into the grueling task of clearing an LZ using chain saws and explosive charges. As Dilger and his men went to work, NVA soldiers converged on the mountaintop by noon. Concealed by dense jungle foliage and with their approach masked by the reverberating sound of buzzing chain saws, enemy snipers positioned themselves around the perimeter and began shooting at members of Dilger's platoon. Unable to see the snipers, yet compelled to finish the radio relay site LZ, the LRRP troopers responded by rolling grenades down the steep slope and by cutting loose with random volleys of M-16 fire at fleeting shadows or at any suspected targets. As this bizarre little battle with an unseen enemy dragged into the late afternoon, the LRRP team members risked all by crawling through mud, twisted, tangled jungle debris, and deadly sniper fire to rescue their wounded and dying comrades and carry them to the top of Signal Hill and the protective shelter of a bomb crater. Outmanned and outgunned, they managed to hang on, but just barely. During the five hours of sporadic battle, enemy snipers killed Sergeant William G. Lambert, Specialist 4 Richard J. Turbitt, Jr., Private First Class James F. MacManus, and Private First Class Robert J. Noto. Corporal Roy Beer was severely wounded through both legs and an arm, while their stalwart leader, Lt Joe Dilger, took an SKS round through the chest and was near death; the entry wound may have been tiny, but the exit wound was enormous. Early the following morning, April 20, a medevac Huey already carrying a badly burned helicopter pilot, set down on Signal Hill to evacuate Joe Dilger and the other LRRP wounded. As the overloaded UH-1 lifted off, the remaining LRRP men on the ground could hear the burned pilot pleading over and over again, "Shoot me! Somebody, for God's sake, please shoot me!"[44]

In the following days after Signal Hill was secured, the 1st Cav airlifted a much-needed battery of artillery to the mountaintop to support infantry assaults in the valley, and along with its vital radio relay mission, the site continued in operation for three weeks. Still opposed by sporadic small arms fire, another helicopter crashed on the peak, severely injuring three other Signal Hill troopers. One was crushed beneath the helicopter's skid; another slammed in the chest by a sailing fuel can; and another, an Air Force meteorologist, had his leg and a foot severed by the swirling rotor blades.[45]

While the top of Signal Hill occasionally enjoyed brief periods of bright sunshine, such was not the case in the valley below. Unbroken cloud layers blanketed the entire length of the valley, with morning fog and afternoon torrential rain limiting visibility to practically zero. The rain kept falling as though there were a hidden purpose to it, some strategic plan by Mother Nature to inundate the entire A Shau, perhaps wash it clean again. The troops on LZ Vicki were in an untenable position, as attempts to sustain them by air had to be abandoned because of the miserable weather. They had left the present behind, the age of planes and hot food and slab sidewalks; they were moving back through time, trapped in the stink of the jungle, the incessant rain, the heat. With no food and only a basic issue of ammunition, Lieutenant Colonel Joseph E. Wasiak personally led his battalion on a four-mile forced march down the valley to LZ Goodman. Slogging through the rain-soaked jungle and the unforgiving elephant grass, the battalion moved at a snail's pace, stopping frequently to fend off small enemy ambushes or to remove the ever-present leeches. Constantly wet from the monsoon rains, many soldiers developed a skin condition called "jungle rot," an infection that targeted their feet, arm pits, groins, or any bare skin cut by the razor-sharp elephant grass. In the case of the 1st of the 7th, the battalion endured those conditions over four consecutive days before finally reaching LZ Goodman. One soldier summed up everyone's attitude when he observed, "Try to imagine grass eight to fifteen feet high, so thick as to cut visibility to one yard, possessing razor sharp edges.

Then try to imagine walking through it while all around you are men possessing automatic weapons who desperately want to kill you."[46]

After three days on the ground in the infamous A Shau, the 1st Cav troops had encountered only sporadic contact with the enemy, who for the most part avoided clashes with the Americans and contented themselves with initiating 122mm rocket attacks against ground targets and scorching antiaircraft barrages against any helicopter foolish enough to fly beneath the low overcasts. As 3rd Brigade patrols ranged out along Route 548, they began discovering large caches of NVA equipment, and one company from the 1st of the 7th stumbled across an enemy maintenance complex, hastily evacuated. They found two trucks, two bulldozers, and assorted engineering equipment—all Soviet manufactured.

On April 24, with a slight improvement in the weather, General Tolson began air assaulting three battalions of his 1st Brigade into the central valley around A Luoi airstrip. As on previous days, enemy gunners reacted fiercely, bringing down two CH-47 Chinooks and one Huey. Nevertheless, the 1st Brigade troops landed, secured the area, and immediately began reconnaissance-in-force operations around the dilapidated airstrip. Contact with the enemy on the ground remained light.

Most in the maneuver battalions of 1st Cav and the 101st Airborne were genuinely surprised by the limited contact with the enemy, since in their minds the American infantrymen had conjured up frightening mental pictures of confronting hordes of fanatical zealots defending what amounted to their home turf—there were probably more VC/NVA per square kilometer in the A Shau than any other place in South Vietnam. So far, the much-dreaded battle for the A Shau Valley had been waged with the legendary nasty weather and not against the vaunted communist combatants from the north. Given the circumstances and the valley's sinister, almost mystical reputation, American soldiers were understandably nervous and edgy as they waited for the proverbial other shoe to drop.

The first sustained ground contact between the 1st Cav and NVA forces occurred on April 25 when D Company, 5th Battalion, 7th Cavalry engaged a large enemy unit at the north end of the Valley of Death on an imposing piece of enemy-held real estate known as Tiger Mountain. Caught in an ambush, Delta Company suffered a significant number of killed and wounded when the company commander led a platoon in a flanking movement and was pinned down and separated from the main body of his unit. The company executive officer, 1st Lieutenant James M. "Mike" Sprayberry, organized and led a volunteer night patrol up the steep side of Tiger Mountain to eliminate the extensive network of enemy bunkers and to rescue the surrounded command element. Facing heavy machine gun fire, Mike Sprayberry, from Sylacauga, Alabama, who had just turned 21-years-old the day before, quickly moved his men to protective cover and without regard for his own safety, crawled within close range of the nearest bunker and silenced the machine gun with a hand grenade. In total darkness it was like fighting wearing a blindfold—he could only identify enemy positions by their muzzle blasts. During breaks in the firing, Sprayberry was so close to enemy soldiers that he could hear them breathing. Locating several one-man enemy positions nearby, Lt Sprayberry immediately attacked them with the rest of his grenades. When NVA soldiers tossed two grenades at his men from a fortified position to the front, Lt Sprayberry charged the enemy-held bunker, killing its occupants. In quick succession, he crawled forward again and took out three more bunkers with grenades. Immediately thereafter, Mike Sprayberry was surprised by an enemy soldier who charged from a concealed position. He killed the soldier with his pistol and neutralized yet another enemy emplacement. Lt Sprayberry then established radio contact with the isolated men, directing them toward his position.

As he waited in the pitch-black night for the link-up with the command element, Sprayberry whistled to several approaching shadows; they whistled back. It was not until the figures were almost on top of him that they began speaking Vietnamese. At point blank range a member of Sprayberry's patrol, Sergeant Delbert Mack, opened fire, killing one enemy soldier. When his M-16 jammed, Sgt Mack attacked and killed two more NVA with his knife. In the savage fighting, Mike Sprayberry dropped the remaining shadowy figures with his pistol. For his gallantry in the fight, Delbert Mack received the Silver Star.

When the two friendly elements made contact, Sprayberry organized his men into litter parties to evacuate the wounded back down the steep road in total darkness. Unfortunately, they were unable to bring out three of their dead comrades: PFC Hubia J. Guillory, Specialist 4 Daniel M. Kelley, and Specialist 4 David L. Scott. As the evacuation was nearing completion, Sprayberry observed an enemy machine gun position which he silenced with a grenade. He then returned to the rescue party, established security, and moved to friendly lines with the wounded. During this vicious firefight and rescue operation, which lasted approximately seven hours, Lt Sprayberry personally killed 12 enemy soldiers, eliminated 2 machine guns, and destroyed numerous enemy bunkers. For conspicuous gallantry and intrepidity in action at the risk of his life above and beyond the call of duty, James M. Sprayberry was awarded the Medal of Honor.[47]

Six days later an OH-6 Loach crew from Bravo Troop, 1st of the 9th Cavalry, volunteered to return to the deadly slopes of Tiger Mountain to recover the three dead Delta Company troopers. As the Loach approached the area at low altitude, a .51 cal machine gun shredded it, sending the bird crashing into the mountainside. Warrant Officer Warren J. Whitmire, Jr., Sergeant Donald P. Gervais, and Corporal Richard D. Martin died in the crash. Along with the three men from Delta Company, their remains have never been recovered from the A Shau Valley.*

Ten miles to the south, in the central valley and along the east wall, nobody was even remotely aware of Delta Company's violent encounter with the NVA; the 1st Brigade's immediate focus was on logistics. On April 26 the buildup at A Luoi continued when, for the first time in days, the cloud cover lifted to about 2,000 feet, permitting aerial resupply by Air Force C-130s. Additionally, huge CH-54 Sky Crane helicopters with out-sized loads slung beneath their odd fuselages joined in the effort by hauling much needed heavy engineering equipment for rebuilding the A Luoi airstrip. The effort, however, did not go unopposed.

Unseen enemy gunners around A Luoi put up a wall of hostile fire, most of it directed at the big C-130 Hercules transports attempting to parachute pallets of supplies into the airstrip. Those dangerous missions highlighted the valor and dedication of the Air Force crews during Operation Delaware. They were faced with the same miserable weather as their rotary-wing Army colleagues, but unlike the helicopter, they could not

---

*In the almost 50 years since the deadly battle on Tiger Mountain, Mike Sprayberry has remained determined to find the six lost men and bring them home. He returned to the A Shau in 2009 and again in 2013. Sadly, he was unable to find the missing men on Tiger Mountain, but he did locate pieces of helicopter wreckage that correlated to the missing Loach. Case number 1153 remains active for the Defense POW/MIA Accounting Agency.

hover or pick holes in the clouds for their descent. Instead, they navigated to the A Shau Valley via a TACAN (tactical air navigation) station at Phu Bai. From there they began an approach through the weather on instruments, using their own on-board radar to avoid the treacherous mountain peaks along the valley walls. Breaking out under a low ceiling, they made their parachute drops at dangerously low altitudes and against a sophisticated network of antiaircraft positions. Perhaps the best tribute came directly from General Tolson when he observed, "No matter how reliable the gauges, it takes a lot of guts to poke your airplane nose into clouds that are full of solid rock!"[48]

During the first 20 airdrops on the 26th, antiaircraft fire hit 7 of the birds. At approximately 2 p.m., a C-130 from the 463rd Tactical Airlift Wing at Clark Air Base in the Philippines broke out of the clouds over A Luoi and was immediately engaged by multiple 37mm and .51 cal machine gun positions spraying green tracers and dark airbursts all around the big Hercules. The entire area sparkled from firing guns, with dirty soot bag explosions bracketing the four-engine transport. The enemy gunners' aim was right on; they hit the maneuvering bird repeatedly. As the crew attempted to jettison the load which had caught on fire in the cargo bay, the pilot, Major Lilburn R. Stow, executed a low altitude 180 degree turn through the deadly ground fire in an attempt to land on the unfinished airstrip. Unfortunately, the Hercules hit some trees short of the runway, crashed and exploded in a huge fireball. All on board, including the six crewmembers and two Air Force photographers, died in the fiery explosion. Two nights later the same guns downed an Air Force O-2 very close to the location of the C-130 crash. The young Rash FAC, Captain James F. Lang, died supporting his troopers of the 1st Cav.[49]

April 26 also saw the tempo pick up for the 101st Airborne's Bravo Company, 2nd Battalion, 502nd Infantry near LZ Veghel along Route 547, a few kilometers east of A Luoi. As was so often the case, the men of the 101st proved once again that they knew how to fight—and how to die. While on patrol in the area, the 3rd Platoon received intense surprise hostile fire from a force of NVA regulars in well-concealed bunkers. With 50 percent casualties, the platoon maneuvered to a position of cover to treat their wounded and reorganize, while one of the Americans caught in the ambush, Private First Class Milton A. Lee, the platoon radio operator, moved through the heavy enemy fire giving lifesaving first aid to his wounded comrades. While advancing with the front rank toward the bunker complex, PFC Lee observed four North Vietnamese soldiers with automatic weapons and a rocket launcher lying in wait for the lead element of the platoon. As the element moved forward, unaware of the concealed danger, PFC Lee, with utter disregard for his own personal safety, passed his radio to another soldier and charged through the murderous fire, overrunning the enemy position, killing all occupants, and capturing four automatic weapons and the rocket launcher. Without hesitation PFC Lee continued his one-man assault on a second bunker through a heavy barrage of enemy automatic weapons fire. Grievously wounded, the 19-year-old soldier continued to press the attack, crawling forward and delivering accurate covering fire to enable his platoon to maneuver and destroy the position. Not until the bunker was knocked out did PFC Lee relent in his steady volume of fire and die from his wounds. For his conspicuous gallantry and intrepidity in action at the risk of his life above and beyond the call of duty on the A Shau's eastern wall, Private First Class Milton A. Lee was posthumously awarded the Medal of Honor.[50]

Over the next few days, all units engaged in Operation Delaware continued to uncover large supply caches left behind by an enemy intent on retreating across the border into Laos. Yet NVA crack artillery units remained in the valley, bombarding American LZs and firebases with some of the heaviest barrages received in Vietnam up to that time. Enemy 122mm rockets targeted U.S. positions in ever-increasing numbers while mortar, recoilless rifle, and RPG rounds crashed around 1st Cav and Screaming Eagle units on a much too regular basis. Endless patrols routinely turned up abandoned NVA positions or a few bags of rice, but little else. In describing actual contact with the elusive enemy, one 1st Cav company commander recalled:

> They were superb at masking their true position. The Americans would move up, you would kill a couple and the rest would run and it was a natural tendency to take off after them. . . . In close terrain against enemy like the North Vietnamese that will get your nose bloodied. . . . They were absolute masters at choosing the right terrain at the right place at the right time to blow your crap away.[51]

By May 2 the 8th Engineer Battalion had finished the airstrip at A Luoi, permitting the first C-7 Caribou transport aircraft to begin landing; by May 4 the first C-130s also landed at what had been named LZ Stallion. Flush with supplies from the airlift, troops from the 1st Cav and the 101st continued to uncover major enemy depots—and they continued to fight a losing battle against the A Shau's unpredictable weather. While dense fog hampered morning ground and air operations, each afternoon brought violent thunderstorms complete with spectacular lightning displays accompanied by rain falling in sheets that produced torrents of red mud. In such a climate anything that did not rot, rusted. The engineering units worked around the clock just to keep LZ Stallion operational. It was yet another situation where nature itself was as formidable an opponent as armed men in different uniforms.

So far during Operation Delaware, NVA units had largely avoided direct contact with American troops by slipping across the border into sanctuaries within Laos. To confirm that theory, MACV once more called on the services of SOG reconnaissance teams. On May 3, RT Alabama, commanded by Staff Sergeant John Allen, inserted along the A Shau's west wall just three miles into Laos to search out an entire NVA division believed to have retreated out of the valley when the 1st Cav swept in. Within an hour after landing, Allen, Specialist 5 Kenneth Cryan, Private First Class Paul C. King, Jr., and six Nungs were being chased by at least 50 NVA soldiers. As the team scrambled up a steep hill, the enemy opened fire, wounding Cryan and killing one Nung. SSgt Allen guided his men into a nearby water-filled bomb crater and began returning fire. As the battle roared around him, John Allen made contact with the circling Covey FAC who immediately brought in much needed close air support. Under the low ceiling, first a pair of F-4 Phantoms dropped Snake Eye retarded-fin 500-pound bombs on enemy positions. Other F-4s, followed by F-100 Super Sabres and A-1 Skyraiders, made pass after pass, riddling the NVA with 20mm cannon fire, cluster bombs, and napalm. When extraction Huey helicopters arrived overhead, the pilot of the lead helicopter radioed the embattled ground team asking, "Is it secure down there?" SSgt Allen laughed, then responded, "Secure? Hell no, it's not secure. And the longer you wait the worse it's gonna get, but I think their heads are down."[52]

As the Huey maneuvered over RT Alabama, the UH-1 took multiple hits from heavy ground fire and accelerated in a climb away from the crater. At the same instant a bullet struck PFC Paul King in the forehead, killing him instantly. By now the helicopters were low on fuel and darkness was settling in. The Covey continued to direct air strikes until it was too dark to continue, promising John Allen he would be back at first light the next morning.

RT Alabama held out through the long night, but at dawn the NVA initiated an all-out assault with massive salvos of RPG rounds as enemy troops fired small arms and automatic weapons in their advance toward the crater. They got close enough to toss at least four Chinese-made grenades into the crater, but the team managed to throw back all four before they exploded. When the charging NVA troops were almost at the edge of the crater, Allen and his men stood up and poured withering fire into them, killing scores of the attackers. Unfortunately, four of the five Nungs also died in the firefight.

The action escalated even more when the Covey worked an F-4 around the bomb crater protecting the survivors of RT Alabama. The Phantom was struck by 37mm fire and exploded in midair. Both pilots ejected and were later rescued. Next an Air Force HH-3 Jolly Green appeared overhead, dropped his penetrator, and went into a hover. SSgt Allen tied Ken Cryan and the Nung to the penetrator and sent them up to their waiting salvation. Then he watched in horror as multiple rounds of small arms fire slammed into the two men being hoisted aboard. Now alone and surrounded, John Allen considered the options: continue to fight an unwinnable battle or bug out. Allen ran full speed downhill killing several enemy soldiers along the way. As he ran past a machine gun pit he leveled his CAR-15 at its startled 5-man crew, killing all of them.

After running for what seemed like miles, SSgt Allen contacted the Covey FAC who directed a Vietnamese H-34 Kingbee to his location. As the Kingbee approached Allen, a .51 cal machine gun blasted the helicopter, sending it crashing into the ground in a fiery explosion. Again running for his life, John Allen changed direction and over the next two hours managed to evade his pursuers with the aid of several additional air strikes. Finally he came upon a large open field where the Covey arranged for another Kingbee helicopter to spiral down to the makeshift LZ and rescue John Allen. Upon his return to Phu Bai, Allen learned that Ken Cryan and his Nung team member, lifted out by the Jolly Green, had died. Each man's body had been riddled by more than 30 bullets. For his gallantry, SSgt John Allen received the Silver Star, no consolation at all for the sole survivor of RT Alabama.[53]

Meanwhile, within the valley itself, 1st Cav units continued patrolling. The 1st Battalion, 7th Cavalry patrols operating several miles northwest of the airstrip engaged in several small, sharp firefights with the NVA. During one such action on May 4, the 2d Platoon, Bravo Company, under the command of 1st Lieutenant Douglas B. Fournet, maneuvered uphill against fortified enemy positions—in the A Shau, every engagement seemed to be fought moving 'uphill.' During the advance the platoon encountered intense sniper fire, making movement very difficult and extremely dangerous. The right flank man suddenly spotted an enemy claymore mine covering the route of advance and shouted a warning to his comrades. Realizing that the enemy would also be alerted, Lt Fournet ordered his men to take cover and ran uphill toward the mine, a deadly anti-personnel device filled with powerful C-4 explosives and hundreds of lethal ball bearings. With complete disregard for his safety and realizing the imminent danger to members of his platoon, the 24-year-old Louisiana native dived on the claymore and used his body as a shield as he attempted to slash the control wires leading from the NVA position to the claymore. Before he could cut the wires, the nearby enemy detonated the mine, killing Fournet instantly. Five men nearest the mine were slightly wounded, but their leader's heroic and unselfish act spared his men from serious injury or death. For conspicuous gallantry and intrepidity in action at the risk of his life above and beyond the call of duty, 1st Lieutenant Douglas B. Fournet was posthumously awarded the Medal of Honor.[54]

The battle against the raging weather over the A Shau continued when, on May 6, the meteorological conditions played a key role in the loss of two Marine A-4 Skyhawks from Chu Lai. After dropping its ordnance in the A Shau, and while climbing back through the thick overcast, a Skyhawk collided with another inbound A-4. Both pilots ejected and were rescued. The next day General Tolson, clearly influenced by the rotten weather and the anticipated start of the southwest monsoon season, decided to begin withdrawing his 1st Cavalry brigades.

Beginning on May 10, as the heavy rains continued, the division began dismantling its firebases in preparation for departure. In many ways the extraction proved to be more difficult than the assault. The problems centered around how to backhaul tons of stockpiled ammunition and supplies, destroy the considerable stashes of captured enemy supplies, and leave behind thousands of mines and booby traps to make the enemy's future work more difficult. By May 11 torrential rains had already washed out a major portion of the A Luoi dirt airstrip, rendering it unusable. Consequently, all men and supplies had to be lifted out by the division's organic helicopter fleet. As the final battalion was extracted—during a driving rainstorm—Operation Delaware terminated on May 17, 1968.[55]

As in the earlier big unit battles like Cedar Falls and Junction City, American senior commanders hailed Operation Delaware as "one of the most audacious, skillfully executed and successful combat undertakings of the Vietnam War."[56] During the 29-day campaign, the 1st Cav and the 101st Airborne divisions had captured incredible amounts of enemy equipment, including 1 tank, 2 bulldozers, 67 trucks, over a dozen 37mm antiaircraft guns, 2,319 individual rifles, and over 71,000 pounds of food. And General Westmoreland's attrition strategy boasted 869 confirmed enemy dead at a cost of 142 Americans KIA, 47 MIA, and 530 WIA.[57]

Yet in some ways the success attached to Operation Delaware turned a blind eye to reality, as evidenced by the statements of a senior general who opined that the A Shau Valley campaign "marked the loss of enemy control of a long-held fortress and demonstrated the control which the U.S. and South Vietnamese forces were re-establishing in the wake of the enemy's Tet Offensive."[58] At best such a view was wishful thinking, at worst, self-delusional. Within a week after American forces departed the valley, North Vietnamese units reoccupied the A Shau and yet again turned it into a heavily defended sanctuary. Unfortunately for Operation Delaware, any long-term success proved to be absolutely minimal.

In a dramatic illustration of the point, just six days after Operation Delaware terminated, SOG inserted RT Idaho onto the west wall opposite A Luoi. The two Americans and four Nungs were never seen or heard from again. When 12-man RT Oregon inserted on the same LZ in an attempt to find the missing men of RT Idaho, a company of NVA attacked, killing one team member and wounding the rest. The survivors were successfully extracted under heavy fire.[59] It became clear, at least to SOG, that by no stretch of the imagination had the NVA lost control of the Valley of Death.

Although ground combat in the A Shau had ended with the with-drawal of U.S. forces, the flak in the area proved to be as deadly as ever. June 9 turned out to be a costly day when enemy gunners in the A Shau brought down Hellborne 215, a Marine A-4 from Chu Lai. Lieutenant Walter R. Schmidt ejected over the north end of the valley, broke his leg on landing, but made radio contact with an Air Force FAC, Trail 33, who initiated a massive search and rescue (SAR) effort for Schmidt. Following several aborted pickup attempts under extremely intense ground fire, Jolly Green 23, piloted by U.S. Coast Guard exchange pilot Lieutenant Jack C. Rittichier, moved in for another attempt. The HH-3 was immediately hit by a barrage of machine gun fire and burst into flames. The big helicopter crashed a few hundred yards away in a fiery explosion; none of the crew survived. The SAR effort for Lt Schmidt continued until dark but was called off when all radio contact ceased and the pilot was observed stretched out on the ground, motionless. The following morning a team inserted into the site found no trace of Walter Schmidt or his parachute. Hellborne 215 was never heard from again.[60]

Back home there was no national grieving for casualties in far away Vietnam. The entire country remained in a state of shock over the June 5th assassination of Senator Robert F. Kennedy in Los Angeles. On both sides of the Pacific, anybody who watched the television coverage somehow knew that the day JFK's younger brother died was the day that a vital part of the United States also died.

By August, the 101st Airborne Division had been reconstituted into an airmobile division. In their latest role, the Screaming Eagles exercised their new capability with a combat assault by the 2nd Battalion, 502nd Infantry, and the 2nd Battalion, 327th Infantry into the A Shau Valley in Operation Somerset Plain. Landing on the valley floor near the old A Luoi and Ta Bat airstrips, this search and destroy operation aimed at eliminating NVA troops trying to reenter the A Shau after Operation Delaware. Running from August 4 to August 20, the operation resulted in sporadic contact with the NVA. When the 101st withdrew, they left behind 171 confirmed enemy dead. The Screaming Eagles lost 19 KIA, 104 WIA, and 2 MIA. Following Operation Somerset Plain, American forces would not return to the A Shau for another five months; the North Vietnamese were back in a week.[61]

Eight thousand miles away and six days after the 101st's exit from the valley, home front attention focused on a different kind of battle—the 1968 Democratic National Convention. Mayor Richard J. Daley of Chicago intended to showcase his and the city's achievements to national Democrats, the news media, and the world. Instead, the proceedings became tarnished by the rioting of 10,000 anti-war demonstrators and the use of excessive force by the Chicago police during what came to be known as the "Battle of Michigan Avenue." The ensuing riots played out on television screens around the world, and as one journalist noted, "The 1968 Chicago convention became a lacerating event, a distillation of a year of heartbreak, assassinations, riots, and a breakdown in law and order that made it seem as if the country were coming apart."[62]

Thirty-seven days after the world's attention had focused on the tumultuous Democratic National Convention in Chicago, the deadly battles in the Valley of Death kept right on coming—and no one even noticed. On October 5, SOG RT Alabama, newly constituted following its disastrous mission back in May, inserted onto the west wall of the A Shau Valley. When the nine-man team departed their Kingbee helicopter, they spotted a large North Vietnamese flag on a pole at the edge of the LZ. They had inadvertently landed in the middle of the NVA regiment they had been sent to search for. Almost immediately the team found themselves under attack by a force of 50 enemy soldiers. The team One-Zero, Staff Sergeant James D. Stride, was killed in the first exchange of fire, along with one of the indigenous team members. The rest of the team formed a perimeter around his body and called for an emergency extraction but were unable to bring SSgt Stride with them as they fought their way to a pick-up area. In the confusion, Specialist 4 Lynne M. Black, Jr., the team's One-Two, or third in command, took charge when the One-One became hysterical. Black stood up firing his weapon on single shot, methodically picking off NVA attackers on top of the small hill to his front. He slammed another clip into his CAR-15 and went down the line, shooting the enemy soldiers one after another. Sometimes they spun around when hit and he shot them a second or third time.

As Lynne Black led the survivors of RT Alabama toward a nearby LZ, hundreds of NVA troops flooded into the immediate area. During the action, an enemy soldier was so close he tossed a hand grenade, which literally hit Black in the head and bounced to the ground. The surprised Green Beret instinctively dived for cover, but the explosion peppered his face with shrapnel wounds and knocked him unconscious. When his team revived him, Black, bleeding and groggy, gamely got to his feet and began coordinating airstrikes with the Covey circling overhead.

Rescue responsibility had been given to the 37th Aerospace Rescue and Recovery Squadron at Da Nang, which promptly dispatched two Jolly Green HH-3 helicopters. On arrival, Jolly Green 28 went into a hover for a hoist recovery of RT Alabama but was badly shot up by the NVA and forced to abort the pick-up. As the first two HH-3s headed back to Da Nang, another pair arrived as RT Alabama attempted to break contact, while the A-1 Sandys blasted the nearest enemy attackers with strafe and napalm. On arrival, Jolly Green 10 went into a hover over the team and was immediately hit by a barrage of fire and RPGs from all directions. The pilot attempted to fly his crippled bird out of danger, but after about a quarter mile the big HH-3 nosed over and crashed in flames. The orbiting Covey FAC was able to make radio contact with Jolly Green 10's PJ and badly injured pilot, both of whom had managed to escape the burning wreckage and evade into a nearby deserted village. The co-pilot and flight engineer died in the crash. Meanwhile, faced with an attack by an additional 100 enemy troops, Lynne Black decided to move RT Alabama to the helicopter crash site to link up with its survivors.

At that point another Jolly Green moved into position in an attempt to rescue them all—provided the recon team could get to the pick-up point in a hurry, and the A-1s could suppress the swarming masses of NVA. The plan worked up to a point. Specialist Black located the two crewmen in the village and led the shot up group to the hovering HH-3, but as he sent the men up on the jungle penetrator, he realized that an indigenous team member was missing. Refusing to leave a man behind, Black sprinted back to a small structure and found his man badly wounded and dying. The young Montagnard told Black to leave him and that he would hold off the rapidly approaching enemy. Black had only run a few steps when the Montagnard emptied his pistol at an NVA squad, then put the gun to his head and pulled the trigger. Black had only moved a few more steps when two young NVA soldiers popped out of the foliage right in front of him, both pointing AK-47s at the SOG man. Black approached the duo with his hands in the air, but at arm's length he grabbed both weapons simultaneously, punching one soldier in the face and smashing the butt of an AK into the face of the other. The incredibly lucky Green Beret, covered in blood, dirt, and sweat, sprinted 100 meters and jumped on the penetrator dangling beneath hovering Jolly Green 32. But just as Lynne Black climbed inside, an RPG exploded on the helicopter's underside. The pilot managed to limp over the next ridgeline and made a controlled crash landing in an open field where another Jolly Green, piloted by Coast Guard exchange officer Lt Commander Lonnie Mixon, immediately landed and picked everyone up except Lynne Black and the One-One. During the rescue, Mixon's bird sustained over 30 hits from enemy ground fire. A Cobra gunship landed to pull out Black and the One-One, both flown to safety sitting on the Cobra's ammo bay doors.

Surviving a deadly ambush, severe wounds, near capture, and a helicopter crash, Black made it out alive; it had been his very first SOG mission. Unfortunately, the A Shau had added three more American lives to its increasingly long list of heroes: SSgt James D. Stride, Major Albert D. Wester, and Sgt Gregory P. Lawrence would rest in the Valley of Death in timeless sleep. For his gallantry in action, Lynne M. Black, Jr. received the Silver Star.[63]

According to SOG veteran and noted military historian John Plaster, in 1968 CCN lost 18 Americans KIA and 18 MIA, almost all of them on operations around the A Shau. Combined with the 199 SOG Americans wounded in Laos, those figures meant that every single SOG recon man was wounded at least once in 1968. Statistically, SOG recon casualties exceeded 100 percent, the highest sustained loss rate since the Civil War.[64] Those staggering losses, however, also reflected the valor that increasingly defined combat operations in the Valley of Death.

As the Year of the Monkey ended, there was no denying one gut-wrenching fact: whether viewed at home within the context of the American domestic scene or from the perspective of the violent battles that raged across the two northern provinces of I Corps, by any yardstick, the year 1968 had indeed been one of heartbreak—the quintessential *annus horribilis.*

chapter 6

OPERATION DEWEY CANYON

The deadliest weapon in the world is a Marine and his rifle!
—GENERAL JOHN J. PERSHING

T he Marines in I Corps inhabited a singularly unique universe with its own rules, values, and its own sense of time. Whereas the other services mandated a 12-month tour of duty in Vietnam, during their 13-month-long tours, young Marines endured bruising battles around hell holes like the Rock Pile, Con Thien, Gio Linh, Hue, Khe Sanh, and Vandegrift Combat Base, but by early 1969 they were about to add another sinister name to the list: A Shau Valley. And ever since the fall of the Special Forces camp there in 1966, top American military leaders had persistently upheld the view that the Valley of Death represented the single most dangerous locale in Vietnam. Yet no matter the battle or operation or the place, Marines tended to shrug off rumors and grisly war stories about the A Shau and instead remained enthralled by and focused on the homes and lives they had left behind in the United States. In their reverie they called it dreaming about "back in the world."

While comparisons are always open to interpretation, a Vietnam Marine's world was every bit as squalid and inhospitable as that of their counterparts in World War II. Although entire battalions sometimes moved by helicopter to hot spots in I Corps, once in the operating area (AO) the Marines deployed on foot just like their World War II brethren had at Guadalcanal, Saipan, and Okinawa. Only in the harsh environs of Vietnam there were no front lines; small units patrolled for weeks at a time through thick jungle and up steep mountains searching for an enemy who hid and only fought on his own terms. Not surprisingly, the tactical advantage on these patrols often rested with the NVA, who would allow the Marines to stumble across their elaborately prepared ambushes in terrain that the enemy knew intimately and that the Americans might in all probability be seeing for the first time. While death might lurk around any curve in the trail, for Marines the battle against the weather and the jungle was just as pervasive and went on 24 hours a day. In the oppressive tropical daytime heat they sweated rivers. The incessant dampness, pelting rain, and the cold mountain air at night made them shiver much more than any fear of the unseen enemy. At night Marines frequently found their bunkers, tents, or foxholes flooded or buried in mud—or rats. One Marine described it thus, recalling, "Fatigues dripping wet with perspiration, clinging to the body . . . forever being tangled in 'wait-a-minute vines,' immobilized by elephant grass, and surrounded by the muffled voices of young marines in the heat muttering under their breath."[1]

Although the youthful Marines patrolling through the mountainous terrain along the border of I Corps may have groused and complained, just as soldiers have throughout recorded history, they were in many respects the finest military force the United States had ever sent to war. Unfortunately, when it came to attitudes about the military, far too many Americans apparently subscribed to the old Chinese proverb, "as you would not use good iron to make a nail, so you would not use a good man to make a soldier." Yet contrary to a widely held opinion in the 1960s that infantrymen were essentially "losers" from the lowest echelons of American society, they were in fact better educated than any soldier or Marine up to that point in American history. During World War II only 24 percent of draftees had completed high school, and 35 percent had never gone beyond grammar school. Among Vietnam era Army and Marine draftees, as many as 78 percent were high school graduates and roughly 30 percent had some college.[2] One Marine gunnery sergeant sarcastically greeted former college students joining his unit in Vietnam with, "Just think of this as your junior year abroad."[3] Unfortunately, the final exam for this latest course would be the toughest of their young lives, a course with a grade of 'live or die' instead of the traditional 'A or F.' And the classroom setting? The remote and deadly A Shau Valley.

By early 1969 some of the staff at MACV, newly arrived and eager to contribute to the war effort, engaged in a frustratingly repetitious rendition of reinventing the wheel—a game that had been going on in the A Shau since 1963. The new intelligence analysts discovered that NVA engineering units, relatively inactive for several months, had begun in January to reopen key roads along the border, specifically Route 922 eastward through Base Area 611 into the A Shau and Route 548 running along the valley floor. There had also been a dramatic surge in vehicle traffic moving into the A Shau. During clear weather, reconnaissance aircraft and FACs sighted hundreds of trucks a day making the run eastward. Whether the new intelligence specialists were aware of Operations Delaware and Somerset Plain is undocumented, but they nevertheless came to the conclusion that their new discovery of NVA activity in and around Base Area 611 and the A Shau suggested an enemy spring offensive and therefore required a sharp American response.[4]

A new, bold campaign in Vietnam seemed not only appropriate, but timely. On January 20 in Washington, DC, Richard M. Nixon took the oath of office as the 37th president—and the new commander-in-chief. Joining the new president were Melvin R. Laird as Secretary of Defense and Henry Kissinger as National Security Advisor. The new team wasted no time in seeking the recommendations from the Chairman of the Joint Chiefs of Staff, General Earle G. Wheeler and from the relatively new MACV commander, General Abe Abrams. Both endorsed a new campaign focusing on the A Shau, hoping a decisive move there could eventually turn things around. Such musings were a pipe dream. In early 1969 President Nixon had no intention of capturing and holding the Valley of Death. He confided to his senior staff, "I'm going to stop the [Vietnam] war. Fast."[5]

The increase in enemy activity infiltrating into I Corps did not go unnoticed by Major General Raymond G. Davis, commanding general of the 3rd Marine Division. In addition to reported NVA movements, two other factors influenced the 3rd Division's leader to act. First, Ray Davis was a scrapper by nature and no stranger to combat. During World War II he had earned Silver Stars on Guadalcanal and at Cape Gloucester, and the Navy Cross at Peleliu. For his actions at the Chosin Reservoir in Korea he was awarded the Medal of Honor. He was thought of by everyone as "a Marine's Marine," a man who relished the prospect of battle for its own sake, who ignored physical danger, and a man who would never stop to count the odds against him. Second, General Davis noted with a certain amount of frustration that the fortress mentality at various bases and the defensive posture of the Marines in I Corps were contrary to the normally aggressive style of fighting that was the hallmark of the Marine Corps. Consequently, with the siege of Khe Sanh behind him, he proceeded to turn the tactical disposition of his division upside down; he ordered Marine units to move out of their combat bases and to engage the enemy. According to General Davis:

> We had something like two dozen battalions up there all tied down to these fixed positions, and the situation didn't demand it . . . . The way to get it done was to get out of these fixed positions and get mobility, to go and destroy the enemy on our terms—not sit there and absorb the shot and shell and frequent penetrations that he was able to mount.[6]

The first test of Ray Davis' philosophy was a bold plan calling for a regimental sweep across the northern end of the imposing A Shau Valley.

Before tackling the thorny and always intimidating A Shau, General Davis first fine-tuned the 3rd Marine Division's unit integrity and concept of mobile operations. For myriad reasons, the regiments within the division had seemingly lost their individual personalities to a practice that allowed any battalion to be assigned to any regiment; the battalions referred to it as being "fragmented." For example, the 12th Marine Regiment might have operational control over a battalion of the 9th Marines, a battalion of the 4th Marines, and only one of its own; there was no unit integrity. Ray Davis changed all that. From that point on each regiment controlled its constituent battalions. Colonel Robert H. Barrow, commander of the 9th Marine Regiment and a future commandant of the Marine Corps, described the turn-around best when he noted that "Regimental size forces no longer consisted of a regimental operational headquarters and several unrelated and ever-changing infantry battalions. The 9th Marines became just that—the 9th Marines. Unit cohesion, teamwork, cooperation, and esprit flourished."[7]

The 3rd Marine Division's new modus operandi evidently drew heavily from the 1st Cavalry Division's air mobility concept: vertical envelopment and the requirement for helicopters—lots of them. General Davis had been tremendously impressed during Operation Pegasus with the 1st Cav's mobile helicopter-borne tactics in the relief of Khe Sanh, and later in the A Shau Valley in Operation Delaware. When he took over the 3d Marine Division in mid-May, Davis insisted on creating a capability to strike at the elusive North Vietnamese units in a series of freewheeling operations throughout the division sector, not just around static enclaves along the DMZ. From the aviation perspective, this created an insatiable demand on the already overburdened and limited number of helicopters and crewmen available. To meet that need General Davis somehow managed to acquire a lion's share of all new D Model CH-46 helicopters arriving in-country, a version that had significantly larger engines than the previous model and could lift more troops. Additionally, General Davis' good relationship with his Army brethren in the newly re-named XXIV Corps produced a promise of Army helicopter support when needed.[8] Thus equipped, the new air mobile capability provided a distinct increase in the combat potential for the 3rd Marine Division. From a tactical point of view, the increased helicopter support gave the Marines a new dimension of warfare in I CTZ—vertical envelopment of the NVA's rear or flanks. Rather than manning static bases or attempting to outflank an enemy on foot, the helicopter allowed Ray Davis to insert troops rapidly across remote, isolated terrain at decisive points in time to shape the outcome of the battle. As had been the case for years, the A Shau was that decisive point.

The 3rd Marine Division's model for air mobility depended not only on the helicopter but also on the wide-ranging use of current intelligence, especially that generated by small reconnaissance patrols. General Davis employed two very different kinds of patrols, both inserted into a target area by helicopter. The first was the "Stingray" patrol, a heavily armed unit that always operated within the range of friendly artillery. Their mission was to "find, fix and destroy the enemy with all available supporting arms and with rapid reinforcement when necessary." The second was the much smaller "Key Hole" patrol, armed only with small arms and trained to operate clandestinely in remote areas beyond artillery range. The primary function of these patrols was to observe. And unlike the Army approach of using fire power and air strikes to blast new LZs or fire support bases (FSB) out of the jungle—a process that invariably tipped their hand to the enemy—Marine Stingray and Key Hole patrols covertly occupied and secured such positions and quietly held them until the air assault into the AO actually launched. According to Ray Davis, the 3d Marine Division "never launched an operation without acquiring clear definition of the targets and objectives through intelligence confirmed by recon patrols."[9]

With unit integrity re-established, helicopters available, and intelligence in hand, the 3rd Marine Division began to implement plans for a regimental-size search and clear operation south of the lower Da Krong River and the northern end of the A Shau Valley, the area where Base Area 611 and Route 922 spilled over from Laos into South Vietnam. Initially codenamed Operation Dawson River South, the codename changed to Operation Dewey Canyon when the scope of the operation expanded. The division's swing regiment, the 9th Marines, supported by the artillery of the 2nd Battalion, 12th Marines, was put on alert to launch the venture as soon as practicable after January 22, 1969.

Planned as a phased operation, Dewey Canyon began as a step-by-step deployment of three battalions into the AO for establishing fire support bases on key terrain features. The concept called for a series of mutually supporting positions approximately 8,000 meters apart with a built-in 3,000 meter firing sector overlap in order to provide Marine units with continuous artillery support. From there the units, once inserted, advanced on foot throughout the area to be searched. Additional FSBs could be constructed as needed for deeper penetration into the AO. Beginning on January 18, the 9th Marines moved out of Vandegrift Combat Base to reoccupy three FSBs, each approximately five miles south of the other. The FSBs, Henderson, Tun Tavern, and Shiloh, all unoccupied since December 1968, were reclaimed and cleared of mines and booby traps by recon teams. Later that day the troops began reconstructing artillery positions and air-lifting 105mm howitzers and ammunition into the parapets.[10]

Phase I of Operation Dewey Canyon also involved extensive patrolling around the fire support bases and consolidation of forces and supplies prior to launching the next phase due south into the area along the Laotian border. In addition to providing security for the two artillery batteries on FSB Shiloh, the Marines of Company A, 1st Battalion, 9th Marines, launched numerous patrols in all directions, encountering little or no contact with the elusive enemy. With the security and the routine well established, the

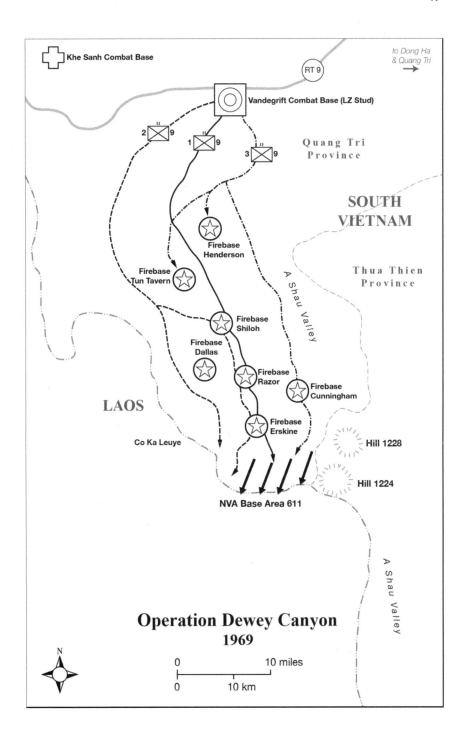

Khe Sanh Combat Base

to Dong Ha
& Quang Tri

RT 9

Vandegrift Combat Base (LZ Stud)

2 9

1 9

3 9

Quang Tri
Province

SOUTH
VIETNAM

Firebase
Henderson

A Shau Valley

Thua Thien
Province

Firebase
Tun Tavern

Firebase
Shiloh

Firebase
Dallas

Firebase
Razor

Firebase
Cunningham

LAOS

Firebase
Erskine

Co Ka Leuye

Hill 1228

Hill 1224

NVA Base Area 611

A Shau Valley

**Operation Dewey Canyon
1969**

N

0   10 miles

0   10 km

company commander, 1st Lieutenant Wesley L. Fox, described his company's time on Shiloh as a "vacation land." In explaining, Fox remembered that:

A platoon a day went off the hill to a small river at the foot . . . for swimming and fishing. Swimming and lying in the sun on a nice sand bar were great, but the real treat was the fish provided by the fishing expedition. The platoons would wind up their day at the river by throwing grenades in the deep holes and simply wading out and picking up the fish that floated to the top.

Once in the heat of combat, however, Lt Fox recalled that "Marines were heard to talk about the good old days back at Shiloh."[11]

Between January 22 and January 25, the 9th Marines began leapfrogging to the south as they constructed FSB Razor and occupied a strategically located ridgeline six kilometers farther south. Shown on their maps as Ca Ka Va, on it they established FSB Cunningham, a key location in the planned AO large enough to accommodate a full battalion and the regimental command post. Except for occasional sniper fire, the landings went unopposed. During the rapid buildup that followed at Cunningham, CH-46 Sea Knight helicopters brought in five artillery units, including two 105mm batteries, two 155mm batteries, and a mortar battery.

The move into the northern end of the A Shau proved to be complicated, dangerous, and miserable. The triple canopy jungle and steep terrain, along with fog and heavy rain, disrupted the heli-lift of troops and resulted in the partial insertion of companies into FSBs. Those who did insert often waited hours or even days for the remainder of the unit to arrive. As the undermanned companies sat there waiting, their Marines endured constant rain, cold, NVA artillery barrages, and doses of frayed nerves—real or imagined—as they contemplated the forbidding, sinister valley where the mist never lifted. The enemy, on the other hand, moved unimpeded at night along roads that were carefully camouflaged during the day with movable trees and shrubs ingeniously planted in containers. As the enemy forces moved, the Marines were pounded by heavy artillery fire from NVA 122mm guns in Laos. Frustrated by the entire situation, General Davis bitterly commented, "It makes me sick to sit on this hill and watch those 1,000 trucks go down those roads in Laos, hauling ammunition down south to kill Americans with."[12]

Phase II of the operation began on January 25 when the 2nd and 3rd Battalions started moving out of FSBs Razor and Cunningham. Their mission was to clear the area around the FSBs and push on to the southern end of the Da Krong River where it abruptly made a sharp turn to the east. The line along the river's east-west axis was designated Phase Line Red, the jumping-off point for upcoming Phase III. Around Phase Line Red, contact with the enemy became much more frequent. While patrolling near the Da Krong, Marines from the 2nd Battalion routinely encountered small groups of NVA support troops in the dense jungle, resulting in short firefights. Company M even discovered a sophisticated four-strand communications wire strung between tree-mounted porcelain insulators. In another find, Company F uncovered the 88th NVA Field Hospital, a huge complex consisting of 8 buildings and capable of accommodating 160 patients. The company also found large quantities of Russian-made surgical instruments, food, and antibiotics; the facility had only been abandoned the day before. With those discoveries and the increased enemy contact, it was clear to all the Marines that they were deep in 'bad guy' country.[13]

Patrolling roughly 3,000 meters apart, the 2nd Battalion moved south along the regiment's right flank while the 3rd Battalion worked the left flank to the east, and in both instances as the units moved closer to the Laotian border, they encountered substantially stronger enemy screening forces. One of the first significant actions involved the 2nd Battalion's Company G, commanded by Captain Daniel A. Hitzelberger. On January 31, the men of Company G launched an attack against Hill 1175, an extremely steep ridge known as Co Ka Leuye. After a short firefight with a small group of NVA soldiers, the company settled into a night defensive position at the base of Hill 1175. The following morning, as the company began a perilous climb via ropes up sheer rock cliffs, the A Shau weather reared its ugly head and deteriorated rapidly. Faced with drizzle, dense fog, zero ceiling, and forward visibility of only a few meters, Company G kept climbing—and the weather kept getting worse.

Once on top of Hill 1175, the members of Company G settled into an existence dominated by the A Shau's incredibly foul weather conditions. Constant drizzle and rain socked in the entire company, preventing any kind of resupply by air. By day three they were out of food and subsisting on a few bananas and rainwater. The weather made their tactical situation even more tenuous; in addition to the constant rain, the low-hanging cloud layers engulfed the Marines in a perpetual shroud of mist, limiting line of sight vision to a maximum of 25 meters. With visibility down to practically zero, Capt Hitzelberger could only wait it out in a surreal world of swirling gray fog while keeping his men poised and alert for enemy activity. To augment extensive patrolling during the day, each night the company commander positioned at least six observation posts, listening posts, and ambushes around his perimeter, and each night those outposts made contact with small NVA parties attempting to probe the Marine position.[14]

With helicopter resupply and medical evacuation halted throughout the Dewey Canyon AO due to weather, the 9th Marines commander, Colonel Robert Barrow, decided to pull his companies back to the nearest FSB for easier support. By February 4 all rifle companies had moved into defensive positions around a fire support base—except Company G, 2nd Battalion. As the company column started down Hill 1175 on February 5, at times actually walking in the clouds, the point element of the 3rd Platoon spotted three NVA soldiers to their right front. In the excitement of the moment, like hounds chasing the fox, the point fire team scrambled after the fleeing enemy, who in actuality represented a typical NVA ploy in the A Shau's dense foliage: the three soldiers acted as bait to draw the Marines into an ambush.

After the point fire team had pursued a short distance, the trap was sprung at 10 a.m. Approximately 30 NVA soldiers, well camouflaged and secure inside bunkers and spider holes, opened fire. Pinned down by the enemy, the Marines of the point team returned fire as best they could and held fast while the remainder of 3rd Platoon moved up. Capt Hitzelberger committed his 2nd Platoon to the left, which immediately came under heavy automatic weapons and RPG fire. Platoon Sergeant Robert D. Gaudioso noted that the enemy soldiers were extremely disciplined, firing at voices or individual Marines rather than spraying the jungle with unaimed volleys. Sgt Gaudioso also speculated that his platoon took casualties because of the terrain. At very close quarters the enemy had the advantage; as the platoon moved down slope, the NVA fired up at exposed Marine legs and silhouettes, while the Marines looking downhill could only see dense foliage.[15]

In the swirling mist on Hill 1175, casualties mounted when unobserved NVA, tied in trees, tossed grenades down on the Marines below. During the firefight Sgt Gaudioso stated that as other Marines attempted to move toward their injured colleagues, enemy soldiers shot to wound them in order to draw more would-be rescuers or corpsmen into the open. He was convinced that the NVA were familiar with the shouted terms 'corpsman' or 'doc,' and consequently targeted a corpsman as he treated the wounded. Men in Company G were briefed not to call out for a corpsman or medic. Instead, they invented their own term—'weasel.' Unfortunately, the chief corpsman was killed as cries for a weasel echoed along the steep, muddy slope.[16]

With four Marines wounded and at least one killed, Capt Hitzelberger deployed his 1st Platoon in a flanking movement to the far left through a small ravine. It was at that point that Lance Corporal Thomas P. Noonan, Jr., a fire team leader, moved from his position of relative security and began maneuvering down the treacherous slope to a location near the injured men, taking cover behind some rocks. Shouting words of encouragement to the wounded to restore their confidence, he then dashed across the hazardous terrain under heavy fire and commenced dragging a corpsman, with blood spurting from a wound in his neck, away from the fire-swept area. Although knocked to the ground by an enemy round and severely wounded, Lance Corporal Noonan nevertheless got up and resumed dragging the man toward the marginal security of a rock. Shielding the other man with his own body, Tommy Noonan was killed in a hail of bullets before he could reach cover. His heroic actions inspired his fellow Marines to initiate a spirited assault which forced the enemy soldiers to withdraw. For conspicuous gallantry and intrepidity at the risk of his life above and beyond the call of duty, Brooklyn native Thomas P. Noonan, Jr. was posthumously awarded the Medal of Honor.[17]

After contact was broken, the men of Company G carefully searched the bunker complex and found two enemy bodies and several blood trails. They occupied the remaining hours of daylight by rigging stretchers to carry the 5 dead and 18 wounded Marines down the hill. Because of the steep, slippery terrain, Capt Hitzelberger was forced to allocate half his company to the effort. "At this time the stretcher cases were moving up and down slopes in excess of 70 degrees," he remembered, "and we had to use six, eight, and at times ten men to carry a stretcher, and it would take us over 30 minutes to move one stretcher case over one bad area." The exhausted and hungry men used ropes to lower the stretchers down the face of an almost vertical rocky cliff. Throughout the movement off Co Ka Leuye, Capt Hitzelberger employed artillery concentrations around the company with an almost continuous walking barrage 150 meters to his rear, which he called his "steel wall."[18]

At the bottom of the steep escarpment, Company G finally linked up with a platoon from Company E which had brought medical supplies and the first rations the survivors of Hill 1175 had eaten in over three days. With the help of the relief platoon and a brief break in the weather, Company G finally loaded its wounded aboard two medical evacuation helicopters that had flown on the deck down the Da Krong River, and with no LZs available, had landed on the rocks in the middle of the river. When the company at last staggered back into LZ Dallas on February 9, they were filthy, exhausted, uniforms ripped to shreds, but in high spirits, and according to their battalion commander, they were ready for a fight. To a man they praised the efforts of the medevac birds, helicopter gunships, and Army CH-47s, but they had few kind words to say about the other Marine choppers. One of the Company G platoon leaders perhaps summed up the general mood when he observed, "The Marine helicopter support was piss poor."[19]

Although complaints about inadequate helicopter support for the rifle companies of the 9th Marines during the first week of February were commonplace, the disparaging comments concerning helicopters were in all likelihood overly harsh for several reasons. First, none of the Marine helicopter pilots had ever experienced anything like the abysmal weather conditions encountered in the A Shau, nor had they ever run up against the heavy volume of interlocking antiaircraft fire. Second, unlike Army helicopters directly assigned to and fully integrated into the 101st Airborne Division, Marine helicopters were assigned to the 1st Marine Air Wing and not to the 3rd Marine Division. The aviators, therefore, operated under their own rules and procedures, a fact that tended to make them less open to, or perhaps unfamiliar with, infantry needs and requirements. Friction and misunderstandings were bound to develop. Finally, comparisons to Army helicopter support tended to be biased; Screaming Eagle aviators had already logged a year of experience in the Valley of Death while their Marine colleagues had none. In the final analysis, General Davis' air mobility concept worked well in clear weather, but in the real world—a world defined by the inhospitable A Shau—the steep learning curve generated not only hard feelings but also cost lives and momentum.

Phase III of Operation Dewey Canyon kicked off on the morning of February 11, when three battalions of the 9th Marines moved out on foot across Phase Line Red and proceeded south toward the Laotian border, approximately five miles away. Unlike Phase II when the NVA generally opposed the Marines with squad-sized units or smaller, enemy contact during Phase III consisted of formidable attacks by entire platoons or companies, all highly disciplined troops who remained in their bunkers or spider holes until they were overrun or destroyed. To meet the larger threat, a Marine rifle company moved forward on line, with a second company following just behind it, said to be 'in trace.' If the lead company became heavily engaged, the company in trace acted as a maneuver element, assisting the lead company as necessary and securing LZs for resupply or medical evacuation. If required, the company in trace could pass through the engaged company and continue to press the attack. According to the 9th Marines' commander, the maneuver worked well "and was masterfully done. Battalion commanders went right along with [their troops], no jeeps obviously, nor any of that nonsense."[20]

Throughout Vietnam, including the A Shau, February 17, 1969 ushered in the Year of the Rooster. In the Chinese zodiac calendar Roosters were noted for becoming overly stubborn and close-minded in their thinking. Considered in that light, it was no surprise that the Rooster was not the most active practitioner of flexibility. The issue surfaced when, in observance of Tet, the North Vietnamese unilaterally declared a weeklong truce, but for some reason the NVA commander in the northern A Shau used the Tet holiday to attack.

At 3:45 a.m. on February 17 an enemy sapper platoon, supported by a reinforced rifle company from the NVA 812th Regiment, launched a vicious attack on FSB Cunningham where the sappers broke through the defensive wire and raced through the firebase, tossing grenades and satchel charges into every bunker. During the initial mortar attack, the officer in charge of FSB Cunningham was partially buried in a caved-in bunker. As he crawled out of the debris he came face to face with one of the sappers. The Marine had a grenade in his hand but was too close to the enemy to use it, so he jumped on the surprised sapper and bludgeoned him to death with the heavy base of the grenade. Just a few yards away the company gunnery sergeant, using only his personal knife, killed several of the sappers in hand-to-hand combat. Initially caught by surprise, Marines of Company L fought off the attack and secured the FSB. Marines from the 106mm recoilless rifle battery, manning a machine gun in the southeast portion of the Cunningham, assaulted and killed six NVA soldiers inside the perimeter. The cooks from India Battery joined the close quarters fight when they manned a .50 caliber machine gun and accounted for 13 enemy killed.

During the initial moments of the attack, 1st Lieutenant Raymond C. Benfatti was severely wounded by an RPG explosion. Ignoring his extremely painful injuries, he refused medical evacuation and, boldly shouting words of encouragement to his men, directed their fire against the marauding NVA sappers. Ignoring the enemy rounds impacting near him, he quickly organized a reaction force and supervised his Marines in evacuating the casualties and in replacing wounded Marines in defensive emplacements. As the large enemy unit continued their attack against the perimeter, Lt Benfatti fearlessly continued leading his company, repeatedly exposing himself to intense hostile fire as he directed the efforts of his men in repulsing the enemy attack, until all were driven off or killed. When the sappers withdrew, he supervised the medical evacuation of casualties and ascertained the welfare of his Marines, resolutely refusing medical assistance until all other injured men had been cared for. His bold leadership and dogged determination inspired all who observed him and were instrumental in his company's accounting for many North Vietnamese soldiers killed. For his conspicuous gallantry Lt Raymond C. Benfatti was awarded the Silver Star.[21]

At first light they found 37 NVA bodies around the FSB, 13 of them inside the perimeter. During the three-hour fight the Marines suffered 4 killed and 46 wounded. Interestingly, on the NVA dead the Marines found significant quantities of marijuana and other drugs. In an interview shortly after the battle at Cunningham, 2nd Lt Milton J. Teixeira explained that

NVA troops hopped up on narcotics "made them a lot harder to kill. Not one of the gooks we had inside the perimeter had less than three or four holes in him. Usually it took a grenade or something to stop him completely."[22]

Some of the heaviest fighting of the campaign occurred on the Laotian border between 18 and 22 February, within a sector assigned to the 1st Battalion. On the 18th, Marines from Company A engaged in a tough fight along a densely wooded ridgeline five kilometers south of FSB Erskine. With assistance from artillery and very limited close air support, the company overran the enemy bunkers, killing more than 30 NVA defenders. A day later Company C moved through Company A's lines, engaging an even larger enemy force hunkered down in yet another camouflaged bunker complex. Not only did the Marines of Company C kill 71 NVA soldiers, they also captured two Russian-made 122mm artillery pieces and a large tracked vehicle used to move those guns. As the attack continued, Company A again took the lead, killing 17 more NVA and capturing a large truck and a stockpile of artillery and antiaircraft ammunition. During these engagements the Marines suffered 6 killed and 30 men wounded.[23]

In the Marine Corps, the valor displayed by Navy corpsmen assigned to each rifle platoon was legendary. In the heat of battle these incredibly brave men, under constant fire and in the open, moved around the battlefield saving the lives of countless wounded Marines. The story of Hospitalman Third Class Mack H. Wilhelm is representative. On February 19, when the 1st Battalion's Company D came under a heavy volume of fire from an enemy force occupying a well-concealed bunker complex in the northern section of the A Shau Valley, Petty Officer Wilhelm observed a seriously wounded Marine lying dangerously exposed to the intense hostile fire and quickly raced across the open terrain to the side of the casualty. Although Wilhelm was painfully wounded in the shoulder, he skillfully administered emergency first aid to his companion, picked him up and, shielding him with his own body, commenced to carry him to a sheltered position. Once again wounded, this time in the leg, Mack Wilhelm nonetheless managed to evacuate his patient to a relatively safe location. The 23-year-old native of Rockport, Texas, then returned through the hail of fire to the side of another critically wounded Marine and was in the process of treating the casualty when he himself was cut down by a lethal burst of enemy AK-47 fire. For his extraordinary heroism Navy Corpsman Mack H. Wilhelm was posthumously awarded the Navy Cross.[24]

Operating on the far western flank of the 9th Marines, Company H of the 2nd Battalion was on the Laotian border by February 20. Sitting on a ridgeline overlooking the border and the all-important Route 922, the Marines watched in disbelief as an enemy truck convoy rumbled unimpeded along the road below. Company commander Captain David F. Winecoff remembered, "The company, of course, was talking about 'let's get down on the road and do some ambushing.' I don't think they really thought that they were going to let us go over into Laos."[25] The Company H Marines were correct: the convoluted rules of engagement did not permit U.S. combat forces to enter neutral Laos. However, there was one small area of interpretive 'wiggle room,' a provision that allowed commanders to execute necessary counteractions against VC/NVA forces in the exercise of self-defense. In the estimation of Colonel Robert Barrow, those NVA forces on Route 922 were moving to attack his men, while 122mm field guns on the Laotian side of the border constantly shelled his troops. "This was a pretty unacceptable situation," he observed, "and it cried out for some sort of action to put a stop to it."[26] The action came the following afternoon when Capt Winecoff received a message from Colonel Barrow directing him to move across the border that night and set up a company ambush along Route 922. The instructions further stipulated that Company H must be back in South Vietnam by 6:30 a.m.

Late on the afternoon of the 21st, Capt Winecoff led his 1st and 2nd Platoons down the ridgeline, leaving his 3rd Platoon as security. The 3rd platoon commander was quite upset that his platoon had been chosen to stay behind; however, since the company's position was periodically being probed by small enemy sapper squads, it was imperative that a platoon be left behind as a rear guard.

Before even setting the ambush in motion, the men were exhausted from the strenuous action on the day before when every squad in the company had been in contact with the enemy. The 1st Platoon's encounter had been the most exciting. They had located a small bivouac area, and while checking it out spotted three NVA soldiers bathing in a creek. The platoon literally ran down and tackled their first live prisoner. When the other two soldiers scrambled for their weapons, a firefight developed. Three addi-

tional NVA soldiers responded to the brief shoot-out—all five resisters died
in a hail of M-16 fire. According to the company commander, such activities were the reason that most of the company's Marines were still worn
out even after a fitful night's sleep. Working the rugged terrain under the
obvious tension of combat in the A Shau was a tiring, emotionally draining
experience. The long night ahead would add to the men's weariness.

In the pitch black of night, Capt Winecoff led his platoons through
the dense jungle in single file with each man holding on to the pack of the
man in front to maintain contact. The column stopped often to listen for
enemy movement, but the only sounds were occasional mortar rounds fired
by the 3rd Platoon and the cacophony of gnats and mosquitoes buzzing
around each man's head, the insect bites becoming ulcerated wounds constantly irritated by salty sweat, and every sore turning into jungle rot. As
the column approached the north side of Route 922 at approximately 8:30
p.m., Winecoff sent the 1st Platoon leader and an experienced sergeant
forward to scout the road for ambush sites. When they finally returned
two hours later and were asked what took so long, their response reflected
the menacing aura surrounding their venture into Laos. The platoon leader
confessed, "Every fallen tree looked like an enemy soldier. We pounced on
one log with drawn knives because we were so sure."

After discussing the ambush site with his scouts, Capt Winecoff, carefully employing a halt-listen-move technique, led his force south across
Route 922. The ambush plan called for establishing the ambushing force
on the Laotian-side of the road so that any assault through the killing zone
would be to the north in the direction of the withdrawal. Halfway across
the road, Winecoff was startled when the drivers of several unseen NVA
trucks just to the west of the crossing site started their engines. The surprised Marines dashed 25 meters up a gentle slope on the far side of the
road; the 1st Platoon commander led his platoon members to the right,
the command group remained in the center, and the 2d Platoon settled in
on the left. The raiding party quickly took up firing positions facing down
on the road. Next, three officers moved forward to place claymore mines
in front of their positions. To achieve maximum damage, the company
commander passed the word along the line that he would not initiate the
ambush against singles or even pairs of trucks—he was after bigger game.

With the ambush in place, a long and agonizing waiting game began.

Several enemy trucks came into view using an unnerving technique. The truck driver would move about 200 meters along the road, then stop, cut his engine and lights, and remain motionless, listening for minutes at a time, a practice known as "recon by silence." Then, at about 1 a.m. on the morning of February 22, the increasingly antsy members of Company H heard shots being fired to their west. The source of that firing turned out to be an enemy patrol working its way along Route 922, firing into suspicious areas as they moved. To preclude his men from triggering the ambush in reaction to the patrol's shots, Capt Winecoff passed the word not to respond to their fire when they walked by. Fortunately, the patrol apparently turned back several hundred meters before reaching the company's location.

At 2 a.m. a single truck entered the killing zone from the west and was allowed to pass. The tired but keyed-up Marines sat in total darkness watching the drama unfold, poised for an ambush but mildly irritated by the sound of chirping crickets and mosquitoes buzzing around their ears. Then, at 2:30 the start up of many engines all at once shattered the silence. Blacked out headlights turned on, which created a visible line as the convoy of eight trucks moved east. As Capt Winecoff watched and waited, the lead truck rounded the corner popping into sight; he allowed it to pass the center claymore into the 1st Platoon's area. Then the next two trucks came into the company commander's field of vision, and when the second truck was abeam his claymore, he triggered the ambush at 3:03 a.m.

Winecoff's claymore lit up the night and caused the center truck to burst into flames, while the 1st Platoon leader's claymore missed the cabin of his truck, failing to stop it. Fortunately a quick thinking NCO observed the miss and fired his light anti-tank weapon (LAW), knocking out the lead truck. The 2d Platoon leader's claymore failed to fire, and the alert driver of the third vehicle threw his engine into reverse and began backing out of the killing zone. At that point all the Marines opened fire with their M-16s and machine guns, shredding the trucks with a hail of lead. The wild scene became even more spectacular when ammunition aboard the burning center truck cooked off. In short order the forward observer also had artillery fire falling on the company's flanks along the road, and in the eerie light of the burning trucks, Capt Winecoff gave the signal to move forward through the killing zone and back across the road to a rally point approximately 500 meters to the north. In addition to the three destroyed trucks, Company H counted eight NVA dead. Not a single Marine had been killed or wounded during the ambush on Route 922.[27]

The decision to send Company H into Laos was not without controversy and appeared to confirm the time-honored adage that it is sometimes easier to ask forgiveness than permission. Such was the approach taken by the 9th Marines commander, Colonel Barrow. He had advocated the raid as early as February 20, but his request had moved at a snail's pace through the chain of command, so he took matters into his own hands—they had their schedule and Barrow had his. When Company H was already 500 meters inside Laos, Colonel Barrow informed his immediate superior of the move, reasoning that "even that much of a minor violation might in itself provide a little bit of assurance of approval." It worked. According to Barrow, "approval came through that yes, we could do what we were going to do, but the implication clearly was you had better make it work."[28] Colonel Barrow also understood what many did not—permitting sanctuary for the enemy was not only illogical, it represented real danger. That same feeling had been incubating for at least four years, ever since the commander of the 1st Cavalry Division, Major General Harry W.O. Kinnard, had bluntly stated:

> When General Giap says he learned how to fight Americans and our helicopters at the Ia Drang, that's bullshit! What he learned was that we were not going to be allowed to chase him across a mythical line in the dirt. From that point forward, he was grinning. He can bring us to battle when he wants and where he wants, and where's that? Always within a few miles of the border, where his supply lines were the shortest, where the preponderance of forces is his, where he has scouted the terrain intensely and knows it better than we do.[29]

The initial reports of the ambush reached the 3rd Marine Division in the form of monitored 9th Marine radio messages. Everyone felt uncomfortable since two days earlier General Abrams, reacting to the earlier request, had stated categorically that all operations into Base Area 611 were to be conducted by SOG forces. As news of the Marine raid made its way up the chain of command, a senior officer at III MAF offered a decidedly positive response when he said, "Good news—who knows where the border is anyway."[30] The day after the highly successful raid, Colonel Barrow sent another message outlining why he had taken the actions he did and emphasizing the success achieved. Furthermore, he requested authority to continue operations along Route 922. In justifying his request, Barrow said, "I put a final comment on my message which said, quote, put another way, my forces should not be here if ground interdiction of Route 922 not authorized."[31] Thus faced with a *fait accompli,* General Abrams finally approved the request on February 24, stipulating however, that there be no public discussion of the Laotian incursion. Whether General Abrams and his staff were focused on the raid and its implications is problematic; their hands were full coping with other issues. The day before, the NVA had launched a "mini Tet," striking 110 cities throughout South Vietnam.

As Company H moved back into South Vietnam during the early morning hours of February 22, Company A of the 1st Battalion at the regiment's center moved along the ill-defined border near the village of Lang Ha. In a sharp firefight, the company's 1st Platoon took on an NVA squad camouflaged in the dense underbrush, killing seven while losing one Marine. In the lull following the battle, Lt Wesley Fox, the company commander, took the opportunity to ask battalion to send a water detail down to a creek near his position since his men were badly in need of water. As the 20-man detail started to fill canteens, they were attacked by heavy machine gun and mortar fire. As 1st Platoon deployed to meet the attack, they discovered they were confronting a reinforced NVA rifle company supported on the ridge above by a bunker complex with a host of automatic weapons and RPGs. Lt Fox immediately moved up his 3rd Platoon and placed it on line with the 1st, but when the attack stalled, he committed the 2nd Platoon through the center. As the close quarters fighting raged, Lt Fox faced a tough choice. He either needed to pull back so artillery could be called in, or he must push through the enemy complex. With his casualties mounting and no possibility of close air support due to low cloud ceilings, Fox reasoned that pulling back, carrying his dead and wounded, would leave no Marines to hold off the enemy; the NVA would wipe out his company. Pressing the attack was the lesser of two evils, so he decided that they would all stay in the Valley of Death together, or they would walk out together.

At that point a mortar round landed in the middle of the command group, killing several and wounding the rest, including Lt Fox. Advancing through heavy enemy fire in spite of his wounds, he personally took out one enemy position and calmly led an assault against a series of hostile emplacements, all the while carrying his own radios since both radiomen were down and out of action. Although wounded a second time, he continued to move through the hazardous area coordinating the activities of his men. From all directions, tracers curved in toward Fox and careened off at wild angles like sparks from an acetylene torch. When the four other company officers were either killed or wounded, Lt Fox reorganized the company and moved from position to position under withering enemy fire to lead his men as they hurled grenades against the enemy and drove the hostile forces into retreat. Wounded again in the final assault, Lt Fox, constantly in the open and under fire, refused medical attention, established a defensive posture, and supervised the preparation of casualties for medical evacuation. For conspicuous gallantry and intrepidity at the risk of his life above and beyond the call of duty while serving as commanding officer of Company A, 1st Lieutenant Wesley L. Fox was awarded the Medal of Honor.[32] In addition to 84 Purple Hearts, the Marines of Company A were awarded 3 Navy Crosses and 6 Silver Stars for their heroic actions on February 22.

By way of explanation, in order to piece together the story of that intense and often times confusing engagement, several primary source documents come into play, none of which gives a complete picture. The first is the 1st Battalion After Action Report, a vital document that provides a brief overview of the "when, where, and what." Unfortunately, AARs rarely provide any insight into the "who, how, and why." For example, here is the 1st Battalion's AAR entry for February 22:

> At 1100H at YD 202052 Company A made contact with an enemy squad in a bunker complex, killed 7 enemy, captured 14 chicom grenades, 1 AK47 rifle, and 3 AK47 magazines while suffering 1 KIA and 1 WIA. At 1300. Company A, on a company combat patrol, came under fire at YD 199049 from RPG's, 82mm mortars, 61mm mortars, machine guns and automatic weapons deployed by an estimated company of enemy troops, well en-

trenched in thoroughly camouflaged bunkers. Company A assaulted through one enemy position at YD 198049 while artillery missions and air strikes were called in on others at YD 204045. Company A suffered 72 WIA and 11 KIA, while killing 105 enemy and capturing 4 machine guns, 2 B40 rocket launchers, 2 7.62 bolt action rifles, 17 AK47 rifles, 47 chicom grenades, 13 RPG rounds, 2 75mm recoilless rifle rounds, 2 VC flags, documents, and 20 brand new packs full of new clothing and gear.[33]

To flesh out the story it was necessary to analyze the lengthy tape-recorded interview with the company commander, Lt Wesley Fox, conducted immediately after the battle. While Lt Fox provided a wealth of detail and insight into the engagement during the interview and in his book, *Marine Rifleman,* his accounts glossed over his own heroic actions, leaving yet another hole in the story. That segment was filled in by Lt Fox's gallantry citation for the Medal of Honor.

Company A's battle on the 22nd was the last large-scale engagement of Operation Dewey Canyon. The NVA lost 105 confirmed killed; the dead, all wearing new uniforms, were apparently highly decorated veterans of other campaigns. Marine casualties in Company A were also high: 11 killed and 72 men wounded.[34] Due to the inaccuracy of the maps of the day, it was impossible to determine on which side of the border the action occurred or where the men died, but for political reasons no public mention was made of Laos.

In spite of the official clampdown on actual battle locations, the 2nd Battalion's Company H once more saddled up and headed back into Laos on February 24 for more ground interdiction of Route 922. The plan called for Company H, followed by Companies E and F, to cross the border and drive east along the road, forcing enemy troops into blocking positions held by the 1st and 3rd Battalions. At approximately 11 a.m., Company H sprang an ambush on six NVA soldiers, killing four. The following day they overran and killed eight enemy soldiers and captured one 122mm field gun and two antiaircraft weapons. Later the same day a company patrol was ambushed by 15 enemy troops, resulting in a short but vicious firefight. Corporal William D. Morgan was a member of a flanking patrol screening Company H's movement along Route 922 when they were temporarily pinned down by an NVA force occupying a heavily fortified bunker complex. Observing that two fellow Marines had fallen wounded in a position dangerously exposed to the enemy fire, and that all attempts to evacuate them were halted by a heavy volume of automatic weapons fire, Cpl Morgan unhesitatingly maneuvered through the dense jungle undergrowth to a road that passed in front of a heavily manned hostile emplacement. Fully aware of the possible consequences of his action but thinking only of the welfare of his injured companions, Cpl Morgan shouted words of encouragement to them as he initiated an aggressive assault against the hostile bunker. To nearby Marines Morgan yelled, "Pull 'em in." Then, with complete disregard for his own safety, he charged across the open road and into the bunker firing his M-60 machine gun from the hip and pouring a stream of hot lead into the bunker. Standing upright, the Pittsburg, Pennsylvania Marine was totally exposed; every hostile soldier in the area turned their fire in his direction, mortally wounding him. His diversionary tactic and deliberate self-sacrifice enabled the remainder of his squad to retrieve their casualties and overrun the NVA position. For conspicuous gallantry and intrepidity at the risk of his life above and beyond the call of duty, Corporal William D. Morgan was posthumously awarded the Medal of Honor.[35]

On March 3, after five days in Laos, the 2nd Battalion began its withdrawal, or phased retraction, back to Vandegrift. While in Laos the battalion sustained 8 killed and 33 men wounded, but in keeping with the subterfuge regarding crossing the border into Laos, all dead were officially reported as having been killed in Quang Tri Province, South Vietnam. Even Corporal William D. Morgan's Medal of Honor citation indicated that the action occurred in Quang Tri Province southeast of Vandegrift Combat Base.[36]

Also on March 3, the 3rd Battalion began its trek north toward FSB Cunningham, yet the move away from the border did not lessen the chance of facing combat. Returning from a reconnaissance-in-force mission, the 1st Platoon of Company M came under intense automatic weapons fire and a grenade attack from a well-concealed enemy force. While the center of the column was pinned down, the leading squad moved to outflank the enemy. Acting as squad leader of the rear squad, Private First Class Alfred M. Wilson, from Odessa, Texas, skillfully maneuvered his men to form a base of fire and to act as a blocking force. In the ensuing firefight, both his machine gunner and assistant machine gunner were seriously wounded and unable to operate their weapon. Realizing the urgent need to bring the machine gun into operation again, PFC Wilson, with complete disregard for his safety, fearlessly dashed through the heavy fire with another Marine to recover the weapon. As they reached the machine gun, an enemy soldier stepped from behind a tree and threw a grenade toward the two Marines. Observing the grenade fall between himself and the other Marine, Mac Wilson, fully realizing the inevitable result of his actions, shouted a warning to his companion and unhesitatingly threw himself on the grenade, absorbing the full force of the explosion with his own body. For conspicuous gallantry and intrepidity at the risk of his life above and beyond the call of duty, Private First Class Alfred Mac Wilson was posthumously awarded the Medal of Honor.[37]

Not all of the retraction missions resulted in combat. As part of the 1st Battalion's phased pullback on March 4, Lt Wesley Fox led Company A on a final sweep through the site of their bitter firefight on February 22. What he encountered was totally unnerving. In that part of the northern A Shau, the undergrowth was so dense that the NVA units had not been able to find and remove all their casualties following the fight. Evidently some of their wounded had crawled into the heavy brush and died; the members of Company A found the enemy KIA by smell—the corrupting stench of death. Lt Fox stated that "all you had to do was follow your nose to find the bodies."[38]

While the gruesome sight and smell of dead bodies at the scene of his A Shau battle were, literally, easy enough to sniff out, according to Lt Fox the larger issue of enemy KIA was not so cut and dried—or completely honest. In a very candid 2012 interview, Wesley Fox opened up and shed considerable insight on the controversial subject of the body count as a yardstick. In the interview he confessed to seeing the practice as a demoralizing culprit. He offered the following explanation about body counts in Vietnam:

If a body count was good, an operation was considered a success. If there really are bodies on the ground, maybe there's something to that. When I'd call in artillery on a contact on a ridge or valley,

I'd have to give a body count. Maybe we killed some, maybe not. When the major or whoever was on the radio would press for a number, I'd just pull it out of my butt. A fellow company commander, Captain Ed Riley, would never do that. He'd say: "If you want a body count, you come out here and get it. I'm not going to lie." Not enough of us were the Ed Riley type.[39]

Although tallying a final body count may have preoccupied some, the 9th Marine Regiment in general found its units fighting yet another wicked battle with the A Shau's unpredictable and always foul weather. As the meteorological conditions turned from marginal to horrendous on March 5, the regiment's withdrawal plan for Operation Dewey Canyon—dependent on helicopter extraction—unraveled. Virtually all chopper flights ceased. When brief holes in the cloud ceiling did appear, the helicopter squadrons scrambled to implement an improvised patchwork scheme for airlift. Unfortunately, many companies and artillery batteries remained stranded for days around FSBs with no rations or ammunition, all the while being constantly probed by aggressive NVA units determined to kill Marines. If a helicopter was lucky enough to make it in, as often as not heavy antiaircraft fire forced the bird to withdraw. When the weather finally broke on March 18, the last of the Marine units was lifted off the A Shau's Tiger Mountain—under a heavy barrage of enemy mortar and antiaircraft fire. Operation Dewey Canyon terminated at 8 p.m. that same day. An anonymous Marine veteran poignantly remembered the campaign in verse:

Eleven days of rain and fog;
Their roof a dark gray sky.
Three days no food and water.
The choppers couldn't fly.
The nights were long and sleepless;
Awake was every man.
The torment dealt by nature,
Was taken in its stride.
And the NVA learned lesson one
About Marine Corps pride.

Pain and hunger, thirst and blood,
Were born by these brave men;
And if you asked them, "Do it again."
They'd only reply, "Say when."[40]

In March of 1969, Laos was not the only neutral country whose border the U.S. violated under the terms of international laws and treaties. Ironically, on the very same day that Dewey Canyon ended and the incursion into Laos became history, President Nixon authorized Operation Menu, the secret carpet bombing of sanctuaries and base areas in eastern Cambodia by Strategic Air Command (SAC) B-52 bombers. On the night of the 18th, a group of 60 of the big bombers departed Anderson Air Force Base, Guam, headed for the border area known as the Fishhook. Although the aircrews were briefed that their target was in South Vietnam, 48 of the B-52s were diverted across the border into Cambodia and dropped 2,400 tons of bombs. For obvious reasons the Nixon administration went to great lengths to keep the mission secret, fearing that widespread national outrage and protests would occur if word leaked out.[41]

During the 56 days of combat in Operation Dewey Canyon, both sides suffered heavy casualties. Enemy losses included 1,617 killed and 5 captured; many more were wounded. The NVA also suffered significant losses of equipment and supplies: 16 artillery pieces, 73 antiaircraft guns, 92 trucks, 1,223 individual weapons, and more than 220,000 pounds of rice. By comparison, the Marines lost 130 killed and 920 Marines wounded, although the official line maintained that all of the losses were in South Vietnam.[42] Knowledge of the incursion into Laos, however, did leak out on March 9 when reporter Drummond Ayres, Jr. of the *New York Times* filed a story disclosing the violation of Laotian neutrality by the Marines. He concluded by writing, "Operation Dewy Canyon seems to indicate that allied commanders operating along borders may dip across lines to secure their flanks."[43] Several days later at a press conference, Secretary of Defense Laird, on a fact-finding trip to Vietnam at the time, initially tapped danced around a question about American troops in Laos by saying that he could not confirm that they were there. Later he admitted that "Marines took up positions in Laos to protect their flank . . ."[44] Oddly enough, raids by the 9th Marines into Laos during Dewey Canyon, while controversial, were essentially ignored by an increasingly disgruntled American public. There was virtually no protest at home about the pinprick raids across the Laotian border; that would occur a year later at the Cambodian border.

Dewey Canyon became the last major Marine combat operation in Vietnam, and it was and still is considered by many to be the most successful of the entire war. Army Lieutenant General Richard G. Stillwell, commander of the XXIV Corps, best captured the spirit of triumph when he stated, "In my possible parochial estimate, this ranks with the most significant undertakings of the Vietnam conflict in the concept and results. . . . The enemy took a calculated risk in massing installations right at the border, misjudging our reach. . . . he lost."[45]

In truth, however, the North Vietnamese in Operation Dewey Canyon, like their predecessors in Operations Delaware and Somerset Plain, only lost tactically. The first clue for the Marines should have been apparent when sizable enemy forces attacked practically every LZ and FSB as Marines boarded their helicopters to leave. That sendoff under fire in no way indicated a defeated enemy, and while the 9th Marines achieved all operational objectives, the self-congratulatory posturing among senior officers in I CTZ and MACV did not mesh with reality. Less than two months after the March 18 retrograde movement terminated, the 6th and 9th NVA Infantry Regiments, the 67th Artillery Regiment, and an assortment of support units had returned to the area and in no time were operating near full strength—the NVA still controlled the Valley of Death and would continue to do so unless permanent "boots on the ground" stopped them. Outsiders like the 9th Marines and the 101st Airborne Division could visit the valley, but they could not and did not remain. That was the inescapable Law of the Valley—it was "Charlie's Law," and he enforced the edict with unyielding determination at the point of a gun. Consequently, as in Operation Delaware a year earlier, any long-term success in Dewey Canyon proved to be negligible.

Nevertheless, as one Marine noted, "In the A Shau we kicked ass and took names." Indeed they had, but unfortunately U.S. policy did not allow them to hold the territory to consolidate the victory. The battle for the A Shau Valley would rage on another three years, and the only certainties to come out of Operation Dewey Canyon were the reinforced ideals of valor and sacrifice among the Americans who fought and died there. Paradoxically, one other certainty emerged—a grudging respect for a tough enemy. A tribute put forward by U.S. Marine advisors best captured the admiration of one warrior for another:

> A toast to the world's finest infantryman. Aggressive in the offense. Tenacious and dogged in the defense. A master of field fortifications, cover, and concealment. Ingenious in his use of supporting arms. Without peer in the application of surprise. Brilliant in his use of terrain. Always courageous and without fear. Defeated only in death. To that miserable little bastard, the NVA and Vietcong grunt.[46]

chapter 7

ELEVEN TIMES UP
HAMBURGER HILL

War is a crime. Ask the infantry and ask the dead.
—ERNEST HEMINGWAY

I n all wars, American soldiers have earned nicknames. In the Revolutionary War they were 'Minutemen' or 'Continentals'; in the Civil War they were 'Johnny Rebs' or 'Billy Yanks'; in World War I, 'Doughboys'; in World War II and Korea, 'GIs,' or in some cases 'Dogfaces.' But in Vietnam, American soldiers—especially the foot soldiers—were known affectionately as "Grunts." Where the term 'grunt' originated is a subject still debated, but the expression always evokes a sense of brotherhood among the American soldiers and marines who fought in Vietnam. Grunt does not so much call to mind a definition as an experience, best captured in a poignant reflection fashioned by veterans themselves:

> To the dirt-eating grunt, Vietnam was an endless succession of bummers. Besides the never-ending fear of death, we had to endure a host of miseries: merciless humps through a sun-scorched landscape packing eighty pregnant pounds, brain-boiling heat, hot house humidity, dehydration, heat exhaustion, sunburn, red dust, torrential rains, boot-sucking mud, blood-sucking leeches, steaming jungles, malaria, dysentery, razor-sharp elephant grass, bush sores, jungle rot, moaning and groaning, meals in green cans, armies of insects, fire ants, poisonous centipedes, mosquitoes, flies, bush snakes, vipers, scorpions, rats, boredom, incoming fire, body

bags, and a thousand more discomforts. Despite all this the grunt did his job well.[1]

If any single location in Vietnam best personified that "endless succession of bummers," arguably the A Shau Valley won hands down.

Grunts in the A Shau debated incessantly an abstract idiomatic metaphor which seemingly had little to do with the mission at hand, but in their conscious thoughts it surfaced repeatedly. They called it "old heads and FNGs." In the world of the "Eleven Bush"—military occupational specialty for the Army infantryman, sometimes referred to by cynical Marines as "Bulletstoppers"—life ebbed and flowed with the constant departure of experienced old friends and the arrival of green replacements, known to all as FNGs—fucking new guys. Although ARVN troops were in the war for extended periods, even for the duration, an American infantry squad's experience level always bounced up or down in a perpetual state of flux as men finished their one year tours, went on R&R, became ill, were wounded, or regrettably died in combat. Tours for infantry officers were even more chaotic since they normally rotated every six months. To the grunts, whether old head or FNG, a new sergeant or lieutenant meant on-the-job training in combat, a learning curve that could prove deadly. With good reason, the grunts saw it as an endless cycle of reinventing the wheel. Many of the old heads felt the same way about the revolving door ventures into the A Shau, a process that had been going on for six bloody years.

That revolving door opened once again on March 1, 1969. Even before the Marines fighting at the northern end of the valley had terminated Operation Dewey Canyon, the XXIV Corps commander, Lt General Richard Stillwell, decided to send the Screaming Eagles of the 101st Airborne Division into the southern A Shau. Famous for its exploits at Normandy and Bastogne during World War II, the division was considered to be one of the best in the U.S. Army, and this was to be its first raid back into the valley since Operation Somerset Plain in August, 1968. Only this time the concept took on a slightly different flavor. Dubbed Kentucky Jumper, the plan envisioned not just a raid, but the subjugation of the entire valley, emulating Civil War General Phillip Sheridan's Shenandoah Valley campaign in 1864—only in this operation the troopers would invade via helicopters instead of on horseback. The 101st vowed not leave the valley until the enemy's supply lines had been cut, his caches uncovered, and his base camps leveled. The intent was to make the A Shau "Screaming Eagle country." MACV, on the other hand, viewed the operation as crucial but temporary.

Specifically, the 2nd Brigade, in coordination with the 3rd Regiment, 1st ARVN Division, "was to conduct a combined airmobile operation in the southern A Shau Valley to interdict Route 548 at the Laotian border, locate, fix, and destroy enemy forces, equipment and caches, with emphasis on a rapid thrust to the border to block enemy withdrawal into Laos followed by a detailed systematic search in assigned battalion AOs to destroy caches and disrupt the enemy logistical system." In addition, the 2nd Brigade was ordered to "expand operations into northwest Quang Nam Province out to Route 614; locate, fix, and destroy enemy forces, equipment, and caches, and disrupt LOC of enemy forces operating in vicinity of Da Nang."[2]

The first segment of the plan, Operation Massachusetts Striker, kicked off on Saturday, March 1, when Air Force C-130 cargo planes from the 463rd Tactical Airlift Wing at Clark Air Base dropped devices off their back ramps called the M121, massive 10,000 pound bombs used to knock down large sections of jungle to create instant landing zones or firebases located along the valley's eastern wall. The 2nd Brigade then inserted a company from the 326th Engineer Battalion onto Hill 831 overlooking the valley. Under the protection of troopers of the 2nd Squadron, 17th Cavalry, they began construction of Fire Base Whip, the proposed forward base camp of the brigade. Unfortunately, the engineers encountered the same stretch of miserable weather that interfered with the 9th Marines' retrograde movement out of their FSBs near Route 922. With rain, fog, and low cloud ceilings blocking aerial resupply, the engineers and their security troops quickly ran out of food and supplies. For days they subsisted on rainwater they could catch in their ponchos. The weather delay not only disrupted the timing of the operation, but the extended pause, in conjunction with the 10,000-pound LZ-busting bombs, gave the cagy NVA units plenty of forewarning about what was to come and time to withdraw across the border.

On March 12 the cloud ceilings lifted just enough for the 2nd Brigade to execute a diversionary combat assault on Fire Support Base Veghel in the high foothills along Route 547. The mission was to re-open the FSB, abandoned the previous year, as a staging area for an unplanned move into the central A Shau to be led by the 1st Battalion, 502nd Infantry. Using three helicopter lifts, Charlie Company landed in late afternoon on Veghel, more than likely anticipating a "cold LZ"—no hostile fire. Instead, they came up against a reinforced rifle company from the NVA's 816th Battalion, 9th Regiment, dug in and well camouflaged on the old firebase. In an unusually sinister ambush, the enemy soldiers had set up rows of U.S. claymore mines around the LZ, all pointed upward. As the helicopters hovered to land, the claymores detonated simultaneously, peppering the choppers with hundreds of 1/8-inch diameter steel balls. All six helicopters were damaged and several of the pilots wounded, but they managed to land and discharge the Charlie Company troopers safely. Almost immediately the NVA assaulted in waves that only ended when the besieged Americans called in a napalm airstrike just 75 meters from their perimeter. Two of the canisters landed so close that many of the grunts had their hair singed by the heat, but the napalm stopped the assault. From there the ground battle raged throughout the rest of the day and night with enemy infantry and sappers crawling through the mud, throwing grenades and satchel charges into American positions; over half the men of 2nd Platoon were wounded. By the next morning the weather cooperated enough to permit another deadly airstrike against the NVA forces, allowing the rest of the battalion to land. After assessing the situation, the battalion commander, Lt Colonel Donald Davis, radioed back that "it seems that we've accidently jumped into a battalion base area." Fortunately, the NVA broke contact and scrambled west out of the immediate vicinity, leaving behind 20 of their dead. A day later the 1st of the 502nd took up the chase and pursued the NVA 816th on foot for over a week into the steep, heavily forested mountains along the east wall of the valley.[3]

On March 20 the 2nd Battalion, 501st Airborne Infantry combat assaulted into the southeast corner of the A Shau and began a sweep to the Laotian border. For the most part they encountered light resistance along the way from small NVA delaying elements of squad or platoon size. During the sweep Delta Company came upon a way-station hospital complex and drove off what apparently was a caretaker platoon. On the night of March 23, however, after the company established its night defensive position in the complex, the enemy platoon returned. About three hours after sunset the night defensive perimeter came under close-in automatic weapons and heavy RPG fire. During the initial volley, a rocket propelled grenade landed only a meter from the company command post. Even though the round had ignited and could have exploded at any moment, Specialist 4 Robert L. Wright, the company radio-telephone operator, ran through the incoming fusillade and threw his body on the round, smothering the fuse and rendering it harmless. Then, in constant exposure to direct hostile fire, he began carrying 81mm rounds to the mortar crews until the perimeter was threatened with penetration. He then immediately commenced firing into the enemy ranks with his weapon until the enemy withdrew. Thanks to Specialist 4 Wright's valor, the attack was repelled, leaving three sappers dead inside the perimeter and many more outside the wire. For his extraordinary heroism, Robert L. Wright was awarded the Distinguished Service Cross.[4]

While three American battalions patrolled and searched the southern A Shau, the 1st of the 502nd continued its dogged pursuit of the elusive NVA 816th Battalion. Over a period of a week they had only covered a straight-line distance of about eight kilometers, yet the chase took them up and down steep mountains and through thick jungle and dense stands of bamboo. The slow going was made even more so by frequent halts to engage snipers during the day or sappers who harassed the American positions each night. Finally, on March 14 the enemy stopped running and decided to make a stand on an obscure mountain with a large razorback finger running to the north. It was on that mountaintop and along the ridge that the 500 men of the 816th Battalion built a series of fortified bunkers connected by tunnels and trenches overlooking expertly cut fields of fire. On tactical maps the stronghold was identified as Hill 801, but the Vietnamese called it Dong A Tay—destined to become the largest single battle of Operation Massachusetts Striker.[5]

On March 19 Lt Colonel Donald Davis sent Alpha Company up the steep slopes of Dong A Tay's ridge for the first time, the assumption being that some kind of small enemy force occupied the high ground. As they climbed, Alpha Company anticipated contact with snipers or perhaps a squad, but in truth they had no idea how many NVA they faced. They ran into an impenetrable wall of machine gun and small arms fire; in the initial fight, Alpha's point platoon had two troopers killed and a number wounded. Dragging their dead and injured, the company had no choice but to retreat back to the foot of Hill 801. Following an hour's worth of airstrikes, Alpha tried again, only to be driven back down the ridge by a formidable NVA counterattack. Next, Bravo Company attempted a charge up the opposite side of the slope only to be repulsed with one man killed and nine wounded.

As the 1st of 502nd continued their assault against Dong A Tay, they encountered a series of deadly ambushes and bunkers. On March 21, while conducting a reconnaissance patrol near the northern tip of the ridge, Bravo Company's point element walked headlong into a hornet's nest of hostile sniper fire. The platoon leader, 1st Lieutenant William L. Dent, at once set up a defensive formation, ordering two machine guns to be brought forward. Suddenly the enemy opened fire with everything they had. Lt Dent moved out under the intense fusillade to retrieve several casualties. When a machine gunner fell wounded, Dent manned the weapon, providing suppressive fire as he directed his men to move back. The 22-year-old Hillsboro, North Carolina soldier operated the machine gun until it malfunctioned. Then he grabbed his M-16 rifle and continued to deliver lethal volleys on the enemy until he was wounded in the head. Having supervised the withdrawal of his men to safety, he followed but was wounded again while providing covering fire. Only after all of his men had reached a secure position did he relinquish command and later succumb to his wounds. During the vicious firefight, three other Bravo Company men died and four were wounded. By the end of the day, the Screaming Eagles began referring to the scene as "Bloody Ridge." For his extraordinary heroism at Bloody Ridge, Lt William L. Dent was posthumously awarded the Distinguished Service Cross.[6]

Over the next few days, casualties continued to mount for the 1st Battalion with little progress toward clearing Dong A Tay. Yet these remarkable young grunts, whether enlistee or draftee, assaulted up Bloody Ridge countless times without asking why. As they stared up at the steep ridge, all they saw was a tangled mass of jungle and trees, rocks and logs, all smashed and broken, a world of rubble providing subterranean hiding places for an enemy bent on killing them. But the men of the 1st of 502nd were single-minded in their determination to make it back up the ridge, and nobody, not even the whole NVA 9th Regiment lined up shoulder to shoulder was going to stop them. In a last ditch effort to break the enemy's back, Lt Colonel Davis called in airstrikes using 1,000-pound bombs with delayed fuses hoping to bust open the intricate network of bunkers and tunnels hiding the enemy soldiers who were killing his troopers. The plan worked—up to a point. The big MK-83 bombs caused the entire top of the ridge to collapse, so Alpha and Bravo Companies assaulted Hill 801 yet again, and yet again they were repulsed by the determined defenders hiding in the debris. One member of Alpha Company remembered the scene "as a truly terrifying experience. Even now when I think about it years later I get goose bumps on my arms, and the hair on the back of my neck stands up."[7]

By late afternoon on the 25th, 1st Battalion finally gained a foothold on the mountain and cleared Bloody Ridge. They had killed at least 90 enemy soldiers and wounded a great many others. In searching the area, the troopers found an enemy hospital on the south side of Hill 801. A document listing names of casualties treated showed that more than half of the 816th Battalion's 500 men had been either killed or wounded in the running battle with the Americans. The hard-fought victory in the A Shau had not come cheap for the men of the "O-Deuce." Before being lifted off Bloody Ridge on April 15, the 1st of the 502nd had suffered 30 killed and over 100 men wounded.[8] In addition to the casualties, the NVA's stand-and-fight tactics shocked the 2nd Brigade, causing the staff to re-evaluate the meaning behind the desperate defense of an insignificant piece of real estate like Bloody Ridge—real estate bought and paid for with American lives.[9]

By the beginning of April, a stretch of tolerable weather permitted the focus of Massachusetts Striker to shift to the original objectives in the southern A Shau. The 2nd Battalion, 327th Infantry boarded a fleet of helicopters and moved into the old airstrip at Camp A Shau, unoccupied since Special Forces Detachment A-102 pulled out in March, 1966. Simultaneously, two other battalions from the 2nd Brigade assaulted into the southeast corner of the valley, establishing Fire Bases Fury, Thor, Pike, and Lash.

As the battalions swept west and south on a reconnaissance-in-force, Colonel John Hoefling, the 2nd Brigade commander, analyzed enemy contacts and saw a disturbing pattern. He reasoned that the transition from fighting in rice paddies along the coastal plains of Thua Thien Province to the heavy jungles and steep mountains of the A Shau had not progressed smoothly. Since his troops were not accustomed to the terrain or to the miserable weather, the circumstances resulted in more friendly casualties than had been anticipated. Furthermore, enemy tactics in the A Shau were unlike those in the coastal plains, where contacts with the enemy were brief and fleeting in nature. On the coast, the NVA rarely attacked or even probed anything as large as a company perimeter unless by indirect fire from rockets or mortars. Not so in the Valley of Death. NVA units occupied well-built bunkers on critical terrain and probed constantly. The enemy also effectively employed snipers in trees, a trick the Screaming Eagles had not encountered before. Although the tactics employed by NVA units were initially a nasty surprise, 2nd Brigade troopers were able to overcome their early inexperience as mountain fighters and take full advantage of the superior firepower available to them. It amounted to the most dangerous kind of on-the-job training.[10]

In the southern A Shau the Screaming Eagles encountered light, sporadic contact with small elements from the NVA's 9th Regiment, but they increasingly found large caches of supplies and equipment hastily abandoned by the enemy. The 1st of the 502nd, re-equipped and supplied with numerous replacements, was airlifted from Bloody Ridge to a location along Route 614, a vital enemy-built supply route that connected the southern A Shau with northern Quang Nam Province. The grunts called it the Yellow Brick Road, named after the mythical thoroughfare in *The Wizard of Oz,* and it was there that they hit the jackpot. They discovered possibly the largest electronic equipment and medical supply cache found in the war—100 tons. The O-Deuce encountered virtually no resistance as they probed and uncovered 14 trucks, over 600 brand new SKS rifles, Chinese Communist radios and field telephones, large stocks of medicine, substantial quantities of assorted supplies and equipment, and documents indicating the location of another cache. Not to be outdone, the 2nd Battalion, 327th Infantry discovered a fleet of 20 Russian trucks, 2 bulldozers, and a fully equipped maintenance garage. And since most NVA units in the south end of the valley had retreated across the border into Laos, the Screaming Eagles took the opportunity to blow up and destroy large stretches of Route 548 and the Yellow Brick Road.[11]

In mid April during Operation Massachusetts Striker, the 101st's 2nd Brigade asked for help from a Project Delta recon team to scout along the valley floor just south of Ta Bat. That six-man team, led by Sergeant Charles F. Prevedel, inserted on April 16. The following day another Delta team leader, airborne on a VR mission, heard a single shout over the radio from Sgt Prevedel, an unusual occurrence since team leaders on the ground almost always talked in whispers. The airborne Delta man immediately realized that his friend was in trouble, so he remained in the area until he ran out of fuel, but there was no more contact with the team. Sgt Prevedel, Specialist 4 Douglas E. Dahill, SSgt Charles V. Newton, and three LLDB troopers were never heard from again. The A Shau had claimed six more warriors.[12]

As the 2nd Brigade continued to focus on the east wall and the southern end of the A Shau, a different unit from the 101st Airborne Division executed a covert mission against the always dangerous west wall. Employed in much the same way as the 3rd Marine Division used its clandestine Key Hole patrols, the 101st sent out six-man Long Range Reconnaissance Patrols, or LRRPs, from L Company, 75th Infantry (Ranger). In an ominous harbinger of things to come, on April 23 one of those teams inserted on the steep slopes of Hill 937, identified on maps as Dong Ap Bia. An experienced team, this one was accustomed to dealing with outrageously weird occurrences in the A Shau, but the one they were about to face took the cake. Travelling as quietly as possible through the heavy jungle with thick underbrush, layers of vines, and dense stands of bamboo, the six Americans discovered an extensive network of trails. As they watched, hundreds of enemy troops looking like a column of ants moved up the hill. The team leader had just begun to send a coded radio message when the low clouds opened up and a deluge of rain pounded the hidden Americans—A Shau weather had once again joined the battle. At that very moment a bolt of lightning struck, surging through every radio and piece of electrical equipment the men carried. The bolt touched off the electrical blasting caps on their claymore mines and sent each team member flying through the air. All were knocked unconscious, burned, and temporarily paralyzed. Miraculously, as they came to, a helicopter appeared overhead and lifted the disoriented LRRP team members out via jungle penetrator.[13] Was this a bad omen, a foreshadowing of what was to come? The Screaming Eagles who assaulted Dong Ap Bia on May 10 might have been inclined to think so.

Although ground combat in the sector during this period remained light, consisting primarily of actions against trail watchers and snipers, such was not the case for the airmen supporting the 2nd Brigade. Unlike the NVA ground forces, which had generally slipped across the Laotian border or moved north along the valley floor, the always dangerous enemy anti-aircraft positions, many of them mobile, remained in action. On May 2, a Navy A-7 Corsair II from the USS *Kitty Hawk* fell victim to ground fire during a late afternoon strike against a storage site at the south end of the A Shau. Fortunately, Air Force SAR helicopters rescued the pilot. A short time later, a Nail FAC flying a Cessna O-2 disappeared while performing reconnaissance over Base Area 607 along the southwest corner of the A Shau. It is believed that Lieutenant Phillip L. Mascari was shot down over this heavily defended NVA sanctuary; no trace of him or his aircraft has ever been found.[14]

When Operation Massachusetts Striker wrapped up on May 8, the 101st's 2nd Brigade box score was indeed impressive. They bagged 34 enemy trucks, 2 bulldozers, 2 armoured personnel carriers, 1 ambulance, 3 antiaircraft guns, 11,697 pounds of rice, thousands of rounds of ammunition, and tons of assorted medical supplies and electronic equipment. For the human box score the body count confirmed 259 NVA killed. The Americans lost 59 killed and 275 wounded. Between Operation Dewey Canyon in the north and Massachusetts Striker in the south, for the first time in the Vietnam War the historically significant supply and infiltration route of the North Vietnamese into the A Shau Valley was denied to them—at least temporarily.[15] While a significant number of enemy troops escaped up the valley to the north, two weeks after the 101st Airborne Division had moved on to another operation, NVA engineers re-entered the southern A Shau and repaired Routes 548 and 614. In spite of the well-planned, aggressively executed efforts of the 101st's 2nd Brigade, the Yellow Brick Road was back in business. The enemy's determination to continue using the A Shau Valley after the pounding they took was militarily baffling, but an even more mystifying development involved the NVA's sudden willingness to stand and fight as they had at Bloody Ridge. That change in tactics set the stage for what many military historians ultimately labelled the toughest single battle of the entire Vietnam War.

On May 10, Lt General Richard Stillwell, commander of the XXIV

Corps, kept the pressure on by initiating phase II of Kentucky Jumper, Operation Apache Snow, intended to destroy NVA bases in the northern end of the A Shau Valley. Apache Snow was the latest in a long series of attempts to neutralize the treacherous valley, which had proved a persistent thorn in the sides of both Generals Westmoreland and Abrams. So far, each effort met with results ranging in degree from temporarily successful to ineffectual. General Stilwell, however, resolved to succeed with his operation and amassed a potent force of three maneuver battalions from the 101st, two from the 1st ARVN Division, and backed up by the 1st and 2d Battalions, 9th Marines assigned the task of occupying the lower Da Krong Valley to prevent any NVA from slipping away from the northern A Shau via Route 922. His plan called for each of the five Army/ARVN battalions, under the operational control of Colonel Joseph B. Conmy, Jr., 3rd Brigade commander, to combat assault onto the valley's west wall by helicopter on May 10 and search its assigned sector for enemy troops and supplies. If a battalion made heavy contact with the NVA, the 3rd Brigade would reinforce it with one of the other units. In theory, the Americans could reposition their forces quickly enough via helicopter to keep the enemy from massing against any one unit. On the other hand, an American force encountering a large NVA unit would engage it in place while the reinforcing battalion flew in to cut off any retreat and assist as necessary. Unfortunately, the 101st Airborne Division and South Vietnamese units participating in Apache Snow only knew that in the Valley of Death they were in for a tough fight, but beyond that they had no first-hand knowledge about the terrain and little knowledge of the enemy's actual strength, units, or dispositions.[16]

Shortly after 7 a.m. on May 10, an armada of 65 Hueys from the 101st Aviation Group airlifted three battalions of the 3rd Brigade to LZs along the west wall of the A Shau. Operation Apache Snow had begun. The 2nd Battalion, 501st, landed on the southwest slope of Hill 1041, just two kilometers east of the Laotian border. Approximately four miles to the southeast, the 1st of the 506th, known by their regiment's World War II nickname, the Currahees, combat assaulted into another LZ. Halfway between those locations, UH-1s carrying three companies of the 3rd Battalion, 187th Infantry, known as the Rakkasans, landed along the northwest slope of Hill 937, annotated on topographical maps as Dong Ap Bia. The Rakkasans—Japanese for parachutists—served in the Pacific during World War II, distinguishing themselves in the Philippines and later in Korea. The 187th Regiment, along with the 3rd battalion, joined the 101st Airborne Division in 1964.

Dong Ap Bia, a stand-alone geological peak, dominated the north central valley and looked down on the old A Luoi airstrip, six kilometers to the east. Winding down from its highest peak were a series of ridges and fingers, the largest extending southwest to a height of 916 meters, another reaching south to a 900-meter peak. The entire mountain complex projected the unassailable image of a rugged, uninviting wilderness covered in double and triple canopy jungle, impassable thickets of bamboo, and dense, tangled underbrush. For the next ten days Hill 937 was to become the main battleground and focus of Apache Snow and was slated to earn the descriptively malevolent name, "Hamburger Hill." Prophetically, the Montagnard tribesmen in the area called it "the mountain of the crouching beast."

The opening day of Apache Snow, May 10, went surprisingly well for the 3rd of the 187th. Alpha, Charlie, and Delta Companies landed without opposition and began a reconnaissance-in-force up the lower slopes of Hill 937. When the battalion commander, Lt Colonel Weldon F. Honeycutt, arrived at 1044 a.m. he immediately requested that his reserve unit, Bravo Company, be brought in. With all his Rakkasans on the ground by early afternoon, he initiated a search in all directions around his command post (CP). The various patrols found evidence of enemy activity: large huts, carefully tended gardens, and well constructed bunkers, but no NVA. The scene reminded the men of their battle two weeks earlier on a remote mountain peak on the east wall of the A Shau: Dong Ngai Mountain. The troopers had found the same sort of NVA evidence there as they charged up the mountain unopposed before stumbling into prepared NVA bunkers and trenches bristling with machine guns. In taking the hill, the Rakkasans suffered 5 killed and 54 men wounded; the enemy lost over 100 killed. To the grunts, the comparison between Dong Ngai and Dong Ap Bia was undeniable.

The first actual contact on Hill 937 did not occur until late afternoon when the point element of Bravo Company came under fire. As the grunts were climbing the side of a small saddleback ridge, an RPG from the trail just ahead roared out of the trees and exploded with a deafening boom

beside the point man, lifting him off the ground and sending him sprawling down the ridge. When he came to, lying in a pulpy-wet matting that
stank of rot and cordite, Specialist 4 Ronald Storm heard the flat, metallic,
pang-pang-pang, the distinctive sound of AK-47 fire. Then he heard that
decidedly mournful cry of pain; three men were down, one of them
screaming over and over again, "I'm hit!" Ron Storm flattened against the
ground as small geysers of earth kicked up around him from the AK-47
fire. Just as his fire team moved up to his position he spotted four or five
enemy soldiers only a few meters away taking cover behind several large
trees. Storm and his point element pulled the pins on their grenades and
tossed them all at once toward the NVA. Following the huge explosion,
all that remained was a gaping hole in the jungle where the enemy soldiers
had been. With sporadic volleys of fire still coming their way, 2nd Platoon
moved back across the saddleback and down the mountain, while the Bilk
FAC orbiting overhead silenced the enemy positions with 20mm strafe

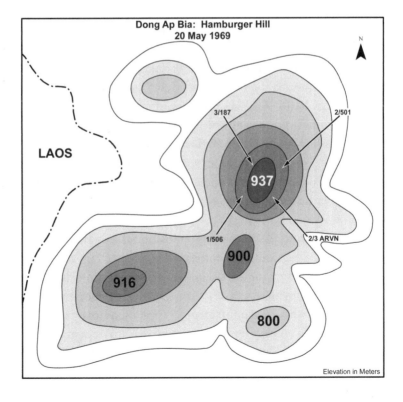

and MK-82 500-pound bombs from a pair of A-1 Skyraiders.[17]

As Lt Colonel Honeycutt's battalion settled into their night defensive positions, the keyed-up troopers tried to eat their C-rations, one hand eating while the other tried to fan away the swarms of flies that always appeared at meal times. And just prior to the 6:30 p.m. nightly harassment and interdiction (H&I) artillery fire that cut loose against suspected enemy positions on Hill 937, the Rakkasans listened to the strange jungle noises around them. Among those sounds came nightly calls from a bird identified as the Blue Eared Barbet. Croaking more like a frog, the unseen bird serenaded the grunts with a deep baritone noise that seemed to echo "reeee-up." Naturally the soldiers called it the Re-Up Bird, a sarcastic swipe at grunts who re-enlisted, or re-upped. The real entertainment occurred when the ever-present geckos, unique among lizards in their vocalizations, chimed in with what the grunts swore sounded like someone shouting "faaa-cuee," so of course they labeled the gecko as the "fuck-you" lizard. Whatever the reason, the weird symphony took their minds off the danger that lurked just outside their perimeter, and in the best traditions of gallows humor the infantrymen allowed themselves to be amused by the jungle refrain: REEE-UP . . . FAAAA-CUEE!

On the morning of the 11th, the battalion commander sent Alpha Company north toward the border and Bravo Company southeast up the northern face of Dong Ap Bia. The mountain loomed above Bravo, its spines and ravines intimidating, even in the soft morning light. Based on the brief fights from the day before, Lt Colonel Honeycutt expected light contact since he still believed that he was up against no more than an assortment of trail watchers and snipers. Surprisingly, there is no evidence that he was ever briefed on the hundreds of enemy sighted by the LRRP team back on April 23.

With the idea of trail watchers as opposition firmly fixed in his mind, Honeycutt pushed his company commanders to speed up the pace of the reconnaissance-in-force, but the troops moved slowly and deliberately, discovering telltale enemy signs at every turn. The first contact finally occurred at mid-afternoon when the point man in Alpha Company's 3rd Platoon spotted a single NVA soldier and opened fire. In return the platoon received several long bursts of deadly RPD machine gun fire. For the men of the 3rd Platoon it was impossible to think with any clarity. The groan and crash of mortars and the popping of rifle and machine gun fire rose to a crashing roar of noise, a stuttering clamor that actually hurt the eardrums. The second trooper in the point element, always called the "slackman," saw an enemy soldier a few meters away in a bamboo thicket aiming an RPG at the platoon. A deadly burst from his M-16 dropped the assailant. As the enemy soldier fell forward, he inadvertently fired his rocket grenade into the ground at his feet, setting off a blinding explosion. The amazed slackman watched in horror as parts of the enemy soldier rained down all over the area.[18]

On Hill 937 Bravo Company's 4nd Platoon also made contact, but with something significantly more hazardous than a few snipers. The point man, Specialist 4 Aaron L. Rosenstreich, called by everyone "Rosey," took fire from the dense brush just to his front. Unable to pinpoint a specific target, he fired several bursts into likely ambush spots. In the exchange of fire, an NVA soldier popped out of a spider hole only a few feet away, fatally wounding Rosey in the chest. At the same instant another NVA emerged from a second hole and fired an RPG round at almost point blank range. The intended target was Specialist 4 John E. McCarrell, a good soldier, well liked, and teased by all for being the company "flower child" because he always wore peace beads around his neck. The rocket hit McCarrell square in the midsection, the explosion also setting off the claymore mine in his rucksack. The resulting blast literally blew the 20-year-old soldier to pieces. In the commotion Specialist 4 Terry Larson raced forward firing his M-16; he fell face first on the trail, wounded in the head. At that point Specialist 4 Donald Mills ran up the trail firing his M-60 from the hip when the same NVA soldier who had shot Rosey showed himself once again and pumped several AK-47 rounds into Mills' chest. The wounded trooper went down for a few seconds, but filled with rage, he got back on his feet and charged his assailant with Terry Larson's M-16 he had picked up on the run. Bleeding profusely, Mills ran to the spider hole and emptied a full 20-round clip into the enemy soldier cowering there.[19]

Peppered with shrapnel wounds, his ears ringing from the horrendous noises of battle and his eyes streaming from smoke and cordite fumes, Lieutenant Charles Denholm crawled through the hell on the mountain to reach the dying Rosey Rosenstreich. As he moved, the platoon leader took fire from still another spider hole. Lt Denholm tossed two grenades with no apparent effect, then moved to his right through tall elephant grass. If ever there was reason to doubt the primeval thickness of the underbrush in the A Shau, Denholm's experience dispelled any such skepticism when an NVA soldier popped out of an unseen spider hole only a foot or so in front of him. There was no time to fire his M-16. Instead, Lt Denholm buried his knife deep in the man's throat and watched as the soldier collapsed back into the hole that was to be his grave.[20]

The battalion commander, radio call-sign "Blackjack," ordered the company to push through the ambush, but with three men dead and nine wounded, Bravo's commander led his battered men back down the mountain. Once they had moved a safe distance, the company forward observer called in a pair of orbiting AH-1 Cobra gunships to engage the enemy positions. The Cobra, the Army's first helicopter designed specifically for attack, sported a lethal package of 7.62mm mini guns, 40mm grenade launchers, and two pods of 2.75-inch folding fin rockets with either high explosive, white phosphorous, or flechette warheads. As the two Cobras, referred internally within the 101st as Aerial Rocket Artillery (ARA), set up overhead, they mistook the battalion CP for the enemy position, and before anyone could wave them off they fired six rockets into the friendly location. The deadly explosions killed one American and wounded 35 others, including the battalion commander and most of his staff.[21] The incident marked the end of the second of 11 costly days for the 3rd of the 187th on the mountain of the crouching beast.

By early morning on May 12, Lt Colonel Honeycutt had already flown to a nearby firebase where a surgeon removed a piece of shrapnel lodged in his back from the ARA incident the day before, bandaged him, and sent the impatient battalion commander back to duty on Hill 937. Sore and irritable, Blackjack was anxious to get Alpha, Bravo, and Charlie Companies on the move, although nobody knew exactly what size force they were facing. Based on Honeycutt's assertive personality, most men in the battalion viewed their commander as "Gung Ho," while some considered him overly aggressive; many of his contemporaries saw him as profane and abrasive. But all who knew him had to concede that Honeycutt was a dynamic combat leader. A mustang, Honeycutt enlisted in the Army at age 16 and in 5 years advanced from private to captain. In the Korean War he commanded a rifle company in the 187th Regimental Combat Team commanded by Brig. General William C. Westmoreland, an association that developed into a lifelong friendship. Earning the nickname "Tiger" for his aggressiveness, he drove his subordinates hard and some claimed ruthlessly.[22]

Honeycutt's reputation preceded him into the battalion. When he took command of the 3rd of the 187th, he did not disappoint. He was disgusted to find that some of his officers were not in the field with their troops but were instead remaining in the rear areas. He quickly changed that and got everyone's attention by ordering every officer into the field, telling them, "From now on this battalion is gonna fight. This battalion is gonna go out and find the enemy and kill him. This bullshit of running and hiding is over."[23]

The hard-charging Honeycutt pushed his troopers out again on the 12th along the finger-like ridges leading to the summit, convinced now that he might be up against an entire enemy company defending the summit of Dong Ap Bia—a force that he outnumbered and should be able to defeat. Some of the battalion staff members were not so sure. Documents captured the day before indicated that the NVA 29th Regiment had entered the area in April and was operating somewhere in that part of the A Shau. Considered one of the best fighting units in the North Vietnamese Army, the 29th Regiment, according to intelligence estimates, possessed around 1,800 men; its confirmed presence on Hill 937 could represent both a tactical and strategic danger.

Throughout the day, enemy snipers harassed Alpha and Bravo Companies as they moved slowly up the steep mountain slopes. When the battalion commander sent Charlie and Delta Companies to the east, they ran up against the same old terrible pattern of interlaced bunkers and sniper fire, necessitating a slow, bitter advance punctuated with the inevitable losses. Much of the day was spent trying to establish a second LZ on the mountain just to the rear of Bravo Company, and during that effort a Huey carrying the construction engineers was hit by a single RPG and crashed into the trees. Men from Bravo Company fought their way to the crash site and eventually rescued the six injured engineers and four crewmembers while Bilk FACs directed multiple airstrikes and Cobra gunship attacks against the west face of Dong Ap Bia.[24]

Dong Ap Bia was not the only hot spot in the valley. At 3:30 on the morning of May 13 at Fire Support Base Airborne on the east wall only seven kilometers from Hill 937, the NVA 806th Battalion and the K12 Sapper Battalion launched one of the bloodiest and most vicious sapper attacks of the entire Vietnam War. A barrage of 82mm mortars and RPG rounds crashed into the firebase, a complex housing three artillery batteries and a security company from the 2nd Battalion, 501st Infantry. After infiltrating through the concertina wire on the north side of the perimeter, the sappers systematically stormed across the northern portion of the firebase, tossing satchel charges and grenades into the bunkers they encountered. Other sappers followed closely behind, firing their AK-47s into the bunkers, literally executing the wounded GIs. The fire directions center of C Battery, 2nd Battalion, 319th Artillery, located in an exposed Conex container, was hit by an RPG round and the men inside began screaming and moaning. One NVA soldier stood on the south side of the container and fired 30 to 40 rounds into the Conex. Both the battery commander and the battery 1st sergeant were killed in this action.

With the first incoming rounds, Staff Sergeant George W. Parker rallied his mortar crews and commenced firing illumination and high-explosive rounds on the hostile fire that rained around his mortar emplacement. As he sprinted through the intense barrage and made his way to warn his platoon leader of the ground attack on two sides of the compound, he was knocked down three times by incoming explosions. At that point an RPG round struck one of the mortar emplacements and knocked it out. Running to the position, SSgt Parker immediately set up the damaged mortar tube and started firing on the enemy by holding it against his shoulder while another man dropped rounds down the tube. During the intense action a satchel charge thrown at his position exploded, wounding all three men in the mortar pit and knocking George Parker senseless. After coming to, he gave first aid to his men and continued fighting, often exposing himself to the enemy barrage to obtain resupplies of ammunition. On one of his trips to the munitions stockpile, through withering fire, he was attacked by four sappers armed with rifles and satchel charges, and he took them out with a well-thrown grenade at point-blank range. For his extraordinary heroism, SSgt George W. Parker was awarded the Distinguished Service Cross.[25]

The one-and-a-half-hour battle ended at first light, revealing a gut-wrenching scene. Amidst the wreckage, debris, and devastation, the exhausted defenders counted 40 enemy bodies scattered around FSB Airborne. They also counted their own losses: 22 of their friends killed and 61 wounded, along with 5 howitzers damaged or destroyed.[26] The debacle at FSB Airborne served to confirm the suspicions of some senior Screaming Eagle officers, namely that the NVA had brought in crack units and intended to mount a vigorous defense to hold the northern A Shau Valley.

Except for the shocking news about Fire Support Base Airborne, the situation for the 3rd of the 187th remained unchanged on the 13th, as the companies conducted operations in their immediate areas, still attempting to slug their way up the rugged terrain. Lt Colonel Honeycutt, however, had again revised his estimate of the enemy force upward. Considering the intensity of the resistance, he now concluded that he was facing an entire NVA battalion. The brigade commander, Colonel Joseph Conmy, thought otherwise. In light of the tragedy at FSB Airborne and more analysis by his intelligence staff, Conmy estimated that the Rakkasans were outmanned on Hill 937 and facing at least three battalions of the NVA 29th Regiment. A long-held military axiom counseled that an attacking force required a three-to-one favorable force ratio against defenders. For Tiger Honeycutt the ratio was reversed; his single battalion attacked three NVA battalions dug in on high ground. Shortly after noon, Conmy ordered Lt Colonel John W. Bowers and his 1st Battalion of the 506th to force-march their way four kilometers north to reinforce the struggling 3rd of the 187th.

Throughout the day the enemy contested Rakkasan movements with small arms, automatic weapons, RPGs, and mortars from well-entrenched positions. The battalion returned fire and saturated the western mountain slope with artillery and tactical airstrikes, but even that concentrated dose of firepower had little apparent effect. In mid-afternoon, an enemy RPG brought down a medevac helicopter attempting to extract Delta Company's wounded. The men of Delta Company stood by helplessly as Medevac 927 burst into flames, burning to death the six men trapped inside. There were other casualties that day as well. During firefights on the 13th, the battalion lost 4 more killed and 33 men wounded.[27]

The first concerted attempt by the Rakkasans to take Hill 937 occurred on May 14. The plan called for Delta Company to attack from the north, Bravo Company would attack from the west, and Charlie Company would advance along a ridge just to the south of Bravo. All companies were supported by artillery prep. Yet by 9 a.m. each company was engaged in heavy contact and sustaining casualties, as it was rapidly becoming one of those days when nothing went right. Bravo Company's lead platoon did manage to reach the top of Dong Ap Bia but was driven back by murderously heavy fire when enemy infantry swarmed down the mountain and attacked from three different directions. With 2 dead and 13 wounded, the 3rd Platoon was forced to pull back. Charlie Company fared no better. As four troopers from the 2nd Platoon carried a wounded buddy down the steep slope, an enemy soldier fired an RPG into their midst. The rocket impacted directly against the man being carried and blew him to pieces; it also killed three of the four stretcher-bearers and severely wounded the fourth. Adding insult to injury, two Cobra gunships, orbiting above a platoon from Alpha Company carrying wounded men down the mountain, mistook them for the enemy and raked the column with mini-gun fire, seriously wounding four troopers. And on the northern face Delta Company was ambushed by an NVA infantry platoon. After the 20-minute firefight, where the crackle and yammer of fire was a continuous, pulsing roar, Delta suffered 10 men wounded. By the end of the 14th, the "battling bastards of Dong Ap Bia" ended up digging into night defensive positions at approximately where they had started that morning. For their efforts they counted 9 of their friends killed and another 74 wounded.[28]

Just before dark, Colonel Joe Conmy's command and control chopper slipped into the LZ near Lt Colonel Honeycutt's CP. After describing the day's actions and explaining that the NVA were moving fresh troops in from Laos each night, Blackjack told his boss, "We're in a goddamn fight here, Joe—and I mean a fight!"

"I agree," the brigade commander said to his friend. "This is the toughest fight I've seen in three years over here. If there's been a tougher one, I don't know what it is." While he concurred with Conmy's assessment, oddly enough Tiger Honeycutt's frustration and anger about the raging battle were not directed toward the enemy but rather toward the 1st Battalion, 506th Infantry. As far as he was concerned, they were not moving fast enough to join the critical fight. The Currahees had only covered 1,500 meters in 40 hours and still had 2,500 meters to go.[29]

During the night, various Rakkasan patrols reported a large group of enemy soldiers moving into a heavily wooded draw halfway down the mountain. Hoping to be unobserved through the persistent morning fog, the NVA force apparently planned to hide in the draw and then attack the rear of the Rakkasans as they assaulted up the mountain. Honeycutt immediately recognized their intention. At first light on May 15 he ordered Alpha and Bravo Companies to begin advancing at a deliberate pace, but when they reached a point roughly halfway up the mountain they were to stop, face to the rear, and take up positions facing the draw. The men of the two under-strength companies peered through the wet murk of the jungle, straining to see until their eyeballs ached, all the while sweating buckets of water and listening to the noisy cries of birds, praying that it wasn't NVA snipers signaling to each other. Honeycutt had guessed right. The surprised NVA walked into a wall of hot lead, and their only recourse was to retreat back down the mud-slick trail into the draw. An orbiting Bilk FAC took over and expended a two-ship of Marine F-4s from Squadron VMFA-115 at Da Nang, call sign Blade. Dropping 500-pound high-drag bombs and multiple canisters of BLU-32 napalm, the F-4s were followed by a pair of Cobras who beat up the target area for 20 minutes. When it was over, an entire NVA company lay sprawled on the ground.[30]

In the brutal fighting that afternoon, Bravo managed to move to within 150 meters of the crest of Hill 937, but the momentum of the assault totally collapsed when another Cobra mistakenly attacked the unfortunate company, yet again killing 2 men and wounding 19 others, including the company commander. When a replacement commander arrived, the battered and dejected men of Bravo were infuriated when Lt Colonel Honeycutt ordered the company to renew the attack. The troopers hated him for it, but Tiger Honeycutt was faced with the draconian law of desperate choices, harsh alternatives that were really no alternatives at all. When the replacement company commander looked into the faces of the men of Bravo, he immediately recognized the signs that they were coming apart: demoralizing fatigue, dulled, vacant gazes, and flashes of unfocused anger—directed against officers and NCOs rather than the enemy. They only managed to advance a few meters before the enemy launched a large counterattack and drove them back down the hill.

The members of Alpha Company, only 75 meters from the crest, also ran into a hornet's nest. Within a matter of a few minutes, half of the 4th Platoon was wounded and out of action. As the men crawled away from the terrible place they found themselves in—a place resembling a moonscape—they observed only smashed terrain full of splintered trees and the mangled remains of a ridge full of shell holes and bomb craters filled with water. For one of the exhausted and demoralized platoon leaders, the sheer decibel level of the noise associated with the sounds of small arms fire and explosions was so loud he could not even hear Blackjack's frantic voice over the company radio urging him to move forward. It was not to be. The epiphany for the gung ho battalion commander occurred when an RPG exploded in his own CP, wounding him yet again in the back, and yet again he refused medical evacuation. That night the 3rd of the 187th took stock of the day's surreal events: 1 soldier KIA and 45 WIA. Additionally, friendly fire from the Cobra attack had killed 2 more and wounded 20.[31]

The Rakkasans held fast on the 16th and 17th, waiting for the 1st of the 506th to arrive at the south base of Dong Ap Bia. During that period the men of both battalions were issued flak jackets since so many of the troopers had suffered shrapnel wounds to the midsection and upper body. Additionally, nearby artillery batteries began firing CS tear gas rounds into enemy bunker complexes hoping to force the defenders into the open. The effort only had marginal effect since soldiers from the NVA 29th Regiment already had gas masks. Oddly enough, most of the Americans did not; they were hastily issued along with the flak jackets.

During the temporary lull, reporters began hitching rides on the choppers that made frequent flights into the LZ near Lt Colonel Honeycutt's CP. Most of them were intelligent and respectful, but in his definitive book, *Hamburger Hill,* Samuel Zaffiri tells the story of one reporter who apparently irritated Tiger Honeycutt to distraction. When he arrived at the CP, one longhaired, bearded man shouted, "Where's the war? I thought there was a fucking war going on out here."

Peevishly, Honeycutt answered, "Come on, I'll show you where the fuckin' war is. Follow me." With the reporter and his photographer in tow, the irritated Blackjack had only walked about 75 yards when an enemy soldier opened up on them with a machine gun. When an RPG round exploded in the trees overhead, the two newsmen jumped to their feet and scrambled back to the CP. Honeycutt called after them, "Hey, don't you want to see the war?"

Running back down the trail, the reporter's pithy reply was, "Fuck the war!"[32]

The morning of May 18 found the Currahees positioned on the south face of Dong Ap Bia with the 3rd of 187th ready to move against the north face. By noon both battalions were in heavy contact. The Rakkasans' Delta Company bore the brunt of the fighting, with every officer in the company killed or wounded. To make matters worse, in the confusion another Cobra mistakenly opened fire on Bravo Company, killing one and wounding four. Angry beyond belief, Lt Colonel Honeycutt ordered all Cobras out of the area.

So far in the brutal fighting, Alpha and Bravo Companies had lost 50 percent of their original strength, while Charlie and Delta Companies had lost a staggering 80 percent. Then, at mid-afternoon a torrent of rain turned Hill 937 into a veritable quagmire, and with no footing due to the mud, both battalions pulled back to avoid taking more casualties. As it was, the Rakkasans suffered 13 KIA and 60 wounded; the ARA attack accounted for another trooper lost and four wounded. The Currahees lost 4 killed and 27 wounded. In view of the casualties and the slow going, that same night the 101st Airborne Division's commander, Major General Melvin Zais, decided to reinforce the effort by air assaulting a company of the 2nd Battalion, 506th Infantry, and a battalion from the 1st ARVN Division to assist the depleted but still scrappy 3rd of the 187.[33]

Although reinforcements might have been necessary, throughout the grueling battle there was no denying the extraordinary valor exhibited by the Rakkasans. The story of Specialist 4 Nicholas W. Schoch nobly illustrates the point and underscores the devotion and love the embattled troopers had for each other, a love that caused them to react to combat in unexpected ways.

A Napa Valley native, Nikko Schoch was an avowed conscientious objector and only averted jail when he agreed to enter the Army as a medic. That decision led to an assignment with Bravo Company, 3rd of the 187th on Hill 937, and his actions on that deadly hill saved numerous lives. Early in the battle his company engaged an entrenched North Vietnamese force, and Specialist Schoch rushed to the area of fiercest fighting and began to administer medical aid to the wounded. Once there, he moved to aid three seriously wounded men lying in an area completely devoid of cover. While treating one of the men, he became the target of a sniper in a nearby tree. He saw the bullets impact the ground next to him, then

heard the shots—a muffled pop that sounded like a crushed paper bag.
Taking the weapon of the man he was treating, conscientious objector
Nikko Schoch realized that the only way to save his buddy would be to
kill the sniper. He did. On May 13 his unit assaulted the enemy stronghold and again came under a heavy concentration of hostile fire. Enemy
machine guns opened up with short, well aimed bursts, while bits of
branches and leaves kept falling around the medic. As Specialist Schoch
was applying first aid to the wounded of the lead element, the medic in
another platoon sustained serious wounds and could not breathe. In the
open, and braving heavy fire from all directions, Schoch coolly and skillfully performed a tracheotomy on his wounded comrade who resumed
breathing and was evacuated. Later as he was treating a casualty, an enemy
fragmentation grenade fell near him and the wounded man. Nikko instantly grabbed the grenade and threw it into a nearby bomb crater and
then shot the enemy soldier who had thrown the grenade. After complet-
ing treatment, he carried the American through a furious firefight to an
LZ for evacuation. On the following day Specialist Schoch treated and
evacuated four more wounded men from his company who had fallen
near the summit of Dong Ap Bia. Then, on May 15 as the battle for the
hill still raged, hostile fire downed a Huey carrying ammunition. Despite
the fact that the burning helicopter might explode at any moment, 21-
year-old Nikko Schoch ran to the wreckage and retrieved an unconscious
survivor and carried him through a barrage of sniper fire to safety where
he administered first aid, saving the man's life. For the remainder of the
day and until May 18, constantly under fire and with no sleep, he took
charge of medical treatment and evacuation on the company's emergency
landing zone. Specialist 4 Nicholas W. Schoch's extraordinary heroism
earned him the admiration of everyone in Bravo Company as well as a
much deserved Distinguished Service Cross.[34]

Just as the battle for Hill 937 reached a climax, another battle, this one
of words, erupted on the home front. Dialog about the war had remained
relatively quiet since the beginning of the year, with what attention there
was focused on the Paris peace talks. In the media, casualty lists and war
stories were routinely buried somewhere on an inside page; for the American public, the Vietnam War seemed to have lost its immediacy. That was
about to change.

On May 18, a 23-year-old Associated Press war correspondent named Jay F. Sharbutt had choppered into the mountain of the crouching beast for a first-hand look. By no means was this young man like the flaky, reckless war-junkie journalists that the Rakkasans had encountered since May 14. He interviewed the generals and the colonels, but mostly he listened to the grunts and wrote about them. Rather than regurgitate a series of bland facts, dates, and statistics, Sharbutt put a human face on the life and death struggle in the A Shau. Unlike many of the reporters who penned innocuous descriptions of the fight in routine terms, Jay Sharbutt seemed to have an insightful Ernie Pyle quality about him, a trait that encouraged the young troopers to open up. In telling the story, Sharbutt's dispatch struck a nerve back in the world, and the opening lines of his article captured the undivided attention of countless readers:

> The paratroops came down from the mountain, their green shirts darkened with sweat, their weapons gone, their bandages stained brown and red—with mud and blood. Many cursed Lt.Col. Weldon Honeycutt, who sent three companies Sunday to take this 3000-foot mountain just a mile east of Laos and overlooking the shell-pocked A Shau Valley. They failed and they suffered. "That damn Blackjack won't stop until he kills every one of us," said one of the 40 to 50 101st Airborne troopers who was wounded.[35]

Many readers were shocked yet mesmerized by Sharbutt's frank characterization of the battle, but others, mostly staunch hawks, were outraged. They accused Sharbutt of being a tool of the anti-war liberal press, that he had sensationalized his dispatch by employing an inflammatory term like "meat-grinder" and for derogatorily referring to the location as "Hamburger Hill." Those accusations were patently false; the reporter never used either term in his article. In all probability the name Hamburger Hill originated with the grunts of the 3rd Battalion, 187th Infantry, the very men who fought and died taking the hill. For them it had indeed been a meat-grinder, informally memorialized on May 20 when a weary trooper scrawled "Hamburger Hill" on the bottom of an empty C-ration carton and nailed it to a shattered tree trunk on top of Hill 937—members of the press undoubtedly picked up on the term and included that unflattering sobriquet in their dispatches. Another grunt cut to the very heart of the matter when he added a P.S. to the sign: "Was it worth it?"

At least one influential person did not think so. A day later Edward M. Kennedy delivered on the Senate floor a stinging condemnation of the battle on Dong Ap Bia, calling it "both senseless and irresponsible to continue to send our young men to their deaths to capture hills and positions that have no relation to ending this conflict. . . . The assault on "Hamburger Hill" is only symptomatic of a mentality and a policy that requires immediate attention. American boys are too valuable to be sacrificed for a false sense of military pride."[36]

While the controversial uproar continued to play out in Washington, on May 20 four allied battalions—three American and one ARVN—finally stormed Dong Ap Bia and secured Hamburger Hill—on the 11th try. The weary troopers inspected some of the log and earth bunkers abandoned by the retreating enemy. Remarkably strong and well built, the dugouts all had that intolerable stink the NVA always seemed to impregnate everything with: a smell of cordite, rotting fish, and untended urinals. A number of dead soldiers lay around the crest, a sign that the enemy had left in a hurry without taking their fallen men with them, as was standard practice for them.

By actual body count the enemy lost 633 soldiers killed, although considerably more probably lost their lives during the battle. A prisoner indicated an 80 percent casualty rate for the NVA 29th Regiment, rendering it ineffective as a combat unit. The Screaming Eagles, however, also paid a steep price. Hamburger Hill cost the Americans 72 killed and 372 wounded. The Rakkasans, the battling bastards of Dong Ap Bia, incurred the lion's share of the casualties with 36 KIA and 329 WIA.[37]

On May 21 a fleet of 101st helicopters lifted the entire 3rd Battalion, 187th Infantry off Hamburger Hill and transported them to Eagle Beach, an in-country R&R center located right on the warm waters of the South China Sea. But the Rakkasans were in pitiful shape: twelve days on Hill 937 in constant combat; boots coming apart, beards, fatigues hanging on them in rags, indescribably filthy and haggard. They had arrived at the battle with all their hope and élan, valor and firepower, and been cut down, and others had come to fill their depleted ranks and been cut down in turn. Arguably the toughest engagement of the Vietnam War, the physical battle for the mountain of the crouching beast—Hamburger Hill—was over. Justifying the victory was a different battle with a different beast, because the tactical success of the battle was lost amid shouts of "senseless slaughter"—some of those shouts from reporters, some from politicians, and some from the men of the 3rd Battalion, 187th Infantry. Specifically in response to Senator Kennedy's Hamburger Hill speech, General Zais commented:

> He's performing to the best of his ability as a Senator in Washington . . . but I know for sure he wasn't here [during the battle] . . . That hill was in my area of operations, that's where the enemy was, that's where I attacked him. If I find him [the enemy] on any other hill in the A Shau, I assure you I'll attack him.[38]

Operation Apache Snow officially terminated on June 7 but unfortunately ended on a sour note. The new commander of the 101st Airborne Division, Major General John M. Wright, created a public relations firestorm when on June 5 he quietly pulled all troops off Dong Ap Bia and abandoned it to the enemy. While Generals Zais, Stillwell, and Abrams proclaimed another unparalleled victory based on kill ratios of 10 to 1, the American public reacted in a totally negative way, just as they had following the Tet Offensive in 1968. And just as in 1968, the Army did not understand the public and political reaction to staggering casualty lists followed by unilateral withdrawal from the battlefield. Instead of holding or neutralizing territory paid for in American blood, MACV had reverted once again to a strategy of attrition, and the Army found it increasingly difficult to explain the strategy to outsiders—especially the media. Yet that approach, represented by the awful expenditure of lives at Hamburger Hill, clearly exceeded the value the American people attached to the war in Vietnam. As one Nixon administration official privately told a reporter, "I don't understand why the military doesn't get the picture. The military is defeating the very thing it most wants—more time to gain a stronger hand." Adding to the critical chorus, a senior political advisor to the Commander-in-Chief, Pacific, astutely explained the situation this way: "This is the tragedy of Vietnam—we were fighting for time rather than space. And time ran out."[39]

Whether fighting for time or a questionable strategy, the Screaming Eagles resolutely continued their campaign in the A Shau. On June 8 they initiated Operation Montgomery Rendezvous, the final push in Kentucky Jumper, the phased pacification of the valley. They signaled their intention to stay when engineers from the 27th Engineer Battalion built a graded road all the way from the division headquarters at Camp Eagle to the valley floor. The 326th Engineer Battalion also rebuilt the old airstrip at Ta Bat; after only 54 hours the strip was operational and the first C-7 Caribou landed in a cloud of red dust. The campaign continued when, on June 20, a procession of 80 tracked vehicles, both tanks and armored personnel carriers, snaked along the road to Ta Bat, the first U.S. armor of the war to enter the Valley of Death. During this period contact with the enemy remained sporadic, but NVA units were still operating in the area, as evidenced by several vicious sapper attacks against Fire Bases Berchtesgaden and Currahee, resulting in 11 Americans killed and 54 wounded.[40]

Unfortunately, the military undermined its own credibility by chronicling the A Shau campaign with less than honest appraisals. In assessing the battle for the A Shau, military documents touted a long-term, sweeping victory. Apparently the authors of those documents put on their rose-colored glasses and wrote the accounts their bosses wanted to read, not the reports that detailed the unvarnished truth. One Project CHECO report, for example, completely misrepresented Operations Massachusetts Striker and Apache Snow by claiming that the 101st Airborne Division had "occupied the valley so effectively that large NVA units in Laos could not break through the allied shield to reach Hue or the coastal lowlands. This allied conquest of the A Shau Valley thus ranked as one of the most successful campaigns of the Vietnam War."[41] Neither claim was accurate.

Official reports notwithstanding, the furor over Hamburger Hill had just begun to cool when yet another media event rocketed the battle back into the headlines. The June 27 issue of *Life* magazine featured an article with photographs of 241 men killed in Vietnam during the preceding weeks. The article also included a short letter written by a soldier on Hamburger Hill: "I am writing in a hurry," he wrote to his parents. "I see death coming up the hill." In reality only five of the pictures were of men who had died during the battle, but many Americans misinterpreted the quote and assumed that all of the 241 pictures were of troopers killed storming Dong Ap Bia. The story was even harder to digest by the unexplained evacuation of Hill 937. The American public's outrage was most definitely exacerbated by the publication of those photographs, so much so that military historian Shelby Stanton came to the conclusion that the *Life* article, like the 1968 Tet Offensive, constituted a major turning point in the flagging support for the Vietnam War. General Westmoreland added more fuel to the controversy over Hamburger Hill when he noted, "Vietnam was the first war ever fought without any censorship. Without censorship, things can get terribly confused in the public mind."[42]

Until press coverage about Hamburger Hill made it infamous, most Americans had never heard of the A Shau Valley. Now the Valley of Death became firmly rooted in the public lexicon, forever linked to Senator Kennedy's charges of a senseless and irresponsible battle. The White House obviously felt the pressure because shortly after the appearance of the *Life* article, General Creighton Abrams was ordered to avoid such large-scale battles, ostensibly to hold down casualties. At the same time, President Nixon instituted what came to be known as "Vietnamization," a strategy whereby the fighting would gradually be turned over to the South Vietnamese. As a first step, on July 8 Nixon ordered an immediate drawdown of 25,000 U.S. troops, to be followed in December by 35,000 more. By November the entire 3rd Marine Division had been withdrawn to Okinawa, a move that dramatically reduced MACV's ability to conduct operations in the A Shau.[43]

While bureaucrats tinkered with the intricacies of Vietnamization in Washington, the 101st Airborne Division's 3rd Brigade pressed on with Operation Montgomery Rendezvous. The toughest fight of the campaign occurred on July 11 at Hill 996, roughly four kilometers southwest of Hamburger Hill. That morning Lt Colonel Arnold C. Hayward led the 1st Battalion, 506th Infantry up the mountain against a well-entrenched NVA bunker complex. Veterans of the battle for Hill 937, the Currahees inched forward as RPG explosions and green tracers filled the air. Seemingly nothing ever changed in the battle for the A Shau. It was always monotonously, cruelly the same. The forward observer, Lieutenant Leonard E. Griffin, had just linked up with Hayward and his radio operator, Private First Class Curtiss Fernhoff, when all three were hit by a volley of AK-47 fire. The three wounded men managed to crawl behind a log where a medic dressed their wounds before moving off to aid others. Lapsing in and out of consciousness, the three men occasionally talked to each other in whispers, but mostly they wondered why they were alone in the dense jungle and where the rest of the Currahees were. All conversation for Lt Griffin ended abruptly when an RPG round exploded a few feet away, with a piece of shrapnel cutting his left ear and rendering him partially deaf for several hours. At some point NVA soldiers brazenly walked through the underbrush shooting any wounded Americans they found. While Lt Griffin played dead, an enemy soldier murdered Lt Colonel Hayward and PFC Fernhoff and kept on walking. In the hours that followed, Griffin remembered a strange, pungent smell, the odor of a large quantity of blood, the smell of death. It had an odd stench to it, an acute copperish, metallic smell, and in the heavy jungle air it reeked of putrefaction, damp-rot, and cordite. When Len Griffin came to after passing out a second time, it was dark. He managed to crawl about 20 yards when he heard American voices; he had survived in the Valley of Death.[44]

At approximately 6 p.m. on July 11, the men of Bravo Company moved up Hill 996 with a vengeance after hearing that the enemy was killing their wounded buddies. Valor and retribution were the orders of the day. As Specialist 4 Gordon R. Roberts' platoon approached the enemy positions, it was suddenly pinned down by heavy automatic weapons fire from camouflaged fortifications on the steep slope above them. The opening volley was so fierce that five members of the platoon were wounded. Seeing his unit immobilized and in danger of failing in its rescue mission, Specialist Roberts crawled rapidly in driving rain toward the closest enemy bunker where the RPD machine gun stopped, started again, and the firing rose to a sudden roar, so loud that no human shouts could be heard above the din. With complete disregard for his safety, he leaped to his feet and charged the bunker, firing as he ran. But there wasn't just one bunker. He saw another behind it to the right and a third stepped back to the left— this was death in echelon. Despite the concentrated enemy fire directed at him, 19-year-old Roberts silenced the two-man bunker with a long burst from his M-16. Without hesitation he continued his one-man assault on a second bunker. As he neared the log and earthen position, a well-placed burst of enemy fire knocked his rifle from his hands. Roberts picked up an M-16 dropped by a comrade and charged forward, killing the defenders in the bunker at point blank range. He continued his assault against a third bunker and destroyed it with well-thrown hand grenades. Even though

Specialist Roberts was now cut off from his platoon and totally alone, he continued his onslaught against a fourth enemy emplacement. He then fought through a hail of tracers to join elements of the adjoining company which had also been pinned down by the enemy fire. Although continually exposed to hostile fire, the Ohio native remained in the open and assisted in moving wounded personnel from exposed positions to an evacuation area before returning to his unit at approximately 10 p.m. For conspicuous gallantry and intrepidity in action at the risk of his life above and beyond the call of duty, Specialist 4 Gordon R. Roberts was awarded the Medal of Honor.[45] When the battle of Hill 996 ended the next morning, 20 of Gordon Roberts' buddies lay dead and 26 more wounded. And it came as no surprise when both opponents followed to the letter the time-honored script for battles in the A Shau—shortly afterwards, the Currahees deployed to the east side of the valley, and the NVA re-occupied Hill 996.

Before the 1st of the 506th left Hill 996, they were joined by a celebrated outfit within the 101st—the Tiger Force platoon of the 1st Battalion, 327th Infantry. As a reconnaissance unit, Tiger Force became the eyes and ears of the battalion commander and was charged with a unique mission: "out guerilla the guerillas." The heart and soul of Tiger Force was 24-year-old Staff Sergeant John G. Gertsch, a legend within the 101st Airborne Division. As platoon sergeant of Tiger Force, Gertsch, on his third tour in Vietnam, had already earned two Silver Stars, three Bronze Stars, and two Purple Hearts. Epitomizing valor, he was considered a soldier's soldier, the best point/recon man in the division, so when Tiger Force combat assaulted into the A Shau on July 15, the Gertsch legend would continue to grow.

Although the NVA may have lost Hill 996 in the fight with the Currahees, enemy strength along the border remained formidable, with combat-tested units moving at will throughout the area. On the 15th, Tiger Force clashed with one of those enemy companies. During the initial phase of an operation to seize a strongly defended enemy position, SSgt Gertsch's platoon leader was seriously wounded and lay exposed to intense enemy fire. Without hesitation John Gertsch rushed to aid his fallen leader and dragged him through a salvo of fire to a sheltered position. He then assumed command of the heavily engaged platoon and led his men in a fierce counterattack that forced the enemy to withdraw. Later, a small element of SSgt Gertsch's unit was reconnoitering when attacked again by the enemy. SSgt Gertsch moved forward to his besieged element and immediately charged into the withering barrage, firing his M-16 as he advanced. His one-man assault forced the enemy troops to withdraw in confusion and made possible the recovery of two wounded men who had been downed by the heavy enemy fire. Sometime later his platoon came under attack by a large enemy force. Sgt Gertsch was severely wounded but refused medical evacuation and continued to command his platoon despite unbearable pain. While moving under fire and leading his men against multiple fortified bunker complexes, he observed a medic treating a wounded officer from an adjacent unit. With enemy soldiers only a few meters away and realizing that both men were in imminent danger of being killed, he rushed forward and took up a position in the open, shielding both men with his body and drawing all enemy fire to himself. While the wounded officer was being moved to safety, the gutsy Tiger Force leader was instantly killed by multiple volleys of enemy fire. For his conspicuous gallantry and extraordinary heroism, Staff Sergeant John G. Gertsch was posthumously awarded the Medal of Honor.[46]

Because of adverse publicity generated by the press coverage surrounding Hamburger Hill, MACV clamped a tight lid on any news concerning Hill 996 and Operation Montgomery Rendezvous. The tactic ultimately proved to be unnecessary since attention on the home front was riveted on the Apollo 11 moon landing, not on Vietnam. A month later, when Montgomery Rendezvous ended on August 14, the campaign, its accomplishments, its sacrifice, and its associated valor never even made the news, either print or television. The youth of America were completely captivated by an iconic cultural/generational phenomenon: the Woodstock Music Festival. Interestingly, the loudest, most boisterous applause from the nearly 400,000 attendees went to Country Joe and the Fish when they performed their anti-Vietnam anthem, "I-Feel-Like-I'm-Fixin'-to-Die Rag." Many in the huge audience joined in the signature chorus:

And it's one, two, three,
What are we fighting for?
Don't ask me, I don't give a damn,
Next stop is Vietnam;

And it's five, six, seven,
Open up the pearly gates,
Well there ain't no time to wonder why,
Whoopee! we're all gonna die.

While Woodstock may have created a symbol for the youth of the time and defined a turning point in American pop culture, it essentially served as a protest message through song—a message filled with anti-war sentiment, anti-establishment reaction, a pro-drug mindset, and radical individualism. Yet in spite of the hoopla and publicity surrounding the Woodstock Music Festival, the message reverberated among the already converted. In Vietnam the war continued, but at a different pace.

On September 24, 1969, the 3rd Brigade's command post at Ta Bat closed and moved back to Camp Evans. By October 1 the entire 101st Airborne Division had left the valley, and with it the earlier plan to make the A Shau "Screaming Eagle Country," which became yet another aborted attempt to subjugate "the place from the beginning of time." The 101st left behind an airstrip, Route 547, and dozens of closed firebases—should the men of the 101st ever need to return. With changing priorities and Vietnamization, however, the 3rd Brigade redeployed along the DMZ to fill in for the departing 3rd Marine Division, while NVA units, battered and bruised though they were, quietly and efficiently set up operations and reclaimed the A Shau Valley. To many Americans, hawk and dove alike, the battles, bloody and obscene, made no sense. As one reporter asked, "When the war is ended, what will be the significance of Hamburger Hill, of Hill 996?"

Adding to the unrest, the anti-war movement captured national headlines when it staged the 'Mobilization' peace demonstration in Washington, one of the largest anti-war protests in U.S. history. Then, in mid-November, support for the war in Vietnam took another nosedive when investigative reporter Seymour Hersh broke the story of an atrocious war crime and cover up. In Quang Ngai Province, about 80 miles south of Da Nang, a platoon from the Americal Division had murdered at least 347 South Vietnamese civilian men, women, and children; equally upsetting, the U.S. Army had covered up the atrocity for 18 months. The horrific episode will forever be remembered as the My Lai Massacre. In the wake of My Lai, memories of Hamburger Hill and the A Shau Valley were conveniently shoved to the collective back of American conscious thought. But the men who fought in the A Shau remembered—they would always remember.

chapter 8

RIPCORD: VALOR IN DEFEAT

*Never send a battalion to take a
hill if a regiment is available.*
—GENERAL DWIGHT D. EISENHOWER

A lmost without exception, Americans transitioning into the year 1970 would never have associated the name "Daniel Boone" with covert operations in the Vietnam War. Some might have remembered the name as an iconic frontiersman and hunter from 18th century American history, but most probably recognized the character from the television series *Daniel Boone,* starring Fess Parker and running from 1965 through 1970. Had the public known about the Studies and Observations Group's (SOG) top secret cross-border raids into Cambodia codenamed "Daniel Boone" (eventually changed to Salem House), the political backlash and anti-war furor may well have paralyzed the entire nation.

Still reeling from reaction to Hamburger Hill, MACV began the year 1970 by maintaining a lower than normal public profile, especially where combat activities were involved; the impression conveyed—whether true or not—was that its heart was no longer fully in the fight. Rather than mount aggressive operations on the offense, most units focused on security roles near cities, towns, major roads, and around key military installations. All the while, U.S. troop drawdown continued: by the beginning of 1970, troop strength had dropped from a high of 543,000 to 428,000. While the de-emphasis on American combat involvement was without a doubt linked to Vietnamization, the unspoken but very real truth included political pressure to hold down casualties as a means to appease the increasingly powerful anti-war movement. One way to accomplish that aim involved employing "black ops" clandestine organizations like SOG, whose units

operated in total secrecy and without the attendant scrutiny of the media—
or Congress.

MACSOG's secret missions into Cambodia began in the fall of 1967
as an attempt to stem the flow of troops and supplies down the Ho Chi
Minh Trail into a locale known as the tri-border area, the point opposite
Kontum Province where the borders of South Vietnam, Laos, and Cambodia briefly touched. The tri-border area, designated Base Area 609, had
developed into a major sanctuary and transshipment point for VC and
NVA forces, and the long-sought authorization to cross into Cambodia
gave birth to top secret Operation Daniel Boone, whose purpose was to
"reduce infiltration of personnel and material and to collect intelligence."
A secondary rationale for Daniel Boone included the objective of obtaining
confirmation that NLF and NVA forces were indeed using neutral Cambodia for military operations against South Vietnam. The reconnaissance
teams of SOG got the job.[1]

One of SOG's first missions of 1970 into Cambodia occurred on January 5, when Staff Sergeant Franklin D. Miller led RT Vermont into Base
Area 609 in search of enemy base camps. Stealthily moving into Cambodia
only several hundred meters south of the Laotian border, Doug Miller's
nine-man team immediately ran into trouble when the point man tripped
a cord across a trail, setting off a booby trap explosion that seriously
wounded four team members. Knowing that the enemy in the vicinity had
been alerted by the blast, SSgt Miller hastily bandaged the wounded and
ordered the second in command to move the battered team to a nearby
hilltop; Miller remained behind in position to cover the withdrawal.

Within a few minutes SSgt Miller observed a 40-man platoon moving
toward his location. Taking on the entire unit with his CAR-15, Miller
single-handedly repulsed two determined attacks by the numerically superior enemy force and caused them to withdraw to regroup. After rejoining
his team he established contact with a FAC and arranged the evacuation
of RT Vermont. However, the only suitable extraction location in the heavy
jungle was a bomb crater some 150 meters from the team location. The
24-year-old Green Beret reconnoitered the route to the crater and led his
men through the enemy controlled jungle to the extraction site. As the
evacuation helicopter hovered over the crater to pick up RT Vermont, the
enemy launched a savage automatic weapon and RPG attack against the

beleaguered team, driving off the rescue helicopter. SSgt Miller led the team in a valiant defense which blunted the enemy in its attempt to overrun the small patrol. Although seriously wounded with a slug in his left arm and with every man on his team a casualty, the Elizabeth City, North Carolina native moved forward to again single-handedly meet the swarm of hostile attackers. From his forward exposed position Doug Miller, wounded and outnumbered 40 to 1, courageously repelled two more attacks by the enemy platoon. His valor saved the lives of his team and allowed a friendly Bright Light team to reach RT Vermont and effect a rescue just across the Laotian border. For conspicuous gallantry and intrepidity in action at the risk of his life above and beyond the call of duty, Staff Sergeant Franklin D. Miller was awarded the Medal of Honor. In keeping with the deception involving cross-border operations, Miller's citation specified that the action had occurred in Kontum Province, South Vietnam.[2]

While sharp firefights continued to occur throughout Vietnam, other events dominated the headlines in early 1970. The Chicago Seven, indicted on a series of riot charges stemming from the 1968 Democratic National Convention, were found not guilty of conspiracy but were convicted of crossing state lines with the intent to incite a riot. The anti-war movement became outraged when all seven men were sentenced to five years in prison and fined $5,000 each; the sentences were overturned two years later.

The population in Vietnam, north and south, focused on the cultural and spiritual observance of Tet. February 6, 1970, marked the beginning of the Lunar New Year, along with the annual promises of a celebratory truce, which each side only observed if convenient to them and then accused the other of violating. Tet ushered in the Year of the Dog, and according to Chinese astrologers, influential people born under that sign were always in danger of being too uncompromising or stubborn in their views. The Dog could also be too intense in its ideals and tended to forbid exceptions in any circumstance. The soothsayers, however, went on to say that in the Year of the Dog, compatibility among warring leaders offered promise. For example, North Vietnam's Le Duan, General Secretary of the Central Committee after Ho Chi Minh's death in 1969, and born in the Year of the Sheep, showed a high degree of compatibility with someone born in the Year of the Pig, namely President Nguyen Van Thieu of South Vietnam. On the other hand, as a Sheep, Le Duan was least compatible with someone born in the Year of the Rat: President Richard Nixon. Whether the astrologers got it right is still subject to interpretation.

As Tet 1970 came and went, the war ground on with a headlong rush to get ARVN units into the battle and American divisions out of the country. In and around the A Shau, the only units operating were SOG reconnaissance teams working the west side of the valley, while 101st LRRP teams ventured into the valley itself and worked the east wall. But in the air, helicopters from the 101st Aviation Group regularly flew over the always intimidating Valley of Death, and on February 19 three Cobra gunships from C Battery, 4th Battalion, 77th ARA, known to one and all as the "Griffins," found out firsthand why the A Shau had never been a healthy place for helicopters. At approximately 2 p.m., as the three Griffins patrolled the west wall of the valley searching for targets of opportunity, they found themselves caught in a wicked crossfire with at least two .51 cal machine guns spitting out streams of tracers. Just inside Laos and due west of Hamburger Hill, several rounds slammed into the Cobra flown by the Griffin battery commander Major Craig H. Leyda and his copilot, Chief Warrant Officer Loren W. Gee. The blinking master caution light on their instrument panel indicated that the oil transmission line had been hit—the two pilots had about a minute to get the bird on the ground before the transmission would freeze up. In a remarkable bit of flying, Leyda managed to settle the dying bird into a large stand of tall bamboo only 300 meters north of the gun that had brought them down.

Inside the second Cobra, Chief Warrant Officers John P. Carter and Edwin D. Billet sized up the precarious situation. It would take a rescue Huey at least 20 minutes to arrive on station, and with the area crawling with bad guys, the pilots realized their friends on the ground did not have that much time. Further complicating matters, Carter and Billet were already dangerously low on fuel, but throwing caution to the wind, they decided to go for a pickup. Although the Cobra only had two seats in tandem for the pilots, there were several documented cases of rescued crewmen sitting outside on the ammo bay doors. While the third Cobra attacked the machine gun positions, John Carter jettisoned his inboard rocket pods and guided his bird to a soft landing on the rim of a bomb crater. Just as Leyda and Gee scrambled on to the ammo bay doors, Carter's emergency fuel low-level light flickered on and the pucker factor soared astronomically—they had about 15 to 20 minutes of fuel to make a 20-minute flight to their base. With superb flying skill and a large dose of luck, John Carter and Ed Billet safely deposited their two fortunate passengers back at Camp Evans. For their daring and valor, both men were awarded the Distinguished Flying Cross.[3]

Yet another Cobra rescue mission involving Ed Billet occurred one month later on March 19, when an indigenous SOG team on the west wall was overrun by a large NVA counter-recon platoon; the only survivor was a single Montagnard trooper. When the supporting Kingbee helicopters could not navigate under an intimidating 300-foot ceiling, one of the orbiting Griffin AH-1G Cobra gunships decided the lone survivor could not be left to his fate. With James E. Mitschke in the front seat and Billet in the back seat, the two Griffins ran a gauntlet of heavy small arms fire to land their Cobra in the A Shau Valley near the frightened team member. Jim opened his side canopy, unstrapped, and climbed halfway out of the cockpit to open the ammo bay door for the small man to sit on. In a panic, the Montagnard instead raced full speed and dived head first into Mitschke's cockpit. Jim recalled that the soldier had been out for four or five days, smelled awful, and kept repeating, "Daiwe [Captain] number one!" With the scared little man sitting on his lap in the cramped, narrow cockpit, Jim Mitschke flew his extremely fortunate passenger back to LZ Star with the canopy half open.[4]

And the dangerously bizarre helicopter missions into the Valley of Death kept right on coming. On March 21, 1970, a Marine UH-1E gunship from HML-167 Squadron flew in support of a SOG RT inserted into Base Area 607 in the southwest corner of the A Shau. The Huey was over the extremely rugged jungle-covered mountains approximately three miles west of the Lao/South Vietnamese border when it was struck by enemy ground fire and plunged into the jungle below.[5]

That violent crash heralded the incredible survival saga of the co-pilot, 1st Lieutenant Larry D. Parsons. While supporting the SOG team, Lt Parsons' Huey, call sign Eagle Claw, was riddled by .51 cal fire from multiple machine guns around the team's position. From low altitude, the bird nosed over and slammed into the jungle in a fiery explosion. According to the team and crew of a second Huey, the resulting explosion was so catastrophic that they determined nobody could have possibly survived the crash. Therefore, no search and rescue operations were initiated due to the location of loss and the fact that for deniability purposes, these top-secret missions in Laos simply did not exist as far as the schedulers and mission planners were concerned. Additionally, because the other flight crew observed no signs of survivors in or around the crash site, 1Lt Robert E. Castle, 1Lt Larry D. Parsons, Sgt David Gonzales, and SSgt Thomas W. Underwood were listed as KIA/BNR—body not recovered. According to other members of Squadron HML-167, when the helicopter went down everyone was prepared to fly back into the Valley of Death to find their friends. This included Marine recon team personnel who were ready to accompany the aircrews in order to secure the area for a SAR operation. Instead, they were told, "there was no way anyone could have lived through the crash" and headquarters was not willing to risk the possibility of losing other aircraft and personnel "just to recover bodies."[6]

On impact Lt Parsons was miraculously thrown clear of the cockpit engulfed in flames; he suffered third degree burns to his arms and legs and a nasty wound to his left arm. Searching the burning wreck, he found Lt Castle dead, but he saw no signs of Sgt Gonzalez or SSgt Underwood in the wreckage or in the surrounding area. Realizing that the crash had attracted the attention of all enemy troops in the area, Larry Parsons found a secure hiding place in the nearby jungle, venturing out only at night. When he departed the crash site, Parsons took some survival pen flares with him and over the next several days fired them at two different flights of helicopters that passed close to his location. Unfortunately none of the aircrews saw his signals. Over the course of his evasion, Parsons heard enemy patrols moving through the jungle and successfully dodged them, but on occasion he heard enemy shots being fired, probably attempts to flush him out of his hiding place.

On April 9, 19 days after Parsons' shoot-down, a flight of ten heli-copters from the 101st Airborne Division was inserting another SOG team just west of the Huey's crash site. As they flew over the rugged terrain on their way in to insert the team, a crewman aboard the last aircraft spot-ted "someone in a small clearing, waving something" at them. The aircraft commander relayed the information to the flight leader who immediately turned around to check out the situation and set up for a possible ex-traction. The pilot of the last Huey reported that he saw a person on the ground who appeared to be a white male with a beard and wearing a flight suit and that he was "in" to pick him up. The lead aircraft commander responded with "be careful, it may be a trap." As the chopper settled into a nearby clearing, Larry Parsons recalled that he had reached the end of his rope. He had no flares left, he was starving, and surrounded by the NVA. He decided to go for broke and ran out into the open field waving what remained of his map in the hope of attracting attention. The brave Huey crew landed under enemy small arms fire, grabbed Larry Parsons and rapidly exited the clearing as the enemy continued to blaze away at the helicopter. When the flight returned to base, the crew counted 34 bullet holes in their fuselage, but Larry Parsons' harrowing ordeal in the A Shau Valley was over.[7]

Some 400 miles to the south, a game-changing event occurred in Cambodia. By 1970 the nationalist and anti-communist sensibilities within Cambodia indicated that Prince Norodom Sihanouk, long-time head of state, and his policy of semi-toleration of Viet Cong and NVA activity within Cambodian borders, had become exasperating if not unacceptable. Sihanouk, espousing a policy of neutrality—regarded by many as "neutrality of the left"—had negotiated a secret arrangement with Hanoi whereby large sections of neutral Cambodia were opened to the North Vietnamese for troop movements and weapons shipments. In actual fact, the penetration of Cambodia by Vietnamese communist forces, complete with their logistic systems, took place along two separate axes. The first was across the Vietnamese borders with Laos and South Vietnam in Base Area 609, while the second was through the Iron Triangle by way of the port of Sihanoukville on the Gulf of Thailand. All the while Sihanouk looked the other way as Hanoi infiltrated 65,000 NVA/VC soldiers and their equipment into his country.[8]

A silent resentment, fanned by rightist defense minister General Lon Nol, spread through the population as the Cambodian people came to realize Prince Sihanouk's duplicity. In a desperate move, he departed Cambodia on January 6, 1970 for France, ostensibly for treatment of a medical condition, following which he would travel to the Soviet Union and the People's Republic of China to discuss economic and military aid. Among political insiders within Cambodia there was general agreement that the two latter visits had no real purpose other than to find some way to resolve the political difficulties caused by the widespread NVA and VC activities ripping the country apart, activities which were becoming more widespread each day. Then, on March 18, with Sihanouk out of the country, the National Assembly deposed Norodom Sihanouk and installed General Lon Nol as the new head of state. Since the coup had essentially followed constitutional provisions rather than smacking of a blatant military takeover, and with anti-communist Lon Nol in firm control, policy wonks in Washington reveled in the spate of prospects opened up by Sihanouk's ouster.[9]

The only offensive campaign in Vietnam planned by MACV for the spring/summer of 1970 called for the 101st Airborne Division to conduct yet another series of operations in the A Shau Valley "to maintain a protective shield beyond the periphery of the populated lowlands of Thua Thien Province." The mission charged the Screaming Eagles with two specific objectives: to seek out and destroy an enemy who was rapidly reinforcing his sanctuaries around the northeast section of the A Shau, and to buy time to allow ARVN forces to develop their fighting skills in order to shoulder a larger share in the Vietnamization process.[10] The latest push, however, varied little from those executed in the valley over the past two years, and considering those operations' very limited, short term successes, a significant reservation surfaced—how could the 101st expect a different outcome by replicating the same strategy and tactics as before? Dubbed Operation Texas Star, the campaign proved to be America's last major ground offensive within the borders of South Vietnam.

Operation Texas Star kicked off on April 1st, six months to the day since units from the 101st had last been in the Valley of Death. During their absence, the NVA's 324B Division began to funnel all its units into a locale the Americans nicknamed the "Warehouse Area," the northeast corner of the A Shau. Those units initially included the 29th Infantry Regiment, veterans of the battle for Hamburger Hill, and the 803rd Infantry Regiment. Each regiment deployed with a supporting artillery battalion and a machine gun company. In addition, the powerful 7th Sapper Battalion operated in the area, and over the following three months the NVA moved ten more battalions into the Warehouse Area. Opposing them would be three battalions from the 3rd Brigade of the 101st Airborne Division.[11]

As a prelude to Texas Star and to re-establish a foothold in the Warehouse Area, the Screaming Eagles actually combat assaulted back into the area in March during the final phase of Operation Randolph Glen. Although primarily a joint pacification campaign with the ARVN 1st Division in the lowlands of Thua Thien Province, Randolph Glen also included some limited objective reconnaissance operations into the A Shau. The crux of this strategy hinged on building/occupying a series of remote fire support bases, each an artificial fortress island located on a key terrain feature. Each temporary FSB, called "Howard Johnsons" by the grunts, came complete with artillery batteries necessary for supporting the search and destroy missions of infantry units. Specifically the plan called for 3rd Brigade units to occupy old Fire Support Base Carol, originally built by the 1st Cavalry Division in 1968 during Operation Delaware; located atop Hill 927, the FSB was renamed Ripcord. Once this key firebase was established to support the upcoming offensive, the 3rd Brigade would seek out and destroy enemy units in the area—an enemy who had been infiltrating into the northeast A Shau for months and whose strength intelligence estimates had woefully underestimated. To counter that buildup, the 2nd Battalion, 506th Infantry, under the command of Lt Colonel Andre C. Lucas, got the job of securing Ripcord. The battalion, a mainstay of the 506th Infantry Currahees of World War II fame, was a close-knit outfit destined to be the principal combatant unit in the last major battle fought by American ground forces in Vietnam. As their leader, Lucas, a 1954 West Pointer on his second combat tour in Vietnam, projected an unmistakable air of professionalism and was considered to be a rising star among battalion commanders in the 101st. He developed a close working relationship with his staff and company commanders but remained somewhat aloof from the grunts in the battalion. Lucas's standoffish demeanor caused some of his troops to view him as a "ticket puncher"—nothing more than another super aggressive commander hoping to use the war to move up the promotion ladder. Rather than spend time with the men of the line companies, Lt Colonel Lucas apparently preferred to lead from overhead in his command and control helicopter. For that reason one grunt wryly observed, "We didn't know who the hell the guy was."[12]

On March 12, Lucas deployed Alpha Company on the initial assault against Ripcord. As the men landed, they came under heavy mortar fire from enemy troops on Hill 1000, just under a kilometer to the west. During the barrage, one of the supporting Hueys took multiple hits from enemy soldiers located at the base of Ripcord and crash-landed on top of the old FSB. Confusion reigned and casualties mounted. Some of the troopers were badly demoralized when an RPG explosion killed their brand new but popular 4th Platoon leader, 2nd Lieutenant Dudley Davis. The lieutenant's radioman, Specialist 4 Daniel N. Heater, wounded behind the left ear by a small piece of shrapnel from the same explosion, initially refused medical evacuation "for just a scratch," only to die on the chopper en route to the hospital. Under constant mortar fire, Alpha dug in and managed to hold out for three days before the company was lifted out so the enemy mortar positions could be bombarded without endangering the friendly troops. Right after the grunts were extracted from Hill 927, a new replacement observed them and noted that the troopers "looked like men gone two steps back toward ape. They Stank. They were bearded. Their fatigues were dirty and ragged. They ate with their hands, hunched over, wolfing down the food. They were quiet, speaking little . . . They had fear written on their faces."[13]

At that point the perennial struggle with A Shau's foul weather brought operations around Ripcord to a screeching halt. Low cloud ceilings and torrential rain grounded virtually all aviation assets and caused one delay after another. When the weather moderated slightly on April 1 and the 3rd Brigade initiated Operation Texas Star, Lt Colonel Lucas called on Bravo Company for the second assault on Ripcord, yet those experienced troopers fared no better than their brothers from Alpha Company two weeks earlier. When Bravo attempted to move across the top of Hill 927, a barrage of intense mortar fire drove them back down the bare, muddy slopes. It was obvious that NVA batteries on nearby hills had pre-registered every position on Ripcord and could land mortar rounds at will with devastating accuracy. When counter battery fire knocked out one enemy position, the NVA simply moved to another and continued the barrage unabated; it proved to be impossible to suppress the deadly mortars. In one instance, when a UH-1 landed to evacuate the most seriously wounded, mortar shrapnel shredded the bird as it lifted off, causing it to crash back on to the LZ. Thus stymied and pinned down by murderous enemy fire and unsupportable by tactical air because of the miserable weather, Bravo Company trudged off Ripcord on April 3rd.[14]

With NVA mortar units occupying all the high ground within a 2,000-

meter radius of Ripcord, the question of ordering a third assault against the hill set off animated discussions among 3rd Brigade and Division staff members. To clear the surrounding hills and to secure such a key piece of real estate for the upcoming offensive, the brigade commander, Colonel William J. Bradley, felt strongly that company-size assaults against Ripcord could not accomplish the mission. He maintained that the 101st should attack Ripcord in strength or not go at all. The brigade operations officer, Major Robert A. Turner, who sided with his boss and minced no words with his outspoken views to the assistant division commander, Brigadier General John J. Hennessey, candidly stated that "we'd gotten our ass kicked out of there twice . . . if we went back in, the enemy was going to respond in force, and then it would take a couple of brigades to hold the damn place," the obvious implication being that a much larger force—with attendant higher casualties—would be required to sustain a third attack. In a briefing to Hennessey, Turner even offered several alternatives including a plan to skip Hill 927 altogether and to launch the offensive from existing firebases. The assistant division commander simply responded, "Well, you're going back to Ripcord."[15]

In spite of Turner's pessimistic prediction, he realized that a large assaulting force against Ripcord amounted to a pipe dream—for two compelling reasons. First, Vietnamization had the Screaming Eagles overextended across the two hottest provinces in the country, forced to defend northern I Corps with a single division, whereas just a year earlier the 3rd Marine Division had been a key element on the team. Inside the 101st Airborne Division, the 1st and 2nd Brigades were fully committed around the DMZ and in the populated lowlands, while the 3rd Brigade in the western part of Thua Thien Province manned the barricades in an AO normally allotted to an entire division; figuratively speaking, they plugged the holes in the dike with their fingers—and as events would prove, NVA soldiers still poured through.

The second reason why it was unlikely that a large force would be deployed against Ripcord also touched on the realities of Vietnamization, but this time the rationale hid a political motive. Because many of the senior commanders in the 101st were still gun shy about the debacle at Hamburger Hill a year earlier, they were under tremendous pressure—whether real or perceived—to hold casualties down by keeping the operation relatively small. The added benefit of a small operation also included keeping the attack off the radar screens of the hordes of press and photographers prowling around in search of another dramatic Hamburger Hill story. As a result, the Currahees from the 2nd of the 506th were destined to go it alone at Ripcord, and by tradition as well as reputation, the battalion was no stranger to that particular predicament: their legendary Currahee name was a Cherokee Indian word meaning "Stand Alone."

On April 8 the Currahees' Delta Company had initiated the third assault on Ripcord's southeast face when they discovered a bunker complex. Almost immediately the attack turned sour. After detecting movement, they popped smoke and called in the Cobras. Unfortunately the smoke drifted as it rose through the thick jungle canopy, resulting in a tragic Cobra friendly fire attack that killed one Delta Company trooper and wounded 14 more. Morale among the Currahees plummeted, fostering what some called the "Hamburger Hill Syndrome," going back after something over and over again. One NCO in Charlie Company bitterly commented, "Hamburger Hill was probably the most shameful thing the 101st ever did. Ripcord was more of the same."[16] Yet over the next few days enemy contact unexpectedly dropped off, and during the early morning hours of April 11, Lt Colonel Andre Lucas moved Charlie and Delta Companies up the south slope of Ripcord. There was no enemy fire as the companies advanced up Hill 927 and onto the old firebase at the top. The conquest may have taken 31 days, but Ripcord now belonged to the Currahees. The question in everyone's mind was, how long could they hold it?

Although NVA units continued to lob rounds of harassing mortar fire into Ripcord, the Currahees threw themselves into the task of building up the firebase perimeter, fully expecting that the enemy would at some point attempt to take the position back. Fortunately for the Currahees, they had the right man in the right place. Charlie Company's indomitable commander, Captain Isabelino Vazquez-Rodriguez, ran a tight ship and brought a wealth of combat experience to the job. A native of Puerto Rico, the diminutive veteran with a heavy accent had fought in Korea as an infantryman and had already served two tours in Vietnam as a Special Forces NCO. He also had very definite views on how to defend a firebase. Instead of fashioning Ripcord's perimeter after other division firebases, Vazquez insisted on modeling his after the border outposts he had occupied during his tours as a Green Beret. He believed strongly that above ground sandbag bunkers stood out like neon signs and advertised their locations to the enemy RPGs and sappers. Instead of bunkers, Vazquez had the men of Charlie Company dig three-man L-shaped fighting positions around the perimeter. As he commented, "At least they were below ground and couldn't be spotted from 500 meters away. They were flat." To further protect the fighting positions, the wily company commander had his platoons string multiple rings of concertina wire embedded with trip flares and claymore mines. When completed, the concertina wire stretching around Ripcord was 50 meters wide, and during every minute of daylight Vazquez had his exhausted men clearing fields of fire. He also employed another Special Forces trick. In front of each fighting position he spotted a 55-gallon drum of thickened fuel known as "phougas." If ignited, the burning gas splashed into the concertina wire, creating illumination for the good guys and a living hell for the bad guys.[17]

With security under control, the 3rd Brigade began airlifting in the *raison d'être* for Ripcord: artillery batteries. Ripcord's perimeter resembled a figure eight in shape, approximately four football fields in size and stretching across the hilltop oriented from northwest to southeast. First to arrive was a battery of six 105mm howitzers to occupy the top of the higher, wider southeast half of the hill. They were followed by a battery of six 155mm guns spotted on a lower, narrower tier at the northwest end of the firebase. Packed in with the security company were a battalion headquarters, aid station, three 81mm mortar platoons, and three helicopter landing pads. Originally no more than a bare hilltop, Ripcord had been transformed into a heavily fortified citadel brimming with firepower—and a festering thorn in the side of an enemy determined to eradicate that thorn.

Any combat news associated with Operation Texas Star instantly took a backseat when, on May 1st, the war expanded spectacularly as a major cross-border offensive into Cambodia launched. With the recent favorable change of governments in Phnom Penh and with an eye toward the eventual departure of American forces under Vietnamization, President Nixon gave the go-ahead for U.S. forces to invade the eastern border regions of Cambodia in order to destroy NVA/NLF bases, sanctuaries, and supply depots. Additionally, the new campaign, Operation Toan Thang 43 for the South Vietnamese Army and Operation Rockcrusher for MACV, would permit the ARVN to demonstrate its ability to challenge one of Hanoi's most formidable strongholds.

Dubbed by the press the "Cambodian incursion," Operation Rockcrusher included elements of the 1st Cavalry Division, the 4th, 9th, and 25th Infantry Divisions, and the 11th Armored Cavalry Regiment, along with numerous ARVN units. While some of the fighting was intense, particularly around traditional hotbed areas like the Fishhook and the Parrot's Beak, for the most part the NVA forces simply eluded allied forces, avoided combat, and retreated deeper into Cambodia. Nevertheless, American and ARVN troops captured and destroyed huge caches of supplies and weapons: 8,000 tons of rice, 1,800 tons of ammunition, 20,000 individual weapons, and 431 vehicles.[18] In critiquing the campaign, however, military historians were mostly unimpressed by what they saw as the ARVN's overall timid and cautious performance. Shelby Stanton, for instance, wrote that "This crash program to mold the South Vietnamese military into an image of the self-sufficient, highly technical U.S. armed forces was doomed to failure." Based on its performance, the ARVN could not and did not savor a victory on the grand scale anticipated by the Americans.[19]

Naturally, the North Vietnamese reaction to the Cambodian incursion included a heavy dose of propaganda rhetoric, complete with assertions that the forces of good had inevitably been victorious over American imperialism and their puppets. In Hanoi's official version, the Military History Institute of Vietnam wrote that "because of their great defeat on the battlefield and in the face of strong opposition from the peoples of the world, including the people of the United States . . . Nixon was forced to announce the withdrawal of troops from Cambodia. The American imperialist invasion of Cambodia had failed."[20]

In spite of its exaggerated propaganda claims, Hanoi was right about the response at home: reaction to the incursion ignited anti-war sensibilities on college campuses across America, sparking protests against what was perceived as an expansion of the unpopular war into yet another country. Emotions reached a fever pitch on May 4 when the unrest escalated to deadly violence as nervous young Ohio National Guardsmen opened fire on and killed four unarmed students during protests at Kent State University. Two days later, at the University of Buffalo, police wounded four more demonstrators. Nationwide, protesters torched or bombed 30 ROTC buildings, and National Guard units were called out on 21 campuses in 16 states. A student strike, highlighted by protests and walkouts involving more than four million students at 450 universities, colleges, and high schools, spread across the country. In the face of such massive home front opposition to the Cambodian incursion, President Nixon attempted to appease American public outrage and Congressional pressure when, on May 7, he issued a directive limiting the distance of U.S. operations to a depth of 30 kilometers inside Cambodia and setting a deadline of June 30 for the withdrawal of all U.S. forces back across the border into South Vietnam.[21] The gesture fell on domestic deaf ears.

While the initial thrusts across the Cambodian border grabbed the headlines, the temporary lull in fighting around Ripcord proved to be an anomaly. NVA sapper units kept up the pressure by moving against Delta Company, 1st Battalion, 506th Infantry, situated approximately five miles south at FSB Maureen, located right on the east wall of the A Shau. Following heavy enemy contact on May 5th and 6th, the company's 2nd Platoon set up its night defensive position within the confines of Maureen. Somehow the determined sappers crept up the hill and infiltrated the perimeter just before dawn on May 7. At that point the night was laced with a crazy quilt of tracers and white muzzle blasts, while satchel charges began exploding everywhere, immediately killing the platoon leader, platoon sergeant, and the radio operator. In the confusion the platoon's brand new medic, Private Kenneth M. Kays, raced across the perimeter to reach his wounded comrades. While moving in the open he found himself on the receiving end of a number of satchel charges, one of which blew his left leg off below the knee. After applying a tourniquet to the stump, Pvt Kays then dragged himself through the perimeter engulfed in small arms fire, administered medical aid to one of the wounded, and helped drag him to an area of relative safety. Despite his severe wound and excruciating pain, Pvt Kays returned to the perimeter in search of other platoon casualties. He treated another wounded comrade, and, using his own body as a shield against enemy bullets and fragments, moved him to safety. Although weak and dizzy from loss of blood, the 20-year-old from Fairfield, Illinois, resumed his heroic lifesaving efforts by crawling beyond the company's perimeter into a hail of enemy fire to treat a wounded American lying there. Only after all his fellow wounded soldiers had been evacuated,

Pvt Kays finally collapsed from loss of blood and was medevaced out. During the vicious sapper attack Delta Company lost six men killed and twelve wounded; without the platoon medic's heroic actions, many more would have died. For conspicuous gallantry and intrepidity in action at the risk of his life above and beyond the call of duty, Kenneth M. Kays was awarded the Medal of Honor.[22]

Throughout the month of June, the Currahees continued to employ one company as a security force on Ripcord while the others executed reconnaissance-in-force missions and ambushes in the hills around the firebase. Even though contact was frequent, the brief skirmishes were with an enemy not quite ready to fight. Patrols regularly detected NVA activity on Hill 1000 approximately 1,000 meters to the west, on Hill 805 2,000 meters to the southeast, and around Hill 902, roughly 2,000 meters south of Ripcord, yet in spite of the aggressive patrolling, the Currahees never pieced together the ominous reality of their situation—and neither did the 3rd Brigade. In actuality, the enemy buildup around Ripcord had been proceeding undetected for some time. In his book, *Hell on a Hilltop,* Major General Benjamin L. Harrison, 3rd Brigade commander during the siege at Ripcord, characterized the limited intelligence provided by higher headquarters as "somewhere between disappointing and disgusting."[23] Confirming that intelligence failure, the 324B Division history indicates that it received its mission order as early as May 19 when tasked by its Military Region Headquarters to "concentrate its main force to attack and destroy Operating Base 935 [Ripcord was Hill 935 on the old French maps used by the NVA] and block and attack enemy elements stationed around the hill and forces sent to relieve the base . . . This would be the first battle in which most of the division's forces would be concentrated in one sector."[24] In carrying out its orders, the NVA 324B Division secretly deployed eight battalions around Ripcord, hoping to replicate a smaller reenactment of Dien Bien Phu. Had they known, the Screaming Eagles inside the perimeter at Ripcord may well have sensed something akin to a 20th-century reenactment of the Alamo.

Just as the fighting was about to heat up at Ripcord, mounting opposition to the Vietnam War sparked a political battle on the floor of the United States Senate, pitting that august body against President Nixon in a clash that shook hawks and doves alike. In the wake of the Cambodian incursion, and in an overt move to flex its political muscle, on June 24th the Senate voted 81 to 10 on an amendment offered by Senator Robert Dole to the Foreign Military Sales Act, to repeal the Tonkin Gulf Resolution, an obvious attempt to limit presidential war powers. The Nixon administration took a neutral stance on the vote, denying that it relied on the Tonkin resolution as the basis for its war-making authority in Southeast Asia. In justifying its actions and policies in prosecuting the war, the administration asserted that it primarily drew on the constitutional authority of the president, as commander-in-chief, to protect the lives of U.S. military forces. The Senate vote nevertheless served as the first step in mandating limits on presidential authority to engage American forces in combat without a formal declaration of war.[25]

A few minutes after 7 a.m. on July 1, General Chu Phuong Doi, commander of the 324B Division, initiated the opening round against Fire Support Base Ripcord, an attack that primarily consisted of harassment by indirect fire from 360 degrees around the hilltop fortress. During the initial volley, the 2nd of the 506th command post received five 82mm mortar rounds, a clear indication that enemy mortar crews had indeed zeroed in on key facilities on Ripcord. Fortunately, the sturdy command post only suffered superficial damage, and its occupants, including Lt Colonel Lucas, escaped with only bad cases of ringing ears. A short time later, an additional barrage of 15 mortar rounds impacted around the 105 howitzer battery, followed by the murderous sound of high-velocity 75mm recoilless rifles drenching Ripcord in dirty smoke, drowning out the shouts of alarm and the cries of the wounded. As the fire continued throughout the day, the newly assigned brigade commander, Colonel Benjamin Harrison, confessed that "I was both surprised and interested in the increase in enemy activity, but did not conclude that something big was about to happen."[26]

Air support from Cobra gunships and a Bilk FAC overhead attempted to take the pressure off by going after enemy mortar positions surrounding Ripcord. With a hail of rockets, the Cobras took out one entrenched mortar located at the base of Hill 805, while the FAC directed a flight of F-4s armed with 'snake and nape' against another position at the base of Hill 902. As the big Phantoms streaked by dumping their lethal loads of ordnance on the valley below, some of the Screaming Eagles on the firebase enjoyed the spectacular show by breaking out their cameras, but the men

THE SIEGE OF FSB RIPCORD, 1–23 JULY 1970

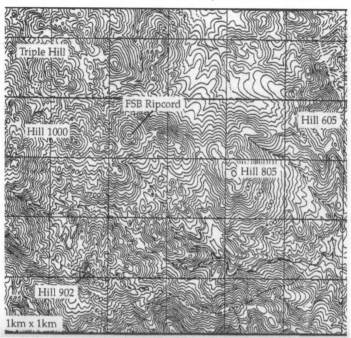

of the howitzer batteries were too busy to watch. During the day the artillerymen and mortar platoons on Ripcord worked unceasingly to deliver counter-battery fire against enemy positions, but since these men were forced to work in the open to fire their weapons, they sustained the only injuries inflicted: 15 artillerymen received minor wounds. With typical bravado and overstatement, the 324B Division history stated that the attack killed 70 Americans and destroyed the ARVN "puppet command post" on the FSB. No Screaming Eagles died at Ripcord on July 1st, and no ARVN troops were even present.[27]

By late afternoon on the 1st, Lt Colonel Lucas put out a desperate call for a resupply to replace the more than 1,000 artillery and mortar rounds his men had fired at enemy positions. While unloading a delivery of ammo, one of the CH-47 Chinooks took so many shrapnel hits from exploding shells that it could not lift off the helipad. Several hours later another Chinook was brought down, not by mortar fire but by a close-range deadly burst from a .51 cal machine gun on the southeast slope of Ripcord. Concealed in a cave, the crew pushed the gun out and opened up on each helicopter that attempted to land. Watching the drama unfold, one of the grunts on Hill 805 noted that "The fast-movers [F-4s] came in and napalmed the whole area, and we thought, boy, nothing can be alive down there—but after the airstrike, the little bastards wheeled that gun back up to the opening and popped off a few more rounds just to let us know they were still there."[28]

The opening NVA ground attack began early in the morning on July 2, not against Ripcord but rather against an outpost two kilometers south located on Hill 902. Defended by two platoons and the command section of Charlie Company, 2nd of the 506th, the bald crest of the hill proved to be a nightmare for the band of Currahee brothers holding it. Most of it was of their own doing. In stark contrast to his predecessor, the hard-nosed and savvy Capt Vazquez, the new Charlie Company commander was evidently still learning the ropes and for whatever reason exhibited a somewhat lackadaisical attitude regarding security for a night defensive position. Apparently many of the troopers in both platoons were not properly dug in, the company had no listening posts manned, and most were asleep. The CO set a poor example by slinging a hammock between two trees right in the open, while a few feet away the rest of the command group unwisely used their ponchos to erect small lean-tos or pup tents above ground. They would pay in blood for their apathetic attitudes.

Taking full advantage of the security lapse, members of the elite 7th Sapper Battalion crept through the darkness dressed only in black shorts and covered head to toe with charcoal camouflage that made them almost invisible in the dark. Undetected and without firing a shot, they somehow slipped inside the perimeter between troopers dozing in their foxholes. More sappers and supporting infantry lay right outside the perimeter.

At 3:46 a.m. the battle erupted when an RPG slammed into the company commander's hammock, literally blowing his legs off and killing him. The same explosion killed or wounded everyone in the command section only a few feet away. Total confusion reigned. Initially, most of the men of Charlie Company assumed the attack originated outside their perimeter. Snapping wide awake, they did as they had been trained, setting off claymores and tossing grenades so as not to give away their positions by firing their individual weapons. Yet in the dark chaos, satchel charges exploded all around them, tossed by an enemy they did not see. The company's wounded radio operator, dazed and deaf from the initial RPG explosion, did manage to request illumination from Ripcord, and when the flares popped overhead and drifted down on parachutes, it was only then in the eerie, flickering light that the defenders realized that sappers behind them and inside the perimeter were tossing the deadly satchel charges.

Arguably the title of luckiest man on Hill 902 belonged to Private First Class Gerald A. Cafferty, Charlie Company's senior medic from West Haven, Connecticut. As was the custom, everyone in the company called him "Doc." During the initial RPG explosion he was peppered by shrapnel, one piece ripping his forearm open from elbow to wrist. Doc Cafferty remembered that satchel charges were exploding everywhere, like waking up on the Fourth of July. As the young medic crawled into the command post foxhole, a sapper tossed a satchel charge into the position; it wedged between Cafferty's back and the shallow wall of the foxhole—inexplicably, it never went off.[29]

In the darkness and confusion, Specialist 4 Robert P. Radcliffe and Sergeant Lee N. Lenz, desperately looking for cover, dived into the small foxhole with Doc Cafferty. "There's too many people in here," Cafferty said. "They know this is the goddamn CP. We're all going to get killed with one grenade. I'm outta here." The Doc had only crawled a few feet when an RPG round exploded in the foxhole he had just left—both Radcliffe and Lenz were decapitated by the blast. Taking cover in the next foxhole he found, Jerry Cafferty literally landed on top of a figure cowering at the bottom, an artillery observer lieutenant who, as next senior officer, should have been leading the defense. Crouching there, half in and half out of the hole, Cafferty started to say something when a hand grenade flying through the air bounced off his helmet and landed only a few feet in front of him. The grenade never exploded. Frightened but still livid with the artillery observer, Doc Cafferty jumped out of the foxhole and immediately spotted several sappers only 30 feet away. With his M-16 on semiautomatic, he dropped them both then cut down several more that had materialized in the shadows.[30]

Private battles continued to rage around the top of Hill 902. Since all the officers and NCOs were either killed or incapacitated, PFC Cafferty assumed the mantle of de facto acting commander of Charlie Company.

First he re-deployed the survivors along the perimeter foxholes, organized litter teams, and began bandaging and treating the wounded. With the approaching dawn, the battle ended at 4:20 a.m. when the NVA attackers melted back into the darkness at the bottom of the hill. They left behind 20 of their dead comrades inside Charlie Company's perimeter. The American defenders suffered seven killed, six wounded, and one missing. When the relief force from Ripcord tried to medevac Doc Cafferty off the mountain, he refused to leave until all of his men were out. And when the relief force pulled out later that afternoon, the Americans forfeited the barren hilltop to the enemy. For his valor, gallantry, and leadership on Hill 902, Gerald A. Cafferty was awarded the Silver Star.[31]

Back at Ripcord, by 10:30 a.m. on July 2nd, it began subtly: at first a distant popping, the individual shots eventually coming so fast they finally blended into a steady, crackling roar, punctuated by the thumps of mortar shells. Almost immediately an incoming round took its toll, bringing down another Chinook. In light of the increased activity, the 3rd Brigade sent reinforcements in the form of the 2nd Battalion, 501st Infantry under the command of Lt Colonel Otis W. Livingston. Known as the "Drive On" battalion, the 2nd of the 501st immediately dispatched patrols southeast of Ripcord, hoping the additional manpower would turn the tide. It did not. On July 4th a trooper from the "Drive On" battalion's Charlie Company unintentionally set off a lethal booby trap—five 82mm mortar rounds strung together in a "daisy chain" known as a mechanical ambush. The deadly explosion killed five men and wounded five more. Then, just after midnight, Charlie Company's trial by fire continued when a substantial force of NVA sappers and infantry attacked around the company perimeter. The "Drive On" men held, driving off the enemy who left five dead behind. Charlie Company's casualties included 1 killed and 17 WIA.[32]

Enemy activity around Ripcord increased dramatically during the first week of July, indicating a substantial NVA buildup, particularly in the vicinity of Hill 1000 due west of Ripcord. Lt Colonel Lucas sent his reconnaissance platoon against the hill on July 6, only to have them suffer five WIA at the hands of a large, well dug in enemy force. The following day Lucas deployed under-strength Charlie and Delta Companies against Hill 1000. Pinned down by a torrent of automatic weapons fire, the men of Delta ran out of fragmentation grenades. Lucas to the rescue! Ordering his pilot to hover at 15 feet above the ground, the battalion commander leaned out into the barrage of tracers and dropped several cases of smoke and fragmentation grenades to his men below. Riddled with holes and losing oil pressure, the chopper limped back to Ripcord where the gutsy commander immediately boarded a second helicopter and repeated the feat. In spite of the resupply, Delta could not advance, losing one man killed, two missing, and 19 men wounded. On the north face Charlie Company met a similar fate, with 1 KIA and 15 WIA. The battered companies tried again on July 8. Moving uphill over totally bare ground offering no cover, the 30 remaining men from Charlie lost two more killed and five wounded. The effort completely unraveled when Lt Colonel Lucas ordered a third attack against Hill 1000. The company commander, Captain Jeffrey D. Wilcox, refused the order. With only 23 exhausted, dehydrated men left in the entire company, Wilcox angrily stated that he would assault the hill alone but that he would not order his men to do so. Lt Colonel Lucas cancelled the third attack but relieved Wilcox of his command.[33]

As the daily pounding on Ripcord continued and the casualties mounted, the 3rd Brigade set its sights on clearing the enemy off Hill 805, approximately 2,000 meters to the southeast. On July 12, Alpha Company, 2nd of the 506, and Delta Company, 2nd of the 501st, captured the crest, only to be swarmed by enemy soldiers in a ferocious attack that night. Delta's M-60 machine gun crews swept the ridge, firing constantly until they burned their barrels out and blistered their hands replacing them. During the violent firefight, with streams of American red tracers crisscrossing the night sky and NVA green tracers ricocheting in all directions, a radio operator from Delta's 2nd Platoon typified the tenacity of the defenders when he was badly wounded in the arm by shrapnel from an RPG explosion. After the medic hastily patched him up, the RTO got right back in the fight, his arm in a bloody bandage, tossing grenades with a vengeance down the slope on the advancing enemy. When the shooting finally stopped, the enemy had retreated back down the hill, leaving 26 Americans wounded but otherwise alive.

Two days later, July 14, 1970, Delta Company, still dug in on Hill 805, received a heavy volume of RPGs, satchel charges, and small arms fire from a large enemy force only a few meters northwest of their perimeter. During the close quarters fighting a satchel charge landed beside Sgt Jack

Godwin from Selma, Alabama, blowing his left leg off. Godwin hunkered in the foxhole with his left leg below the knee gone, plus multiple injuries to his right leg and back. The air thick with smoke and tracer rounds, platoon leader 1st Lieutenant Terry A. Palm bolted down the hill and through the hail of fire to help Godwin. An NVA soldier near the foxhole shot Palm in the chest, causing him to fall into the foxhole on top of Sgt Godwin. Fortunately for Godwin, the NVA observed no movement and assumed he had killed everyone. As the enemy soldier ran up the hill, another Delta trooper, Paul "Rat" Guimond, cut him down with a long burst from his M-60 machine gun. "Rat blew him all to pieces," said Godwin. As the melee continued, a medic, although wounded, made it to the foxhole. According to Jack Godwin, "The medics didn't realize that the LT [Palm] had been shot right through the heart and it bored a hole in his back. I put my hand in it trying to get him off me. When his heart exploded, he just covered me with so much blood."[34]

Over the next three days, the Screaming Eagles on Hill 805 were subjected to constant attacks. Out-manned and out-gunned, they could not hold on without reinforcements—none came. After suffering 9 more killed and 23 wounded, the two battered companies finally relinquished Hill 805 to the enemy on July 17. In the aftermath, the commander of Delta Company, Captain Christopher C. Straub, bitterly commented, "Often times a special degree of valor is required to get yourself out of a situation that you wouldn't have been in in the first place if not for command stupidity."[35]

One of the most remarkable soldiers on Ripcord tuned out to a tough, pint-sized artillery officer serving his fourth year in Vietnam: Captain David F. Rich, B Battery Commander from 2nd Battalion, 319th Artillery. Exposed to incoming mortar and recoilless rifle fire each day during the siege of Ripcord, Capt Rich was everywhere, encouraging his men and directing return fire against the enemy. Because counter-battery fire was at that time much more of an art than a science, and a dangerous one at that, during each barrage Capt Rich typically dashed from crater to crater to analyze the impact angles in order to plot the trajectories back to the firing location. Although wounded on seven different occasions, the Buffalo, New York artilleryman continuously pinpointed enemy positions for his men and assured that all the wounded received medical treatment before he did. During a particularly intense barrage of enemy 120mm mortar fire on July 17, Capt Rich conducted accurate crater analysis amid the hail of enemy shrapnel. Although painfully wounded yet again in the arm, chest, and eye, with multiple shrapnel wounds and a fracture to one of his legs, he refused to relinquish the command of his battery and continued to direct the defensive fire of his men. Inspired by his leadership and determined efforts, Capt Rich's men never left their guns, resolutely resisting the enemy barrage while maintaining a high level of fighting spirit throughout the ordeal. For his extraordinary heroism, Capt David F. Rich was awarded the Distinguished Service Cross.[36]

On July 18 David Rich's beloved 105mm battery lost its battle on Ripcord in a bizarre ending. At approximately 1:30 p.m., a CH-47 Chinook hauling a load of ammunition suspended in a sling under the aircraft came under fire from an enemy .51 cal machine gun located at the base of Hill 927. As the Chinook attempted to land, bullets from the gun ripped through the bird, igniting the entire aft section of the big helicopter. The CH-47 plummeted into a 105mm ammunition storage area and burst into flames. The resulting fire and exploding artillery ammunition included Willy Pete rounds that blasted the area with burning chunks of white phosphorus along with choking clouds of tear gas from exploding CS shells. The fires and explosions lasted for three hours, ultimately destroying five 105mm howitzers and badly damaging the sixth. Battery B was out of business, and the fate of Ripcord hung in the balance.[37]

Directly impacting Ripcord's future, Alpha Company, 2nd of the 506th, made a startling discovery on July 21 when it located an enemy telephone line strung along the western base of Hill 805. Tapping into the line, the company interpreter listened excitedly as the enemy revealed that Ripcord was surrounded by four NVA regiments. After digesting the disquieting information, Brigadier General Sidney B. Berry, acting commander of the 101st Airborne Division, wrote the following letter to his wife early in the morning of July 22, fully realizing that within the prevailing political atmosphere accompanying Vietnamization, it simply did not make sense to accept heavy casualties to claim victory in a single battle:

We've now reached the point when we must question the continued use of Ripcord. Is it worth the casualties for the purpose it is serving? Now we are taking constant casualties from incoming mortar rounds, particularly among our artillerymen on top of the hill. We are taking constant casualties among our rifle companies operating in the mountains and jungles around Ripcord.[38]

Evacuating Ripcord would prove to be easier said than done. In addition to the firebase itself, there was the daunting task of extricating Alpha Company, still mired in the jungle and under fire over 1,000 meters to the east. En route to the rocky hill designated by Lt Colonel Lucas for the extraction, Alpha ran headlong into three NVA battalions—it was Little Big Horn time for the Currahees. According to the company commander, Capt Charles F. Hawkins, "Enemy soldiers started boiling out of the brush from as close as 50 meters . . . They came at us in a massed attack, crouching low, running through the undergrowth, shouting and shooting . . ."[39] As Hawkins prepared his men to counter attack the enemy, a squad from the 1st Platoon, led by Sergeant John W. Kreckel, began receiving heavy fire from an enemy machine gun emplacement located on higher terrain. Without hesitation Sgt Kreckel ran into the fusillade and began administering aid to his wounded men. He then organized half a dozen stragglers into an assault force and led them up the hill toward the enemy position. As the assault force neared the enemy emplacement, intense fire forced them to take cover. At this time Sgt Kreckel observed a grunt standing directly in the line of fire of an enemy RPD light machine gun. Leaving his covered position, the 22-year-old Milwaukee man ran to the soldier and pushed him to the ground just as the RPD opened fire. Shot in the head, John Kreckel took the burst that was meant for the other trooper; he died a few minutes later. For his extraordinary heroism, John W. Kreckel was posthumously awarded the Distinguished Service Cross.[40]

For Alpha Company the battle raged for five hours. Clinging to the very bottom of their makeshift foxholes, the exhausted grunts, soaked to the deepest marrow of their bones, shaking with malaria, jungle ulcers covering their bodies, their guts gripping with spasms of amoebic dysentery, fought valiantly in the darkness to stop the determined enemy. With help from Cobra gunships, the small band held out through the night with only 20 men who could still fight, and all but six of them were wounded. When Hueys lifted them out the next day, the men of Alpha Company had suffered 12 killed and 51 wounded. They counted 61 dead NVA soldiers.

The evacuation of Ripcord began at 6:32 a.m. on July 23 when dozens of Hueys and Chinooks landed on the firebase to lift out the artillery pieces and the men. At 7:40 a.m., the operation degenerated into mass confusion when a CH-47 crashed in flames on the firebase's large lower landing pad, preventing the other Chinooks from lifting out the rest of the men, artillery, and heavy equipment. With only the smaller upper pad available, the remaining grunts and artillerymen would have to be evacuated by UH-1 Hueys which could carry only six men at a time. As a dozen UH-1s milled around aimlessly trying to figure out what to do, Huey pilot Capt Randolph W. House instinctively knew that a costly screw-up was in the making unless something could be done quickly to help the troopers stranded below. Orbiting above Ripcord, acting as a controller and traffic cop, Randy House directed each chopper into the pad, at least turning pandemonium into organized turmoil. As the evacuation continued throughout the morning, enemy mortar shells constantly rained down on the hilltop while automatic weapons fire tore into the vulnerable helicopters, downing another Chinook and damaging two Cobras and 12 Hueys. The fierce incoming fire was so heavy that it forced everyone on the besieged firebase to take cover—except one man. Leading by example and attempting to calm everyone's nerves in the chaos and confusion of battle, Lt Colonel Andre Lucas was standing in the middle of Ripcord at 9:15 a.m. when a 120mm shell landed at his feet, the blast severing both his legs. The battalion surgeon loaded Lucas aboard a Huey, but the tough commander died on the medevac ramp at Camp Evans. For his numerous acts of extraordinary valor during the battle of FSB Ripcord, Lt Colonel Andre C. Lucas was posthumously awarded the Medal of Honor.[41]

There was little time to mourn as the evacuation continued. By noon, only 18 fighting men remained at Ripcord from an original force of nearly 400—and they were almost out of time. They could see NVA soldiers swarming up the mountainside like ants, breaching the lower perimeter wires less than 100 meters away. Hueys lifted the last men out at 12:14 p.m., and Hill 927 now belonged to the NVA 324B Division. At approximately 2 p.m., a B-52 Arc Light strike leveled what was left of the impregnable fortress known as Fire Support Base Ripcord.[42]

Several days after the evacuation, General Berry visited with each of the battalions involved, giving impromptu pep talks and doing his best to present the battle as a victory, telling the men that their hasty departure from Ripcord constituted "the most brilliantly planned and executed airmobile operation of the war." Most of the grunts, especially the Currahees, greeted his comments less than enthusiastically. According to the 2nd of 506th chaplain, "There was a lot of anger from the troops at that time," feeling that they had been used as bait and left hanging. "The one thing that many people were angry about," noted the chaplain "was that they didn't feel we had gotten the support from the higher-higher [division] that we should have."[43] The bitterness manifested itself in numerous threats to refuse to return to the field on the battalion's next operation—strange behavior for troops who had just been told they had won a major battle. One disgruntled trooper perceptively compared the Currahee ordeal on Ripcord to a stanza from Tennyson's famous *The Charge of the Light Brigade*:

Cannon to right of them,
Cannon to left of them,
Cannon behind them
Volleyed and thundered;
Stormed at with shot and shell,
While horse and hero fell,
They that had fought so well
Came through the jaws of Death,
Back from the mouth of Hell,
All that was left of them,
Left of six hundred.

Arguably one of the most compelling and insightful critiques of Ripcord came from a survivor, Major Herbert E. Koenigsbauer, the Currahee battalion operations officer during the siege. He stated, "Lucas and I made repeated requests that division commit additional forces to the action ... but higher command was not prepared to follow through and do what was required to win the battle, and I must admit to a certain sense of disillusionment that after all the sacrifices that had been made to take and hold Ripcord, we just turned around and gave it back to the North Vietnamese."[44]

Few people outside the 101st Airborne Division were aware of the dissention and bad feelings. Certainly the media had no inkling; during the battle they had not been allowed to visit FSB Ripcord. What information there was about the battle filtered up to higher headquarters in after action reports that staff members put a positive spin on, then fed to senior commanders who predictably publicized another hard-won victory over the North Vietnamese. Apparently reverting to Westmoreland's attrition strategy, senior commanders ignored the tactical reality of Ripcord by touting a 30 to 1 kill ratio against the enemy—an unsubstantiated claim since the Americans lost 75 KIA/MIA around Ripcord against a body count of 125 NVA. Whereas the enemy undoubtedly lost many more men—Berry estimated over 500, Harrison 2,400—in the absence of data from Hanoi, American estimates remained guesses.

Essentially the story of Ripcord languished buried and forgotten until Keith Nolan's definitive book *Ripcord: Screaming Eagles Under Siege* appeared in 2000. His detailed and unvarnished account sparked renewed interest along with a modicum of debate. While some saw the valor and tragedy of Ripcord, still others rehabilitated the finger pointing game, accusing the liberal press, anti-war protesters, revisionist historians, and Washington politicians of turning an American victory into a defeat. Did we win or did we lose? Theories and opinions poured in from all quarters. Claims of a U.S. victory at Ripcord began to take a decidedly convoluted turn into the twilight zone when a former company commander, who ran a tour agency after the war in Vietnam, was thrust forward as an expert. He maintained that since Hanoi only lionized the battles they claimed to have won, the simple fact that Ripcord went unreported proved that the battle was an embarrassing failure to the North Vietnamese. Adding fuel to the fire, he also offered emotionally unsupported claims—that of all the significant engagements fought during the U.S. troop drawdown, "Ripcord stands as a monument of success during that entire period of time." Somehow linking the battle to the Easter Offensive of 1972, he speculated that "Without the success of Ripcord that offensive would have been advanced a full year."[45]

Since Keith Nolan's book, most discussions about Ripcord have tended to focus much more on the bravery and glory of the Currahees than on the military blunders involved, with a perverse effect that, according to noted psychologist Norman Dixon, "did much to strengthen those very forms of tradition which put such an incapacitating stranglehold on military endeavor."[46] A U.S. victory at Ripcord became urban legend unsupported by facts.

Consequently, for over 40 years the mantra among Vietnam veterans has been "We won every battle but lost the war," a myth that still persists. The tour agency operator's unsubstantiated claims notwithstanding, Ripcord seems to shoot a gaping hole in that time-honored axiom. The enemy initiated the attack with ferocity backed by overwhelming numbers, and at the end of the day the Screaming Eagles, valorous men all, evacuated Hill 927, leaving the NVA in control of the battlefield. As General Berry wrote at the end of the siege: "I made the most difficult professional decision of my life: to get out of Ripcord as quickly as possible."[47] His admission does not sound much like a victory statement. The battle's outcome was and remains a bitter pill to swallow—the United States was defeated at Ripcord.

The evacuation of FSB Ripcord did not equate to a lull in the fighting for the Screaming Eagles. Operation Texas Star pressed on with its efforts focused just north of the A Shau around Fire Support Base Barnett, a joint U.S.-ARVN position overlooking the Khe Ta Laou River in Quang Tri Province. Some of the toughest fighting took place on August 19 when Bravo Company, 2nd Battalion, 502nd Infantry, attacked a small hill infested with enemy soldiers dug in and ready to fight. As the lead platoon, under heavy enemy fire, approached the hilltop, Private First Class Frank R. Fratellenico crawled right up to the first bunker and tossed a fragmentation grenade through the firing port, killing all five of the enemy soldiers inside. Without hesitation he was moving to a second bunker when the 19-year-old trooper from Connecticut took a machine gun burst in the chest. Stunned and knocked to the ground, PFC Fratellenico dropped the grenade he was about pitch into the bunker. Realizing the imminent danger to four of his friends in the immediate area, PFC Fratellenico had the presence of mind to retrieve the grenade and pull it under his body an instant before it exploded. For conspicuous gallantry, extraordinary heroism, and intrepidity at the cost of his life, above and beyond the call of duty, Frank R. Fratellenico was posthumously awarded the Medal of Honor.[48]

With NVA units once more controlling the inhospitable A Shau by late summer of 1970, American ventures into the valley reverted to small patrols by the 101st and clandestine raids by LRRP and SOG recon teams—all of those missions as frightening and as deadly as ever. The month of September proved to be particularly unnerving. For example, just before dawn on September 11, a LRRP team from the 101st tangled with an enemy unit just northeast of their position on the A Shau's east wall. The NVA counter-recon platoon was delivering a hail of B-40 rockets and automatic weapons fire on the team until a pair of Marine A-4s came to the rescue. The on-scene FAC worked the Skyhawks in close, but on his second napalm pass the lead A-4 was struck by 23mm fire, burst into flames, and crashed into the ground. The pilot, 1st Lt Bernard H. Plass-meyer, did not have time to eject.[49]

Later that same day, a Screaming Eagle platoon from the 1st Battalion, 501st battled with NVA soldiers in yet another bunker complex. When the enemy opened up with automatic weapons and RPGs, five out of eight men in the point squad had been wounded. After medevacing their injured friends, the severely depleted platoon, now with only 14 men remaining, called on the services of one of the most lethal standoff weapons of the entire war. Cruising just off shore, the battleship USS *New Jersey* aimed her massive 16-inch guns, firing 2,000-pound projectiles into the A Shau Valley and the enemy bunker complex. Immediately after the first shells hit, one of the platoon members standing over a kilometer away from the impact point felt a rush of hot air past his head. He was amazed to discover a glowing red, four-pound piece of shrapnel on the ground nearby—a souvenir from the *New Jersey.*[50]

Just two days later SOG inserted RT Moccasin into Base Area 607 on the southwest corner of the A Shau. The team's mission was to observe enemy troop concentrations fording a fairly large river. The following day the RT made contact and called for an extraction, but the only open area near them turned out to be a clearing situated on a steep mountain slope. Under covering fire from two Cobra gunships, the lead Huey moved in for the pick-up. Rather than land on the steep incline, Lead tossed out a ladder and went into a hover while half the team attempted to hook on. At that instant a B-40 rocket exploded in some tree branches just above the hovering chopper, pelting the entire area with deadly shrapnel. The damaged helicopter staggered like a wounded animal, went into an uncontrolled turn to the right and slammed into the ground, flipping over several times as it rolled down the steep hill. While the Cobras beat up the tree lines suppressing the small arms fire, the second Huey hovered over the wreckage and managed to rescue all four crewmembers. Next, the third UH-1 picked up half the team while the fourth plucked out the remaining members of RT Moccasin and flew them back to Firebase Birmingham. Later it was learned that one of the indigenous team members had been crushed to death when the chopper rolled down the hill, pinning him underneath the wreckage. Ironically, the team One-Zero did not seem that upset at the loss of one of his men; he suspected the dead soldier was actually an NVA infiltrator.[51]

In mid September, SOG's most successful mission—and its most controversial—launched from Kontum. Most people simply refer to it as "Operation Tailwind." As originally conceived, Tailwind began as a diversion to draw NVA units away from devastating attacks against Royal Laotian forces operating along Route 23 on the Bolovens Plateau, approximately 100 miles south of the A Shau. The job went to Hatchet Force commander Captain Eugene McCarley. The Hatchet Force was SOG's strike arm, either quick reaction platoons or companies whose short duration missions involved a reconnaissance-in-force against lucrative enemy targets. For Operation Tailwind, McCarley led a Hatchet Force whose mission was to create a diversionary ruckus around the strategic area of Chavane, a key sector right on the Ho Chi Minh Trail. By SOG standards, McCarley fielded a huge contingent composed of 16 Americans and 110 Montagnards. The size of the company and the distance to the objective precluded the use of Hueys, so SOG enlisted the help of much larger U.S. Marine Corps CH-53 Sea Stallion helicopters. On September 11 the raiding party boarded four CH-53s escorted by 12 Marine Cobra gunships and flew to the target area.[52]

Approaching Route 165 near Chavane, Laos, the Sea Stallions began taking heavy ground fire. Bullets ripped through the floor of one bird, wounding three Montagnards. In spite of the intense fire, the Marine choppers successfully landed on a large LZ and disembarked the Hatchet Force. At that point a running gun battle erupted, one that lasted for three days. The first firefight occurred only a quarter of a mile from the LZ. Amazingly, in the middle of the fight the raiding force heard telephones ringing.

Upon further investigation they discovered a huge bunker complex over 500 yards long containing thousands of 122mm and 140mm rockets. McCarley had his men blow up their find. The Hatchet Force then continued moving and fighting throughout the remainder of the day and night, and by morning nine of the sixteen Americans had been wounded, along with an even larger number of Montagnards.[53]

To evacuate the most seriously wounded, McCarley again called on the Marine CH-53s. Before being able to load any casualties aboard, however, the first bird was hit by an RPG that did not explode, but the fuel tank ruptured, forcing the big chopper down about five miles away. The second CH-53 took a number of .51 cal rounds and also made a forced landing. A third helicopter rescued both crews.

To keep from being surrounded, Capt McCarley kept his force trekking west. With over two dozen wounded, the Hatchet Force medic, Sergeant Gary M. Rose, patched them up and kept them moving. Throughout the ordeal, Covey FACs from Pleiku directed dozens of airstrikes around the raiding party, using A-1s from Da Nang and F-4s to pummel enemy positions with bombs, CBU, and strafe. On the second night a B-40 rocket impacted just meters from Sgt Rose, knocking him off his feet and inflicting wounds throughout his body. Ignoring his own injuries, Rose struggled to his feet and continued to administer medical treatment to the other wounded soldiers. All through the night and into the next day, the NVA pounded the allied force with a continuous barrage of B-40 rockets and mortars, yet despite the deadly volleys falling around him, Sgt Rose displayed a calm professionalism as he remained in the open administering medical treatment to countless men. Sergeant Rose, though exhausted and wounded, refused evacuation until all other casualties were safely out of the area. For his extraordinary heroism, Gary M. Rose was awarded the Distinguished Service Cross.[54]

On September 13 McCarley's men routed an enemy platoon in a sharp firefight and then overran a huge base camp containing many maps and hundreds of pounds of documents. The raiders continued moving west, hauling their wounded and the stash of NVA documents. Since the Covey overhead observed massive enemy reinforcements moving in on two sides, the decision was made to get out. As the CH-53s landed in a large field of elephant grass to extract the raiding party, Cobras and A-1s pounded the surrounding area with ordnance, including CBU-30 tear gas cluster bomb units. The Marine choppers landed, protected by the devastating might from the air umbrella, and lifted out the entire Hatchet Force. The highly successful mission had, however, been costly. Three Montagnards had been killed; 33 were wounded, along with all 16 of the Americans. During the fighting, the Hatchet Force killed 144 NVA, with almost 300 more estimated to have been KBA—killed by air. Eugene McCarley and three of his NCOs were nominated for the Silver Star.[55]*

During the month of September, the Air Force also had its share of bizarre encounters around the A Shau. On September 23, a flight of two F-105s attacked the same river ford in Base Area 607 where RT Moccasin had fought its way out ten days earlier. Hit by 37mm fire during the strike, the pilot of Dallas 01, Capt John W. Newhouse, guided his burning aircraft out of Laos before ejecting over the northeast corner of the A Shau, just east of Ripcord. Landing on the bank of a streambed, the pilot sank up to his armpits in the sticky mud. When a 101st OH-6 Loach could not pull the pilot free, the orbiting FAC called on the services of an Air Force Jolly Green. Fifty-five minutes later, in an area crawling with enemy soldiers, the big HH-53 finally freed the very fortunate Capt Newhouse and flew him to Da Nang. Ironically, the A Shau had claimed the last of 169 F-105s lost during the war by the 355th Tactical Fighter Wing.[56]

In early October the battle against North Vietnamese forces in the A Shau experienced a significant reversal when the 1st ARVN Division aban-

---

*The raid on Chavane remained classified and lay dormant for almost 30 years until a mind-boggling controversy erupted in 1998 when television's CNN aired a story about Operation Tailwind called *Valley of Death*. Based on an interview with a disgruntled former SOG team member, the televised segment alleged that the true purpose of the Tailwind mission was to eliminate a group of Americans who had defected to the enemy. In the process of taking them out, SOG had ordered the use of deadly Sarin nerve gas. It also claimed that over 100 civilians had been killed. In effect, the CNN story accused SOG and the Pentagon of war crimes, including genocide. Three weeks later an internal investigation by CNN admitted that the reporting was deeply flawed; a public retraction was aired and apologies made. The two producers of the program were fired outright and the on-air reporter received a reprimand. None of the CNN allegations were true, but the intimations forever placed a tainted legacy around Operation Tailwind and the brave men of the Hatchet Force who went "in harm's way" to carry out the incredibly daring and dangerous mission.

doned FSB O'Reilly, about seven kilometers northwest of Ripcord. Eerily similar to the Ripcord siege, the two-month-long battle at O'Reilly had once again pitted the NVA 324B Division against the ARVN's 1st Regiment in another standoff. After 92 enemy artillery barrages and numerous infantry probes against the firebase, the ARVN troops evacuated the fortress, ostensibly due to the onset of the northeast monsoon. Whatever the reason, the occasion marked the last time a major allied unit ventured into the Valley of Death.

As the 1st ARVN Division left the east side of the valley, SOG continued its dangerous mission by inserting a team into Base Area 611, due west of the village of Ta Bat. Late on the afternoon of October 5, a Prairie Fire Covey FAC, Capt Evan J. Quiros, monitored an emergency transmission from the One-Zero of RT Fer-de-Lance, Staff Sergeant David "Babysan" Davidson. Already a legend within SOG, 23-year-old Babysan had been running recon for three years and had even made a night combat parachute jump into Cambodia. Now, when Babysan advised his FAC that he had heavy enemy movement around his team, it was clear he was in the center of a very precarious situation. With no chance of slipping in under the heavy weather that shrouded the hills and mountain peaks on the west wall of the A Shau, Evan Quiros set up an orbit over the approximate location of the RT, hoping the sound of his circling OV-10 would keep the enemy off balance long enough for the team to make a run for it. After exhausting most of his fuel, he had no choice but to return to Quang Tri for gas.

Launching out of Quang Tri at dark, Evan returned to the team's general location using a fix he had plotted on his TACAN. As he approached, his blood ran ice cold when he heard a voice whispering over the radio. In a hushed tone, the One-One, Sergeant Fred A. Gassman, asked Evan to mount an emergency extraction. What was left of the seven-man team was in heavy contact on three sides and low on ammo. He whispered that Babysan had been shot and had fallen over a cliff.

Faced with unworkable weather and darkness, Quiros knew a rescue was out of the question, but to keep the team's spirits up, he told them to keep their heads down while he armed up his HE rockets. Counting on a big dose of luck, he began firing blindly through the low cloud deck, praying his rockets would explode close enough to break the contact without hitting the team. The first few salvos landed well south of the target area, exploding harmlessly in the thick jungle; directions from Gassman based strictly on sound proved to be ineffective. Finally, the gutsy One-One realized the hit-or-miss tactic would not work. In a perfectly calm voice he said to Evan, "Covey, we're out of ideas and time. Got any suggestions?"

At first the Covey FAC could not think of a positive answer to the hopeless question. Then he recalled that a few of the teams carried small portable radar beacons. Keying off that signal, sophisticated sensors aboard an AC-119 Stinger gunship could lay down a deadly wall of mini-gun fire, theoretically to within just a few yards of friendly troops. It was their only chance. Quiros told the trapped team, "I've ordered up a Stinger gunship. You've got to hang on another 45 minutes. In the meantime, I want you to get your beacon set up."

His voice heavy with dejection, Gassman replied, "No good. The One-Zero had the mini-ponder on him. He's somewhere down on the rocks below us."

The FAC shouted, "Your best bet is to find that beacon. You've got to retrieve that beacon!"

After the truth of Evan's words sank in, the One-One answered, "I'll give it a try. Here goes nothing—wish me luck."

Evan Quiros continued to circle in the darkness for several long minutes, hoping beyond hope that the courageous Green Beret below would find the all-important radar beacon. When his radio receiver finally crackled, Evan's heart sank into his boots. In a quivering, weak voice, Fred Gassman said simply, "I've been hit—and in the worst way." There were several groans then the radio went dead.[57]

The following day a SOG Bright Light team launched a search for RT Fer-de-Lance.* During the attempted insert, however, the supporting A-1s—call sign Spad—had taken a lot of ground fire, and a few of the rounds must have found their mark. The Spad pilot, Major John V. Williams, Jr., was advising the FAC, "The cylinder head temp is off the charts, and she's starting to smoke. I'm gonna have to get out."

---

*The remains of David Davidson and Fred Gassman have never been recovered. For years Hanoi continued to deny any knowledge of the two men, but after normalization of relations in 1995, American researchers found pictures in Hanoi's files of Davidson's body taken at the scene of the firefight where he died. NSA/DIA intercepts indicated that Gassman may have actually been captured alive.

The Covey answered, "I copy, Spad Lead. If you can, stay with her until we cross the border and clear the A Shau. That way we'll have a chopper waiting for you when your feet touch the ground."

Seconds after that transmission, John shouted, "Okay, I can't wait. I'm punching out." A long pause followed, then the Spad wingman chimed in, "John, get out of it! Get out now!"

"I can't. The Yankee [ejection system] didn't work."

"Don't you have anything?"

In a low-pitched, angry-sounding voice, Williams replied, "I don't have a damn thing."

The orbiting FAC, in a cool voice, talked to the rapidly descending A-1. "Spad Lead, try to go for the pass between those two ridges directly in front of you. You've got a good glide going. Hold her steady on a heading of about 120 degrees. Looking good." Then the Covey's voice jumped up about three octaves. "Lead, no! No, for Christ's sake. Back to your right! To your right!"

When quite near the ground, the A-1 plunged into a vertical dive and then exploded in a great sheet of orange flame, followed by a swiftly rising column of black smoke and thin white plumes of exploding ammunition. Somebody else came up on frequency. "He went in. Big fireball on the east wall. Negative 'chute."

Everyone in the package saw it. Bright orange-red flames consumed a football field-sized area just below the rim of the small ridge on the A Shau's east wall. A pall of sooty black smoke floated straight up above the inferno. The Covey FAC was still in control but obviously shaken by what he had witnessed. When he talked on his FM radio to another Covey in the area he sobbed, "If he'd just stayed on that heading. He had it made. Why didn't he listen? He just went into a left bank and held it. He wouldn't listen to me. Why didn't he listen?"[58]

SOG managed to recover John Williams the following day when the Spad commander, Lt Colonel Melvin G. Swanson, jumped on a helicopter and joined the Bright Light team in retrieving his pilot's remains. There was barely time for a short memorial service before the top-secret reconnaissance teams suited up again for more missions into the A Shau; operational requirements mercifully left no time for extended grieving.[59]

For the remainder of 1970, U.S. and ARVN mainline units stayed clear of the Valley of Death, just as they had during the period 1966 to 1968. Following Ripcord and O'Reilly, the NVA pushed more troops than ever into the valley, all of them better armed, better supplied, and ready to fight, but there was nobody there to oppose them—nobody except SOG.

The only headline-grabbing event involving Special Forces occurred on November 21, not in the A Shau but at a small village 23 miles west of Hanoi. Former SOG commander Colonel Arthur "Bull" Simons led 56 Green Berets on a daring mission to Son Tay to rescue 61 American POWs believed to be held there under brutal and primitive conditions. The Son Tay raiders pulled off a textbook mission, but they departed without a single POW; all the prisoners had been moved prior to the raid. Incredulously, just hours before the raiders departed from Thailand on the mission, Defense Intelligence Agency analysts learned that the POWs had been relocated, yet the raid on Son Tay launched anyway on the outside chance that a few of the men might still be in camp. While the mission was clearly a tactical success, it proved to be a painful intelligence failure. Called Operation Kingpin, the Son Tay raid ironically mirrored American campaigns throughout the entire Vietnam War: undeniable valor, ingenious planning and execution, but the operation failed to achieve the goals that the command authorities in Washington had set for it.

By the end of 1970, enemy domination west of the A Shau was so complete that SOG chose to stay clear of the deadly area along Route 922, known as Target Oscar Eight. Seventh Air Force, however, kept a watchful eye on that key infiltration point. The enemy's interlocking antiaircraft defense in the area proved to be as formidable as ever, as the crew of Stormy 03, an F-4 from the 366th Tactical Fighter Wing at Da Nang, discovered on an armed reconnaissance mission on December 2. Their aircraft shredded by intense ground fire, the crew ejected at an altitude of approximately 1,500 feet. The crewmen landed about a mile apart on a rolling, muddy ridge full of trails. When a Nail FAC located them, he called in the Jolly Greens, but as was typical around the A Shau, the cloud deck was so low that the big rescue helicopters could not find a way under the 300-foot overcast and into the rugged terrain. Following several aborted attempts, the Jollies backed off while an Army medevac UH-1 dropped below 200 feet and snaked its way into Oscar Eight. Piloted by Chief Warrant Officer Steven S. Woods, Dustoff 509 located the backseater's parachute and then established radio contact with the downed crewmen. After four hours on the ground in one of the most dangerous areas in Laos, both crewmen were hoisted aboard Dustoff 509. For the fortunate Phantom crew, a potentially disastrous situation terminated in a happy ending, in large part due to the efforts from everyone involved in a perfectly executed SAR. The only visible evidence remaining to mark the scene in Oscar Eight were two parachutes draped in the tops of the trees and the shattered wreckage of a five million dollar F-4E.[60]

To show their appreciation for rescuing two of their own, the Gunfighters at Da Nang threw a wild party for the crewmembers of Dustoff 509. The Army medic recalled the evening:

> The party was hard to forget . . . a Hall filled with food that us Army Fly Boys don't see! . . . roast beef, turkey, potatoes, jello, salads and only God knows what else . . . the Champaign we had to chug-a-lug (which I haven't touched since that time) . . . the wheel barrow with the gold balls that were hung on our zippers by a Lady in a flight suit . . . saying we had BRASS BALLS . . .[61]

To close out its year in the A Shau, CCN inserted a team into deadly Base Area 611 on Christmas Eve. The mission turned tragic on the 28th when the supporting FAC and his Covey rider ran afoul of the valley's always-dangerous guns and weather. Flying an OV-10 Bronco, Captain James L. Smith, accompanied by Staff Sergeant Roger L. Teeter, maneuvered his aircraft around the far northwest corner of the A Shau in an attempt to reach the team, completely socked in by a low overcast of clouds. The team reported radio contact with the Covey overhead at 12:40 p.m., but because of the low cloud deck there was no visual contact. On one of the passes they heard several long bursts from what sounded like a 14.5mm ZSU heavy machine-gun. Approximately one minute later the team heard the distinctive turbo prop engines increase to full power, followed by two muffled explosions. The One-Zero estimated the map coordinates, based strictly on sound, to be about three kilometers northwest of his position, and according to that plot the explosions were near a steep cliff socked in by mist and fog. The missing crew remained undetected until January 8 when another Prairie Fire Covey located the wreckage of their OV-10. A Bright Light team was inserted into the crash site, and after two hours of searching they recovered the bodies of Jim Smith and Roger Teeter. There were no indications that the enemy had been at the scene of the crash.[62] Like so many of the other losses in and around the A Shau, there was no plausible reason other than guts and valor that could explain the sacrifice of yet two more American lives in the Valley of Death.

chapter 9

A SHAU *FINI:* THE NINTH YEAR

We shall not cease from exploration
And the end of all our exploring
Will be to arrive where we started
And know the place for the first time.
—T.S. ELIOT

"**B**ack burner" characterized MACV's attitude about the A Shau Valley in 1971. While always a perennial American concern in I Corps, recently re-designated Military Region I, the Valley of Death, after eight years of tough fighting, had evolved into an imbroglio with no cogent strategy or viable solution. At least half a dozen different military operations had been launched against the formidable enemy bastion, all with mixed results varying from temporary headway to not any. Consequently, on the planning staffs at MACV, XXIV Corps, and the 101st Airborne Division, especially in the aftermath of the controversial battles at Hamburger Hill and Ripcord, few if any jumped at the chance for another crack at the old nemesis, the A Shau. At least one component in that reluctance could be attributed to Vietnamization, where along with the escalating drawdown of American troops, other priorities and reduced forces dictated the operational focus in Military Region I—and that focal point no longer included the "Ah Shit Valley."

With overall American troop strength down to 280,000, the vaunted 101st Airborne Division no longer found itself participating in far-ranging enemy hunting expeditions near the Laotian border. Instead, the Screaming Eagles transitioned into a concept dubbed "Dynamic Defense" by MACV. The 101st actively participated in Operation Jefferson Glenn, a joint campaign with the 1st ARVN Division designed to shield the coastal lowlands of Thua Thien Province by concentrated patrolling of enemy rocket belts along the eastern edge of the mountains. The most westerly move in the operation occurred when the 1st Brigade of the 101st feigned a thrust toward the A Shau, stopping at Fire Support Base Granite, nine kilometers east of Ripcord.[1]

By the end of January the remaining 101st brigades moved north to bolster the defenses of Quang Tri Province, while many ARVN units stood down for the Tet Lunar New Year. January 27th heralded the beginning of the final sign of the Chinese zodiac, the Year of the Pig. Individuals born under that sign were said to be compassionate, diligent, and generous, but they had a tendency to be overly trusting and naïve, thus easily drawn into traps. The soothsayers even predicted enemy ruses during the year; ARVN senior commanders, secret plans in hand, hoped to spring their own colossal trap against their foes from the North in spite of the fact that the South's president, Nguyen Van Thieu, had been born under the sign of the Pig. As the initial step in executing that trap, the U.S. Army's 1st Brigade, 5th Mechanized Infantry Division, launched Operation Dewey Canyon II on January 29, moving from Vandegrift Combat Base along Route 9 toward Khe Sanh with an armored cavalry/engineer task force. The 5th Mech was to clear the way for the move of 20,000 South Vietnamese troops along the highway to reoccupy 1,000 square miles of territory in northwest South Vietnam and to mass at the Laotian border in preparation for Lam Son 719, the invasion of Laos.

Planning for Lam Son 719 actually began in early December 1970, when General Creighton Abrams and the MACV staff convened a secret meeting with their South Vietnamese counterparts to discuss the possibility of an ARVN cross-border attack into southeastern Laos. Detailed planning for the attack fell into the lap of the XXIV Corps commander, Lieutenant General James W. Sutherland, Jr. The operation would consist of four phases: during Phase One, the U.S. 1st Brigade of the 5th Mech would push out along Route 9 and reopen it all the way to the old Khe Sanh combat support base. Next, a strong ARVN armor/infantry force would pass through the American positions on the border and strike into Base Area 604, its ultimate target the vital crossroads of Tchepone, some 25 miles into Laos. In Phase Three the plan called for ARVN troops to disrupt or even completely destroy this vital staging area on the Ho Chi Minh Trail.

Finally, before the beginning of the southwest monsoon in May, the South Vietnamese force would backtrack to the east along Route 9 or south through Base Area 611 to exit through the A Shau Valley.[2]

ARVN units participating in Lam Son 719 crossed the border into Laos at 7 a.m. on February 8, 1971, right on the heels of a massive artillery barrage and a dozen B-52 Ark Light sorties. While the 1st Armored Brigade task force pushed due west along Route 9, the ARVN 1st Infantry Division, considered the best in the South Vietnamese Army, leapfrogged via helicopter to temporary firebases along the left flank of the main advance. Simultaneously, the elite ARVN 1st Airborne Division combat assaulted into key terrain on the north side of Route 9. The operation represented the acid test for Vietnamization. Due to the Cooper-Church Amendment passed in late December, a move born from the antiwar backlash following the Cambodian incursion, U.S. ground troops, including American advisors, were prohibited from entering Laos. Lam Son 719 was an all ARVN show—except in the air. The 101st Airborne Division was tasked to "provide helicopter support for all U.S. and ARVN units committed to the operation, on both sides of the border." For security reasons, the Screaming Eagle aviation units only learned of the actual mission on February 7 when the assistant division commander, Brig General Sid Berry, briefed the assembled aviation commanders on the invasion of Laos. One shocked battalion commander mumbled to himself, "I'll be a son of a bitch. I thought we were going into the A Shau."[3]

Under the command of Lieutenant General Hoang Xuan Lam, Lam Son 719 made good progress until February 12 when Lam's troops slammed into a large contingent of NVA forces, forces who, unlike in Cambodia, stood their ground and fought. Supported by Soviet PT-76 and T-54 tanks, as many as five NVA divisions—including the 304th, 308th, and 320th— used massed ground attacks to isolate individual firebases before wiping out ARVN units piecemeal. The South Vietnamese quickly went from the offensive to the defensive. By the first of March over 40,000 NVA soldiers—twice the number of ARVN troops—were attacking General Lam's units strung out along and beside Route 9. Besides ravaging ARVN positions with tanks and long-range artillery, the enemy employed vicious antiaircraft fire to decimate helicopters attempting to reinforce and resupply the South Vietnamese troops who depended on the 101st's airmobile assets for their very existence. In addition to automatic weapons, the enemy deployed twelve triple A battalions with over two hundred 23, 37, and 57mm antiaircraft guns. The effectiveness of those guns shocked everyone when, on March 3, a battalion from the 1st ARVN Division air assaulted into LZs near Tchepone. In a single day enemy gunners shot down 11 helicopters and damaged 44 others.[4]

Those same enemy gunners had equal success against F-4 Phantoms. On February 25, Major Richard K. Somers from the 366th Tactical Fighter Wing at Da Nang was on his fourth bombing pass at 1,000 feet when ground fire struck his cockpit. His backseater ejected, but Major Somers never got out of his aircraft. At approximately 4 p.m. that same afternoon, over the same target, a burst of green tracers from a .51 cal machine gun hit a second Phantom. The two pilots ejected just before their aircraft exploded in a fireball and crashed. Both were rescued three days later.[5]

Like a giant sponge, Lam Son 719 continued to soak up men and equipment. Internal bickering among senior ARVN commanders also muddied the command and control lines since two of the generals with units involved actually outranked General Lam. As Henry Kissinger described it later, "The operation, conceived in doubt and assailed by skepticism, proceeded in confusion."[6] By late February it became obvious that General Lam had underestimated his opponent on two crucial points: the speed at which Hanoi could reinforce its units in Laos, and the ferocity of their counterattack. When he finally achieved his objective at the bombed-out crossroads at Tchepone, General Lam, concerned about a rout, disengaged and started the deadly return to the border, again via helicopter. Earlier thoughts about turning south and carrying the battle into the A Shau were summarily dismissed. While a few units carried out their missions admirably and with valor, the 1st Airborne Division, the showpiece of Vietnamization, performed ineffectively and entirely failed in its flank security mission. Adding to the worsening drama, the highly regarded Vietnamese Marines abandoned key positions without much of a fight, although other accounts had them battling valiantly at LZ Delta. At any rate, the retreat was on. Mobbed by frightened ARVN troops, some helicopter crews resorted to greasing the skids of their Hueys to prevent panicky soldiers from clinging to them during the evacuation process. Yet in spite of the dire situation, dangerously overloaded American UH-1 Hueys and CH-47 Chinooks shuttled back and forth to hell holes named LZ Lolo, Liz, and Sophia Two, the valiant chopper crews keeping at it until they dropped from exhaustion or from enemy ground fire.

For the ARVN troops fighting for their lives along Route 9, close air support was vital to keeping the enemy forces at bay, but extremely heavy antiaircraft fire took its toll among the pilots attempting to help. On March 6, enemy gunners poured a stream of white-green tracers into the right wing of an A-1H on its ninth pass, causing the aircraft to burst into flames. The pilot ejected and was picked up by a Jolly Green rescue helicopter. Ten days later a 37mm gun brought down a FAC working airstrikes over an allied unit. The O-2 Skymaster nosed into the ground, killing both crewmen. And on March 22, a flight of F-100s attacked four NVA tanks on Route 9. Capt Peter G. Moriarty was on his first pass when a .51 cal machine gun found the range. The Super Sabre crashed before the pilot could eject.[7]

At the height of the evacuation on March 18, as ARVN positions were being overrun, U.S. helicopters ran a deadly gauntlet of fire to save the allied soldiers. During one particularly harrowing mission, Cobra pilots Captain Keith A. Brandt and co-pilot Lieutenant Boffman A. Brent from D Company, 101st Aviation Battalion, repeatedly flew through the lethal fire, leading Huey after Huey into hot LZs. The two pilots, call sign Music 16, remained over the besieged 88-man ARVN unit all afternoon, refueling and rearming three times. On the doomed Cobra's last run, NVA antiaircraft fire exploded around the AH-1G. Brandt's Cobra shuddered and he radioed, "I've lost my engine and my transmission is breaking up. Goodbye. Send my love to my family. I'm dead." Then, Music 16 exploded in a ball of fire and crashed in the trees.[8] By the time Lam Son 719 ended, many other American fliers had suffered a similar fate: 215 KIA with 38 MIA. U.S. aviation units lost a total of 168 helicopters shot down and another 618 damaged.[9]

By March 24 the last ARVN troops had been lifted out of Laos, and all that remained was the withdrawal from the border back to Dong Ha and Quang Tri. And as in all major battles, the leadership trumpeted the notion that our side had pulled off another lopsided victory. In a televised speech on April 7, President Nixon told the American people "the South Vietnamese demonstrated that without American advisors they could fight effectively against the very best troops the North Vietnamese could put in the field . . . Tonight I can report that Vietnamization has succeeded."[10] Not to be outdone, President Thieu addressed the survivors of the invasion and claimed that the operation in Laos was "the biggest victory ever."[11] The reality was that Lam Son 719 played out as an incredibly costly and humiliating evacuation for South Vietnamese forces—as Winston Churchill remarked 30 years earlier following the tragedy at Dunkirk, "Wars are not won by evacuations." Tactically, the assault into Laos had sputtered to a halt when determined NVA forces routed the best the ARVN had. The operation amounted to an unmitigated disaster for the ARVN, decimating some of its best units and destroying their confidence and morale. Furthermore, it became clear to the pragmatists that Vietnamization had not prepared the South Vietnamese military to the point where it could effectively stand on its own and challenge the NVA *mano a mano*, especially in traditional enemy strongholds like Base Area 604.

Approximately 30 miles south of Base Area 604 and Tchepone, an unpublicized but particularly violent part of Lam Son 719 played out in a top-secret battle along the west wall of the A Shau. In anticipation of an ARVN withdrawal through the infamous valley, SOG inserted several of its reconnaissance teams to tie down enemy forces and gather intelligence. One of those teams, RT Intruder, was led by Captain Ronald L. Watson. Known to his men as "Doc," Watson, a Military Intelligence officer with a PhD from Stanford University, seemed an unlikely sort to run one of the most dangerous clandestine missions in the U.S. Army. Nevertheless, he pushed ahead with his plan to check out as a One-Zero so he could write a book on the subject, perhaps replicating T.E. Lawrence's famous wartime memoir, *Seven Pillars of Wisdom,* a blueprint for guerrilla warfare in the twentieth century. In short order Doc Watson won over the doubters in SOG; they quickly recognized that he had the intellect of a scholar, the soul of a poet, and more importantly, the heart of a warrior. To some he did, indeed, conjure up visions of Lawrence of Arabia.

On the morning of February 18, Doc Watson loaded RT Intruder aboard two UH-1s at Phu Bai for the short flight to the A Shau. The team included Sergeant Allan R. "Baby Jesus" Lloyd as the One-One, Sgt Raymond L. "Robby" Robinson as the One-Two, and five Bru Montagnard mercenaries. By coincidence, SFC Samuel D. "Sammy" Hernandez and

SFC Charles F. "Wes" Wesley had wandered into the tactical operations center (TOC), only to be ordered to accompany RT Intruder to evaluate them for an upcoming special mission. As the two men gathered their weapons and equipment, Wes cursed Sammy and said, "See, I told you we shouldn't go down to the TOC. I was in the A Shau Valley as a platoon sergeant with the 101st back in 1968. All the bad guys in the world are in that valley."[12]

The Hueys inserted RT Intruder into a rocky clearing on a ridgeline overlooking the southwest rim of the valley, just across the border in Laos, and once the choppers departed, the team hunkered down to give their ears a chance to attune to jungle noises. Then the arduous trek began: RT Intruder took three hours to cover 300 meters. Shortly after moving out and crossing the border back into Vietnam, the team heard signal shots to their right and left, indicating that the enemy was aware of their presence. Threading their way slowly through the wait-a-minute vines and heavy underbrush, RT Intruder literally stumbled across a major high-speed trail easily large enough to handle truck traffic. The overhanging tree boughs had been tied together, making the road virtually unobservable from the air. Also strung out beside the road were a dozen strands of communication wires, indicating a major line of communication. As Doc Watson studied the trail, one of the Bru on the left flank signaled "people coming"; a five-man NVA porter crew came into view. From their ambush positions the team opened fire, killing two NVA while the others abandoned their loads and fled into the dense jungle. Watson and his men quickly gathered up the enemy booty, and since the shots clearly compromised their location, he called the nearby Covey FAC to arrange an immediate extraction.[13]

Orbiting just east of the valley, Covey 275, 1st Lieutenant James L. "Larry" Hull, piloted his O-2 toward RT Intruder. Although new to the Prairie Fire operation, Hull was eager to help—he felt the connection deeply. The invisible bond between that team on the ground and that FAC circling above was beyond explanation. People like Larry Hull would break every rule and take any chance to help a reconnaissance team. When the action turned super-hot, the One-Zero never gave a second thought to friendly machine-gun fire or rockets kicking dirt up at his feet, as long as it came from one of his Prairie Fire FACs. That mutual respect and commitment formed the lifeblood of SOG operations in the secret parts of Laos.

The SOG troops evidently saw something of themselves in Larry Hull because they idolized him, partly as warrior and partly as mascot. For reasons known only to them, the Green Berets decided the young, blond lieutenant reminded them of "Woodstock," the small yellow bird from the *Peanuts* cartoon strip who became best friends with everyone's favorite beagle, Snoopy. They called him Woodstock, and the name naturally stuck. Sitting in Woodstock's right seat was Sergeant First Class Jose Fernandez, a brand new Covey rider on his very first mission. When Jose and his pilot headed for Hill 1528 on the west wall, both men agonized about the rapidly deteriorating weather along the ridgeline. Jose summed up the situation when he commented to Larry, "Nothing is ever easy in the A Shau." With that terse observation they waited, mostly in silence, for the extraction helicopters to arrive approximately 30 minutes later.

Three Hueys from A Company, 101st Aviation Battalion, contacted Covey 275 and moved into position to extract RT Intruder. Known as the Comancheros, the crews displayed nerves of steel, hovering at treetop level in the clouds while moving forward a few feet at a time attempting to locate the SOG team in the dense jungle below, knowing that at any moment NVA troops close by could blast their vulnerable birds out of the sky. With no LZ available, the first Comanchero hovered and dropped an aluminum ladder out the troop door. Sergeants Robinson and Wesley, along with two Bru, snapped their rucksacks to the first rungs of the ladder, then climbed up and snap-linked themselves to the rickety, swaying contraption. In the thin mountain air and high altitude, the Huey struggled to lift the heavy load of men and equipment, inadvertently dragging the ladder through the trees. The struggling UH-1 was just seconds away from crashing when the four dangling team members jumped off the ladder, a split second before the crew chief cut it loose from the overloaded chopper. Strangely, Robby and Wes landed right on top of the NVA they had just killed. As they ran back to the team's perimeter, a second Huey approached, dangling four long ropes anchored to its floor. This time the two Green Berets and the two Bru attached the ropes to their STABO rigs, a nylon harness with two snap rings at the shoulders. Referred to as "coming out on strings," in time-critical situations with no LZ available, the STABO harness might be a team's only option, and if done correctly, three or four men could hook up to the ropes and be lifted out at the same time, leaving the team members' hands free, enabling them to fire their weapons. As an added bonus, a wounded or unconscious troop could be extracted with no danger of slipping off the rope. Once hooked up to the "strings," Robby and Wes gave the crew chief a thumbs up and away they went, dangling precariously in the open as the Huey sped them to safety. Almost immediately another Comanchero pulled out the three remaining Bru. Only Doc Watson, Baby Jesus Lloyd, and Sammy Hernandez remained on the ground.

Unfortunately, the rescued men were not out of danger. When the Huey with Robinson and Wesley dangling beneath it arrived at Phu Bai, the pilot approached the landing pad too low, inadvertently dragging the suspended men through the camp defensive perimeter concertina wire, cutting them to ribbons. In the process of being dragged, Robby Robinson hit a metal engineer stake used to hold the razor sharp concertina wire in place; the stake drove deep into his leg. After landing, another chopper evacuated Robby to the 95th Evac Hospital while a second lifted Wes and the two Bru to the SOG compound. It was then that they learned the fate of their teammates on RT Intruder.[14]

Orbiting overhead while orchestrating the rescue, Larry "Woodstock" Hull observed several streams of telltale green tracers tracking the last helicopter. To suppress the threat, he asked another Prairie Fire FAC in an OV-10 Bronco to work the area over with high explosive rockets. As the last UH-1 moved into position, the three Americans on the ground engaged in a bitter firefight with the converging enemy. On their stomachs facing outward in a small wheel formation, Watson, Lloyd, and Hernandez set off their last claymores and continued firing their CAR-15s and M-60 machine gun while simultaneously trying to grab the dangling STABO lines. In a truly remarkable display of bravery, the last Comanchero Slick, piloted by Warrant Officers George P. Berg and Gerald E. Woods, went into a stationary hover while the three team members hooked up the strings. Then the three Americans felt the violent yet reassuring tug as the Huey began clawing for altitude. But the intense small arms fire coming from all directions proved to be more than even the agile Cobras could handle. Probably riddled with bullets, the hovering Huey lurched forward in a drunken fashion, inadvertently snagging the strings, along with the three clinging team members, in the tops of the trees. Acting like an unbreakable leash on a straining dog, the tangled strings jerked the chopper up short, sending it plunging nose first into the dense jungle. At first contact the rotor blades sprayed branches and wood chips in all directions. Then the UH-1, tail number 68-15255, evaporated in a huge orange fireball right on the Laotian/Vietnamese border.

As twilight and weather closed in on the scene, a disconsolate Larry Hull sent the rest of the package back to Phu Bai, while he trolled the treetops along the west wall of the A Shau searching for survivors. The crash site was located right on the Laos-Vietnam border on the down slope of a heavily forested ridge running northwest from Hill 1485. Trying to pinpoint the exact map coordinates using 20-year-old maps in an area covered with mile after mile of featureless jungle was a chore made even tougher by a constant stream of green tracers from at least half a dozen automatic weapons sites. Enemy gunners shot the OV-10 assisting in the mission full of holes, forcing Covey 275 to escort the pilot "feet wet" for the flight back to Da Nang. Woodstock returned to the scene and remained on station until dark, shooting off all his remaining willie pete rockets at the sporadic ground fire still coming from the ridge. For all his troubles, he caught a few AK-47 rounds in the passenger door. It was a miracle that his Covey rider in the right seat, SFC Jose Fernandez, escaped being hit.[15]

Just before dawn the next morning, a different FAC, Covey 221, headed directly to the crash site and began a slow low-altitude search on the outside chance that someone from the crew or team might still be alive. As the sun rose above the hills on the east wall of the A Shau, the FAC picked up what looked like a mirror flash several hundred meters up the slope from the crash. On his second pass at treetop height, the Covey spotted a lone figure step out of the shadows and wave. The pilot rocked his wings to acknowledge the signal, and an hour later a helicopter package rendezvoused with the FAC in the middle of the A Shau. Since he could not be sure there were no other survivors wandering around the area, the Covey gave strict orders to the Cobras and the Slick door gunners: the only permissible use of guns was to return fire for fire. There would be no LZ prepping and no suppressing fire. Under the circumstances, everyone in the rescue package was extremely nervous as Slick Lead inched over the spot verbally marked by the Covey. Fighting the heavy rotor wash, the survivor limped out of his hiding place and climbed aboard his waiting salvation. The Huey pilot, working his collective to perfection, skillfully lifted his precious cargo up and clear of the trees before transitioning into forward flight. Everyone flew alongside the incredibly lucky Sammy Hernandez all the way back to Phu Bai where he debriefed his ordeal. During the nightmare the day before and hanging from the STABO rig below the Huey, Sammy heard gunfire erupt from directly underneath him. He remembered that he "was high enough almost to run across the treetops, and the next thing I knew, I'd come back crashing through the trees," falling 30–40 feet into the jungle canopy below. SFC Hernandez's rope had snagged in the trees and snapped under the added weight of carrying two gear bags. As darkness approached and weather conditions deteriorated, Sammy, initially knocked unconscious by his perilous fall, heard NVA troops moving through the surrounding jungle; he hid in the dense undergrowth and went undetected. By the next morning he had returned to the small clearing used the day before to insert the team, and when he heard an OV-10 overhead, SFC Hernandez crawled into the open and signaled it. In an hour, Sammy Hernandez found himself back at the team's base camp at Phu Bai.[16]

By mid-morning on the 19th, CCN had launched a Bright Light team from Da Nang to search for other survivors from the Huey crash. RT Habu, led by SSgt Charles W. Danzer, included SFC Jimmy Horton, Sgt Lemuel D. McGlothren, SSgt James Woodham as the chase medic, and six Bru Montagnards. Accompanying the team as additional members, or "strap hangers," SSgt Cliff Newman insisted on going along, and SFC Wes Wesley volunteered since he had been on the ground with RT Intruder and knew the approximate location of the crash. The insert went off without a hitch, although several batteries of 37mm guns along the mid-section of the A Shau fired 30–40 rounds at the package as they crossed the valley. Once on the ground, RT Habu was forced to move at a snail's pace through the double canopy jungle, hindered by layers of smaller trees all interwoven in a tangle of vines, thick brush, and virtually impenetrable stands of bamboo. While the team moved, the Covey ordered two flights of F-4s and went back after the guns that had just fired at his helicopters, fearful that the triple-A positions would play havoc with other SOG packages attempting to work the west wall of the A Shau. Using CBU-24, the fighters destroyed one gun and damaged another. At that point a 57mm battery opened up. The second flight of Phantoms knocked out another gun and silenced the others.[17]

Shortly after noon, Larry Hull relieved the on-station Covey. As he headed in to land at Phu Bai, Covey 221 cautioned Woodstock over the secure radio, "The Bright Light has a long way to go. My guess is they'll need lots of air support as they move and when they extract. Be on the lookout for a ZPU [14.5mm heavy machine gun] somewhere on the ridge just above the team. He could give your choppers problems."[18]

SFC Jose Fernandez was once again flying right seat in the O-2A Sky-master as Covey rider for Woodstock—this was his second Covey mission. Fernandez informed Danzer that he had the crash site spotted, and since it was only a short distance over the side of the hill in the direction of the A Shau, he would direct the team to it. The thick undergrowth slowed their progress, and they had to snake their way through the wait-a-minute vines and deadfall while Wes used his signal mirror to let Covey know their location. With help from Jose, the team made a couple of course corrections and found the crash site. Then the unexpected happened.

Covey 275 was orbiting above the team gathering information about the crash from Charlie Danzer. On his last pass over the team, Woodstock, from Lubbock, Texas, was in a sharp left hand bank avoiding some heavy machine gun fire—the team could see the top of the Cessna's wings. Seconds passed and then the team heard a crashing sound; the noise of the O-2's engines abruptly stopped.

Realizing they had probably lost two more Americans, the members of RT Habu continued with their grisly job at the helicopter crash site. The team found both Comanchero pilots still strapped in their seats. One door gunner, Specialist 4 Gary L. Johnson, was hanging from a tree; Wes and Cliff carefully lowered him down to the ground. Meanwhile, Mc-Glothren and Horton put the two pilots, George Berg and Gerald Woods, in body bags. They also found a single leg but not the rest of the body. It was assumed the body part was that of Specialist 4 Walter E. Demsey, Jr., and that he had been trapped under the helicopter which caught fire when it crashed. The engine and transmission had completely melted into molten metal. The only recognizable part of the Huey was the tail section and rotor mast, without its rotor blade. With darkness and the weather closing in fast, RT Habu placed the body bags on top of the burned out helicopter wreckage and moved off to find a suitable night defensive position.[19]

Covey 221 located Woodstock's aircraft with no difficulty. The crash site sat on top of the west rim of the A Shau at an elevation of about 4,700 feet, just inside Laos. From the air, the plane seemed to be partially intact with both wings and the empennage still attached, appearing to have come down in some kind of crash landing. Devastated by the tragedy unfolding in the Valley of Death, everybody stood by anxiously while CCN put together a second Bright Light team. When the choppers finally arrived late that afternoon, the Covey led them to the scene and orbited while the Bright Light team inserted next to the O-2. On the ground, Captain Frederick C. Wunderlich had repelled down from the hovering chopper to the crash with three other team members. They found the damage to be much more extensive than could be seen from above. Wunderlich stated that "The whole top and wing section was shredded down, exposing the cockpit. Both Jose and Woodstock were dead and the crash had broken nearly every bone in their bodies." With a great deal of difficulty they managed to remove and recover Jose Fernandez's body. In Jose's lap they even found the gold baht chain and Buddha amulet Jimmy Horton had given him for safekeeping until Horton returned from the mission. But no matter how hard they tried, they could not get Larry's body out of the twisted wreckage. As it began to get dark and the team started receiving sporadic ground fire, they put Fernandez in a body bag, strapped him to the jungle penetrator, and hoisted him up, leaving Woodstock still sitting at the controls of his Oscar Deuce.*[20]

As the daylight faded, RT Habu spotted two STABO ropes. After moving a short distance downhill the team discovered two bodies still attached to ropes hanging approximately 40 to 50 feet over the edge of a steep cliff. At the bottom of the rock face they could just make out the lifeless forms of Doc Watson and Allen Lloyd. In the darkness, the team followed the cliff for another 30 meters and set up a perimeter with their backs to the overhang. Danzer, standing at the edge of the cliff staring down at the heartbreaking scene below, sent a 'team okay' to the Covey and advised that they would recover the bodies of their friends in the morning.

---

*In 1997 a joint US/Lao team located a crash site believed to be that of Larry Hull. Various pieces of aircraft wreckage and life support equipment found definitely correlated this site to Larry's O-2 aircraft. Unfortunately, the team was unable to recover any remains. The site was finally excavated in 2006, and Larry's remains recovered. He was buried at Arlington National Cemetery with full military honors on 13 November, 2006.

For RT Habu, the action began just after dawn on February 20, when the One-Zero asked for an air strike against a concentration of enemy troops to his west. For the past two hours his team had heard sporadic fire close by, including a few rounds from an 82mm mortar. The Covey obliged by controlling Bennett Flight, a two-ship of F-4s, against suspected enemy positions around his team. The blast patterns from the 500-pound bombs looked spectacular, probably because each MK-82 sported a three-foot-long fuse extender protruding from the nose. Instead of burrowing into the dirt making a crater, the 500-pounders detonated when the fuse contacted the surface, lethally blasting the surrounding jungle. With each explosion, the FAC could hear the Bright Light team cheering over the radio. At that point the Covey stood by awaiting the arrival of a large Air Force HH-53 helicopter, call sign 'Knife,' to haul out the 12 RT Habu team members, plus the dead crew and team members from the helicopter crash. Waiting on the ground, Jimmie Horton asked Wes Wesley for a cigarette and Wes said, "As soon as we light one, we'll get hit." At that very moment all hell broke loose as an NVA counter-recon company attacked RT Habu in force. The scene immediately turned into a close-quarters firefight of unimaginable ferocity and of human survival against the odds. The area erupted in a hail of automatic weapons fire and Claymore mine explosions. Hand grenades rained down on the team, one of them exploding right next to Jimmy Horton; his foot was nearly blown off and was just dangling by shreds.[21]

In the turmoil, Cliff Newman picked up Horton and what was left of his foot and jumped over the ledge. While attempting to contact the orbiting FAC, Charlie Danzer was also blown over the same cliff by an RPG explosion, his radio smashed beyond repair. Newman got on his URC-10 survival radio and made contact with Covey 221, explaining the grave situation and directing the Covey's low-level machine-gun strafe against the ridge line just a few yards above his position. The FAC had already launched a set of slicks and Cobras to the area and called on the services of a flight of VNAF A-1 Skyraiders.

After what seemed like an eternity, the two-ship of VNAF A-1s came up on frequency. Even though Newman stood in the open under heavy fire and popped a smoke for his FAC, only small whiffs of yellow sifted up through the jungle canopy. Had the smoke drifted? Was it in the right

place? There was no time to make sure since RT Habu was taking murderous fire from three sides. As the Covey fired a willie pete rocket down
one side of the team's perimeter, the big A-1s dropped a string of CBU-25
bomblets down the other. Complicating the situation, typically the rear-
ejecting sub-munitions did not drop in a straight line after release but
drifted toward the left for 15 feet or so for every 100 feet of altitude. Unfortunately, the shrapnel from a few of the exploding bomblets wounded Sgt
Lemuel McGlothren in the back, along with several other Bru team members. At that point, in the middle of a vicious firefight, Wes Wesley ran out
into the middle of the clearing with Cliff Newman and popped another
smoke, holding it high above his head on the butt of his CAR-15. This
time, with corrections from the totally exposed Newman, the FAC pinpointed the team's exact location and the A-1s did the rest, pounding the
NVA on the ridge above the team with Mk-81 250-pound bombs and
20mm strafe.[22]

With virtually all strike aircraft being funneled into the Lam Son 719
battles just to the north, somehow the Covey obtained another set of F-
4s, putting their MK-82s in as close as he dared, about 150 meters east of
the team. In a split second the concussion and shock waves from the 500-
pound bombs raced over RT Habu, but they were apparently unhurt by
the bombs' lethal force. With some of the ground fire suppressed by the
bombs, the Covey next moved the ordnance in much closer to the team,
employing the 20mm cannons on the F-4s. Known as the M-61 Vulcan,
this six-barrel Gatling gun, firing an incredible 6,000 rounds per minute,
stripped the trees almost bare of leaves and cut a swath through the jungle
around RT Habu about five meters wide.

Jimmy Horton's injury required immediate medical attention, so RT
Habu called a single Huey into the battle area to medevac their badly
wounded friend while the A-1s were still available to provide covering fire.
Since there was no LZ, the plan was to take Horton out on a string. The
plan, although a noble one, went haywire from the beginning. As the Huey
hovered, one of the Bru team members, evidently unaware of the plan,
brashly hooked his STABO rig onto the string and away he went, leaving
the badly injured Jimmy Horton on the ground with the remainder of the
Bright Light team. At that same moment, an RPG was fired at the UH-1
from the ridgeline and exploded, sending hot shrapnel into the helicopter,

wounding the pilot and the right door gunner. For its trouble, the Huey sustained 50 more hits from the intense ground fire as it pulled away.[23]

Some minutes later the Heavy Hook HH-53 arrived with a second set of A-1s. As the big Sikorsky helicopter pulled the team out three at a time via a hoist and jungle penetrator, the FAC worked the Skyraiders 'danger close' around the hovering bird. As the HH-53 started to pull the jungle penetrator up with the last three team members attached, the winch suddenly slipped due to the combined weight of the three Americans. Upon being slammed back on to the ground, SSgt Newman, fully aware that his action might lead to certain death or capture, unhooked from the penetrator and elected to stay on the ground by himself in order that the other two team members could be extracted safely. Now the sole target of every NVA soldier in the immediate area, Newman remained on the ground alone, shouting ordnance corrections to the FAC and singlehandedly battling the entire counter recon company. When the penetrator finally came back down, Cliff Newman was the last man out, firing his weapon at the charging NVA soldiers the entire time he was being hoisted. He got a much-needed assist from the Knife door gunner who turned his lethal mini-gun loose against the enemy. Through it all, the first two Bru team members lifted aboard positioned themselves on the open back ramp of the helicopter and used their M-79s to fire CS tear gas grenades to slow down the NVA attackers. Finally, with RT Habu safely onboard, the HH-53 headed for the Air Force hospital at Da Nang while four A-1 Skyraiders did victory rolls over the big helicopter before heading back to Thailand.*[24]

Across the valley, members of another SOG recon team were desperately fighting for their lives on abandoned Firebase Thor. Captain James E. Butler led RT Python, with SSgt Leslie A. Chapman as the One-One. SSgt Larry Brasier and Sgt Reuben Prophett joined the team on their first missions, along with 10 Montagnards. They were inserted the same day as RT Intruder and had been in constant contact, surrounded by hundreds of NVA from the first day.

---

*In early June 2015, Cliff Newman joined a team from the Defense POW/MIA Accounting Agency on another mission into the A Shau to search for the remains of the missing men from RT Intruder and the helicopter crew lost during the extraction. Unfortunately, the DPAA team could not locate the site. Case 1706 remains active.

Jim Butler's choice of Firebase Thor as the insert LZ proved to be unorthodox as well as controversial. CCN had originally wanted him to insert on the valley floor, but from experience Butler knew that the valley offered no cover and that the tall elephant grass cut visibility to just a few feet. On February 12, he jumped in the back seat of a Covey OV-10 to perform his own aerial reconnaissance of the target area, and as he had suspected, the valley LZs were totally unacceptable. Butler did, however, find a location that suited his mission perfectly: the remnants of old Firebase Thor on the east wall of the A Shau approximately six kilometers due east of the insert LZ for RT Intruder. Armed with a new plan, the leader of RT Python injected his own security precaution into the mission. Butler was convinced that a "mole" somewhere in the chain of command was tipping off the North Vietnamese about LZs, so he announced to all his intention to use the LZs on the valley floor as his primary and backup insertion points. In actuality, he and his Covey FAC were the only ones who knew that Thor was to be the LZ. When the Covey reminded Butler that the six square kilometer "No Bomb Line" boxes—no ordnance could be expended inside the box unless a Prairie Fire FAC controlled the strikes—would be around the wrong LZs, the cagey One-Zero replied, "I'll take care of it."[*][25]

At 11:30 a.m. on February 18, four Hueys carrying RT Python departed Phu Bai with one American team member aboard each chopper. The additional airlift was necessitated by Butler's plan to "go in heavy." Besides carrying food and water for a week, each man carried at least 3 claymore mines, 4 ground flares, 2 white phosphorous grenades, 20 minigrenades, and 1,000 rounds of CAR-15 ammunition. The team also hauled in four M-60 machine guns with 5,000 rounds of ammo each, along with a 60mm mortar with 50 HE rounds. In addition, Butler lugged in a powerful PRC-77 radio and antenna.

En route to the A Shau, Jim Butler aboard the lead UH-1 told his pilot about the change in LZ. The news initially rattled the pilot who balked at the idea of landing on Thor; most of the abandoned firebases had been

*Butler's suspicions had been correct. The mole was later identified as a very high level ARVN colonel attached to the Joint General Staff who participated in the monthly SOG targeting meetings. Evidently the individual communicated real time information about SOG targets directly to Hanoi.

mined and booby-trapped when the 101st pulled out of the valley in 1969 during Operation Massachusetts Striker. When the chopper went into a hover just above the surface, Butler jumped to the ground and began stomping up and down and running around Thor to demonstrate that there was no problem. The lead Slick reluctantly landed in a cloud of red dust. One of Butler's first actions after landing was to break out the radio and attach a 30-foot "292" antenna, to the top of which he carefully hooked a small American flag. Since the new location did not enjoy the protection of the No Bomb Line provision, Butler hoped the American flag would alert any marauding helicopter hunter-killer teams of his presence. The flag also served another purpose: it announced to the NVA in the area, "We're here, and we're staying."[26]

The immediate task for RT Python was to dig in and fortify the dilapidated remnants of Thor. Situated on the barren top of Hill 1084, the former firebase sported a few crumbing sandbag walls and not much else. As seen from the rim, steep fern-covered inclines sloped downhill 30 to 100 meters before intersecting with heavy jungle. The NVA would certainly be expected to approach from 360 degrees using that jungle for cover, but at that point they would have to traverse uphill on open ground to get at the 14-man team. To greet the attack they knew would come, the members of RT Python carefully placed a barrier of claymore and M-14 toe-popper mines around their perimeter and positioned their machine guns on four sides of their makeshift Alamo, while Les Chapman dug in the 60mm mortar near the center so he could adjust fire in any direction. In short order the team had in place its plan for channeling enemy movement into four distinct kill zones. Orchestrating the defense from the center of Thor, Jim Butler set up his command post and made radio contact with the FOB at Phu Bai, thanks to his tall 292 antenna. He also established contact with RT Intruder just across the valley on the west wall, a vital link since Intruder had no direct communication with the FOB.

The initial TIC occurred at 9:43 p.m. when RT Python heard enemy troops moving up the mountain. The team set off several claymores and opened fire, driving the NVA away, but several hours later the team members braced when in the darkness they heard the distinctive pop-pop-pop, as enemy soldiers dropped HE rounds into mortar tubes and opened up from all directions. Simultaneously, sniper fire raked Thor, wounding several of the defenders. Butler returned the favor by calling on the services of an AC-119 Stinger gunship. Stinger 08 repelled the attackers with a lethal barrage of mini-gun and 20mm cannon fire.

That first night, RT Python watched the valley floor to their west as a procession of truck headlights moved unimpeded down Route 548, accompanied by long lines of troops carrying flashlights. Observing those movements, Jim Butler instinctively knew that the harassment fire he was receiving represented only the prelude to a massive attack by hundreds of enemy soldiers. To even the odds, he unleashed an AC-130 gunship equipped with a state of the art system called "Black Crow," which could detect spark plug impulses in truck engines up to ten miles away. According to Butler, "There were more lights than I could count. I was now working with Spectre, the incredible AC-130, my favorite. We brought him on target via offset UPN transponders [radar beacons] and it was a turkey shoot. We could hear the NVA screaming on the valley floor from our position. The more they screamed, the more I hit them. They turned their lights off."[27]

Throughout the day on the 19th, harassing enemy mortar rounds crashed into Firebase Thor, wounding still more of the RT Python defenders. In a small victory, Butler did succeed in making radio contact with RT Habu, the Bright Light team across the valley attempting to reach the downed helicopter. With almost everyone on Thor wounded and the enemy massing for a final assault, Capt Butler thought about calling for an extraction, but since he was the only direct radio link for RT Habu, he decided to gut it out and continue the mission. Possibly Jim regretted that decision when during the night a heavy mortar attack preceded the long awaited ground assault. At 9:40 p.m., at least 60 determined NVA soldiers stormed out of the darkness and up the steep southwest slopes of Hill 1084. Claymores and 60mm mortar fire stopped 13 of them, but the human waves kept coming. At the height of the attack Butler made radio contact with the CCN Mobile Launch Team at Quang Tri; they sent in the cavalry. Within minutes a Stinger gunship arrived overhead, followed at 1 a.m. by an AC-130, Spectre 05. The 25-minute aerial pounding from the 20mm Vulcan cannons cut down the NVA. Even in the pitch-black night the enemy could not hide from the Spectre's low-light-level-TV and forward-looking infrared sensors. Butler then turned the gunship loose on an enemy column on the valley floor, decimating their ranks and igniting ten sec-

A view of the infamous A Shau Valley looking south. American forces fought along the valley's forbidding terrain and in perpetually miserable weather for nine years.—*National Archives*

An aerial view of Special Forces Camp A Shau looking east to west. The runway can be seen in the foreground with the triangular-shaped camp in the upper center. The camp fell to the NVA on 10 March 1966.—*U.S. Air Force*

Left: Majors Bernie Fisher and Jump Myers photographed in front of their A-1E following the miraculous rescue at Camp A Shau. For his actions on 10 March 1966, Fisher was awarded the Medal of Honor.—*U.S. Air Force*

Below: Troopers from the 1st Cavalry Division combat assault into the west wall of the A Shau during Operation Delaware.—*U.S. Army*

A flight of Air Force A-1H Skyraiders escorting an HH-53 Jolly Green on a sortie over Laos. Both aircraft teamed up to run some of the most dangerous rescue missions of the war in Target Oscar 8, just a few miles west of the A Shau Valley.—*U.S. Air Force*

Major General John Tolson, commander of the 1st Cavalry Division, confers with his counterpart, Major General Ngo Quang Truong, 1st ARVN Division, and an unidentified aide during Operation Delaware.—*U.S. Army*

A mortar crew from Bravo Company's 2nd Battalion, 7th Cavalry, 1st Cavalry Division preparing to evacuate a landing zone in the A Shau on 23 April 1968 during Operation Delaware. Note the crashed Huey just to their rear.—*Bettmann/Corbis*

When no landing zone was available, UH-1 Hueys often rescued SOG or Project Delta personnel using any means available. Here, members of a reconnaissance team ride out on ladders after an emergency extraction from Laos.—*Richard Madore*

A CH-47 Chinook with supplies suspended in a net beneath its fuselage delivers its load to 101st Airborne troopers on Fire Support Base Berchtesgaden in the A Shau Valley during Operation Somerset Plain.—*U.S. Army*

Marines from 3rd Battalion, 9th Marines, slog their way up the steep slopes of Tiger Mountain during Operation Dewey Canyon, a search and destroy sweep through the north end of the A Shau.—*U.S. Marine Corps*

Above: Route 922 on the Ho Chi Minh Trail. This bomb-cratered segment was located in the northwest corner of the infamous A Shau Valley. —*Author's collection*

Left: Marines stop to inspect some of the 606 enemy rifles captured in the A Shau on 28 February 1969 during Operation Dewey Canyon.—*U.S. Marine Corps*

Right: Marine Corps 1st Lieutenant Wesley L. Fox earned the Medal of Honor during a ferocious firefight in the A Shau Valley on 22 February 1969.—*1st Battalion 9th Marines*

Below: This is the view that greeted Screaming Eagle troopers as they waited for orders to advance yet one more time up Dong Ap Bia—a place they would dub Hamburger Hill.—*U.S. Army*

During Operation Apache Snow a Screaming Eagle platoon leader talks on his PRC-25 radio while one of his troopers engages the enemy with his M-16.—*U.S. Army*

Troopers from the 3rd Battalion, 187th Infantry, 101st Airborne Division, assault an enemy bunker near the top of Hamburger Hill.—*Bettmann/Corbis*

Scribbled on the bottom of a C-rations carton, this iconic sign gave the battle for Hill 937 its unflattering name.—*U.S. Army*

Weary troopers from the 3rd Battalion, 187th Infantry, collapse on the top of bloody Hamburger Hill after finally securing the summit on 20 May 1969 during Operation Apache Snow.—*U.S. Army*

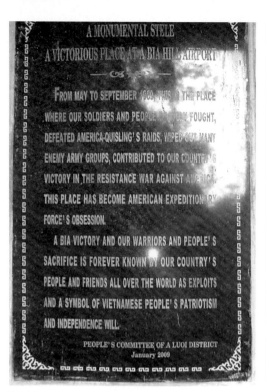

A MONUMENTAL STELE
A VICTORIOUS PLACE AT
A BIA HILL AIRPORT

FROM MAY TO SEPTEMBER 1969, THIS
IS THE PLACE WHERE OUR SOLDIERS
AND PEOPLE BRAVELY FOUGHT,
DEFEATED AMERICA-QUISLING'S
RAIDS, WIPED OUT MANY ENEMY ARMY
GROUPS, CONTRIBUTED TO OUR
COUNTRY'S VICTORY IN THE RESIST-
ANCE WAR AGAINST AMERICA. THIS
PLACE HAS BECOME AMERICAN
EXPEDITIONARY FORCE'S OBSESSION.
    A BIA VICTORY AND OUR WAR-
RIORS AND PEOPLE'S SACRIFICE IS
FOREVER KNOWN BY OUR COUNTRY'S
PEOPLE AND FRIENDS ALL OVER THE
WORLD AS EXPLOITS AND A SYMBOL
OF VIETNAMESE PEOPLE'S PATRIOTISM
AND INDEPENDENCE WILL.

PEOPLE'S COMMITTEE OF
A LUOI DISTRICT
JANUARY 2009

This English version of a 2009 memorial plaque placed on Hamburger Hill by the "People's Committee of A Luoi" uses bombastic rhetoric to tell their version of the battle for Dong Ap Bia. A heavy dose of propaganda permeates the text, seen at right.—*John Podlaski*

A close up view of a camouflaged enemy bunker on Hill 996, just a few kilometers south of the infamous Hamburger Hill. These dugouts all had a distinctive odor the NVA always seemed to impregnate everything with: a smell of cordite, rotting fish, and untended urinals.—*U.S. Army*

A patrol from the Screaming Eagles motors along a rough trail toward Ta Bat in mid June, 1969 during Operation Montgomery Rendezvous.—*U.S. Army*

In the heat of battle, Cobra pilots on occasion rescued fellow fliers. In this shot Loren Gee hitches a ride on the ammo bay door of an AH-1 after his Cobra was shot down in the Valley of Death on 19 February 1970.—*Author's collection*

During a sapper attack in the A Shau at Fire Support Base Maureen, Private Kenneth M. Kays, a medic with the 1st Battalion, 506th, 101st Airborne Division, earned the Medal of Honor on 7 May 1970 for saving the lives of his wounded comrades in Delta Company.—*U.S. Army*

Members of a battery from the 2nd Battalion, 11th Artillery, 101st Airborne Division, man the 155mm guns on Fire Support Base Ripcord, July 1970.—*U.S. Army*

An Air Force OV-10 Bronco, call sign Covey, marks a target in Laos. The Covey FACs flying the Prairie Fire mission supported SOG reconnaissance teams on their dangerous journeys into the A Shau Valley.—*U.S. Air Force*

A patrol from 2nd Battalion, 506th Infantry, returns through concertina wire strung around Fire Support Base Ripcord on 7 July 1970.—*U.S. Army*

In this shot of the rugged west wall of the A Shau, the "1706" is the case file designation for the Huey crew lost on 18 February 1971 during the attempted rescue of RT Intruder. In June 2015, Cliff Newman returned to the site to resume the search for his missing comrades.—*JTF-FA photo*

Heavy black smoke billows from Ripcord on 18 July 1970 after a CH-47 Chinook crashed into the 105mm howitzer battery on the southeast corner of the FSB. Enemy machine gunners at the base of the hill brought the Chinook down.—*U.S. Army*

Troopers from Charlie Company, 1st Battalion, 506th Infantry, refill canteens at a stream along the east wall of the A Shau.—*U.S. Army*

A Huey Dustoff lands on Ripcord to evacuate the wounded.—*U.S. Army photo*

ondary explosions. Thanks to the gunships, RT Python would live to fight another day.[28]

Another reconnaissance team also took part in the operation, entering the Valley of Death in support of Lam Son 719 early on the morning of February 20. RT Louisiana, led by Capt Duane Ramsey, inserted into the valley floor against a notorious target that Jim Butler referred to as the "Freak Show." Since Ramsey and his One-One, John Houser, were both African Americans, the team had acquired the unofficial nickname "RT Africa," and after the movie *M*A*S*H* came out, everyone called John Houser "Spear-Chucker," the nickname of Fred Williamson's character in the iconic film. Within minutes after inserting, RT Africa was mauled by a large NVA force. It was to be Ramsey's first and last mission with CCN. He lasted 27 minutes on the ground and would have stayed in the A Shau permanently if Spear-Chucker had not carried his wounded One-Zero out.[29]

At 6:30 a.m. on the 20th, NVA infantry began pummeling the men on Firebase Thor with automatic weapons fire and RPG rounds from 360 degrees. In no time at all every member of RT Python had been wounded at least once, yet they held their ground until notified that RT Habu across the valley had been rescued. Almost on cue an entire NVA battalion attacked, leaving Jim Butler no choice but to declare a Prairie Fire and an emergency extraction. In response, the Covey who had just run the extraction of RT Habu dashed across the valley to help RT Python. When he arrived overhead, Butler explained in measured tones that his team was up against a massive attack in force and that the lead enemy elements were already on the northwest perimeter about to spill over the top. Prophetically, he told the Covey, "We can't hold 'em much longer. Get us out of here."

Arming up the HE rockets, the FAC spiraled down to treetop level. Sure enough, a pocket of enemy troops sat huddled just outside and below the sandbag fortification. Every few seconds several more raced out of the brush at the base of the hill and scampered 20 or 30 yards up the slope to join their buddies. Diving in from the north at a shallow angle in his OV-10, the Covey let the gunsight pipper drift up to the crouching figures before squeezing off several HE rockets. Pulling up in a hard rolling turn to the west, he did not observe the rockets' impact, so he asked Butler, "How was that?"

Laughing, Jim shouted, "You're blowing dirt and rocks all over us. It's great! Keep it coming."[30]

Unfortunately, the enemy troops were climbing the entire hill perimeter faster than the team or the FAC's rockets could mow them down. As if in answer to a prayer, a two-ship of A-1s en route from Thailand to Da Nang came to the rescue. Within ten minutes the Covey had the Skyraiders dropping napalm canisters 'danger close' on the hiding troops at the base of the hill. Then they worked over the slopes and tree lines with CBU-25 and strafe. Just as the A-1s departed, the One-Zero's shouts alerted the FAC to another pending disaster; Butler was beside himself. NVA formations were attacking the north end of Firebase Thor with infantry and a barrage of B-40 rockets. One of the explosions had blown an indigenous member of RT Python down the slope of the hill into the advancing enemy troops. The One-One, SSgt Les Chapman, with complete disregard for his own safety, climbed over the barricade and charged down the hill to retrieve his unconscious comrade. Although already wounded, Chapman ran directly into the middle of an enemy squad, killing four of them in close combat. Reaching the wounded soldier, he threw the injured trooper on his back and started up the steep slope under murderous enemy fire. Although wounded again and knocked down by exploding grenades, he managed to carry the soldier back inside the perimeter where he administered first aid to the Montagnard, refusing medical attention for himself. For his extraordinary heroism, Leslie A. Chapman was awarded the Distinguished Service Cross.[31]

Because of the intense fighting along Route 9, all 101st Airborne Division helicopter assets were heavily committed to Lam Son 719, so CCN's Phu Bai FOB could only round up two Hueys to effect the rescue of RT Python—not a single Cobra gunship was available, meaning the vulnerable unarmed Slicks would have to run the gauntlet at Thor alone. The Covey managed to scare up two sets of fighters that were coming off the refueling tanker and would be overhead in about 15 minutes, but RT Python just didn't have that kind of time—the rescue had to occur now or never. With the men trapped on top of that hill laying down their maximum rate of covering fire, the Hueys began their approach supported by the lone OV-10. The Covey concentrated his HE rockets in the southern quadrant and tree lines while the door gunners fired their M-60s along the steep slope.

As the lead Huey crossed the hilltop perimeter, the chopper shook violently from the blasts of several RPG explosions, but the pilot held on and touched down in a blinding cloud of red dust. After an agonizingly long wait, Lead lifted off, covered by the FAC who laid down a wall of strafe from one end of the eastern slope to the other, then racked his Bronco into a high-G climbing turn to the west to link up with Slick Two. In formation, they ran a carbon copy of the original effort, with the Covey firing off all his remaining rockets and the last few rounds from his machine guns as Slick Two slid into the LZ. When the Huey finally lifted off, the unopposed enemy troops on the eastern slope riddled it from stem to stern. Somehow, the courageous crew kept their chopper flying.[32]

As the shot-up formation departed the A Shau, the team took a head count and discovered they were a man short. In the confusion they had left one of their own on the LZ. Although out of ammunition, dangerously low on fuel, and bleeding from numerous shrapnel wounds, the Covey led his airborne package back to Firebase Thor. He then covered the lead UH-1's approach by executing multiple treetop-level passes, drawing all ground fire toward his own aircraft while pickling off his external stores, sending the four empty LAU-59 rocket pods and the external fuel tank tumbling end over end into the red dirt. The ploy silenced two heavy machine guns and at least forced the enemy troops to keep their heads down, thus enabling the vulnerable helicopter to land and rescue the stranded team member.[33] Alive but bloodied by their ordeal, the members of RT Python mostly rode in silence back to Phu Bai, all wounded with one Montagnard dying en route. On the slopes of Firebase Thor they left 42 enemy soldiers dead and an estimated 300 KBA.[34] Later that afternoon, another Covey put in multiple airstrikes against Thor to destroy the equipment RT Python had to abandon during their emergency extraction.

Even before the ARVN invasion of Laos concluded, American troop withdrawal moved forward at an accelerated pace and continued throughout the year. In early March the 5th Special Forces Group officially returned to Fort Bragg, followed by the 1st Brigade of the 5th Mech, which returned to Fort Polk, Louisiana. Two brigades from the Americal Division left and the division was deactivated, while the entire 1st Marine Division returned to Camp Pendleton. The only remaining U.S. division in Military Region I, the 101st Airborne Division, found itself confined to "dynamic defense" duties as it gradually disengaged from active combat and prepared to return to Fort Campbell beginning in December 1971. The rapid disengagement in Vietnam also signaled a shift in Army emphasis back toward the traditional Cold War European battlefield.[35] And what about the A Shau Valley, the place that time forgot? After nine years of bitter fighting, MACV forgot about it, too—it was now an ARVN problem.

For reasons never explained or justified, SOG continued to insert U.S.-led reconnaissance teams into the valley, more than likely because they remained "the only game in town" willing to take on the dangerous assignment. By and large most of the missions did not accomplish their goals, although not from a lack of valor, sacrifice, or initiative on the part of the individual team members going in harm's way. Nevertheless, their impact on the enemy was far out of proportion to their size. Presumably any intelligence the teams gathered made its way up the chain of command to MACV, but what value it offered became a moot point since the American headquarters had no intention of acting on the information.

Albert Einstein is credited with saying that "insanity is doing the same thing over and over again and expecting different results." By Einstein's definition, the planners at SOG in 1971 must have suffered from chronic insanity after repeatedly ordering what amounted to a standard mission profile. The organization suffered from an incurable operational mentality, one that did not attempt to analyze lessons learned, nor did it come up with methods to offset North Vietnam's efforts to counter SOG teams. Invariably, the results rarely changed, especially in the A Shau. As team members continued to be killed, even a few senior officers within SOG agitated against the accepted modus operandi. For example, Lt Colonel Raymond Call, deputy chief of OP-35, the Ground Studies Group responsible for sending teams against the Ho Chi Minh Trail, felt strongly that the program had become stale. In discussing the mission, he noted that "It became redundant and a waste of resources. If you double the size of something like OP-35 it doesn't mean it's going to be twice as good." After his second tour with OP-35, Call reflected, "I don't think we accomplished anything my second tour . . . but the issue then was to put numbers on the board . . . never mind if you didn't get any intelligence."[36]

In spite of Raymond Call's warning, recon teams continued to be inserted into the Valley of Death—with predictable results. For instance, on

May 3, 1971, RT Asp ventured into the southeast corner of the A Shau: the three Americans and five Montagnards were never seen again. Years later the lone Montagnard survivor from RT Asp turned up and revealed that a 40-man local VC militia force tracked down the team and engaged them in a prolonged firefight. When the VC ordered the team to surrender, the members of RT Asp kept fighting until they ran out of ammunition, at which point the three Americans and five of the six Montagnards were captured and executed. The lone survivor managed to evade and made his way into Laos.[37]

On May 7 CCN executed a different entry into Base Area 611, this time via parachute. In an effort to insert teams at night when no LZ watchers operated, SOG decided to attempt its second combat HALO (high altitude, low opening) parachute drop in the A Shau. The concept resembled sport parachuting free-fall jumps, including a steerable parachute; however, unlike the sport, in HALO the free fall was only a means to a very hazardous end. In the predawn darkness, the four members of the all-U.S. RT Manes leaped from the tailgate of a C-130 at 18,500 feet. Two team members were injured on landing and subsequently extracted, but the two remaining continued their mission throughout their four-day stay in the area. The team was targeted against a storage area which, unfortunately, they could not locate. Nevertheless, the HALO insert apparently went undetected.[38]

Evidently expecting a different result, on May 18, 1971, CCN also inserted RT Alaska into the A Shau on the northeast corner of Base Area 611. Almost immediately the team of three Americans and three Nungs made contact with a large NVA force and called for an emergency extraction. Sgt Dale W. Dehnke, Specialist 5 Gary L. Hollingsworth, and one of the Nungs apparently died in the early fighting; it was Dehnke's 23rd birthday. During the firefight the One-Zero, Lieutenant Danny D. Entrican, and the two remaining Nungs evaded while they waited for the rescue helicopters to arrive. First on the scene was a UH-1 piloted by Warrant Officers David Soyland and Dale A. Pearce. As they passed over the team and banked the aircraft to the right, it was hit by an RPG which severed the tail boom, causing an immediate crash. The aircraft impacted on its right side on a slope, sliding downhill until it stopped at the bottom of the hill. Warrant Officer Pearce was killed in the crash, but the other three crewmen were able to exit the demolished chopper. Heavy enemy fire precluded rescue until the next day when a Bright Light team was inserted in an attempt to recover the survivors of both RT Alaska and the downed Huey. The two surviving crewmen and the two Nungs were found alive, and while Pearce's remains were identified, the rescue party lacked the tools needed to free his body from the wreckage. The Bright Light team recovered the bodies of Hollingsworth, Dehnke, and the Nung trooper. Hollingsworth and the Nung, however, had been stripped naked and both had been shot in the temple, a strong indication that they had been captured alive and then executed. One of the survivors reported that he saw a man, believed to be David Soyland, running on the crest of a nearby ridge, and although search efforts continued until May 27, the searchers were unable to locate either Lt Entrican or Warrant Officer Soyland. Both were listed as MIA.[39]

Between May 19 and May 23, the heaviest large unit battles in the A Shau occurred under the auspices of Vietnamization, when a South Vietnamese Marine battalion took on an NVA battalion in a series of sharp firefights along the east wall. Using artillery and air strikes, the South Vietnamese destroyed numerous bunker complexes and captured large stashes of enemy supplies. U.S. involvement in the battle was limited to helicopter and close air support, but at a cost. Ground fire downed three 101st helicopters and one Air Force O-2 FAC aircraft.

Just north of the A Shau, the depleted American combat presence endured another surprising shocker inflicted by aggressive, confident NVA forces. By the summer of 1971, a CCN (recently renamed Task Force 1 Advisory Element) radio relay site on Hill 950 just north of the old Khe Sanh combat base represented the only U.S. contingent left in northwestern Military Region I. Code named "Hickory," the top-secret site offered the perfect location for a highly classified operation, the National Security Agency's Polaris II radio intercept station. The defense of Hickory, a tiny enclave in an enemy controlled region, fell to a SOG contingent consisting of 27 U.S. personnel and 67 Vietnamese/Montagnard members from the Special Commando Unit, SCU. On June 4, a large NVA force scaled Hill 950 undetected and launched a fierce surprise attack on Hickory. During the hand-to-hand fighting, Sgt Jon R. Cavaiani orchestrated the helicopter evacuation of the NSA team and all wounded except for 23 SCU, Sgt John R. Jones, and himself. When enemy forces finally overran Hickory at 4 a.m. on June 5, Jones, already wounded but still fighting, was shot in the chest at close range and presumably died. Badly wounded and burned, Cavaiani ordered the remaining SCU troopers to attempt escape while he provided them with covering fire. He then retrieved a machine gun, stood up, completely exposing himself to the heavy enemy fire directed at him, and began firing the weapon at two ranks of advancing enemy soldiers. Through Sgt Cavaiani's valiant efforts, the majority of the remaining platoon members were able to escape down the hill. While inflicting severe losses on the advancing enemy force, Sgt Cavaiani was wounded numerous times before finally sliding down the face of a cliff. He crawled and dragged himself eastward for ten days before the NVA captured him. When released in 1973, Jon Cavaiani was awarded the Medal of Honor. Sgt Jones was posthumously awarded the Silver Star.[40]

At the south end of the A Shau, RT North Carolina ran into yet another large NVA unit on the Laotian border near the village of Ta Ko, a few miles southeast of Base Area 607. In the early morning on August 13, the team ambushed a large enemy force that had been sweeping the area searching for them. As the firefight erupted, Sgt Mark H. Eaton immediately began placing a heavy volume of CAR-15 fire on the advancing force, inflicting heavy casualties on them. The enemy then regrouped and aggressively assaulted the RT again, utilizing small arms, hand grenades, automatic weapons, and RPGs. Valiantly, Sgt Eaton rallied his team while repeatedly exposing himself to a hail of hostile fire in order to direct the defense of the team's position. Again he inflicted heavy losses on the enemy, thwarting the vicious assault until he was mortally wounded in a barrage of NVA small arms fire. For his gallantry, Sgt Mark H. Eaton was posthumously awarded the Silver Star.[41] Although the records are sketchy, Mark Eaton may well have been the last SOG combat death in the A Shau.[42]

Ground action might have diminished in the A Shau, but communist antiaircraft gunners kept up the pressure and made the area as deadly as ever. On September 30, a Stormy "fast FAC" F-4 from the 366th Tactical Fighter Wing at Da Nang flew a low-level mission along the southwest corner of the A Shau. The aircraft had refueled twice from KC-135 tankers before going down in the rugged terrain of Base Area 607. Capt Michael L. Donovan and Lt Ronald L. Bond have never been found.[43]

Throughout 1971, SOG inserted approximately 30 teams in and

around the A Shau Valley, all of them fighting for survival as they attempted to document a continuing NVA buildup. Whether that intelligence information was worth the lives it cost is still debated, but during the fall of 1971, SOG dutifully dispatched the data to MACV where it was rushed to a waiting courier plane and flown to American negotiators in Paris, who used it in their deliberations with their North Vietnamese counterparts. While the stalemated peace talks droned on, the deadly cat and mouse games continued in the A Shau. By November, the tactical situation had become so grim that recon teams who inserted on five-day missions ended up spending fewer than two hours on the ground before NVA counter recon companies forced them out. In December, one last recon team penetrated the valley, called in airstrikes on NVA trucks and tanks along Route 548, and made it out safe and sound.[44] With that mission—after nine years—the U.S. combat role in the A Shau Valley came to a quiet, contentious end.

chapter 10

A BARD FOR THE GRUNTS

The tumult and the shouting dies;
The captains and the kings depart:
Still stands Thine ancient sacrifice,
An humble and contrite heart.
Lord God of Hosts, be with us yet,
Lest we forget—lest we forget!
—RUDYARD KIPLING

Many of the grunts, marines, and airmen who battled the weather and NVA in and around the A Shau Valley have, over the years, found it almost impossible to share their wartime experiences either verbally or in writing. The Valley of Death numbed their minds and choked off their words. The trauma of combat ate into their souls and plagued them with war-related readjustment problems: flashbacks to combat, the inability to relate to friends and family, feelings of alienation, even unbearable doses of survivor's guilt. But one grunt managed to capture and bring to light the savagery, the friendship, the valor, and the internalized voices of a generation—and he did it through poetry.

Gary Jacobson served as a grunt infantryman in the 1st Cavalry Division in 1967. He was badly wounded when a booby-trapped artillery shell exploded, sending shrapnel through his skull and deep into his brain. While recovering and as a cathartic release, Jacobson began writing poetry, at first not realizing that his poignant feelings penned in verse encapsulated the suppressed thoughts of many other grunts.

Perhaps inspired by a Vietnamese legend that says, "All poets are full of silver threads that rise inside them as the moon grows large," Gary Jacobson confessed that he wrote because "It is that these silver threads are words poking at me—I must let them out. I must! I write for my brothers who cannot bear to talk of what they've seen and to educate those who haven't the foggiest idea about the effect that the horrors of war have on boys-next-door."

Author of several books on the Vietnam War, including a mesmerizing volume of poetry called *My Thousand Yard Stare,* Gary Jacobson has become for many the poet laureate of Vietnam. With his permission, his captivating, gut-wrenching poem *A Shau Ripcord* is included in its entirety:

A SHAU RIPCORD
by Gary Jacobson

A Shau Valley
Death walks this shadowed alley
Where the rain never stops
Fierce
In rustic tangled wood
Inaccessible
Nigh impenetrable
Wall-to-wall
Dense obstructive green
Concealing well the malignant
Virulent rebel
Malevolent NVA
Warriors in the jungled screen
Sprayed with toxins obscene
Leech infested streams
101st Airborne
Enveloped by the valley
Searching
For hostiles . . .

Hostile
Men look to kill men
Enmeshed in hate

Murderously filled with it
Boys from both sides secreting furies
To poisonously harm
Boys on the other side
Conducting half-blind
Clashes contending for the right
To life
Snarled by evil
Fierce nose to nose
So quickly lost
In the darkening wild lair
Setting the knotty jungle snare
Initiating each other into hell.
Battling for the A Shau throne

Ripcord
Twisted forest whipcord
Is the rain never going to stop?
Obsessed generals,
In pitched battle for control
Vying for one last victory
One last gasp
Last chance for glory in this war
To hone their skills
In the Nam's last dance
Before the war is through
To themselves console
Before withdrawal
Before Vietnamization.
Obsessed generals,
Playing God, by God!
Pumping technology
Into gnarled greenwood
Seeking an edge they thought
They'd win
A grunt's life catapult

Flung into the fray
In the midst of infantry foes
With Charley
Slugging it out toe to toe . . .
Filling the road
On the pathway to hell . . .
"Whatcha gonna do,
Send me to Nam?"
If we only knew
Life there in Hell
Known as the A Shau
Was dependent on the gun
Under a blistering sun . . .
Blistering our innocence . . .
Look to skies supernal
For rescue by the eternal . . .
But find no relief infernal
As in multifaceted battalions
Sneakin' and peekin',
The latest in a series
Of Long
Hot
miserable
Days . . .
In verdant jungle dark
Many men lay slaughtered
Thrown at each other
Torn from sacred life
Unto sanctified death
Down in the valley
Mid matted corkscrew
With a considerable body of troops . . .
Not ours
Where life could vanish
In a twinkling . . .

Is the rain ever going to stop?
Patrolling the dark A Shau
Slip and slide up one hill
Skim down the other side
In fevered breath
Awaiting
Fated death
Ah shit . . .
Fresh prints in the muddy track
Everyone on edge
Sniff the air for waiting ambush
Could this be the day we die?
Is the rain ever going to stop?

Is the rain ever going to stop?
Running in rivulets red
Flowing
Everywhere endless
Pop, pop, pop,
Pesky VietCong
Fire a couple rounds and di di
Harassment maddening
Frustrated
Taut jawed
Barbed wire lips . . .
Clash and dash
Get adrenalin roaring
Then bring it back down
No one around
Charley
Blends with the shadows
Until the next turn in the trail
Frustrated . . .
Waiting for "show time . . ."

Secure another LZ

On the highground
Nestled in rocks on the ridgeline
Before fast closing dark
Just another wet miserable day
As a grunt
A groundpounder
My God . . . a shortimer . . .
Listening to cricket rhythms
Hearing something small
Moving in underbrush
Harsh alarm of a monkey
Nightbirds singing low
Trembling rage still eats at me
Protected
Under the surface below . . .

I hate the quiet time
Too much time
For thinking
For fearing
Rivulets of sweat merging
With tears from my eyes
Trying to discern
The deadly sounds . . .
Again adrenalin pumping . . .
Be absolutely quiet
In this life or death moment . . .
Can anyone hear
My primal scream?
Is the rain never going to stop?
Good morning Vietnam!
Another routine morning
Check for leeches
Dislodge other crawlies
Tend your jungle rot
No such thing as dry

Clear booby traps
And trips
Check claymores
See if they've been turned
By those practical jokers
Tricky VietCong

Try to calm
Stark fear stifling
Set jangled nerves
To survive another day
Saddle up that heavy pack
Loaded with lots of things
That go boom . . .
Clean the mud off your rifle
Y'wanta make it home?
It's going to be a long
Long day
Expecting the enemy to open up
On every rise
At every bend in the trail
To bring on the hurt
Make boiling blood pump . . .
Another adrenalin dump . . .

Still we make the turn
Take each forsaken step
Past trembling bush
Over muddied ground
Past silent sound
God only knows why . . .
Or how . . .
Each minute dragging by
Seems like a year . . .
Playing hide and seek with the Cong
The stakes in this game

So high. . . .

Heroic grunts
Negotiating hell and shadow.
Good men
Brave men
Beloved men
Brothers . . .
Lost in obsidian thoughts
Slowly dying as former companions
Omnipresent jungle closing in
Chilling hot
Sweet and sour
Surrounded within . . .
In this bamboo wood
You can't find the Vietcong
Unless he wants to find us.
Napalm will ferret him out . . .
I'd rather be in Hell
Can't be any hotter than this
But perhaps we're already there
Knocking at the southern gates . . .
Look at the FNG
How long is this one gonna last?
Oh how fragile
These men of war . . .

As NVA assaulted
Sloping mountaintop
Left no choice but to bail
Out of the fiasco
Now as we left
That blood soaked ground
Picked up by the Huey's
Wearied unto death . . .

Turn out the lights
The parties over . . .
Look out your six
Charley hates to see you go . . .
Wave goodbye
It's closing time . . .
As gunships blast surrounding hills
Watch Uncle Sam's parting gift
Given by high-flying B52's
Leaving nothing for the enemy
Bombing Ripcord into extinction
Napalming it
Like it never was . . .

EPILOGUE

Generations that know us not and that we know
not of, heart-drawn to see where and by whom
great things were suffered and done for them, shall
come to this deathless field, to ponder and dream;
and lo! The shadow of a mighty presence shall wrap
them in its bosom, and the power of the vision
pass into their souls.
—JOSHUA LAWRENCE CHAMBERLAIN

Forty-plus years after the echoes of war last resonated along its steep walls, the A Shau has returned to it primordial roots, once again a remote, pristine valley, a place from the beginning of time. For the most part, the valley floor today conjures up visions of a pastoral setting with only a few overgrown bomb craters scarring the bucolic landscape. Hill 937—the infamous Hamburger Hill—rendered bare by the savage battle on its steep slopes, is totally reclaimed and covered by double canopy jungle. Route 548, once a dilapidated dirt road for NVA trucks hauling weapons of war, is now a two lane paved highway with telephone wires strung beside it. Truck and automobile traffic is at present somewhat sparse, but steady streams of motorbikes travel along the route, now called the Ho Chi Minh Highway. A Luoi, smashed and deserted during the war, has been transformed into a bustling town with one hotel, nine guesthouses, seven restaurants, and a beautiful three-story town hall. From all indications the valley residents—at least those old enough to remember—have managed to move on with their lives and block out the carnage that raged around them for nine years. In moving on they have presumably never given a second thought to the many Americans who died there. Yet those

same inhabitants, especially the younger ones, greet American visitors—
mostly returning Vietnam veterans—cordially and talk of going to the
United States to visit or study. According to one American visitor, "The
preschool-age kids are already learning English: they can count from one
to ten and proudly recite their ABCs."[1] The veterans themselves take in
the panorama and still marvel at the mystical qualities that the now tran-
quil A Shau holds for them. But in spite of the awe-inspiring new vistas
before them, they cannot and will not forget their brothers who died in
the Valley of Death.

While those aging survivors will forever remember their lost friends,
most cannot recall the strategy behind the specific operations that hurled
them into combat in the A Shau, operations that repeatedly sent them into
the shadowy valley over the course of nearly a decade. Most of those distant
campaigns—Delaware, Dewey Canyon, Massachusetts Striker, Apache
Snow, and Texas Star—went down in American history as successes, although after 40 years, numerous historians now regard the operations as
short-term expedients that accomplished little in stopping a determined
enemy from occupying a vital piece of real estate. The problem was the
lack of a coherent strategy, the limited objectives, and the shortsighted execution. The main flaws were clear from the outset, like periodically attempting to neutralize the A Shau without occupying and holding the ground,
then trying the same tactic again six months later—and expecting a different result. For that reason the various campaigns in the valley did not
achieve their objectives, but as historian John Correll cogently notes, it is
essential to remember that "North Vietnam was fighting a war. The United
States was sending signals."[2] Those signals notwithstanding, one must ask
how MACV could have hoped to force Hanoi into backing off without
eliminating the strategic A Shau Valley from the equation, certainly not
by a stratagem that periodically reacted by poking a finger in a hole in the
dike. That misstep was not just a miscalculation—it amounted to intellec-
tual negligence by military leaders who unfortunately became enamored
with their own rectitude.

In that self-imposed ethos of infallible judgment among tone-deaf senior U.S. leaders and planners, war in the A Shau—always inherently more
subjective than objective—proved to be both perplexing and unmanage-
able. American efforts around the Valley of Death came to resemble peri-

odic production-line campaigns where success was measured by statistics. Body counts, kill ratios, overly optimistic after action reports, and bomb damage assessments produced perceptions of success and only the illusion of victory—Operation Delaware prevented a second Tet attack on Hue; Dewey Canyon shut down infiltration along Route 922; Apache Snow defeated the communists on Hamburger Hill; without the success of Ripcord the 1972 Easter offensive would have been advanced a full year. Such bravado and counterfactual thinking, linked to false standards of success, fooled many into believing U.S. forces were winning the war in the A Shau.

Furthermore, given Hanoi's commitment to long-range objectives and a willingness to absorb punishing losses, North Vietnam repeatedly demonstrated the institutional fortitude to outlast the United States. Despite America's enormous expenditure of firepower and men, MACV's strategy for winning in the A Shau was neither realistic nor focused enough to ensure a successful outcome. Only taking and holding territory could have done that, something that was never seriously considered by American leadership. In effect, self-delusion substituted for strategy.

After the A Shau, one Columbia University professor astutely observed that when it comes to the use of force, "America should either bite the bullet or duck, but not nibble." That notion was reiterated by Army Chief of Staff General John A. Wickham's views on the A Shau in particular and Vietnam in general when he stated, "Once we commit force, we must be prepared to back it up as opposed to just sending soldiers into operations for limited goals."[3] MACV failed on most counts in the A Shau Valley and never did devise a strategy appropriate to the war at hand—they nibbled. Why that happened will remain the subject of rancorous discussion for years to come.

On reexamination, the 1970 battle for Fire Support Base Ripcord encapsulates in microcosm the long, bloody U.S. effort in the A Shau. The operations officer of the 2nd Battalion, 506th Infantry at Ripcord, Major Herb Koenigsbauer, offered a profound and emotional analysis that resonates even today:

> I cannot reconcile in my mind that the chain of command could not foresee the impact the opening of Ripcord would have on the NVA. The potential for a major enemy response must have been

realized at the highest levels. If the political climate was so clear to people above battalion and brigade that evacuation was the only viable option when the enemy massed around the firebase, it makes no sense that the battalion was ever committed to taking Ripcord. There had been no change in the political situation from the time we were ordered to take Ripcord and the time we were ordered to evacuate. To write Ripcord off made clear to those of us fighting the war that there was no national commitment to fight and win . . . The evacuation saved U.S. lives, but it was also one more step towards our tactical, operational, and strategic defeat in Vietnam.[4]

Yet in no way does that defeat reflect on the grunts, marines, and airmen who did the fighting and the dying. Their extraordinary heroism and devotion to duty are in keeping with the highest traditions of the armed forces of the United States. They consecrated the ground known as the Valley of Death with their blood, sweat, tears, and sacrifices. Retrospectively, Admiral Chester W. Nimitz's observation about Marines on Iwo Jima applies equally well to the gallant men who fought in the A Shau Valley: "Uncommon valor was a common virtue."

ACKNOWLEDGMENTS

This project could never have been undertaken without the support and encouragement of many friends, colleagues, researchers, and scholars across this wonderful country. I am indebted to all of them. I especially want to thank those who shared with me their own stories and writings: in particular Jim Butler, John Carter, Loren Gee, Jim Mitschke, Cliff Newman, Evan Quiros, Robby Robinson, Mike Sprayberry, and Don Taylor.

Still more people helped in other ways. I benefitted greatly from numerous individuals who assisted with tracking down hundreds of primary source documents. Steve Sherman and John Plaster, two Special Forces veterans and well-known Vietnam scholars, generously shared their data with me by bringing after action reports and valor citations to my attention. Rick Blythe from the Ripcord Association, Gary Roush from the Vietnam Helicopter Pilots Association, and Cal Rollins from the Special Operations Association guided me through the mountains of literature on operations in the A Shau Valley. Information and insights provided by Rick Blythe, Jason Hardy, Bill Kindred, and Gary Robb have been invaluable.

My endeavor has been greatly facilitated by the tireless efforts of staff members in various government agencies and universities. I owe a special debt to Dr. Fred Allison, chief of the Marine Corps Oral History Archives, for providing hours of taped interviews with participants in Operation Dewey Canyon. The same holds true for Barry Spink and Archie DiFante of the Air Force Historical Research Agency, Sharon Edgington at the Congressional Medal of Honor Society, and Dr. Janet McDonnell, senior historian at the Defense Intelligence Agency. Thanks also to Tim Nenninger, Holly Reed, Marcus Martin, and all the dedicated folks at the National

Archives for their assistance and patience as I proceeded to drive them to fits of distraction with my constant demands for more information and photographs. I am also beholden to the U.S. Army Center of Military History and to the Texas Tech University Vietnam Center and Archive for allowing me access to their outstanding databases. And a special 'hats off' to Professor Ian Ward and graduate assistant Jeff Huewinkel in the Department of Geography at George Mason University who were instrumental in creating maps for *A Shau Valor*, and to Dr. Richard Diecchio, geology professor at GMU, who graciously spent time tutoring me on the geological origins of the A Shau Valley.

I chose Casemate from among the publishers who bid for *A Shau Valor* because of the company's impeccable reputation for producing top quality military history books. I am particularly grateful to Casemate's editorial director, Steve Smith, for guiding and nurturing this project. The other Casemate personnel who assisted in the book's publication—publicity director Tara Lichterman and production editor Libby Braden—were committed and supportive from the beginning. Throughout the project they worked with unbounded energy and efficiency.

Behind the scenes three individuals have played key roles in bringing this manuscript to life. Thanks to Gary Jacobson, the "poet laureate of Vietnam," for inspiring me and allowing me to reprint his gut-wrenching poem, *A Shau Ripcord*. Also, I offer my profound thanks to a trusted friend: former Air Force nurse, Vietnam veteran, and Da Nang colleague Naomi Fisher, who read the manuscript carefully and critically—her moral compass always pointed true north and helped keep me on track. Finally, every step of the way I relied on the good judgment and counsel of my long-time literary agent, Ethan Ellenberg, who backed the project with enthusiasm from concept to completion. I thank them all. As the incomparable New York Yankees manager Casey Stengel said after his team won the 1958 World Series, "I couldn't a done it without 'em."

NOTES

PREFACE

1 Arnand S. Khati, *Jim Corbett of India* (Noida, India: Pelican Creations International, 2008), p. 103.

2 T.R. Yarborough, *Da Nang Diary: A Forward Air Controller's Gunsight View of Flying with SOG* (Havertown, PA: Casemate Publishers, 2013), p. 24.

3 Keith W. Nolan, *Ripcord: Screaming Eagles under Siege, Vietnam 1970* (New York: Ballantine Books, 2000), p. 4.

4 L.V. Averyanov, "Phytogeographic Review of Vietnam," *Komarovia*, March 2003, pp. 3–6.

5 *Minority Groups in the Republic of Vietnam,* (Washington, DC: Department of the Army Pamphlet 550–105, 1966), p. 9–6.

6 Shelby L. Stanton, *Green Berets at War: U.S. Army Special Forces in Southeast Asia 1956–1975,* (Novato, CA: Presidio Press, 1985), pp. 38–41.

7 Nikolas Arhem, *In the Sacred Forest: Landscape, Livelihood and Spirit Beliefs Among the Katu of Vietnam* (Götenberg, Sweden: Götenberg University, SANS, 2009), p. 12.

8 Ibid, p. 13.

9 Ibid, p. 15.

10 Ibid, p. 17.

11 Yarborough, *Da Nang Diary,* p. 119.

12 John Prados, *The Blood Road: The Ho Chi Minh Trail and the Vietnam War* (New York: John Wiley & Sons, 1999), pp. 9–10.

13 Michael D. McComb, "Fading Photographs from My Mind's Own Album," *NamVet Newsletter,* November 8, 1994, p. 91.

14 John Laurence, *The Cat From Hue: A Vietnam War Story* (New York: Publicaffairs, 2002), p. 501.

15 Bernard B. Fall, *Hell in a Very Small Place: The Siege of Dien Bien Phu* (Cambridge, MA: Da Capo Press, 2002), pp. 431–432.

16 Fredrick Longevall, *Embers of War: The Fall of an Empire and the Making of America's Vietnam* (New York: Random House Trade Paperbacks, 2013), pp. 488–489.

17 For works that explore this battle, see Harold G. Moore and Joseph L. Galloway,

We Were Soldiers Once . . . and Young (New York: Random House, 1992); Shelby Stanton, *The 1st Cav in Vietnam: Anatomy of a Division* (Novato, CA: Presidio Press, 1999).

18 Bernard B. Fall, *Street Without Joy: The French Debacle in Indochina* (Mechanicsburg, PA: Stackpole Books, 1994), p. 34.

CHAPTER 1: INTO THE VALLEY OF DEATH

1 Mark W. McChord and Nguyen Thi Dieu, *Culture and Customs of Vietnam* (Westport: Greenwood Press, 2001), pp. 9–16.

2 Robert S. McNamara with Brian VanDeMark, *In Retrospect: The Tragedy and Lessons of Vietnam* (New York: Random House, 1995), p. 49.

3 Ibid, p. 50.

4 Malcolm W. Browne, *The New Face of War* (New York: Bantam, 1986), pp. 79–85.

5 Colin L. Powell and Joseph E. Persico, *My American Experience* (New York: Random House, 1995), p. 83.

6 Ibid, p. 89.

7 Stanton, *Green Berets at War*, p. 65.

8 1st Special Forces Group, *Monthly Operational Summary,* 20 Nov 1963–20 Dec 1963.

9 McNamara, *In Retrospect,* pp. 84–85.

10 Lyndon Baines Johnson, *The Vantage Point: Perspectives of the Presidency 1963–1969* (New York: Holt, Rinehart, and Winston, 1971), p. 45.

11 For a full discussion of LLDB incompetence, see Stanton, *Green Berets at War,* pp. 76–83.

12 5th SFGA, *Detachment B-410 Debriefing,* 18 Dec 1964.

13 William C. Westmoreland, *A Soldier Reports* (New York: Doubleday & Company, 1976), pp. 60–61.

14 Gordon L. Rottman, *Special Forces Camps in Vietnam 1961–70* (New York: Osprey Publishing, 2005), pp. 47–48.

15 Justo Bautista, "Green Beret from Lyndhurst Earns Posthumous Salute," *North Jersey News,* March 9, 2003.

16 Gerald Hickey, *Window on a War: An Anthropologist in the Vietnam Conflict* (Lubbock: Texas Tech University Press, 2002), p.137.

17 Extracted from *Houston Distinguished Service Cross Citation,* Military Times Hall of Valor, http://www.projects.militarytimes.com/citations-medals-awards. Accessed 23 May 2014.

18 Extracted from *Donlon Medal of Honor Citation,* U.S. Army Center of Military History, Ft. McNair, DC.

19 Hickey, *Window on a War,* p. 144.

20 "Battle of Nam Dong," http://www.wikipedia.org/Battle_of_Nam_Dong, n.d. Accessed 12 May 2014.

21 W.C. Westmoreland, *Command Report on the War in Vietnam, January 1964–June 1968* (Saigon: Military Assistance Command Vietnam, 1968), p. 93.

22 LBJ, *The Vantage Point,* p. 118.

23 Westmoreland, *A Soldier Reports,* p. 194; See election discussion in McNamara, *In Retrospect,* pp. 145–160.

24 Thomas Preston, *Pandora's Trap: Presidential Decision Making and Blame Avoidance in Vietnam and Iraq* (Lanham, MD: Rowman & Littlefield Publishers, Inc., 2011), p. 196.

25 5th Special Forces Group, *Monthly Operational Summary,* 1–31 Dec 1964; Christopher M. Hobson, *Vietnam Air Losses 1961–1973* (Hinckley, England: Midland Publishing, 2001), p. 13.

CHAPTER 2: THE RISE AND FALL OF CAMP A SHAU

1 Arthur J. Dommen, *The Indochinese Experience of the French and Americans: Nationalism and Communism in Cambodia, Laos and Vietnam* (Bloomington: Indiana University Press, 2001), p. 636.

2 Carl Berger, ed., *The United States Air Force in Southeast Asia* (Washington, DC: Government Printing Office, 1977), p. 89; for Administration thoughts on planning and implementing "Rolling Thunder," see McNamara, *In Retrospect,* pp. 171–177.

3 Jack Shulimson and Major Charles M. Johnson, *U.S. Marines in Vietnam: The Landing and Buildup 1965* (Washington, DC: USMC History and Museum Division, 1978), pp. 9–15.

4 Nigel Cathorne, *Vietnam: A War Lost and Won* (London: Arcturus Publishing Limited, 2003), p. 4.

5 Tyrone G. Martin, "Old Ironsides in Vietnam," *USS Constitution Museum,* n.d. http://www.ussconstitutionmuseum.org. Accessed May 20, 2014.

6 John D. Blair IV, "Defense of Camp A Shau," After Action Report, U.S. Army Infantry School, Fort Benning, GA, 2 January 1968, p. 27.

7 Ibid, p. 18.

8 John T. Correll, "The Lingering Story of Agent Orange," *Air Force Magazine,* January, 2015, pp. 50–51.

9 James G. Jones, "Smokey Bear in Vietnam," *Environmental History,* 2006, pp. 598–603.

10 5th SFGA *Monthly Summary of Operations,* February 1966.

11 Blair, AAR, pp. 29–30.

12 Ibid, pp.33–34.

13 "The Saigon Thi Party," *Time,* March 18, 1966, pp. 10–11.

14 Blair, AAR, pp. 22–26.

15 Extracted from *Hall Distinguished Service Cross Citation,* Military Times Hall of Valor, http://www.projects.militarytimes.com/citations-medals-awards. Accessed 12 May 2014.

16   Blair, AAR, pp. 39–40.

17   Victor C. Underwood "Battle of A Shau," After Action Report, 5th Mobile Strike Force Command Collection, 22 June 1967, pp. 46–47.

18   John L. Frisbee, "Valor in Two Dimensions," *Air Force Magazine,* January, 1988, p. 116.

19   Extracted from *Peterson Air Force Cross Citation,* Military Times Hall of Valor, http://www.projects.militarytimes.com/citations-medals-awards. Accessed 23 May 2014.

20   Kenneth Sams, "The Fall of A Shau," Project CHECO Report, HQ PACAF, 18 April 1966, pp. 4–5.

21   Blair, AAR, pp. 45–46.

22   Ibid, p. 48.

23   Extracted from *Stahl Distinguished Service Cross Citation,* Military Times Hall of Valor, http://www.projects.militarytimes.com/citations-medals-awards. Accessed 12 May 2014.

24   Extracted from *Adkins Distinguished Service Cross Citation,* Military Times Hall of Valor, http://www.projects.militarytimes.com/citations-medals-awards. Accessed 13 May 2014.

25   Hobson, *Vietnam Air Losses,* p. 52.

26   Laurence, *The Cat From Hue,* p. 365.

27   Underwood, AAR, p. 47.

28   John T. Correll, "Into the Valley of Fire," *Air Force Magazine,* October, 2004, p. 52.

29   Ibid, p. 54.

30   Extracted from *Fisher Medal of Honor Citation,* U.S. Army Center of Military History, Ft. McNair, DC.

31   Underwood, AAR, pp. 49–50.

32   Richard Camp, "Rescue in Death Valley," *Vietnam,* April 2012, p. 32.

33   Underwood, AAR, p. 59.

34   Blair AAR, pp. 64–65.

35   Extracted from *Berger Navy Cross Citation,* Military Times Hall of Valor, http://www.projects.militarytimes.com/citations-medals-awards. Accessed 3 June 2014.

36   Blair, AAR, pp. 66–67.

37   Hobson, *Vietnam Air Losses,* p. 52.

38   Camp, "Rescue," p. 33.

39   Steven Sherman, e-mail message to author, 22 May 2014.

40   Laurence, *The Cat From Hue,* p. 368.

CHAPTER 3: PROJECT DELTA INVADES THE A SHAU

1   Shelby L. Stanton, *The Rise and Fall of an American Army: U.S. Ground Forces in Vietnam, 1965–1973* (New York: Ballantine Books, 1985), p. 132.

2   General Bernard W. Rogers, *Cedar Falls-Junction City: A Turning Point* (Washington, DC: Department of the Army, 1989), p. 39.

3   Ibid, p. 79.

4   Stanton, *Rise and Fall*, p. 133.

5   The Military History Institute of Vietnam, *Victory in Vietnam: The Official History of the People's Army of Vietnam, 1954–1975*. Translated by Merle L. Pribbenow (Lawrence, KS: The University Press of Kansas, 2002), p. 199.

6   David Schoenbrun, *As France Goes* (New York: Atheneum, 1968), pp. 232–235.

7   Extracted from *Leonard Medal Of Honor Citation*, U.S. Army Center of Military History, Ft. McNair, DC.

8   Stanton, *Green Berets*, pp. 195–196.

9   R.C. Morris, *The Ether Zone: U.S. Army Special Forces Detachment B-52, Project Delta* (Ashland, OR: Hellgate Press, 2009), p. 18.

10   Jack Shulimson, *U.S. Marines in Vietnam, An Expanding War, 1966* (Washington, DC: USMC History and Museum Division, 1982), p. 13.

11   B-52, *Operation Pirous After Action Report* (AAR), 16 June 1967, p. 89.

12   Ibid, p. 7.

13   Extracted from *Siugzda Commendation Medal for Heroism*, General Order 3017, 21 Jun 1967, provided by Steve Sherman, Radix Press, Houston, TX.

14   Donald J. Taylor, "The A Shau," http://www.ProjectDelta.net. Accessed 25 June 2014.

15   Extracted from *Robinette Silver Star Citation*, General Order 4714, 17 Sep 1967, provided by Steve Sherman, Radix Press, Houston, TX.

16   Stanton, *Green Berets*, p. 202; Morris, *The Ether Zone*, p. 294.

17   Jim Morris, "Death-Dealing Project Delta, Part 3," *Soldier of Fortune Magazine*, September 1981, pp. 47–51.

18   Hobson, *Vietnam Air Losses*, p. 99.

19   General Hugh Shelton with Donald Levinson and Malcolm McConnell, *Without Hesitation: The Odyssey of an American Warrior* (New York: St. Martin's Press, 2010), pp. 57–61.

20   Extracted from *Markham Silver Star Citation*, General Order 4330, 25 Aug 1967, provided by Steve Sherman, Radix Press, Houston, TX.

21   Donald J. Taylor, "Remembering the 281st AHC," http://www.ProjectDelta.net, 2005. Accessed 8 June 2014. Sgt Maj Taylor provided additional background on his article in correspondence with the author on 20 June 2014.

22   B-52, *Operation Pirous AAR*, pp. 39–41.

23   Ibid, pp. 169–170.

24   Ibid, pp. 167–168.

Chapter 4: SOG: West of the A Shau

1   Yarborough, *Da Nang Diary*, p. 117.

2   Richard H. Shultz, Jr., *The Secret War Against Hanoi* (New York: Perennial,

2000), pp. 73–74.

3 Lt Col Raymond Call interview with Dr. Richard H. Shultz, Jr. *MACV Studies and Observations Group Documentation Study and Command Histories* (Houston: Radix Press, 2002). CD-ROM, p. 26.

4 Yarborough, *Da Nang Diary*, p. 33.

5 For the definitive account of the extraordinary courage and dedication displayed by SOG reconnaissance teams going in harm's way in Laos and Cambodia see John L. Plaster, *SOG: The Secret Wars of America's Commandos in Vietnam* (New York: Simon & Schuster, 1997).

6 Yarborough, *Da Nang Diary*, p. 126.

7 MACSOG *Documentation Study, Appendix D: Cross-Border Operations in Laos* (Washington, DC: Joint Chiefs of Staff, 1970), p. 51.

8 William D. Waugh, "The Story of Target Oscar 8," pp. 1–2. http://www.mac-sog.cc/traget_oscar-8. Accessed on 3 July 2014.

9 Hobson, *Vietnam Air Losses*, p. 103.

10 Although several eyewitnesses on the ground and an airborne Covey rider observed this crash, there is no record of an F-4 loss on that date.

11 Mike Law, "Member Accounts Crucial to History," *Vietnam Helicopter Pilots Association Newsletter*, Jan–Feb 1998, p. 9.

12 Ibid, p. 10.

13 Plaster, *SOG*, p. 92.

14 Ibid, pp. 93–94.

15 Robert M. Gillespie, *Black Ops in Vietnam: The Operational History of MACV-SOG* (Annapolis: Naval Institute Press, 2011), p. 117.

16 "Nov. 15, 1969: Anti-Vietnam War Demonstration Held," *The New York Times Learning Network*, http://www.learning.blogs.nytimes.com/2011/11/15/Nov. Accessed 14 Jul 2014.

17 Extracted from *Baxter Distinguished Service Cross Citation*, Military Times Hall of Valor http://www.projects.militarytimes.com/citations-medals-awards. Accessed 3 June 2014.

18 John L. Plaster, *SOG: A Photo History of the Secret Wars* (Boulder: Paladin Press, 2000), p. 108.

19 John L. Frisbee, "Into the Jaws of Death," *Air Force Magazine*, May 1987, p. 218.

20 Plaster, *Photo History*, p. 108.

21 Terry P. Arentowicz, *That Empty Feeling: The Real Story of One 72-Hour Rescue Mission in Laos* (Bloomington, IN: AuthorHouse, 2013), p. 68.

22 Donald K. Schneider, *Air Force Heroes in Vietnam* (Washington DC: U.S. Government Printing Office, 1979), pp. 34–38.

23 John L. Frisbee, "A Hillside Near Khe Sanh," *Air Force Magazine*, July 1985, p. 136.

24 U.S. Military Assistance Command, Vietnam, Studies and Observations Group, *Annex G, Command History 1967*. Saigon: MACV-SOG, 1968, p. G-IV-2.

CHAPTER 5: *ANNUS HORRIBILUS*: 1968

1   LBJ, *Vantage Point,* pp. 382–383.
2   Extracted from *Gonzalez Medal of Honor Citation,* U.S. Army Center of Military History, Ft. McNair, DC.
3   Extracted from *Hooper Medal of Honor Citation,* U.S. Army Center of Military History, Ft. McNair, DC.
4   Erik Villard, *The 1968 Tet Offensive Battles of Quang Tri City and Hue* (Washington, DC: U.S. Army Center of Military History, 2008), p. 60.
5   Jack Shulimson et al, *U.S. Marines in Vietnam: 1968 The Defining Year* (Washington, DC: HQ USMC History and Museum Division, 1997), p. 213.
6   Villard, *Tet Offensive Battles,* p. 81.
7   Westmoreland, *A Soldier Reports,* p. 321.
8   Ibid, p. 234.
9   Karnow, *Vietnam,* p. 534.
10 "Tet Offensive Begins," n.d. *1968 Timeline,* http://www.NYU.edu. Accessed 23 July 2014.
11 Milton J. Bates, Lawrence Lichty, Paul Miles, Ronald H. Spector, ed., *Reporting Vietnam, Part 1: American Journalism, 1959–1969* (New York: Library of America, 1998), p. 582.
12 Cathorne, *Vietnam: A War,* p. 242.
13 Westmoreland, *A Soldier Reports,* p. 344.
14 Berger, *USAF in SEA,* p. 52.
15 Extracted from *Thomas Navy Cross Citation,* http://www.HMM-364.org. Accessed 24 Jul 2014.
16 Westmoreland, *A Soldier Reports,* p. 346.
17 Gillespie, *Black Ops,* pp. 146–147.
18 Extracted from *Calhoun Distinguished Service Cross Citation,* Military Times Hall of Valor, http://www.projects.militarytimes.com/citations-medals-awards. Accessed 3 Aug 2014.
19 Detachment B-52 (Project Delta), *Samurai IV After Action Report,* 7 Apr 1968, p. 3.
20 Ibid, pp. 43–46.
21 Ibid, pp. 57–60.
22 Rick Newman and Don Sheppard, *Bury Us Upside Down: The Misty Pilots and the Secret Battle for the Ho Chi Minh Trail* (New York: Ballantine Books, 2006), pp. 245–248. Newman and Sheppard incorrectly identify the date as 17 March instead of 14 March.
23 Ibid, p. 248.
24 *Samurai IV AAR,* pp. 85–89.
25 Bill Byrd, "A Shau Valley," http://www.USAFhpa.org, n.d. Accessed 31 Jul 2014.
26 Extracted from *Griggs Air Force Cross Citation,* Military Times Hall of Valor, http://www.projects.militarytimes.com/citations-medals-awards. Accessed 3

Aug 2014.

27 LBJ, *The Vantage Point*, p. 435.

28 Edward F. Murphy, *The Hill Fights: The First Battle of Khe Sanh* (New York: Presidio Press, 2003), pp. 239–240.

29 Westmoreland, *A Soldier Reports*, p. 345.

30 Ronald H. Spector, *After Tet: The Bloodiest Year in Vietnam* (New York: The Free Press, 1993), p. 119.

31 Lt General Willard Pearson, *The War in the Northern Provinces 1966–1968* (Washington, DC: Department of the Army, 1975), pp. 85–87.

32 "Victory at Khe Sanh," *Time Magazine*, April 12, 1968, p. 12.

33 Lewis Sorley, *A Better War: The Unexamined Victories and Final Tragedy of America's Last Years in Vietnam* (New York: Harcourt, 1999), p. 7.

34 Lewis Sorley, "The Abrams Tapes: Insight to the MACV Headquarters During the Vietnam War," *Vietnam Magazine*, December 2005, p. 36.

35 Peter Brush, "Battle of Khe Sanh: Recounting the Battle's Casualties," 26 Jun 2007. http://www.Historynet.com. Accessed 11 Aug 2014. Other sources put Marine casualties during Operation Scotland II at 270.

36 Spector, *After Tet*, p. 118; p. 138.

37 Pearson, *War in Northern Provinces*, pp. 90–91.

38 159th Squadron, 9th Cavalry, *Combat After Action Report*, 4 Jun 1968, p. 4.

39 Stanton, *The 1st Cav*, p. 145.

40 Oral History Interview with Michael Ward, 19 Apr 2003. http://www.virtualarchive.vietnam.ttu.edu. Accessed 30 Aug 2014.

41 Philip R. Shafer, *Case Synopsis*, virtual.vietnam.ttu.edu. Accessed 30 Aug 2014.

42 Lt General John J. Tolson, *Airmobility, 1961–1971* (Washington. DC: Department of the Army, 1999), pp. 185–186.

43 Robert C. Ankony, "No Peace in the Valley," *Vietnam Magazine*, October, 2008, p. 28.

44 Ibid, p. 29.

45 Ibid, pp. 30–33.

46 Bernard Edelman, *Dear America: Letters Home from Vietnam* (New York: Norton, 1985), p. 50.

47 Extracted from *Sprayberry Medal of Honor Citation*, U.S. Army Center of Military History, Ft. McNair, DC; *The M.I.A.'s on Tiger Mountain*. Dir. Norman Lloyd. Commitment and Sacrifice Foundation, 2015. DVD; telephone interview with LTC Sprayberry, 18 Nov 2015.

48 Tolson, *Airmobility*, p. 188.

49 Hobson, *Vietnam Air Losses*, p. 146.

50 Extracted from *Lee Medal of Honor Citation*, U.S. Army Center of Military History, Ft. McNair, DC.

51 Spector, *After Tet*, p. 79.

52 Plaster, *SOG*, p. 185.

53 Ibid, pp. 186–190.
54 Extracted from *Fournet Medal of Honor Citation,* U.S. Army Center of Military History, Ft. McNair, DC.
55 Tolson, *Airmobility,* p. 190.
56 Ibid, p. 191.
57 1st Cav Division, *Combat Operations After Action Report,* 11 Jun 1968, Tab 1. The most extensive list of captured enemy equipment/supplies is contained in 1st Cav Division Periodic Intelligence Report NR 5-68, pp. 1–3.
58 Pearson, *War in Northern Provinces,* p. 92.
59 "Recon Team Idaho," http://www.Task Force Omega.org. Accessed 9 Aug 2014.
60 Ken Freeze, "The Last Mission of Hellborne 215," http://www.Check-Six.com, pp. 1–6. Accessed 5 Jul 2014; "Lead Sheet, Case 1205 (Schmidt): Recommendation of Case for CAT 1-JTFFA Activity." Found in LOC POW/MIA Database, Item 84.
61 "Operation Somerset Plain," Vietnam Helicopter Pilots Association, 6 Mar 2011.
62 Haynes Johnson, "1968 Democratic Convention: The Bosses Strike Back," *Smithsonian Magazine,* August, 2008, p. 41.
63 Extracted from *Black Silver Star Citation,* Department of the Army General Order Number 5852, dated 26 Dec 1968; Jack Murphy, "Across the Fence with MACV-SOG: You Shot me Three Times," http://www.sofrep.com/27914. Accessed 21 Mar 2015. For a detailed television account of this action, see the Military History Channel's "Heroes Under Fire: Jungle Ambush," airdate 1 Nov 2005.
64 Plaster, *SOG,* p. 195.

CHAPTER 6: OPERATION DEWEY CANYON

1 Spector, *After Tet,* pp. 46–47.
2 Andrew J. Rotter, *Light at the End of the Tunnel: A Vietnam War Anthology* (Lanham, MD: Rowman & Littlefield, 2010), pp. 393–394.
3 Spector, *After Tet,* p. 36.
4 Charles R. Smith, *U.S. Marines in Vietnam: High Mobility and Standdown 1969* (Washington, DC: USMC History and Museums Division, 1988), p. 27.
5 Shultz, *The Secret War Against Hanoi,* p. 331.
6 Gen Raymond G. Davis Interview, 2 Feb 1977, pp. 17-18 (USMC Oral History Collection, History Division, Quantico, VA).
7 Robert H. Barrow, "Operation Dewey Canyon," *Marine Corps Gazette,* Nov 1981, p. 87.
8 Jack Shulimson et al, *U.S. Marines in Vietnam: 1968 The Defining Year* (CreateSpace Independent Publishing, 2013), pp. 516–517.
9 Smith, *High Mobility,* p. 17.
10 Ibid.
11 Ibid, pp. 30–31.
12 C. Douglas Sterner, "Operation Dewey Canyon," 2001, p. 2. http://www.1stbat

talionin9thmarinesfirebase.net. Accessed on 16 Oct 2014.

13 Lt Walter J. Wood Interview, 5–9 Mar 1969, Sound Recording (USMC Oral History Collection, History Division, Quantico, VA).

14 Capt Daniel A. Hitzelberger Interview, 5–9 Mar 1969, Sound Recording (USMC Oral History Collection, History Division, Quantico, VA).

15 Sgt Robert D. Gaudioso Interview, 5–9 Mar 1969, Sound Recording (USMC Oral History Collection, History Division, Quantico, VA).

16 Ibid.

17 Extracted from *Noonan Medal of Honor Citation,* U.S. Army Center of Military History, Ft. McNair, DC.

18 Hitzelberger Interview.

19 Lt Robert S. Lankford Interview, 5–9 Mar 1969, Sound Recording (USMC Oral History Collection, History Division, Quantico, VA).

20 Smith, *High Mobility,* p. 38.

21 Extracted from *Benfatti Silver Star Citation,* Military Times Hall of Valor, http://www.projects.militarytimes.com-citations-medals-awards. Accessed 20 Nov 2014.

22 Lt Milton J. Tiexeira Interview, 5–9 Mar 1969, Sound Recording (USMC Oral History Collection, History Division, Quantico, VA).

23 Smith, *High Mobility,* p. 40.

24 Extracted from *Wilhelm Navy Cross Citation,* Military Times Hall of Valor, http://www.projects.militarytimes.com-citations-medals-awards. Accessed 21 Nov 2014.

25 Capt David F. Winecoff Interview, 5–9 Mar 1969, Sound Recording (USMC Oral History Collection, History Division, Quantico, VA).

26 Col Robert H. Barrow Interview, 8 Apr 1969, Sound Recording (USMC Oral History Collection, History Division, Quantico, VA).

27 Dave Winecoff, "Night Ambush!" *Marine Corps Gazette,* January 1984, pp. 47–52.

28 Barrow Interview.

29 Moore, *We Were Soldiers,* pp. 341–342.

30 Smith, *High Mobility,* p. 44.

31 Barrow Interview.

32 Extracted from *Fox Medal of Honor Citation,* U.S. Army Center of Military History, Ft. McNair, DC.

33 1st Battalion, 9th Marines, *Combat Operations After Action Report,* 31 Mar 1969, pp. 11–12.

34 Smith, *High Mobility,* p. 46.

35 Extracted from *Morgan Medal of Honor Citation,* U.S. Army Center of Military History, Ft. McNair, DC.

36 Smith, *High Mobility,* p. 47.

37 Extracted from *Wilson Medal of Honor Citation,* U.S. Army Center of Military

History, Ft. McNair, DC.

38 Lt Wesley L. Fox Interview, 5-9 Mar 1969, Sound Recording (USMC Oral History Collection, History Division, Quantico, VA).

39 "Wesley Fox Lessons Steeled in Combat," *Vietnam Magazine*, April 2012, p. 18.

40 Beth Crumley, "Green Hell—Operation Dewey Canyon," 22 Aug 2011. http://www.mca-marines.org. Accessed 25 Sep 2014.

41 Department of Defense, *Report on Selected Air and Ground Operations in Cambodia and Laos,* 10 Sep 1973, pp. 5–9, as presented in "Bombing in Cambodia," Hearings Before the Committee on Armed Services, United States Senate, 93rd Congress, 1st Session, July 16–20, 1973.

42 Smith, *High Mobility,* p. 50.

43 Drummond Ayres, Jr., "Hilltops in Laos Seized by Marines," *New York Times,* March 9, 1969, A1.

44 "Laird Foresees a Troop Cut by U.S. in Vietnam," *New York Times,* March 11, 1969.

45 Smith, *High Mobility,* p. 51.

46 Tom Campbell, *The Old Man's Trail* (Annapolis: Naval Institute Press, 1995), p. vi.

CHAPTER 7: ELEVEN TIMES UP HAMBURGER HILL

1 "American Grunt," http://www.vetswithamission.com. Accessed 24 Sep 2014.

2 2nd Brigade, *Combat Operations After Action Report, Massachusetts Striker,* 25 May 1969, pp. 3–4.

3 "Division History: Massachusetts Striker," http://www.ripcordassociation.com, p. 28. Accessed 8 Nov 2014.

4 Extracted from *Wright Distinguished Service Cross Citation,* Military Times Hall of Valor, http://www.projects.militarytimes.com-citations-medals-awards. Accessed 9 Nov 2014.

5 Several web sites and Samuel Zaffiri's book *Hamburger Hill,* incorrectly identify the dates for the battle of Bloody Ridge as 17–20 April, 1969. The actual dates, confirmed by all after action reports, were 19–25 March.

6 Extracted from *Dent Distinguished Service Cross Citation,* Military Times Hall of Valor, http://www.projects.militarytimes.com-citations-medals-awards. Accessed 8 Nov 2014.

7 Samuel Zaffiri, *Hamburger Hill: The Brutal Battle for Dong Ap Bia, May 11–20, 1969* (New York: Ballantine Books, 2000), p. 58.

8 1st Battalion, 502nd Infantry, *Annual Historic Supplement,* 22 Mar 1970.

9 2nd Brigade, *AAR,* pp. 14–16.

10 Ibid, pp. 10–12.

11 Lt. Frank Hair, "The Summer Offensive in the A Shau Valley Massachusetts Striker" Originally published in *Rendezvous With Destiny Magazine,* Summer 1969, http://www.101st-Airborne-ranger.com. Accessed 3 Nov 2014.

12 Taylor, "The A Shau," n.d.

13 Larry Chambers, *Death in the A Shau Valley: L Company LRRPS in Vietnam, 1969–70* (New York: Ivy Books, 1998), pp. 11–12.

14 Hobson, *Vietnam Air Losses,* p. 180. Phil Mascari and Yarborough were pilot training classmates together at Laughlin AFB, TX, 1967–1968.

15 2nd Brigade, *AAR,* pp. 6–7; p. 17.

16 *101st Fact Sheet,* "Summer of Action and Results," 24 May 1969, pp. 4–5.

17 Zaffiri, *Hamburger Hill,* pp. 71–72.

18 Ibid, p. 85.

19 Ibid, pp. 87–88.

20 Ibid, pp. 88–89.

21 22nd Military History Detachment. *Narrative: Operation "Apache Snow,"* 10 May–7 June 1969. p. 5.

22 Harry G. Summers, Jr., "Battle of Hamburger Hill During the Vietnam War," Originally published in *Vietnam Magazine,* June 1999, http://www.historynet.com, p. 5. Accessed 13 Nov 2014.

23 Zaffiri, *Hamburger Hill,* p. 66.

24 *Narrative: Operation "Apache Snow,"* pp. 6–7.

25 Extracted from *Parker Distinguished Service Cross Citation,* Military Times Hall of Valor, http://www.projects.militarytimes.com-citations-medals-awards. Accessed 23 Nov 2014; AAR, "Sapper Attack on FSB Airborne—13 May 1969," http://www.alphaavengers.com/firebase-airborne. Accessed 23 Nov 2014.

26 *Narrative: Operation "Apache Snow,"* pp. 8–9.

27 3/187, *After Action Report, Apache Snow, 20 June 1969,* pp. 28–29.

28 Ibid, pp. 30–31.

29 Zaffiri, *Hamburger Hill,* p. 167.

30 Ibid, pp. 175–176. The strike aircraft information was extracted from the Combat Air Activities File, Southeast Asia Data Base, http://www.aad.archive.gov/aad/series. Accessed 25 Nov 2014.

31 3rd Battalion, 187th Regiment, *AAR,* pp. 32–34; *Narrative,* p. 21.

32 Zaffiri, *Hamburger Hill,* pp. 203–204.

33 3/187, *AAR,* pp. 40–41.

34 Extracted from *Schoch Distinguished Service Cross Citation,* Military Times Hall of Valor, http://www.projects.militarytimes.com-citations-medals-awards. Accessed 26 Nov 2014.

35 Jay Sharbutt, "U.S. Assault on Viet Mountain Continues, Despite Heavy Toll." *The Washington Post,* May 20, 1969, A15.

36 Edward M. Kennedy, "Hamburger Hill Speech," 20 May 1969. http://www.tedkennedy.org. Accessed 26 Nov 2014.

37 *Narrative: Operation "Apache Snow,"* p. 232.

38 David Hoffman, "Hamburger Hill: The Army's Rationale," *The Washington Post,* May 23, 1969, p. A1.

39 Summers, "Battle of Hamburger Hill," p. 5.
40 101st Airborne Division, Operational Report—Lessons Learned, Period ending 31 Jul 1969, pp. 6–7, 9 Dec 1969.
41 Col Bert Aton with William Thorndale, "A Shau Valley Campaign: December 1968–May 1969." HQ PACAF, Directorate Tactical Evaluation, CHECO Division, p. 1, n.d.
42 *Time Magazine,* April 5, 1982, p. 12.
43 Zaffiri, *Hamburger Hill,* pp. 279–280.
44 Len Griffin, "Hill 996—July 11, 1969." http://www.old.506infantry.org. Accessed 1 Dec 2014.
45 Extracted from *Roberts Medal of Honor Citation,* U.S. Army Center of Military History, Ft McNair, DC.
46 Extracted from *Gertsch Medal of Honor Citation,* U.S. Army Center of Military History, Ft McNair, DC.

CHAPTER 8: RIPCORD: VALOR IN DEFEAT

1 MACSOG *Documentation Study, July 1970, Appendix E,* pp. 12–14.
2 Extracted from *Miller Medal of Honor Citation,* U.S. Center of Military History, Ft. McNair, DC.
3 John S. Carter correspondence with author, 24 Jan 2015.
4 James E. Mitschke correspondence with author, 5 Sep 2012. Mitschke duplicated the feat in July 1970 when he earned the Silver Star for rescuing two Cobra pilots deep in Laos on the Ho Chi Minh Trail.
5 U.S. Military Assistance Command, Vietnam, Studies and Observations Group, *Annex B, Command History 1970.* Saigon: MACV-SOG, 1971, p. B-66.
6 HML-167 Command Chronology, 1 Mar-31 Mar 1970, pp. 3–5; SOG *Annex B, Command History 1970,* p. B-72; "Rescue of Larry D. Parsons," http://www.taskforceomegainc.org, n.d. Accessed 8 Dec 2014.
7 "Pilot Rejoins the Living," *Pacific Stars and Stripes,* 14 Apr 1970; SOG *Annex B,* p. B-72.
8 Lt General Sak Sutsakhan, *The Khmer Republic at War and the Final Collapse* (Washington: Department of the Army, 1978), p. 18.
9 Ibid, pp. 13–17.
10 101st Airborne Division, *Operational Report—Lessons Learned,* 15 Aug 1970, pp. 1–3.
11 M/Gen Benjamin L. Harrison, *Hell on a Hilltop: America's Last Major Battle in Vietnam* (New York: IUniverse, Inc., 2004), pp. 41–47.
12 Nolan, *Ripcord,* pp. 113–118.
13 Ibid, p. 79.
14 101st Airborne Division (Airmobile), *Combat After Action Report: Firebase Ripcord, 23 July 1970,* n.d. pp. 1–3.
15 Nolan, *Ripcord,* pp. 88–89.

16 Ibid, p. 91.

17 Capt Isabelino Vazquez-Rodriguez Interview, Video Recording, 2013 (Grand Valley State University Veterans History Project, Allendale, MI).

18 John M. Shaw, *The Cambodian Campaign* (Lawrence, KS: University of Kansas Press, 2005), p. 162.

19 Stanton, *Rise and Fall,* p. 339.

20 Military History Institute, *Victory in Vietnam,* p. 257.

21 "Cambodian Campaign," http://www.Wikipedia.org/Cambodian_Campaign. Accessed 5 Feb 2015.

22 Extract from *Kays Medal of Honor Citation,* U.S. Army Military Center of History, Ft. McNair, DC.

23 Harrison, *Hell on a Hilltop,* p. 72.

24 Ibid, p. 67.

25 "Gulf of Tonkin Resolution is Repealed Without Furor," *The New York Times,* January 14, 1971. President Nixon signed the Foreign Military Sales Act in January 1971. Congress passed the War Powers Resolution in 1973, over Nixon's veto.

26 Nolan, *Ripcord,* p. 27.

27 Harrison, *Hell on a Hilltop,* p. 77.

28 Nolan, *Ripcord,* pp. 36–37.

29 Jim Shelton, "Induction as Distinguished Member of the 506th Infantry Regiment," *New Haven Register,* May 1, 2014.

30 Nolan, *Ripcord,* pp. 59–60.

31 Shelton, "Induction."

32 101st Airborne Division *Combat After Action Report: Operation Texas Star,* 1–23 Jul 1970, pp. 19–20.

33 Nolan, *Ripcord,* pp. 228–233.

34 Bill Colclough, "Delta Blood," *Coastguard Heartland,* 5 Aug 2013, http://www.heartland.coastguard.dodlive.mil. Accessed 8 Feb 2015.

35 Nolan, *Ripcord,* p. 243.

36 Extracted from *Rich Distinguished Service Cross Citation,* Military Times Hall of Valor, http://www.projects.militarytimes.com/citations-medals-awards. Accessed 31 Jan 2015.

37 AAR, *Ripcord,* p. 2.

38 Harrison, *Hell on a Hilltop,* pp. 120–121.

39 Nolan, *Ripcord,* p. 429.

40 Extracted from *Kreckel Distinguished Service Cross Citation,* Military Times Hall of Valor, http://www.projects.militarytimes.com/citations-medals-awards. Accessed 31 Jan 2015.

41 Extract from *Lucas Medal of Honor Citation,* U.S. Army Military Center of History, Ft. McNair, DC.

42 Tom Marshall, "Rescue from FSB Ripcord," http://www.screamingeagles.org/ripcord pp. 6–8. Accessed 10 Dec 2014.

43 Nolan, *Ripcord*, pp. 474–475.

44 Ibid, p. 485.

45 Harrison, *Hell on a Hilltop*, pp. 213–216.

46 Norman Dixon, *On the Psychology of Military Incompetence* (London: Jonathan Cape, 1976), p. 41.

47 Harrison, *Hell on a Hilltop*, p. 121.

48 Extracted from *Fratellenico Medal of Honor Citation*, U.S. Army Military Center of History, Ft. McNair, DC.

49 Hobson, *Vietnam Air Losses*, p. 208.

50 Allen B. Clark, *Valor in Vietnam 1963–1977: Chronicles of Honor, Courage, and Sacrifice* (Havertown, PA: Casemate Publishers, 2012), pp. 230–231.

51 MACSOG, *Annex B, Command History, 1970*, p. B-112.

52 Gillespie, *Black Ops*, p. 205.

53 MACSOG, *Annex B, Command History, 1970*, pp. B-VIII-8-9.

54 Extracted from *Rose Distinguished Service Cross Citation*, Military Times Hall of Valor, http://www.projects.militarytimes.com/citations-medals-awards. Accessed 3 Apr 2015.

55 MACSOG, *Annex B, Command History, 1970*, pp. B-VIII-10.

56 JOPREP 230225 Sep 70, Rescue Opening/Closing Report; Mission Narrative Report, 30 Sep 70.

57 Evan J. Quiros, Sworn Statement, 23 Oct 1970; Taped interview with author, 1 June 1990.

58 Yarborough, *Da Nang Diary*, pp. 191–192.

59 Telephone interview with Mel Swanson, 17 Nov 2014.

60 3rd Aerospace Rescue and Recovery Group, *Rescue Opening/Closing Report, 2 Dec 70*, pp. 1–4.

61 Phil Marshal, "There Was No Billboard That Said Welcome to Laos," http://www.vhpa.org/stories/billboard.pdf p. 9. Accessed 31 Jul 2014.

62 MACSOG, *Annex B, Command History, 1970*, p. B-76; Yarborough, *Da Nang Diary*, pp. 246–247.

CHAPTER 9: A SHAU *FINI:* THE NINTH YEAR

1 101st Airborne Division (Airmobile), *Operational Report—Lessons Learned,* period ending 31 Oct 1971, p. 3.

2 Dave R. Palmer, *Summons of the Trumpet* (Novato, CA: Presidio Press, 1995), p. 240.

3 Keith W. Nolan, *Into Laos: The Story of Dewey Canyon II/Lam Son 719, Vietnam 1971* (New York: Dell Publishing Co., 1988), pp. 119–123.

4 Stanton, *Rise and Fall*, p. 351.

5 Hobson, *Vietnam Air Losses*, pp. 212–213.

6 Karnow, *Vietnam*, p. 629.

7 Hobson, *Vietnam Air Losses*, p. 213.

8   Vietnam Helicopter Pilots Association, ed. *Vietnam Helicopter History 1961–1975* (Citrus Heights, CA: VHPA, 2008). CD-ROM, pp. 1135–1136.

9   Nolan, *Into Laos*, pp. 366–367.

10   Karnow, *Vietnam*, p. 630; Transcript: Address to the Nation on Situation in Southeast Asia (April 7, 1971), http://www.millercollection.org, n.d. Accessed 23 Mar 2015.

11   Earl H. Tilford, Jr., *Setup: What the Air Force Did in Vietnam and Why* (Maxwell AFB, AL: Air University Press, 1991), p. 203.

12   Raymond L. Robinson and Charles F. Wesley, "The Missing Men of RT Intruder," unpublished document, 2006, p. 2. The author obtained a copy from the Special Forces Association. It can be found on-line by searching the title.

13   "RT Intruder," p. 1, http://www.taskforceomegainc.org. Accessed 31 Dec 2014.

14   Robinson, "Missing Men," p. 5.

15   Yarborough, *Da Nang Diary*, pp. 282–283; "Field Investigation Report Concerning Case 1706," pp. 1–8, 28 May 1992. Found in LOC POW/MIA Database, 1706, Item 1.

16   "RT Intruder," p. 2.

17   MACSOG, *Annex B, Command History, 1971–72*, p. B-97.

18   Yarborough, *Da Nang Diary*, pp. 285–286.

19   Robinson, "Missing Men," pp. 7–8.

20   Frederick C. Wunderlich Eyewitness Account, hhtp://www.macvsog.cc/1971, n.d. Accessed 8 Mar 2015; "Detailed Report of Investigation of Case 1707," pp. 185–188, 28 May 1992. Found in LOC POW/MIA Database, 1707, Item 16.

21   Yarborough, *Da Nang Diary*, pp. 288–289.

22   Clifford M. Newman correspondence with the author, 28 Oct 2012.

23   Robinson, "Missing Men," p. 10.

24   Ibid, p. 11.

25   James E. Butler correspondence with the author, 11 Mar 2015.

26   Ibid.

27   Ibid, p. 3.

28   Mike Perry, "When RT Python Ruled the Valley of Death," June 22, 2014. http://www.specialoperations.com. Accessed 17 Dec 2014.

29   Butler written account to author, 28 Apr 2015, p. 1.

30   Yarborough, *Da Nang Diary*, p. 292.

31   Extracted from *Chapman Distinguished Service Cross Citation*, Military Times Hall of Valor, http://www.projects.militarytimes.com/citations-medals-awards. Accessed 10 Mar 2015.

32   Yarborough, *Da Nang Diary*, pp. 294–295.

33   Extracted from *Yarborough Silver Star Citation*, HQ Seventh Air Force Special Order G-1035, 5 May 1972.

34   MACSOG, *Annex B, Command History, 1971–72*, p. B-112.

35   Stanton, *Rise and Fall*, pp. 354–357.

36 Call interview, p. 64. Col Lawrence Trapp, Deputy Commander of OP-35, voiced almost identical opinions during a separate interview with Shultz, p. 41.
37 Kenneth Conby and James Morrison, "The Rise and Fall of Recon Team Asp," *Vietnam Magazine*, August, 2001, p. 24.
38 MACSOG, *Annex B Command History, 1971–72*, p. B-141.
39 Robert L. Noe, "Chronological Listing of MACSOG MIA/KIA," *MACV Studies and Observations Group, Documentation Study and Command History 1964–1973* (Houston: Radix Press, 2002). CD-ROM, pp. 198–200.
40 Extracted from *Cavainai Medal of Honor Citation*, U.S. Army Military Center of History, Ft. McNair, DC.
41 Extracted from *Eaton Silver Star Citation*, Military Times Hall of Valor, http://www.projects.militarytimes.com/citations-medals-awards. Accessed 28 Mar 2015.
42 The most comprehensive list of SOG losses is contained in Robert Noe's "Chronological Listing of MACSOG MIA/KIA."
43 Hobson, *Vietnam Air Losses*, p. 216.
44 Plaster, *SOG*, p. 338.

EPILOGUE
1 David Demsey, "The Long Journey Home," journal entry extracted from http://www.vietvet.org/ashau. Accessed 11 May 2015.
2 John T. Correll, "How Rolling Thunder Began," *Air Force Magazine*, March 2015, p. 68.
3 David H. Petraeus, *The American military and the lessons of Vietnam* (Doctoral Dissertation). Princeton University, 1987, p. 128.
4. Nolan, *Ripcord*, p. 485.

BIBLIOGRAPHY

BOOKS

Ankony, Robert C. *LURPS: A Ranger's Diary of Tet, Khe Sanh, A Shau, and Quang Tri*. Lanham, MD: Hamilton Books, 2009.

Bates, Milton J. et al. *Reporting Vietnam, Part 1: American Journalism, 1959–1969*. New York: The Library of America, 1998.

Browne, Malcolm W. *The New Face of War*. New York: Bantam, 1986.

Chambers, Larry. *Death in the A Shau Valley: L Company LRRPS in Vietnam, 1969–70*. New York: Ivy Books, 1998.

Dougan, Clark, and Stephen Weiss. *The Vietnam Experience: Nineteen Sixty-Eight*. Boston: Boston Publishing Company, 1983.

Fall, Bernard. *Street Without Joy*. Harrisburg, PA: The Stackpole Company, 1961.

Fox, Wesley L. *Marine Rifleman: Forty-Three Years in the Corps*. Washington, DC: Brassey's Inc., 2002.

Gillispie, Robert M. *Black Ops in Vietnam: The Operational History of MACV-SOG*. Annapolis: Naval Institute Press, 2011.

Guilmartin, John, and Michael O'Leary. *Helicopters, The Illustrated History of the Vietnam War*. Toronto: Bantam Books, 1988.

Harrison, Benjamin L. *Hell on a Hilltop: America's Last Major Battle in Vietnam*. New York: iUniverse, Inc., 2004.

Herring, George C., ed. *The Pentagon Papers*. New York: McGraw-Hill, Inc, 1993.

Hickey, Gerald C. *Window on a War: An Anthropologist in the Vietnam Conflict*. Lubbock: Texas Tech University Press, 2002.

Hobson, Christopher M. *Vietnam Air Losses: United States Air Force, Navy and Marine Corps Fixed-Wing Aircraft Losses in Southeast Asia 1961–1973*. Hinckley, England: Midland Publishing, 2001.

Johnson, Lyndon B. *The Vantage Point: Perspectives of the Presidency, 1963–1969*. New York: Holt, Rinehart and Winston, 1971.

Karnow, Stanley. *Vietnam: A History.* New York: Penguin Books, 1984.

Laurence, John. *The Cat From Hue: A Vietnam War Story.* New York: PublicAffairs, 2002.

Logevall, Fredrik. *Embers of War: The Fall of an Empire and the Making of America's Vietnam.* New York: Random House, 2012.

McChord, Mark W. and Nguyen Thi Dieu. *Culture and Customs of Vietnam.* Westport: Greenwood Press, 2001.

McNamara, Robert S. with Brian VanDeMark. *In Retrospect: The Tragedy and Lessons of Vietnam.* New York: Random House, 1995.

Military History Institute of Vietnam. *Victory in Vietnam: The Official History of the People's Army of Vietnam, 1954–1975.* Translated by Merle L. Pribbenow. Lawrence, KS: The University Press of Kansas, 2002.

Morris, R.C. *The Ether Zone: U.S. Army Special Forces Detachment B-52, Project Delta.* Ashland, OR: Hellgate Press, 2009.

Murphy, Edward F. *Vietnam Medal of Honor Heroes.* New York: Ballantine Books, 2005.

Newman, Rick and Don Sheppard. *Bury Us Upside Down: The Misty Pilots and the Secret Battle for the Ho Chi Minh Trail.* New York: Ballantine Books, 2006.

Nolan, Keith. *Into Laos.* New York: Dell Publishing Co., 1986.

_____. *Ripcord: Screaming Eagles Under Siege, Vietnam 1970.* New York: Ballantine Books, 2003.

Palmer, Dave R. *Summons of the Trumpet: U.S.-Vietnam in Perspective.* Novato, CA: Presidio Press, 1995.

Plaster, John. *SOG: A Photo History of the Secret Wars.* Boulder, CO: Paladin Press, 2000.

_____. *SOG: The Secret Wars of America's Commandos in Vietnam.* New York: Simon & Schuster, 1997.

Powell, Colin L. with Joseph E. Persico. *My American Journey.* New York: Random House, 1995.

Prados, John. *The Blood Road: The Ho Chi Minh Trail and the Vietnam War.* New York: John Wiley & Sons, Inc, 1999.

Preston, Thomas. *Pandora's Trap: Presidential Decision Making and Blame Avoidance in Vietnam and Iraq.* Lanham, MD: Rowman & Littlefield Publishers, Inc., 2011.

Shelton, Hugh with Ronald Levinson and Malcolm McConnell. *Without Hesitation: The Odyssey of an American Warrior.* New York: St. Martin's Press, 2010.

Shultz, Richard H., Jr. *The Secret War Against Hanoi.* New York: Perennial, 2000.

Sorley, Lewis. *A Better War: The Unexamined Victories and Final Tragedy of Amer-*

ica's Last Years in Vietnam. New York: Harcourt, 1999.

Spector, Ronald H. *After Tet: The Bloodiest Year in Vietnam.* New York: The Free Press, 1993.

Stanton, Shelby. *Green Berets at War.* Novato, CA: Presidio Press, 1985.

_____. *The Rise and Fall of an American Army: U.S. Ground Forces in Vietnam, 1965–1973.* New York: Ballantine Books, 1985.

Veith, George J. *Code-Name Bright Light: The Untold Story of U.S. POW Rescue Efforts During the Vietnam War.* New York: The Free Press, 1998.

Westmorland, William C. *A Soldier Reports.* New York: Doubleday, 1976.

Wilbanks, James H. *A Raid Too Far: Operation Lam Son 719 and Vietnamization in Laos.* College Station: Texas A&M University Press, 2014.

Wirtz, James J. *The Tet Offensive: Intelligence Failure in War.* Ithaca: Cornell University Press, 1991.

Zaffiri, Samuel. *Hamburger Hill: The Brutal Battle for Dong Ap Bia, May 11–20, 1969.* New York: Ballantine Books, 2000.

MILITARY AND GOVERNMENT PUBLICATIONS

Comas, Graham A. *MACV: The Joint Command in the Years of Escalation, 1962–1967.* Washington, DC: Center of Military History, U.S. Army, 2006.

Minority Groups in the Republic of Vietnam. Washington, DC: Department of the Army Pamphlet 550-105, 1966.

Nalty, Bernard C. *The War against Trucks: Aerial Interdiction in Southern Laos, 1968–1972.* Washington, DC: Air Force History and Museums Program, 2005.

Pearson, Lt. Gen. Willard. *The War in the Northern Provinces 1966–1968.* Washington DC: Department of the Army, 1975.

Rogers, Gen. Bernard W. *Cedar Falls-Junction City: A Turning Point.* Washington, DC: Department of the Army, 1989.

Schlight, John. *Help from Above: Air Force Close Air Support of the Army 1946–1973.* Washington, DC: Air Force History and Museums Program, 2003.

Smith, Charles R. *U.S. Marines in Vietnam: High Mobility and Standdown—1969.* Washington, DC: History and Museums Division, HQ USMC, 1988.

Sutsakhan, Lt Gen Sak. *The Khmer Republic at War and the Final Collapse.* Washington, DC: Department of the Army, 1978.

Tilford, Earl. *Setup: What the Air Force Did in Vietnam and Why.* Maxwell Air Force Base, AL: Air University Press, 1991.

Tolson, Lt. Gen. John J. *Airmobility, 1961–1971.* Washington, DC: Department of the Army, 1999.

Villard, Erik. *The 1968 Tet Offensive Battles of Quang Tri City and Hue.* Washington, DC: U.S. Army Center of Military History, 2008.

GOVERNMENT DOCUMENTS

1st Battalion, 9th Marines, *Combat Operations After Action Report,* 31 Mar 1969.

1st Cavalry Division, *Combat Operations After Action Report,* 11 Jun 1968, Tab 1.

1st Special Forces Group, *Monthly Operational Summary,* 20 Nov 1963–20 Dec 1963.

2nd Brigade, *Combat Operations After Action Report, Massachusetts Striker,* 25 May 1969.

3rd Battalion, 187th Regiment, *After Action Report, Apache Snow,* 20 June 1969.

5th SFGA, *Detachment B-410 Debriefing,* 18 Dec 1964.

5th Special Forces Group, *Monthly Operational Summary,* 1–31 Dec 1964.

5th SFGA *Monthly Summary of Operations,* February 1966.

22nd Military History Detachment, *Narrative: Operation "Apache Snow,"* 10 May–7 June 1969.

101st Airborne Division (Airmobile), *Combat After Action Report: Firebase Ripcord,* 23 July 1970, n.d.

101st Airborne Division *Combat After Action Report: Operation Texas Star,* 1 Apr–5 Sep 1970, n.d.

101st Airborne Division, *Operational Report—Lessons Learned,* 15 Aug 1970.

159th Squadron, 9th Cavalry, *Combat After Action Report,* 4 Jun 1968.

Aton, Col Bert with William Thorndale, "A Shau Valley Campaign: December 1968–May 1969." HQ PACAF, Directorate Tactical Evaluation, CHECO Division, n.d.

Blair, John D. IV. "Defense of Camp A Shau," After Action Report, U.S. Army Infantry School, Fort Benning, GA, 2 January 1968.

Detachment B-52 (Project Delta), *Operation Pirous After Action Report,* 16 June 1967.

Detachment B-52 (Project Delta), *Samurai IV After Action Report,* 7 Apr 1968.

HML-167 *Command Chronology,* 1 Mar–31 Mar 1970.

MACSOG Documentation Study, *Appendix D: Cross-Border Operations in Laos.* Washington, DC: Joint Chiefs of Staff, 1970.

MACV-SOG *Annex B, Command History, 1970.* Saigon: MACVSOG, 1971.

MACV-SOG *Annex B, Command History, 1971–72.* Saigon: MACVSOG, 1972.

Report on Selected Air and Ground Operations in Cambodia and Laos, 10 Sep

1973, pp. 5–9, as presented in "Bombing in Cambodia," Hearings Before the Committee on Armed Services, United States Senate, 93rd Congress, 1st Session, July 16–20, 1973.

Sams, Kenneth. "The Fall of A Shau," Project CHECO Report, HQ PACAF, 18 April 1966.

Underwood, Victor C. "Battle of A Shau," After Action Report, 5th Mobile Strike Force Command Collection, 22 June 1967.

Westmoreland, Gen. William C. *Command Report on the War in Vietnam, January 1964–June 1968*. Saigon: Military Assistance Command Vietnam, 1968.

ARTICLES

Ankony, Robert C. "No Peace in the Valley," *Vietnam*, October, 2008.

Ayres, Drummond Jr., "Hilltops in Laos Seized by Marines," *New York Times*, March 9, 1969.

Barrow, Robert H. "Operation Dewey Canyon," *Marine Corps Gazette*, Nov 1981.

Bell, Kelly. "Capt. Roger Donlon & His Stand at Nam Dong," *Modern War*, Jul–Aug 2015.

Camp, Richard D. "Rescue in Death Valley," *Vietnam*, April 2012.

Conby, Kenneth, and James Morrison. "The Rise and Fall of Recon Team Asp," *Vietnam*, August 2001.

Correll, John T. "Into the Valley of Fire," *Air Force Magazine*, October, 2004.

_____. "The Long Retreat," *Air Force Magazine*, October, 2014.

Frisbee, John L. "A Hillside Near Khe Sanh," *Air Force Magazine*, July 1985.

_____. "Valor in Two Dimensions," *Air Force Magazine*, January, 1988.

Hair, Lt. Frank. "The Summer Offensive in the A Shau Valley: Massachusetts Striker," *Rendezvous With Destiny Magazine*, Summer, 1969.

Hoffman, David. "Hamburger Hill: The Army's Rationale," *The Washington Post*, May 23, 1969.

Morris, Jim. "Death-Dealing Project Delta, Part 3," *Soldier of Fortune Magazine*, September 1981.

Petraeus, David H. "The American Military and the Lessons of Vietnam," Doctoral Dissertation, Princeton University, 1987.

Sharbutt, Jay. "U.S. Assault on Viet Mountain Continues, Despite Heavy Toll." *The Washington Post*, May 20, 1969.

Shepherd, Mike D. "A Valley Soaked in Rain & Blood," *Vietnam*, October, 2015.

Sorley, Lewis. "The Abrams Tapes: Insight to the MACV Headquarters During the Vietnam War," *Vietnam*, December 2005.

Summers, Harry G., Jr. "Battle of Hamburger Hill During the Vietnam War," *Vietnam*, June 1999.

"Wesley Fox: Lessons Steeled in Combat," *Vietnam*, April 2012.

Winecoff, David F. "Night Ambush!" *Marine Corps Gazette*, January 1984.

INDEX

Note: Vietnamese personal names consist of three elements, the family name being first. Vietnamese individuals in this index are alphabetized by family name—for example, Vo Nguyen Giap.